Yale Historical Publications

Harold E. Selesky

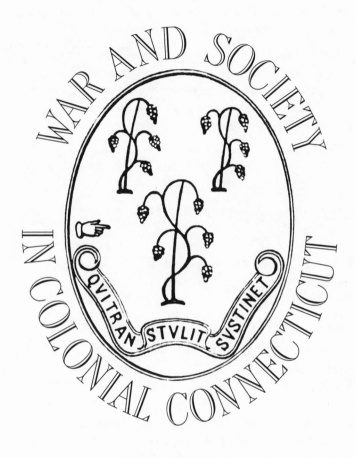

Yale University Press

New Haven and London

Published under the direction of the Department of History of Yale University with assistance from the income of the Frederick John Kingsbury Memorial Fund.

Designed by Nancy Ovedovitz and set in Garamond No. 3 type by Brevis Press. Printed in the United States of America by BookCrafters, Inc., Chelsea, Michigan.

Library of Congress Cataloging-in-Publication Data
Selesky, Harold E.
    War and society in colonial Connecticut / Harold E. Selesky.
       p.   cm.—(Yale historical publications)
    Bibliography: p.
    Includes index.
    ISBN 0–300–04552–2 (alk. paper)
     1. Connecticut—History—Colonial period, ca. 1600–1775.
  2. Connecticut—History, Military. I. Title. II. Series.
F97.S45   1990
974.6'02—dc20   89–35958
                                        CIP

The paper in this book meets the guidelines for permanence and durability of the Committee on Production Guidelines for Book Longevity of the Council on Library Resources.

10   9   8   7   6   5   4   3   2   1

For my mother and to the memory of my father

Contents

Part Two
THE FINAL FRENCH AND INDIAN WAR

Preface

The definition of military history has grown in recent years to en-
compass the study of how war is related to society. It is now widely
accepted that societies wage war in ways that reflect the character
of their people and institutions, and that they are in turn greatly affected
by having to devote men and resources to making war. Historians of
colonial America have just begun to investigate these relationships, and
they have focused on the culminating event, the American Revolution.
Less well understood is the military heritage the colonies possessed on the
eve of their rebellion, the experience which enabled them to survive the
crucial first year of their revolutionary war. This book tells the story of
how one of those colonies learned to organize and use military force in
the 140 years before 1775.

In the earliest days of settlement, the colonies relied for their defense
on a militia composed of all their able-bodied men. But the militia was
a home defense force, a framework for rapid reaction in case of attack by
local Indians or rival French, Spanish, or Dutch colonists. As an institution, it could be called into active service only for a limited time in an
emergency; men engaged in subsistence agriculture could not be made to
remain away from home for extended periods. Because the colonies did
not want to wait to be attacked, much military activity involved taking
the fight to the enemy. They quickly learned to organize a portion of their
manpower into temporary units which were institutionally distinct from
the militia and which were disbanded as soon as the campaign for which
they were raised was over. The most important military organizations in
colonial America were the ad hoc companies raised for specific short-term

purposes. The colonies developed this system during their early wars against the local Indians and expanded it after 1689 when they were drawn into the great Anglo-French contest for dominance in North America. The militia's most important role was to act as a register of men who could be drafted for active service in emergencies, and even this function faded after the middle of the eighteenth century as the colonies replaced draftees with volunteers in the campaigns against the French.[1]

Despite considerable military activity and the widespread ownership of firearms, the colonists themselves were not particularly good soldiers. Most of them knew how to use guns, but they were amateur and temporary warriors, not sharpshooting woodsmen able to fight tough and crafty opponents over forbidding terrain; only a few possessed the Indian-fighting skills later made legendary by such men as Daniel Boone and Davy Crockett. Several consequences flowed from their lack of military ability. The colonists were rarely able to force hostile local Indians to engage in battle and generally had to wage a war of attrition to grind them into submission. After 1689, they had great difficulty defending their frontier settlements against French and Indian raiders. They understood from the outset that only the conquest of Canada would end the menace at its source, but they also knew that most of them were not adept at moving through the hundreds of miles of wilderness which separated their population centers along the Atlantic seaboard from the French in the St. Lawrence valley. Their desire to strike a decisive blow, plus a lack of confidence in their ability to brush aside hovering French war parties, made them reluctant to advance with anything less than overwhelming strength. Slow-moving armies tied to long supply lines—Western-European–style campaigning in the forests of eastern North America—meant that the expeditions were trammeled by logistical obstacles that made war against the French time-consuming, hideously expensive, and indecisive; an attack by sea up the St. Lawrence was potentially more decisive, but, if anything, was even more expensive and complicated than an overland invasion. As war in colonial America became primarily a logistical enterprise, the colonies looked to Britain to provide the financial, naval, and military assistance without which they could not hope to conquer Canada.

All of the colonies participated to a greater or lesser degree in the process outlined above. Connecticut's military problems were similar to those of Massachusetts and New York, although it was subject to fewer

1. The best introduction to the nature of the military system in colonial America is still Shy, "New Look."

internal distractions and less external influence because of its location, social and economic structure, and privileges of local self-government. Geography was the most important factor shaping the way Connecticut made war. After defeating the local Indians, the colony faced no major danger close to home until the Revolution; French and Indian raiders did not pose a fundamental threat to its security. Distance from the frontier freed it from the border war that plagued its neighbors, and allowed it to consider carefully how to invest its military resources. Ethnic and economic homogeneity facilitated agreement on what to do, but the lack of a commercial center like Boston or Manhattan limited its ability to generate large sums of capital on short notice, and made it reluctant to undertake anything but the most essential military activity.

Connecticut always tried to reduce to a minimum the demands the imperial government made on its military resources. Imperial officials had suspended the charter government for twenty months in 1687–89, and fear that they might do so again prompted the colony to evade integration into an imperially mandated defense system along the frontier with Canada. It succeeded for twenty years after 1689 only because the French never endangered the frontier enough so that London was forced to step in to unite and control the military resources of New England and New York. Imperial officials became increasingly impatient with Connecticut after the turn of the century, and the colony decided it had to participate in imperially sponsored expeditions against Canada in 1709, 1710, and 1711 to earn London's tacit agreement to allow it to regulate most of its internal affairs, the bargain it used to define its place in the empire for the rest of the colonial period.

Although the northern colonies did cooperate militarily without imperial prompting as late as 1745, when New England troops captured Louisbourg, the French fortress on Cape Breton Island, after mid-century imperial officials made all the major military decisions. Between 1758 and 1760, Britain finally invested the resources necessary to dismantle the French empire in North America, and called on the colonies to assist its regular troops with the largest, most complex, and most expensive military activity they had ever undertaken. Contrary to its reaction in the 1690s, in the 1750s Connecticut responded enthusiastically to London's initiatives, in part because it knew it needed imperial help in removing what it viewed as the continuing French threat to the security, expansion, and prosperity of the colonies, but also because it wanted its share of the enormous subsidies Parliament paid the colonies for their help. Connecticut strained its resources to help Britain expunge the French menace, and earned a reputation in London as a generally hard-working and co-operative colony.

This book examines the relationship between war and society in colonial Connecticut in two ways. My first purpose is to explain how the leaders understood and responded to their military problems. Because they were subject to frequent popular review, they had to tailor their commitments to what their neighbors would bear, and were reluctant to take action for which there was little popular support. The government of Connecticut was managed by a collective leadership centered in a representative assembly, unicameral and called the General Court before 1698, bicameral and called the General Assembly thereafter. The leaders nearly always acted together to reach decisions, at times in councils of as few as a half-dozen men, but not infrequently bringing vital issues of policy and finance before the entire assembly. The records, unfortunately, rarely indicate which man suggested what action. While the leaders were intelligent and pragmatic in fitting their decisions to the strengths and weaknesses of their society, they never developed a sophisticated assessment of their military situation, and generally proceeded by applying to each new situation the lessons they or their predecessors had learned in prior wars.

My second concern is to create a social portrait of the men who went to war, and to examine how the composition of the forces changed as Connecticut grew from a cluster of tiny frontier settlements into a relatively prosperous colony with an increasingly complex and mature social structure. Invariably, the most difficult problem was raising troops. As long as local Indians were the principal threat, the leaders could compel their neighbors to undertake military service. They were always willing to draft men to meet emergencies along the frontier in western Massachusetts, but they were reluctant to use impressment to raise troops for an invasion of Canada because the French threat to Connecticut was neither immediate nor nearby. To avoid straining their authority by making men undertake unpopular military service, the leaders began in 1709 to offer financial incentives to encourage voluntary enlistments, and thereafter invoked impressment only when enough men did not volunteer. Twenty-five years of peace after 1715 promoted both population growth and economic activity, and enabled Connecticut to use larger bounties to tap an expanding manpower pool. While the sheer size of the imperial demands on the colony's manpower increased after mid-century, raising troops got comparatively easier.

Officers were the linchpin in the colony's military system, and their principal qualification was always the kind of popularity that would induce their neighbors to serve willingly in the ranks. Like their neighbors, the men appointed as officers were amateur soldiers with negligible training. Because militia officers had been elected to their positions, the leaders generally named them to lead men they drafted from their own companies to war against local Indians or French raiders, but when the leaders had to raise troops to garrison the frontier or to invade Canada, they chose as officers men who could attract volunteers, even though these men generally lacked the social status and broad appeal needed to win election to militia rank. They raised their companies by force of personality, and held them together by compromise, persuasion, and example; they could not maintain strict discipline for fear the soldiers would desert or refuse to serve again. Expeditionary officers rarely rose to prominence after their service— martial glory was not a path to political power in Connecticut—and they influenced the political process only in 1765, when some of them led the armed opposition to the Stamp Act, an attempt by the imperial government to increase its control over the colonies. Veteran officers of the final French and Indian war rendered their most important service in 1775, when the leaders called on them to raise the troops that made armed rebellion against Britain possible. Their success gave the new states time to develop new ways of creating military forces and kept the Revolution alive through its first year.

In the course of 140 years, the way Connecticut made war evolved from a focus on self-defense into an ability to raise and project substantial forces hundreds of miles beyond its borders. The first three chapters of this book examine how Connecticut's military system changed from a local defense force drawn by impressment from the militia into an expeditionary army raised largely by voluntary enlistment and designed for use against Canada. Chapter 1 explains how the colony defended itself against local Indians and European competitors from its settlement in 1635 until it helped defeat the last great Indian challenge in 1676. Chapter 2 examines its participation in the first round of the Anglo-French conflict after 1689, and shows how the campaigns against Canada between 1709 and 1711 began to transform the way the colony made war. Chapter 3 explains how a growing society turned war into an economic activity after 1715, and focuses on the capture of Louisbourg in 1745, the pinnacle of colonial arms.

The last three chapters examine Connecticut's role in the final French and Indian war (1755–62), the crowning achievement of its colonial military system. Chapter 4 explains how the leaders responded to Britain's decision to send across the Atlantic the resources necessary to conquer

Canada, and shows how a war of unprecedented scope and scale affected their military attitudes and decisions. Chapter 5 examines how Connecticut created the largest and most complicated armies of its colonial period, and provides a social portrait of its soldiers and officers. Finally, chapter 6 examines how the war contributed to the deterioration of the colony's relations with the imperial government, and ends by showing how Connecticut adapted its colonial military system to the demands of the opening year of a revolutionary war.

This book could not have been written without the records preserved in the Connecticut State Library, especially in the series "War, Colonial" of the Connecticut Archives, and in the Connecticut Historical Society. Archivists and staff in both repositories were unfailingly helpful and generous with their time and resources. Quotations from all sources have been modernized, and abbreviations have been expanded. An earlier version of the first section of chapter 5 was presented to a colloquium entitled "War and Society in Early America" at the Shelby Cullom Davis Center at Princeton University in March 1983, and will be published in John M. Murrin, ed., *Military and Society in Colonial America.*

My principal scholarly debt is to Edmund S. Morgan, on whose good sense, encouragement, and advice I have come to rely. The late William B. Willcox helped to shape the dissertation on which this book is based, and Robin W. Winks gave important last-minute advice. Richard V. Buel nurtured my undergraduate interest in American colonial history and especially in the military history of colonial and Revolutionary Connecticut. Don Higginbotham and Fred Anderson offered kind words and expert criticism as I transformed a dissertation into a book. Chuck Grench and Harry Haskell, of Yale University Press, were gracious, helpful, and understanding beyond the call of duty.

My principal personal debt is to my parents, Edna L. Selesky and George H. Selesky. Mothers love and are proud of their sons, whatever they do. Fathers are a bit more demanding. My father never ceased to prod, to question, and to care about what I was doing. My greatest regret is that he did not live to see this book. Responsibility for its contents is, of course, my own.

Abbreviations in Notes

See Bibliography for full citations.

CHS	Connecticut Historical Society, Hartford
CSL	Connecticut State Library, Hartford
CA	Connecticut Archives, Connecticut State Library
MHS	Massachusetts Historical Society, Boston
YU	Yale University, New Haven

Roman numerals (where given) are volumes, Arabic numerals or dates are documents:

CA-CM	Crimes and Misdemeanors
CA-Ecc	Ecclesiastical
CA-FC	Finance and Currency
CA-For	Foreign Correspondence
CA-FTA	Finances, Treasurer's Accounts
CA-Ind	Indians
CA-Mil	Militia
CA-Mis	Miscellaneous
CA-TL	Towns and Lands
CA-TM	Trade and Maritime
CA-War	War, Colonial
CHS-GA	General Assembly Papers
CHS-IP	Israel Putnam Papers
CHS-JT	Jonathan Trumbull, Sr., Papers
CHS-RW	Roger Wolcott Papers
CHS-WY	Wyllys Papers
CSL-AB	Treasurer's Account Books

CSL-JT   Jonathan Trumbull, Sr., Papers

CSL-LH   Journals of the Lower House

CSL-RW   Robert C. Winthrop Collection

CSL-TA   Account Book of Treasurer Joseph Talcott

CSL-UH   Journals of the Upper House

MHS-FP   Francis Parkman Papers

MHS-IW   Israel Williams Papers

SPC   Great Britain, *Calendar of State Papers, Colonial*

YU-ES   Ezra Stiles Papers in Beinecke Rare Book and Manuscript Library

YU-MS   Manuscripts and Archives in Sterling Memorial Library

Roman numerals are volumes, Arabic numerals are pages:

CHC   Connecticut Historical Society, *Collections*

CPR   Connecticut, *Public Records of the Colony*

DNY   O'Callaghan, *Documents Relative to the Colonial History of New York*

MHC   Massachusetts Historical Society, *Collections*

NHC   New Haven Colony, *Records*

NHT   New Haven Town, *Records*

UC   United Colonies, *Acts of the Commissioners*

WO-34   Public Record Office, War Office, Class 34

Roman numerals are microfilm reels, Arabic numerals are frames:

CHS-FIW   CHS, French and Indian War Papers

CO-5   Public Record Office, Colonial Office, Class 5

PART ONE

From Self-Defense
to Self-Interest

Chapter One

Apprenticeship
at Arms

INDIAN CONSPIRACIES AND IMPERIAL RIVALRIES

Like all Europeans who emigrated to North America in the seventeenth century, the Connecticut settlers had to be ready to defend themselves against potentially hostile natives. Although the local tribes had been ravaged by European diseases, they still had the numbers and knowledge of the land to threaten the survival of the settlements. While geographical isolation made local control of military affairs a necessity, the settlers did not organize their colony along military lines. A handful were professional soldiers, and a few more may have learned to use firearms at the annual militia muster in England, but they had neither the training nor the skill to meet the Indians as military equals.[1]

The settlers had two advantages, but neither was clear-cut. They wanted to manipulate existing intertribal rivalries for their benefit, but an unquestioned belief in their own cultural superiority made it hard for them to understand the complex relations among tribes. They compensated for their blindness by suspecting the intentions of all Indians, and were always ready to believe that some tribes were conspiring against them. The

---

1. The most balanced summary of Indian-settler interaction is Vaughan, *Frontier,* pp. 3–121. A more caustic view is Jennings, *Invasion,* pp. 177–85. On early conflicts, see Washburn, "Indian Wars," in Trigger, *Handbook,* XV/89–100. On the settlers' military experience, see Underhill, *News,* p. 3; French, "Arms and Military Training," pp. 8–9; and Boynton, *Elizabethan Militia.* I disagree with Webb's assertion that the colony was organized as a military garrison (*Governors-General,* pp. 437–38).

presumption that their survival depended on overawing all the local tribes primed them to overreact the first time any tribe committed hostile acts. Their other advantage was a military technology that the Indians could not match. Bullets flew faster and farther than arrows, and inflicted more damage if they found their mark. But their weapons were not decisively superior. Matchlock muskets were so heavy and prone to misfire that hitting a moving target was more a matter of luck than of skill. An Indian archer could aim and fire faster than a musketeer, and, if he got close enough, kill efficiently with his arrows. The settlers protected themselves with upper-body armor and helmets, but this equipment severely restricted their maneuverability and endurance. If they ever went to war, they would face the challenge of adapting their European military technology to the forests of eastern North America.[2]

By early March 1636, 250 settlers had created three towns on the west bank of the Connecticut River about forty miles from its mouth. The six leaders of the new colony did not organize a militia at their first formal meeting on 26 April, and no evidence suggests that they thought military training was necessary. They relied on a monopoly of firearms to deter Indians from disturbing their peace, and were seriously concerned when a settler bartered a gun for food. It soon became apparent that prohibiting settlers from trading arms and ammunition to the Indians would not be enough to preserve their security. By early June, rumors were circulating that the Pequots, a tribe with a reputation for bellicosity that lived along the eastern shore of Long Island Sound, were harboring Indians accused of murdering Englishmen. In response, the leaders directed each town to institute a watch and ordered every inhabitant to procure a supply of powder and shot.[3]

Ironically, the principal danger to Connecticut was the irresponsibility of Massachusetts in trying unilaterally to call the Pequots to account.

---

2. On technology and tactics, see Underhill, *News,* pp. 5–6, 23–25, 27; Vincent, *Relation,* p. 35; and Winthrop, *History,* pp. 235–36. Flintlocks began to replace matchlocks after mid-century (Brown, *Firearms*).

3. On settlement, see Andrews, *Colonial Period,* II/82–91; and Vaughan, *Frontier,* pp. 55–56. The settlers left temporary homes around Boston because better lands were available in the Connecticut valley. On population, see Mason, *History,* p. ix. Benjamin Trumbull assumed Mason meant 250 *men* and asserted that "the whole consisted, probably, of about eight hundred persons" (*History,* I/ 68). Most historians accept Trumbull's assertion, but a smaller population better explains the settlers' actions. On defensive preparations, see CPR:I/1–3.

While the Connecticut leaders agreed that the provocation was sufficient, they did not want to go to war until "we get more strength here about us." Their distant neighbors rejected this sound advice, and in mid-August sent one hundred men to apprehend the accused murderers and punish their hosts. Massachusetts wanted to defeat the Pequots in a single decisive battle, but it had not devised a way of making them engage in a European-style contest they knew they could not win. While the Massachusetts farmers showed considerable skill in maintaining their defensive formations on open ground, they could not pursue the fleeing Pequots without risking ambush and defeat in detail. They were reduced to plundering whatever possessions the Pequots could not carry away because they had no other way of trying to force the tribe to sue for peace.[4]

The Connecticut settlers feared a lengthy and debilitating guerrilla war, and hoped the Pequots would not retaliate against them for the actions of Massachusetts. The leaders ordered the settlers to join together once a month for military training, a measure which was intended to increase their familiarity with firearms and which also marked the beginning of the militia, but otherwise the towns waited to see what the tribe would do next. The Pequots may have chosen deliberately to limit their response, or they may have been concentrating on recovering from the blow struck by Massachusetts; whatever the reason, they spent the fall and winter of 1636–37 doing nothing more than harassing the nearest Englishmen, the small garrison of Saybrook fort at the mouth of the Connecticut River. Even this small-scale response showed how dangerous they would be if they turned their attention to the towns upriver. The settlers knew the Pequots did not have to "come to open battle" with them, "only fire our houses, kill our cattle, lie in ambush and shoot us as we went about our business, so we should be quickly forced to leave this country, and the Indians not exposed to any great hazard."[5]

With the coming of spring, the Pequots for unknown reasons decided

4. On the Massachusetts expedition, see Winthrop, *Papers,* III/270–71, 284–85; Gardener, "Relation," pp. 138–39 (quotation); Winthrop, *History,* pp. 189–93; and Underhill, *News,* pp. 6–8, 10, 26. On the response of Englishmen to the wilderness, see Salwen, "Indians," in Trigger, *Handbook,* XV/ 160–76; and Axtell, *School,* pp. 245–81.

5. On the Connecticut response, see CPR:I/3–4; Gardener, "Relation," pp. 141–48; and Mason, *History,* Introduction by Thomas Prince, p. iv (quotation). In late spring, Connecticut sent twenty men to reinforce Saybrook fort for a month (Mason, *History,* p. ix).

to expand the conflict, and on 23 April 1637 they launched the attack Connecticut had been dreading. A war party raided some outlying farms at Wethersfield, killing nine people and taking two young women captive, and frightened the anxious and desperate settlers into all-out retaliation. Not knowing when or where the Pequots might strike next, the settlers turned their towns into armed camps on constant alert. They thought they faced a stark choice: either they must destroy the tribe or it would destroy them. The need to act was underscored by local tribes, undoubtedly for their own reasons. As Thomas Hooker, the most influential minister in the Connecticut towns, explained to his colleagues in Massachusetts: "The Indians our friends were so importunate with us to make war presently that unless we had attempted some thing we had delivered our persons unto contempt of base fear and cowardice, and caused them to turn enemies against us. Against our minds, being constrained by necessity, we have sent out a company." The settlers were in too exposed a position to risk appearing to be unable or unwilling to act decisively; help from Massachusetts could never arrive in time to save them from an all-out Pequot attack. Behind stern words lay a fear of weakness that prompted them to strike against the Pequots as though their survival depended on complete victory.[6]

The need to respond to the Pequot raid forced the six original leaders to expand participation in decision making: war was the catalyst that made them create representative government. Each town elected three deputies, and on 1 May 1637 all fifteen leaders met in a general court and agreed to raise ninety men, about three-quarters of the colony's adult males, for "an offensive war against the Pequots." That was the largest percentage of its population that Connecticut ever sent to war at one time, and it included all the men capable of service. To meet the requisition, the towns even impressed men who were physically unfit, and were left dangerously undermanned, "so gleaned," reported an older man who stayed behind, "that those that remain are not able to supply our watches,

6. On Connecticut's attitude, see Mason, *History,* pp. ix-x; Underhill, *News,* p. 15; Vincent, *Relation,* pp. 35–36; Winthrop, *Papers,* III/407–08 (quotation); MHC:2, VIII/235–36; and Stiles, *Windsor,* I/136–37. Contrary to what Jennings asserts (*Invasion,* pp. 198, 202), the settlers did not go to war "til they were impelled to it by blood" (Gardener, "Relation," p. 152). Massachusetts was distracted by a religious controversy which crippled its ability to mobilize its military resources. On the Antinomian Controversy, see Morgan, *Puritan Dilemma,* pp. 134–54.

which are day and night." It took two weeks to organize the expedition. Most soldiers were under thirty years old, many in their early twenties, and none over forty. Bachelors outnumbered married men, reflecting the social structure in frontier towns, and servants probably served alongside their masters. The men provided their own weapons and equipment, and, like all soldiers of the period, expected to rely on swords as much as on firearms; each man carried only twenty bullets. All-out war was enormously expensive. To "defray the charges," the Court later levied the first colony-wide tax—the extraordinary sum of 620 pounds, roughly 5 pounds per adult male—to be paid in specie, Indian wampum, or beaver skins. Each soldier received about 2 pounds for thirty days' service, 3 pounds if he supplied his own food, and had his wages credited against the taxes he owed.[7]

Connecticut's gamble succeeded because its chief officer, thirty-seven-year-old Captain John Mason, a tall and portly veteran of England's wars in the Netherlands, understood the military realities of New England. Mason knew that without the knowledge and skills of Indian allies, his men were no better able to fight the Pequots than the Massachusetts farmers had been. To overcome this deficiency, he accepted the help of Uncas, the sachem, or chief, of the Mohegans. Uncas had "revolted" after he lost a bid to become chief sachem of the Pequots, and he and his followers were now bitter enemies of the parent tribe. While it cannot be proven that he deliberately vilified his cousins, he did nothing to change the unflattering opinions the settlers held about the Pequots. Uncas proved his fidelity by sending Mohegan warriors to kill four Pequots who were scouting around Saybrook fort, and joined Mason's force with between fifty and one hundred warriors.[8]

7. On organizing the expedition, see CPR:I/9–10; Gardener, "Relation," p. 149; Vincent, *Relation,* p. 41; and MHC:2,VIII/235 (quotation). Although Andrews, the most influential historian of colonial Connecticut, claimed the leaders wanted to base government on "a broader foundation" of political participation (*Colonial Period,* II/88), they did not do so until war forced their hand. For a reconstructed muster roll, see Shepard, *Soldiers;* also Jacobus, *Lists.* For vital statistics, see Savage, *Genealogical Dictionary.* On taxation in February 1638, see CPR:I/11–12 (quotation). The term *pound* refers to local currency, whose value against the English pound sterling was not established.

8. On Mason and Uncas, see Mason, *History,* pp. iii, v, 1–2; Underhill, *News,* pp. 15–19; and Gardener, "Relation," pp. 148–49. Mason probably did not have extensive combat or command experience. Twenty men from Saybrook fort joined Mason's force, allowing Mason to send twenty men back upriver

Mason's most difficult problem was deciding how to employ his forces. Speed was vital, since the towns were vulnerable as long as the men were absent; he could not wait to see what help Massachusetts might send. But he faced a dilemma. Although the Court had ordered him to lead his men ashore at the Pequot (now Thames) River, he knew they did not have the military ability to force a landing against Pequot opposition. Instead, he gambled on a time-consuming strategy that seemed to offer a better chance of success. He used the mobility conferred by his three ships to take his army east to Narragansett Bay, where it landed in the territory of the Narragansett tribe and marched west to attack the Pequots. Mason correctly assumed that because the Narragansetts disliked the Pequots, they would permit his men to pass through their lands. The settlers would have courted disaster, however, if they had advanced into Pequot territory without Indian allies to probe ahead for ambushes. At this critical point, Uncas reassured Mason of Mohegan support and thereby earned Connecticut's undying gratitude. The danger was actually less than Mason feared because the Pequots, who had seen the ships sail past their river, did not send scouts to find out where the settlers had gone.[9]

Early on the morning of 23 May 1637, the settlers took advantage of Pequot complacency to trap half the tribe in one of its forts where it could not avoid a decisive battle. The settlers broke into the enclosure intending to kill the warriors and capture the noncombatants, but this plan quickly went awry. The Pequots fought "most courageously" and English casualties mounted as the melee continued. With two men dead and twenty wounded, Mason knew that the longer the fight lasted, the greater were his chances of losing it. With disaster staring him in the face, he ordered his men to burn the fort and save themselves. At least four hundred Pequot

---

(Mason, *History,* pp. 1–2). Vincent said there were fifty Mohegans (*Relation,* pp. 35–36), while Winthrop reported that Roger Williams had said there were one hundred (*History,* p. 266).

9. On strategy, see Mason, *History,* pp. 2–7, 21; and Underhill, *News,* p. 23. According to Underhill, the settlers were "unexpert in the use of their arms" (Underhill, *News,* p. 23). The Narragansetts rejected an alliance with the Pequots: "Being more afraid of the Pequots than of the English, they were willing they should weaken each other, not in the least imagining the English could destroy" the Pequots (Mason, *History,* Introduction by Thomas Prince, p. iv). Some Narragansetts accompanied the settlers, but neither they nor their temporary allies, the Mohegans, did much fighting (Underhill, *News,* p. 26; and Vincent, *Relation,* pp. 36–37, 39).

men, women, and children died trying to escape; the settlers cut down some who tried to fight their way out. Warriors from a second fort nearby almost overwhelmed Mason's men as they made their way to the shore a few miles away, where their three ships, coasting west from Narragansett Bay, had arrived in the nick of time. The settlers kept together, used their firearms to keep the Pequots at bay, and after hard fighting managed to reach the safety of their ships.[10]

Civilized Englishmen slaughtered the Pequots because they thought it was the only alternative to their own destruction. According to one participant, "every man . . . fell upon the work without compassion, considering the blood they [the Pequots] had shed of our native countrymen, and how barbarously they had dealt with them." The settlers excused their conduct by claiming that "severe justice must now and then take place." In the heat of the moment, they fought with an uncivilized ferocity to protect their families from a tribe with which they could no longer live in peace. They understood that anything less than a complete victory would leave them vulnerable to reprisals and that help from Massachusetts or England would arrive too late to save them. They acted to eliminate the menace as quickly and as completely as possible.[11]

The Connecticut victory raised the prestige of English arms to undreamt-of heights and ended the best chance the Indians would ever have of reversing the tide of settlement in southern New England. The dimensions of the triumph stunned the surviving Pequots, who chose to scatter rather than fight again, and led the Mohegans and Narragansetts to protest that the bloodthirsty English had killed "too many men." In early June, the Court capitalized on the terror Mason had sown by sending thirty men to harry the remaining Pequots, who were fleeing west along the shore of Long Island Sound, and to prevent a belatedly dispatched Massachusetts army from claiming lands which "God by conquest hath given us." Thereafter, the settlers left the work of rounding up the fugitives to the Mohegans and Narragansetts, because diverting manpower from farm-

10. On the fight, see Mason, *History,* pp. 7–8, 10–13; Underhill, *News,* pp. 23–27 (quotation 24); and Winthrop, *History,* p. 225. The only prior instance of deliberate cruelty was when Mason allowed some Mohegans to torture a Pequot prisoner in retaliation for Pequot torture of an Englishman captured at Saybrook fort (Vincent, *Relation,* p. 36). Winthrop reported that Englishmen tortured the prisoner (*History,* p. 226).

11. Quotations are from Underhill, *News,* p. 25; and Vincent, *Relation,* p. 37.

ing had already created a food shortage in the towns. They survived by
buying corn from the local Indians, who were too overawed to cripple the
colony by withholding food.[12]

The Pequot war shaped New England's attitudes about military force
for decades to come. By winning so decisively and so quickly, the settlers
lost the incentive to learn the military skills needed to defeat future Indian
threats. The obliteration of the Pequots removed any pressing need to
think about how to fight a mobile enemy, and left Connecticut dependent
on its Indian allies. Mason had exploited an extraordinary situation without solving the tactical problems that had baffled Massachusetts. Over the
next forty years, the Indians gradually mated firearms with their superior
knowledge of the land to create a new style of hit-and-run fighting that
emphasized speed, stealth, and surprise. When some tribes rose up against
English domination in 1675, the settlers found they still could not match
the military skills of the Indians.[13]

Victory over the Pequots gave the settlers the upper hand for the moment, but their farms were still vulnerable if other tribes overcame their
awe of English power. A sense of danger permeated daily life. In New
Haven, founded on Long Island Sound in April 1638, town leaders strictly
enforced watch regulations: a man had to hire a substitute if he could not
mount guard himself. The town required all men to keep arms and
perform militia duty, refused to allow militia officers to leave town, and
in June 1640 established a night watch to detect Indians sneaking into
town after dark. The threat of Indian attack initially led Connecticut to
concentrate political authority to ensure speed of response; a committee
of six senior leaders generally managed military affairs between sessions
of the Court. As the colony grew, some of the two dozen deputies elected
by the towns claimed a greater role in deciding how to maintain the
psychological edge won in 1637. Everyone was alert to any rumor that
tribes might be conspiring against Connecticut, and wanted to quash
every challenge before it grew into a real threat. The leaders occasionally
sent up to forty militiamen to confront various tribes, and although their
efforts were heavy-handed, their willingness to act established their reputation for strength and vigilance so convincingly that no tribe attacked

12. On the aftermath, see Underhill, *News,* pp. 27–28 (quotation); Mason,
History, pp. 14–18, 22; CPR:I/10–12 (quotation); Gardener, "Relation," p. 151;
Vincent, *Relation,* p. 39; and MHC:5,IX/1–3, 117–18, 121.

13. On Indian adaptations, see Malone, "Changing Military Technology."

Connecticut again, even when war engulfed the other New England colonies in 1675–76.[14]

Connecticut's choice of Indian allies lay at the heart of southern New England's military problems in the 1640s and 1650s. The colony continued to rely on Uncas for information about other tribes and for assistance if attacked. The leaders took seriously every hint of conspiracy he passed along, even if they suspected him of slanting the reports in his favor. Uncas thus had considerable freedom to attack his traditional rivals, the Narragansetts, with the implicit promise of Connecticut's support, and he drew the colony into military problems it would not have encountered otherwise. Connecticut and New Haven responded to rumors of Narragansett hostility by renewing injunctions against selling arms and ammunition to Indians and by barring settlers from living with any tribe, restrictions that made it hard for them to learn the skills which would have reduced their dependence on Uncas. Fear of attack also induced Connecticut, New Haven, Massachusetts, and Plymouth to confederate in May 1643. Although the partners pledged to aid one another to defeat all threats, in practice Massachusetts would not help Connecticut and New Haven attack Indians on their western borders or the Dutch at New Netherlands. On the other hand, all four agreed that the centrally located Narragansetts might pose a common danger.[15]

14. On New Haven, see NHC:I/33–34, 74–75, 131, 381–82, 459, 483, 485, 495; NHT:I/97, 145–46, 175–76, 179–80, 184–91, 194, 199–200: and NHT:II/143, 177, 181, 312–13. The senior leaders in Connecticut were elected by all voters and included the governor, deputy governor, and (at this time) up to eight assistants. The towns handled most organizational details, while committees of assistants and deputies coordinated measures among towns (CPR:I/ 22–23, 241–43, 261–64). In August 1639, Connecticut sent forty men to disperse Pequot refugees who had returned to the Pequot River, and to assert its ownership of lands also claimed by Massachusetts (CPR:I/31; and Mason, *History*, pp. 18–20). New Haven Colony, a loose federation of towns near New Haven, did not always support Connecticut. It refused in August 1639 to help apprehend Indians accused of murdering Englishmen in the lower Connecticut valley for fear of starting a new war (CPR:I/31–32; and Trumbull, *History*, I/111–12). Connecticut forced a union on the smaller New Haven Colony in May 1665.

15. On prohibiting arms sales, see CPR:I/73–75; and Vaughan, *Frontier*, p. 159. Connecticut renewed the law seven times before 1649 (CPR:I/74, 78– 80, 113–14, 138, 145, 163, 197–98). New Haven banned sales for the first time in November 1641 (NHC:I/60, 206). On reports of conspiracy, see MHC:3,III/161–64. On the Confederation, see CPR:I/31; UC:I/3–4, 7, 9, 12;

Connecticut always convinced its partners that their safety depended on Uncas. When the Narragansetts attacked the Mohegans in midsummer 1643, the colonies construed this as the start of a conspiracy against them. When Uncas captured the Narragansett chief sachem Miantonomo, the colonies allowed Uncas to execute him because they believed "Uncas cannot be safe while Miantonomo lives." Since the leadership of a tribe depended largely upon the personality of its chief sachem, the death of Miantonomo crippled the Narragansetts; they never retaliated against the colonies, presumably because that kind of action had brought disaster to the Pequots. Although the Narragansetts continued to harass Uncas, the dispatch of a few soldiers always made them back down. Because they never provoked a major confrontation, Connecticut and New Haven could never persuade Massachusetts to act against them.[16]

England's declaration of war against the Dutch in the summer of 1652 opened a new era of imperial war, and forced Connecticut and New Haven to confront new problems. They feared the Dutch would encourage Narragansett hostility and would raid their coastal towns, and wanted to remove the threat by conquering Manhattan. Massachusetts rejected the idea, in part because the Dutch were good trading partners, but also because it realized New England did not have the fleet, the financial resources, or the trained soldiers for such an expedition. Frustrated by their neighbor's lack of cooperation, Connecticut and New Haven appealed to England for help in late 1653. Their request fell on responsive ears, and in early June 1654 a small fleet arrived at Boston to begin England's first joint military venture with New England. The two colonies enthusiastically agreed to provide the largest force either had ever raised, 200 men from Connecticut and 133 men from New Haven, about 25 percent of each colony's militiamen. They were ready to draft their soldiers from among nearly all men under sixty years old, including "seafaring men" who were not "freed from trainings" in the militia until May 1658, and

---

and Ward, *United Colonies,* pp. 30–59. Rhode Island was excluded because its neighbors considered it unorthodox in religious matters.

16. On Miantonomo, see UC:I/10–12 (quotation), 14–15; Trumbull, *History,* I/129–36; Andrews, *Colonial Period,* II/94; and Sainsbury, "Miantonomo's Death." On military action, see NHC:I/167–69; CPR:I/128; and UC:II/33, 35, 38–40, 55, 114, 125–26, 131–32, 149–52, 193. Connecticut never sent out more than twenty-five men, 5 percent of its militiamen. It tried to reduce dependence on Uncas by reconstructing a small Pequot tribe (UC:II/134, 142–43; and CPR:I/292).

Indian and black servants who trained until May 1660. Both colonies named militia officers to command the companies; although a few officers had fought the Pequots seventeen years earlier, popularity was more important than experience. All of these preparations were halted on 20 June, however, when the two colonies learned, to their intense frustration, that England had been at peace with the Dutch since April.[17]

England took a more active interest in North America after the restoration of Charles II in 1660. The first fruit of this new imperialism was the conquest of New Netherlands in August 1664, a surprise attack launched from England that began the Second Dutch War. While Connecticut was thankful that New Netherlands had become New York, a Dutch fleet sent to retake Manhattan would pose a major threat to its coast. The senior leaders pledged to help Manhattan if the Dutch attacked, but they would not commit themselves "beforehand" because local Indians were again "in an hostile posture," or do anything that might be construed as accepting subordination to New York. The Court created four committees to manage local defenses around the colony, and these bodies raised companies of dragoons to respond quickly to any attack. When Dutch ships seemed poised to strike in May 1667, the Court in panic empowered each committee to negotiate with the enemy, the only time it failed to meet its obligations for the defense of the colony.[18]

Even if militiamen could muster fast enough to catch Dutch raiders (an almost impossible task, even for dragoons), they lacked the training to repel an attack. Many inhabitants did not take military drill seriously, and the training they did receive was not suited to local conditions. As

17. On the expedition, see CPR:I/237–43, 248–49, 259–62, 265, 548; and NHC:II/4–11, 37, 100–02, 107–09. On eligibility, see CPR:I/15, 62, 75, 316 (quotation), 349. New Haven prohibited twenty-six-year-old Thomas Stevens of Guilford from ranking higher than corporal "because he is not a freeman" (NHC:II/108–09 (quotation); CPR:I/261; and Holmes, *Steevens Genealogy*, p. 14). He was later a deputy from Killingworth. Four of seven New Haven officers were Pequot War veterans.

18. The best history of the new imperialism is Lovejoy, *Glorious Revolution*. On helping Manhattan, see MHC:5,VIII/97, 99 (quotation); and CHC:XXIV/ 12–13 (quotation). The boundaries in the royal charters to Connecticut and New York overlapped. On the committees, see CPR:II/19–21, 34–35, 69, 81–82, 169, 191; and MHC:5,VIII/117–19. The Court divided the colony into four counties along the lines of the committees in May 1666. The first militia troop of horse had been established in Hartford, Windsor, and Wethersfield in March 1658 (CPR:I/309–10).

late as June 1663, the New Haven company divided in half to practice forcing back a tightly packed opponent by "pushing of pikes." Moreover, the militiamen were inept: one man inadvertently "cast his pike . . . into the other part" of the company and "struck one on the face that had it been an armed pike [steel-tipped] it might have been hazardous to the man's life." Despite having lived for thirty years in a wilderness radically different from their homeland, the colonists clung to the military training which reminded them they were Englishmen. Although the Law Code of 1650 required each town to provide enough gunpowder for target practice on training days, the colonists did not cultivate the marksmanship and woodscraft which would have made them a match for the Dutch and the Indians.[19]

Connecticut's military problems were complicated in July 1666 by news that England was also at war with France, temporarily a Dutch ally. The colony avoided attempts by the imperial government to commandeer its resources for an invasion of Canada and the relief of English islands in the West Indies, but the leaders knew they could not openly defy royal commands. Unlike their counterparts in Massachusetts, however, they won royal approval with words while doing little of substance to follow the king's wishes. They also parried a request from New York for three hundred dragoons to help defeat a French attack on the Mohawks, the firmest English allies in the Iroquois Confederacy. They claimed to be unable to raise so many men, and worried that helping the Mohawks, "inveterate enemies to the Indians around us," would alienate the local tribes. They suggested that "the French and Mohawks try it out a while," and reasoned that if Dutch merchants at Albany could "be kept from supplying" the French, the Mohawks would "put them in so bad a condition that they may be far easier" to defeat later. The idea of having the Mohawks fight their battles for them appealed to Connecticut's leaders. They were genuinely concerned about their relations with the local Indians, and they knew their fellow colonists did not have the military ability to help stop the French. But their vision remained limited to Connecticut when it should have embraced New York as well. While they claimed to be "very sensible of the danger of invasion of any of the plantations though it should be remote" from Connecticut, they did not appreciate the fact

19. On New Haven, see NHT:II/47–48 (quotation), 90–91. On 31 July 1666 a committee of the Court ordered at least twenty of every hundred militiamen to be armed with pikes (CPR:II/46). On the Law Code, see CPR:I/554–55. On Englishness, see Demos, *Remarkable Providences*, p. 247.

that the Mohawks, the best buffer against Canada, could not be left to defend themselves without both reducing their power and alienating them from the English. As it turned out, the French did not catch the Mohawks, although they hurt the tribe badly by burning its houses and food supplies.[20]

The Court did a better job of managing military affairs when England went to war with the Dutch for a third time in June 1672; the only problem was coastal defense now that France was an English ally. When a Dutch fleet, overwhelmingly strong by North American standards, recaptured New York in late July 1673, the Court delegated authority to act between its sessions to a "Grand Committee" of twenty senior leaders and deputies. This body was the culmination of what the Court had learned in the last thirty years about managing military affairs in an emergency, and it served as the prototype of the system the colony would use for more than a century. The Court also took the unprecedented step of ordering 500 militiamen to procure horses and be ready to ride "to any town assaulted" along with the 184 members of the four existing militia troops of horse. The fact that the colony was able to mount a total of about a third of its militia on horseback shows how prosperous it had become since its precarious early years. This prototype also proved to be highly successful, for the colony would use similar dragoon forces to respond to frontier emergencies for the next eighty-five years.[21]

Connecticut became more aggressive after the Dutch fleet departed in late September 1673. On 22 October, Hartford leaders allowed volunteers to reinforce Long Island, and on 27 November the Court began to organize an expedition against Manhattan. It appointed inspectors to correct the "intolerable insufficiencies and gross defects in arms and ammunition" among the militiamen, again named "a standing Council of War" as its surrogate, and appointed officers who were more prominent than such previous appointees. It was well along in its preparations when Massachusetts vetoed the attack, as it had done on each occasion since the 1650s. New England lost nothing by its inaction, however, since the

20. On the imperial projects, see SPC:II/1134, 1136; and CPR:II/514–15. On helping New York, see SPC:II/1232, 1236, 1295, 1474; NHT:II/180; CPR:II/514–16; MHC:5,VIII/99–101 (quotation), 108, 112 (quotation); and Eccles, *Canadian Frontier,* pp. 62, 64.

21. On the defensive measures, see CPR:II/182–83, 205–08; MHC:5,IX/ 88–96; and MHC:6,III/436–44. The three oldest dragoon officers were Pequot War veterans.

Dutch returned New York to English control at the peace in July 1674. The Third Dutch War demonstrated that locally superior seapower would be decisive in any contest along the Atlantic seaboard, and showed that the outcome of an imperial war rested ultimately with the principal parties in Europe.[22]

By 1675 Connecticut had encountered in some form all the military problems it would face during the colonial period. Although the colony had not fought a pitched battle in the wilderness since 1637, it had accumulated considerable experience in responding to military challenges from Indians and European competitors. The second generation had built upon the methods inherited from the original settlers to create an effective and flexible way of organizing its military forces, a system it would put to good use when the last great Indian war engulfed southern New England in July 1675. The new leaders had also inherited some of the bellicosity of their fathers, but the actual outbreak of hostilities was a sobering prospect that made them more careful and conservative in their use of force.

THE LAST INDIAN CHALLENGE

Southern New England's only protracted war against the local Indians began in early July 1675, the product of pressure by Plymouth Colony towns on a tribe led by a sachem the colonists called King Philip. Connecticut feared that the first major Indian war since 1637 might spread westward. That did not happen, but the memory of how easily the original settlers had crushed the Pequots made King Philip's War more frightening than it would have been for a battle-hardened people. Connecticut was fortunate once again: it survived its most difficult military challenge before the American Revolution in better shape than any of its neighbors.[23]

22. On the preparations, see CPR:II/214–19 (quotation 217); CHC:XXIV/17; and MHC:6,III/444–45.

23. The best account of King Philip's War is Leach, *Flintlock.* Just as the war began, Connecticut had to stop Governor Edmond Andros of New York from annexing its western half. The Court sent Thomas Bull of Hartford, a seventy-year-old Pequot War veteran, to gather militiamen at Saybrook and fight if necessary; the show of force called Andros's bluff. The Council augmented Saybrook's defenses twice in the next three months, when rumors circulated that Andros might return. See CPR:II/261–64, 334, 339–43, 582–85; MHC:6,III/3–4; and MHC:5,VIII/279.

The need to respond quickly to unexpected dangers reduced the number of leaders who were involved in decision making. The Court met in special session only once during the war, on 9 July, and delegated authority to act between its sessions to an eighteen-member Council, similar to the ones it had created during the Third Dutch War. The Council met most frequently early in the war when the crisis was at its height, an average of almost six days in ten through October, declining to an average of once every four days by the following summer. Because the Council met at Hartford, it was dominated by the five Hartford county leaders who attended most often; by May 1676, three or four constituted a quorum. They were all prominent men whose new responsibilities were an extension of an existing leadership role. Connected by marriage, business interests, and common public service, they had helped direct military affairs during the last two Dutch wars, and had as much experience making military decisions as anyone in the colony.[24]

Although the Hartford leaders controlled Connecticut's war effort, they tried whenever possible to broaden participation in managing the war. They asked leaders from the other counties to join them at Hartford, but distance made it difficult; New Haven, Fairfield, and New London county leaders usually stayed home to help organize their own counties' military affairs. The fourteen men who made the most important decision of the war—to join Massachusetts and Plymouth in an attack on the Narragansetts in December 1675—formed the largest and most representative Council of the war, but it still lacked someone from New London county, the region most directly affected by the decision. The dominance of a few Hartford county leaders raised questions about the extent of the Council's authority. In January 1676 New Haven county leaders objected to the

24. On the Council, see CPR:II/261, 275, 278, 284, 351–52, 369, 382–86, 401, 442–44, 470; and CHC:XXI/230–31, 245. Twelve senior leaders attended in July, average for a regular session, along with twenty-two deputies, fewer than the average of forty-one for regular sessions over the past decade. When Governor John Winthrop, Jr., went to Boston in mid-August as Commissioner to the United Colonies, Deputy Governor William Leete of Guilford, who had been the last governor of the New Haven Colony, moved to Hartford to chair the Council; he was elected governor of Connecticut after Winthrop died on 5 April 1676 (Dunn, *Puritans and Yankees*, pp. 185–86). The five most active Hartford county leaders included four assistants from Hartford (John Allyn, John Talcott, Samuel Wyllys, and James Richards) and a deputy from Farmington (John Wadsworth). These men, plus Leete, were the only ones who attended at least half of the 160 meetings held between 14 July 1675 and 6 October 1676.

Council's levying the enormous tax of 12 pence on the pound of rateable estate, but in May the Court approved the decision—all leaders realized that unprecedented taxation was needed to pay for a full-scale war—and reiterated the Council's right to act as events might require.[25]

When the war broke out, Connecticut's principal concern was to guard against surprise attack. Most towns instituted a watch of some sort. In Windsor, where the population was scattered, it was double-strength; in New Haven it was "only a single watch." Towns strictly enforced watch regulations, fining men for not standing watch and for alarming the town unnecessarily by "unseasonably shooting" their guns. Many towns began to erect fortifications for the first time. The pace was slow at Hartford, even after the burning of Springfield on 5 October 1675 showed how hostile Indians could devastate an unprepared town. New Haven voted in mid-October to garrison some houses and to construct a palisade around the entire town, but the cost, as well as debate over whose houses to protect, ensured that the project was still incomplete when the war ended. The Council and Court expected every town to defend itself, even the frontier towns most vulnerable to attack. In October the Court told the men of Derby to move their families, their belongings, and their corn to "some bigger town" and to defend what remained. A few small and exposed towns were abandoned temporarily, but the contraction of settlement did not threaten the survival of Connecticut. The colony suffered its only major property loss when hostile Indians burned the "great part" of the abandoned town of Simsbury on 26 March 1676.[26]

The most important advice the Court and Council gave towns was to deal fairly with the local Indians. This policy was a pragmatic response to a war the leaders were not sure they could win, and it succeeded because

---

25. On taxation, see CPR:II/269, 292, 322, 401. The rate had reached two-and-a-half pence during the Third Dutch War (CPR:II/186, 212, 218). Despite the Court's reaffirmation of the Council's authority, some dragoons objected when the Council sent them north to meet an emergency in the upper Connecticut valley in late May instead of east into Narragansett country as the Court had directed (CPR:II/442–55).

26. On home defense, see NHT:II/338–44 (quotation 339), 346, 348–53 (quotation 350); CPR:II/268–69, 361, 372–73, 375 (quotation), 380, 389, 410, 412–13, 416–17; CHC:XXI/232–34; and CA-War:I/11e-f, 52. A man could fire his gun in self-defense or to destroy "a wolf or such ravenous beast" (CPR:II/361). On Derby and Simsbury, see CPR:II/266–67, 269, 412, 423, 491. After the war, the Court remitted colony taxes for two or three years to men living in frontier towns (CPR:II/309; and CPR:III/2, 10).

the towns generally did not give the Indians "any just cause of provocation." The local Indians in turn pledged "to be enemies to our enemies."
By eschewing harsh action, Connecticut avoided the kind of confrontation
that had plunged its neighbors into war, but a moderate policy was not
always easy to follow. At the start of the war, Massachusetts offered a
bounty for the head of any enemy, and the Council followed suit when
friendly Indians brought these tokens of "faithfulness" to New London in
late July. Although the Council later offered to pay twice as much for a
live enemy as for his head alone, any form of bounty hunting increased
the chance that a colonist might kill a friendly Indian.[27]

The leaders knew they should not overreact, but they could not ignore
the possibility that hostile Indians might attack Connecticut inhabitants.
In early September 1675, the Council instituted patrols between towns
in Hartford county, ordered men to go armed and in company to the
fields, and reluctantly gave travelers wide latitude to kill armed Indians.
Since friendly Indians could demonstrate their peaceful intentions by dis-
arming themselves, the Council hoped to avoid any confrontations. The
burning of Springfield on 5 October prompted towns to increase their
supervision over the local tribes. In Hartford, no Indian was to be "abroad
after sunset, and none [was to] be absent but by leave" or with some
colonists; such measures were occasionally enforced by the taking of hos-
tages. Still, the Court urged colonists not to "rashly, unjustly, or impru-
dently" injure friendly Indians. It empowered county leaders to agree with
local tribes about the times when Indians could approach the towns, and
reminded them not to impose "any unrighteous or intolerable terms."
Even after fighting flared up in early March, the Council advised local
leaders to "carry so tenderly towards the Indians that they may not receive
any just provocation to stir them up against us. We have enemies eno',
and let us not by any harsh dealings stir up more yet."[28]

Keeping the peace with the local Indians allowed Connecticut to take
the offensive. The colony wanted to send soldiers to "pursue and destroy"
hostile Indians because it could not remain on the defensive indefinitely.
The situation in 1675 was much as it had been in 1637. Connecticut

27. On fair dealing, see NHT:II/339; CPR:II/360 (quotation), 364, 370
(quotation); and CHS-WY:I/44. On bounty hunting, see MHC:6,III/447 (quotation); and CPR:II/345, 348, 370, 374, 408.

28. On dealing with local Indians, see CPR:II/272 (quotation), 359, 374,
376 (quotation), 378–79, 419 (quotation); CA-War:I/13, 52; and CHC:XXI/
213–14.

could not endure a guerrilla war or risk losing the goodwill of local tribes by doing nothing to stop Philip. The Council accepted the advice of Uncas, still the leader of the Mohegans, that the colonists must "make excursions with competent numbers" to surprise the enemy. But the leaders also realized that the colonists knew little about war in the wilderness, and they looked to Uncas to fill their need for Indian allies. Although one New London county leader thought "it will be well if he [Uncas] proves not as bad as Philip," most colonists trusted Indian warriors, principally Mohegans, to protect them against ambush on the march and to help them seek out and defeat the enemy in battle. Connecticut took pains to see that Massachusetts did not mistake its allies for enemies, and warned friendly Indians "to be wary in going amongst the English, lest through inadvertency they should receive some damage." It understood military realities better than Massachusetts, which was slow to employ Indian allies in part because it lacked suitable Indian friends.[29]

This offensive strategy was not as successful in 1675–76 as it had been in 1637. Where the Pequot War had been a short, decisive encounter, King Philip's War turned into a war of attrition. The colonists could not end the war quickly because hostile Indians refused to fight when they were outnumbered or had lost the element of surprise. Connecticut soldiers were cautious and unskilled, and were never able to trap the enemy. Indeed, in the fall of 1675 the Court prohibited them from operating in the field "without sufficiency of strength." The more enterprising New London county leaders quickly learned that "a smaller force will move with more speed and secrecy than greater bodies for the surprise of the enemy, and without by surprisal we shall do little good . . . ; experience teacheth that if the enemy be either alarmed or have intelligence, great bodies must be content with little success." Nonetheless, the Council, concerned with minimizing the danger to soldiers on the march, continued to send out large forces that could not find any enemy to kill and so failed to achieve their primary goal. Because the soldiers risked ambush without a screen of friendly Indians, the Council always called the companies home when the warriors grew weary of the service: "It was not safe for us and

29. On taking the offensive, see CPR:II/271, 335–37, 345–51 (quotation 350), 359–62, 366 (quotation), 381, 441 (quotation); CHC:XXI/209–11, 216–17, 221–23, 227–28 (quotation), 240; MHC:5,VIII/279–80, 401–03; MHC:6, III/447–48; and CA-War:I/1e, 9. John Pynchon, the principal military officer in western Massachusetts, understood the value of Indian allies, but was correct not to trust the local tribes (Pynchon, *Papers,* I/137, 152, 154–55).

the health of the colony's interest in the Indians to break with them."
The colonies were reduced to ravaging the homes and food supplies of
their enemies in order to destroy their capacity to make war; starvation
was a major weapon in winning the war.[30]

Failure to end the war quickly put tremendous strain on relations among
the colonies. Although they sought to coordinate their military activity,
each partner was free to pursue its own interests. Connecticut always
complained that Massachusetts did not send enough help to the upper
valley, but the Council itself regarded the defense of Connecticut as its
first priority, and did less than it might have done to aid western Massachusetts. Before allowing the dragoons to ride north, it insisted that
they make sure no enemy Indians were "skulking about the plantations,"
ordered them to return immediately if Connecticut towns were threatened,
and refused to allow them to remain for extended periods in the upper
valley.[31]

The most serious case of lack of cooperation among the colonies forced
Connecticut into war with the Narragansetts. In early November 1675,
Massachusetts and Plymouth overreacted to rumors that the most powerful
tribe in southern New England might join Philip's cause in the spring,
and, without consulting Connecticut, decided to launch a preemptive
attack while the tribe was concentrated for the winter. After thirty years
of clamoring for action against the Narragansetts, Connecticut ironically
did not want to fight when the chance came. But it could not remain
aloof while its partners stirred up a hornet's nest so close to its eastern
towns, and on 22 November 1675 the Council reluctantly agreed to
contribute 315 men to a 1,000-man army. The attack was successful only

30. On caution in the field, see CPR:II/377–78 (quotation). On the abilities
of the soldiers, see CA-War:I/96 (quotation); CPR:II/409, 411–12, 448, 450,
453, 458–59 (quotation), 465–66; and CHC:XXI/246, 248. On starvation as
a weapon, see Pynchon, *Papers,* I/167. The Council ordered towns to train militiamen for the first time in June 1676 (CPR:II/452). One officer suggested
using dogs to hunt the enemy (CPR:II/443).

31. On reinforcing western Massachusetts and hunting enemy Indians, see
CPR:II/267, 357–60, 363–67, 372–74, 377–82, 411, 422–26, 429–31, 438,
464; CA-War:I/71; MHC:6,III/448–49; NHT:II/342 and Pynchon, *Papers,* I/
138–45, 148, 161–62. For the tribulations of one town in the upper valley, see
Sheldon, *Deerfield,* pp. 81–178; also Melvoin, *Outpost,* pp. 92–123. Connecticut
spitefully refused to send Mohegans to Maine in 1677 because Massachusetts
had been slow to help the valley in 1675–76 (CPR:II/497–98, 502–03; and
UC:II/462–64).

because the Narragansetts chose not to scatter during a cold spell. On 19 December the intercolonial army trapped the tribe in its stronghold in the Great Swamp near Kingston, Rhode Island, and forced it to fight a decisive battle. As in Mason's victory over the Pequots in 1637, the Indians were routed only when the colonists burned them out. The victory broke the tribe's power, but it turned the survivors into implacable foes. Connecticut men were involved in the brutal work of tracking them down well into the fall of 1676.[32]

The difficulty in coming to grips with hostile Indians raised the moral costs of the war. At the outset the Council had offered "just and honorable terms of concession or quarter," exempting from pardon only "grand contrivers and murderers," and had demanded that the behavior of its soldiers "be sober, Christian, and comely." In early September 1675, Connecticut dragoons were shaken by the cruelty that hostile Indians displayed when they ambushed a Massachusetts company in the upper valley, and all thoughts of proper conduct evaporated in the heat of a deadly and frustrating war. Burning out the Narragansetts was only the largest episode of cruelty between the combatants. When starvation forced enemy Indians to surrender, they often got a harsh reception. Brutality was most common in eastern Connecticut, where fear of enemy Indians was greatest. New London leaders chose not to investigate when two Narragansett warriors captured in late January 1676 were "shot dead in the prison, by two wounded soldiers it is said." Some men took literally the exhortation of their ministers to kill the enemy "according to the utmost power God shall give you," and even Council members opposed sparing the enemy "lest their preservation should prove a reservation for further future scourge." By the fall of 1676, the war had degenerated into hunting down helpless refugees.[33]

32. On the campaign, see CPR:II/380, 383, 390–92 (quotation 391), 409, 421–24, 426–27, 453; UC:II/357–59, 456–58; MHC:5,IX/99–100; and Hubbard, *Narrative,* p. 47. Massachusetts raised 525 men and Plymouth 160 men, numbers based on proportions agreed upon when they had joined Connecticut in reviving the Confederation of New England in 1673 (UC:II/349).

33. On proper conduct, see CPR:II/357–58 (quotations). On terms of surrender, see CPR:II/440. The dragoons saw the results of the ambush at Northfield (Sheldon, *Deerfield,* pp. 97–98). On the murdered Narragansetts, see CPR:II/403 (quotation); one New London county leader complained that it was a "pity so rude and barbarous [an] act should be passed by without due witness against it," but he was in the minority. On killing the enemy, see CHC:XXI/250 (quotation); CPR:II/444 (quotation), 458–59; and Trumbull, *History,* I/343–45.

King Philip's War was the first major test of Connecticut's ability to raise soldiers. Over the course of the war manpower demands grew to unprecedented levels, but the initial commitment was small and intended to meet short-term emergencies. On 1 July 1675, Governor Winthrop and his Hartford colleagues sent 40 horsemen to New London county, and on 5 August the Council sent 40 Hartford county dragoons to western Massachusetts. The next day, the Council regularized its military system on the model of the Third Dutch War by impressing 230 dragoons in the three western counties (10 percent of the colony's 2,300 militiamen) to be ready to ride "upon an hour's warning" to any town in danger; only half of them were to be sent out at one time. Each man supplied his own weapons and equipment, and normally rode his own horse or one impressed by his town. To keep down expenses, the Court paid him wages based on a pay scale it had not increased since 1655; a private got 1 shilling, 4 pence a day, less than what he could earn in civilian life. Beginning with the Narragansett campaign in December, the leaders distributed the burden of service among all four counties, with Fairfield county, farthest from the danger, always contributing the highest proportion of dragoons. A higher percentage of Connecticut men was under arms during the summer of 1676 than at any time since the Pequot War— 350 dragoons in the field and 240 more on call at home, more than 25 percent of the militiamen. Records do not show how many men served at least once during the war, but the the number must have been enormous, probably over three quarters of all able-bodied men performing in some sort of military capacity. The inhabitants met these demands because, said one veteran, they were "willing to adventure . . . [their lives and fortunes] in so good a cause, being both the cause of God and of the republic."[34]

34. On the dragoons, see CPR:II/266–68, 278–79, 290, 331–32, 345–47 (quotation 347), 355–56, 384, 386–87, 392, 395, 400, 410–11, 443; CHC:XXI/210; and Trumbull, *History,* I/351. The 1 July reinforcement included ten troopers, the only occasion members of the elite militia troop were specifically drafted for service. On the number of militiamen, 15 percent of fifteen thousand people, see Trumbull, *History,* I/351; and CPR:II/290. New Haven county always raised the fewest dragoons because its leaders claimed to fear attack by local tribes (CHC:XXI/223–25). Three men shared a horse during the Narragansett campaign because forage was difficult to obtain in winter (CPR:II/386). On wages, see CPR:I/273; CPR:II/386; and CPR:III/300–301. On the veteran, see CA-War:I/135 (quotation).

Some towns bore a larger share than others. The Council refused to reduce Saybrook's quota when the town complained in March 1676 that the 20 dragoons it had in service were "one-third" of its men. (Saybrook contained 85 militiamen, but only three-quarters of them, or 60 men, seem to have been liable to impressment.) The Council reasoned that it was not always possible "to observe the rule of proportion exactly, as in the case of a house on fire," and concluded that Saybrook was as safe "as any place in this colony." There was no reason, however, to make frontier towns bear the greatest burden. Although the Council asked New Haven county to "favor small plantations in the press," Derby and Wallingford later complained they "had more proportionable to our numbers" in service "than (we suppose) any other town in the colony." While frontiersmen may have been better woodsmen, and thus better soldiers, than men from more established towns, this policy weakened the very towns most liable to be attacked.[35]

Selection of individual soldiers was left to the towns, and presumably they did not impress men who provided essential services, like judicial officers, ministers, physicians, schoolmasters, and millers, all occupations the Council later exempted from the watch. Most towns seem to have drafted young bachelors first, thereby placing the heaviest burden on their least affluent members. For most of these young men, poverty was a temporary condition; they could look forward to earning or inheriting more wealth as they grew older. Not all soldiers had bright prospects, of course, but neither were the companies filled with "lowly expendables." Several examples illustrate the mix. Norwalk's soldiers were mostly unmarried men in their twenties. Many were sons of freemen, and, in Stamford at least, they included scions of prominent families. Stratford, on the other hand, impressed at least one eighteen-year-old servant, and Fairfield drafted an older married man who did not own the farm he worked. Four of the five soldiers from Windsor who died fighting the Narragansetts were comfortable for their age and status, including three young bachelors with estates under 67 pounds and a married man in his thirties who left his widow and seven children an estate worth 185 pounds. They died alongside a man who left his widow and four children an insolvent estate

35. On Saybrook, see CPR:II/290, 422 (quotation). On Derby and Wallingford, see CPR:II/346; and CA-War:I/115 (quotation). In Hartford county, the Council sent out men from the largest towns first (CPR:II/360). Norwich and Stonington on the eastern frontier were occasionally excused from raising dragoons (CPR:II/267, 450–51).

of only 65 pounds. As might be expected, officers from Windsor were substantially better off. Captain Samuel Marshall left his widow and nine children an estate of 903 pounds.[36]

To increase the level of expertise, the Council wanted veteran dragoons to serve as often as possible, and generally ordered them to "remain under press." While at home, they had to be ready to march "at a day's warning" and "perform equal duty" on the watch, but were otherwise free "to attend to their necessary business." Many veterans went out several times, after being resupplied by their towns with clothing, arms, and horses, and were joined by "other sufficient able men" to replace those who had been "disenabled for service." But hard campaigning drained the pool of experienced soldiers. Eighty men were killed or wounded fighting the Narragansetts in December 1675 (25 percent of 315 men), a higher casualty rate than for the other colonies; more were disabled by cold and snow. In early January 1676, New Haven and Fairfield county leaders complained that the new quotas were "as many as we can well raise and spare and that not without some difficulty." The Council knew it could not demand too much of the veterans or they would refuse to serve again. When some soldiers returned from the Narragansett campaign "without pass or leave," the Council felt it could not punish them for seeking refuge "in such an extreme season."[37]

36. On men excused from the watch, see CPR:II/361. On Norwalk and Stamford, see Hall, *Norwalk,* p. 62; Huntington, *Stamford,* pp. 113–14; and Jacobus, *Fairfield,* I/238, 242, 291, 297, 329, 357, 526, 661. The term "lowly expendables" is from Main, *Society,* p. 31. Apparently few men evaded service. In Hartford county, the Council released fifty-one-year-old Sergeant Jonathan Kilbourn of Wethersfield from service, but demanded that another man take his place (CPR:II/375; and Stiles, *Wethersfield,* II/467–68). On categories of wealth, see Main, *Society,* pp. 66, 69, 70, 113. On the Windsor soldiers, see Bates, *Windsor,* pp. 15, 31, 34, 59, 65, 84–85. On their estates, see Manwaring, *Probate Records,* I/187, 193, 198, 218, 226, 232. Money was calculated in "country pay," a Connecticut system whose values were, according to the most careful student, twice those of sterling (Main, *Society,* p. 42).

37. On veterans, see CPR:II/360 (quotation), 382 (quotation), 384. On casualties, see Trumbull, *History,* I/341; and MHC:5,IX/97. Massachusetts lost a hundred men (20 percent) and Plymouth twenty (15 percent). On the difficulty of raising dragoons in January, see CPR:II/400; and CHC:XXI/229–30 (quotation). On returning without leave, see CPR:II/394–95 (quotations), 398. The Council imprisoned a man for coming home but released him when he promised to return (CPR:II/396, 399). On furloughing the dragoons in the spring, see

The Council set discipline at a level that allowed it to control the troops without making them decline or desert the service. To "keep the soldiers to their duty" in the future, in early January it borrowed twenty rules from those which Massachusetts had adapted from the "Articles of War" used to govern England's New Model Army in the 1640s. The principal changes involved reducing the severity of punishment; New Englanders wanted to maintain order among farmers, not impose iron discipline on a professional army. Although the Council was reluctant to test the new rules by sending the troops back to Narragansett country in the depths of winter (to "march so far" when the enemy is "at our doors . . . doth seem intolerable"), the dragoons did what they were asked to do. The New London county volunteers, who went out with the Mohegans to track down Narragansett survivors after February 1676, were more difficult to control. While the Council let them keep any plunder they could find, and gave them food, ammunition, and pay as the "[im]pressed soldiers have," it warned them not to claim the goods of "innocent persons." The Council rejected the idea that the volunteers, a cross-section of the county's younger men, would obey only their own officers, for "order must be upheld and a due submission to authority maintained, or ruin will come in." In late May the dragoons solved the problem by taking over the pursuit of the Narragansett refugees.[38]

Connecticut kept 350 dragoons continuously in service from late May to mid-August 1676, the first time it had maintained such a large force in the field for so long. The Council tried to boost the morale of the dragoons by granting them ammunition, additional provisions, and "all the plunder they can get . . . provided they do orderly behave themselves," but searching for the enemy in the wide arc from Narragansett country

---

CPR:II/415, 425–27, 434 (quotation), 456. The Council recalled them in April because sickness was "proving mortal to many" (CHC:XXI/242–43; NHT:II/353; and CA-War:I/60).

38. On the regulations, see CPR:II/392–94 (quotation); Hutchinson, *History*, I/251–52; and Firth, *Cromwell's Army*, pp. 279–80, 400–412. On the severity of the weather in January, see CPR:II/391–92, 395–97 (quotation 395), 399, 401–03. On the New London volunteers, see CPR:II/407, 412–13, 417–18 (quotation), 420–21 (quotation), 423, 427–28 (quotation), 429, 431, 438, 503–04; CA-War:I/57; CHC:XXI/255–57; Trumbull, *History*, I/343–45; Minor, *Diary*, pp. 130–37; and Wheeler, *Stonington*, p. 22–23. They could "kill ˈnd destroy" all hostile Indians and "all such who have already surrendered and

in the east to the upper Connecticut valley in the north proved to be "tedious with little or no plunder gained." After midsummer, the dragoons all had "pressing occasions" at home. The harvest season soon hampered efforts to raise soldiers, especially in New Haven and Fairfield counties, where leaders reported that "our old soldiers . . . implead incapacity . . . to go forth again."[39]

Leadership was the most important element in keeping the dragoons together. Command was based on deliberation and consent as in the militia, and decision-making authority was vested in a council of senior officers chaired by the chief officer. During the most difficult part of the conflict, from August 1675 through the following spring, Connecticut relied on fifty-three-year-old Assistant Robert Treat of Milford as its chief military officer. He was a good choice: popular, energetic, courageous, willing to cooperate with officers from other colonies without loosing sight of his responsibilities as Connecticut's commander. He was elected deputy governor in May 1676, and, worn out from months of hard campaigning, he retired from active service. The Court replaced him with forty-five-year-old Assistant John Talcott of Hartford, who, as colony treasurer and a senior member of the Council, was one of the half dozen men directing the colony's war effort. As Hartford county militia commander, he had played an important role in gathering information about the military situation in the upper valley, but he seems to have had little experience in leading dragoons against hostile Indians. The Court valued political popularity over military experience because it wanted to boost morale and ensure that a war of attrition which required doggedness more than skill would be pushed to its conclusion.[40]

During the early months of the war, militia captains in the three western counties left the job of leading the dragoons to their middle-aged

---

39. On organizing the army during the summer, see CPR:II/278, 455, 456 (quotation), 458–59 (quotation), 460 (quotation), 465 (quotation); and CA-War:I/104 (quotation).

40. On Treat, see CPR:II/266, 354, 356–58, 383, 388, 411. He had been second-in-command of the New Haven county militia. Service was hard, even for senior officers: Treat was struck by a spent musket ball at Northfield on 6 September (Sheldon, *Deerfield,* p. 97) and was one of many who succumbed to the illness sweeping Connecticut in April 1676 (CA-War:I/60). On Talcott, see CPR:II/279–80; and Pynchon, *Papers,* I/144–45, 148, 167. Officers were appointed five times (CPR:II/266–68, 279, 347, 355–56, 386–87, 395, 400, 411, 443; UC:II/457; and CA-War:I/18, 141).

subordinates who were promoted to higher rank on active service. One of the hardest-working dragoon captains was Thomas Watts of Hartford, a fifty-five-year-old militia lieutenant who had been a selectman only three times between 1657 and 1667. He and other men who were second-rank leaders in peacetime turned out to be effective officers in wartime. Against the Narragansetts, they inspired the dragoons to fight "with as gallant a resolution" as the men from Massachusetts and Plymouth. But the price was high: three of five captains were killed and a fourth was mortally wounded; only Watts survived.[41]

The need to appoint new officers to lead the western dragoons through a tough winter brought a temporary rise in the prominence of the captains. They were now younger and more popular, like thirty-four-year-old, four-time Selectman Moses Mansfield of New Haven and thirty-four-year-old Jonathan Selleck, a well-educated militia captain, deputy, and tavern-keeper from Stamford. Subordinate officers, most of whom were promoted from noncommissioned rank, supplied the experience. By midsummer 1676 these captains had seen enough of active service, and the western counties once again relied on less prominent commanders. Fairfield county leaders were "in great straits to pitch upon a meet person" before they selected forty-one-year-old John Minor of Stratford, whose most important credential seems to have been his father's prominence in New London county. As long as Minor had the confidence of the men in the ranks, it did not matter that he lacked the political popularity and militia rank of his predecessor. Officers like Watts and Minor, who kept their companies together through the danger and tedium of pursuing hostile Indians across forbidding terrain, were at the heart of the colony's military system. Second-rank leaders like them would play an even greater role during the conflict with Canada after 1689, when Connecticut's military problems moved further away from the colony.[42]

41. On Watts, see CHC:VI/95, 101, 115, 123, 137, 151, 164; CPR:II/ 210, 251, 346; and Pynchon, *Papers,* I/148. Connecticut officers occasionally refused to obey the orders of Massachusetts leaders in the upper valley (Sheldon, *Deerfield,* p. 122). On officer casualties, see Hubbard, *Narrative,* p. 52 (quotation); CPR:II/395; and Trumbull, *History,* I/338–41. Captains John Gallop, Samuel Marshall, and Nathaniel Seely were killed, and Captain John Mason, Jr., was mortally wounded (Bodge, *Soldiers,* p. 191). The commander of the sixth company, from New Haven county, was apparently Lieutenant John Miles of New Haven; he survived.

42. On Mansfield, see NHT:II/289, 303, 318, 337; and CPR:II/400. On

In New London county, where the danger was closer than in the western counties, the officers were always more prominent. Through the spring of 1676, men who maintained good relations with the local tribes, including twenty-nine-year-old John Mason, Jr., son of the Pequot War commander, led mixed companies of colonists and friendly Indians. The criteria changed in May when the Council needed a man who could control the former volunteers who were now being drafted into the county's dragoon company. It chose fifty-six-year-old Captain George Denison of Stonington, a veteran of the English Civil Wars and a former leader of the volunteers, and even named him second-in-command of the army, despite the fact that the Court had earlier barred him from holding public office for protesting too vigorously Stonington's lack of local autonomy. The subordinate officers were generally men in their mid-sixties who had a record of public service not matched by their western counterparts. First-rank leaders continued to lead the New London county dragoons because Narragansett raiders kept a frontier mentality alive in eastern Connecticut.[43]

After the war ended in the late summer of 1676, Connecticut for the first time had to deal with a substantial number of veterans who sought compensation for injuries suffered in the service. In addition to paying for lost or damaged horses, guns, and equipment, the Court eventually gave wounded men a limited amount of "cure and diet" at the colony's expense. When "many soldiers" clamored for relief in October 1676, the Court said it was willing to allow them "some equitable reparation," but by February 1677 it had granted small sums to only five veterans. Ex-soldiers occasionally petitioned the Court directly and got a more favorable response: Samuel Hall received 2 pounds, 3 shillings to pay his back taxes and 7 shillings more for the loss of coat, shirt, stockings, cutlass, and Bible; and Thomas Trill got 2 pounds, 10 shillings for damage done to his corn while he was "in the country's service." The Court also granted land to veterans, some of it long after the war. In the most lavish bequest, it gave thirty-six square miles in eastern Connecticut to former New

---

Selleck and Minor, see Jacobus, *Fairfield,* I/534 and 412. On Fairfield county, see CA-War:I/104 (quotation). The leaders hoped Minor was "competently accomplished for the work," and were thinking about promoted a drafted sergeant to be his lieutenant.

43. Mason was mortally wounded in the Great Swamp Fight in December 1675. On Denison, see Baldwin and Clift, *Descendants,* pp. 6–7; and CPR:II/ 36, 159, 236, 249, 258, 279, 310, 407, 418, 444.

London county volunteers in 1696. A few grants were made as late as 1713 to the heirs of veterans. Towns also gave land to their ex-soldiers. Norwalk allotted it according to the difficulty of their service, up to twelve acres for a man who had served in December 1675. New Haven offered them land in a distribution in 1680 according to "the time they were out," and even included three young veterans who were not "admitted inhabitants." (The grants were small, only six acres on average, much less than the forty acres allotted on average to full inhabitants.) Officers in New Haven received land according to their wartime rank, which corresponded to their place in society. A junior officer got as few as twenty-eight acres while a captain received over one hundred.[44]

Military service occasionally boosted an officer's political popularity. Robert Treat is the best example of upward political mobility through military service in Connecticut history: he went from the eleventh-ranking assistant to deputy governor largely on his showing as the chief military officer during the early part of the war. A few others, men who were rising in public esteem for traditional reasons, gained political power sooner than otherwise might have been the case. Captain Moses Mansfield of New Haven, for example, was elected a deputy eight times after October 1676, and town selectman and treasurer after April 1678. But no man became a significant public figure on the basis of military service. Thomas Watts was chosen a Hartford selectman only once more before he died in 1683; John Minor was elected a deputy from Stratford only in October 1676; and thirty-six-year-old Lieutenant John Miles of New Haven, a militia ensign and fence viewer before the war, rose to nothing more prestigious than highway surveyor thereafter. He returned to public office only in 1689, when war with Canada made military experience important once again. The only formal recognition ex-officers got was exemption "from training as private soldiers" in the militia. The Court required them to help train their local company in the rank "they bore in the

44. On relief from the Court, see CPR:II/284–85 (quotation), 288 (quotation), 298–99, 307, 484–85. For petitions from individuals, see CA-War:I/124, 135, 137; CPR:II/320, 326–27; and CPR:III/5–6, 14, 22, 29 (quotation). Amounts are in country pay. The land granted to the New London volunteers was laid out in October 1700 and named Voluntown in May 1708 (CPR:IV/186, 335; and CPR:V/47). For other petitions for land, see CA-War:I/146–49. On Norwalk, see Hall, *Norwalk,* p. 62. On New Haven, see NHT:II/389–90 (quotation), 402–03 (quotation), 407, 409–10.

wars," but subordinated them to militia officers to avoid creating resentment or subverting the social order.[45]

King Philip's War was New England's most traumatic military experience of the colonial period, but the war never threatened to do more than slow the growth of settlement. The position of the Indians who tried to stop English expansion by force of arms was fatally weak. They had no defensible homeland where they could rest, recuperate, and repair the firearms on which they had come to depend. They were refused refuge by the Mohawks of New York, and faced such relentless pressure from the colonial dragoons that they eventually ran out of ammunition, food, and places to hide within New England. They could hurt the colonies, but they could not regain the upper hand the Pequots had enjoyed before their destruction in 1637.

Connecticut survived the war in better physical, economic, and emotional shape than its neighbors because the Indians who lived among its towns were satisfied with the status quo and chose not to join Philip's cause, and because hostile Indians did not attack simultaneously along the eastern frontier and down the Connecticut valley. Fighting the war cost Connecticut 30,000 pounds, roughly 30 percent of what it cost all of New England. While absorbing these costs contributed to an overall decline in wealth in the 1680s, the economic situation was not desperate for a colony that suffered comparatively little property damage and found a ready market for its surplus food in its harder-hit neighbors. Although taxes levied in the eighteen months after July 1675 totaled an astounding 30 pence on the pound, or 12.5 percent of assessed valuation, tax rolls recovered their prewar level by 1678. War slowed population growth but did not stop Connecticut's expansionism. The dust had hardly settled before people were clamoring to acquire the lands of the defeated Narragansetts. The war was far more difficult in religious and psychological terms than it was as a military or economic problem. Indians had scourged

45. On Mansfield, see NHT:II/289, 303, 311, 318, 326, 337, 353–54, 358, 360, 367, 375, 388, 406, 412–13, 416–17, 419, 430; NHT:III/1, 7, 16, 28, 50; CPR:II/292; CPR:III/112, 127; and CPR:IV/65. He was also elected a militia lieutenant in October 1676, and, although referred to as "captain," he was not elected a militia captain until October 1683. He became an assistant in 1692, twelve years after his first nomination. On Watts, see CHC:VI/180. On Minor, see CPR:II/286. On Miles, see NHT:II/264, 311, 352, 401, 409. On ex-officers, see CPR:II/315 (quotation).

New England, and colonists everywhere searched their souls to find out why God had allowed it. A long and hard war did much to erode their hitherto unswerving confidence that God had a special mission for His people in New England.[46]

King Philip's War was the last time Connecticut faced a major military threat nearby until the Revolution a hundred years later. But while one danger had been overcome, the war created new perils, especially by drawing the attention of the imperial government to the need to provide for the defense of the colonies. The military experience gained in 1675–76 was vital in helping Connecticut meet the challenge of Anglo-French tension along the frontier in the 1680s and 1690s, but the imperial government's attempts to curb the colony's privileges of internal self-government posed a greater threat to Connecticut's integrity, sense of purpose, and survival as a self-governing entity than hostile Indians ever did. King Philip's War was the last conflict the colony waged without an imperial dimension.[47]

46. On the cost of the war, see UC:II/394; CPR:III/300–301; and Leach, *Flintlock,* p. 244; amounts are in local money. For the impact on economic prosperity, see Main, *Society,* pp. 69–70. On taxes, see CPR:II/269, 292, 322, 401. On tax rolls, see CPR:II/236, 265–66, 290, 320; and CPR:III/17, 36. The number of taxables increased from 2,300 in 1676 to 2,490 in 1678 (SPC:V/1447). On the religious and psychological impact of the war, see CPR:II/280–83, 328–29; and the relevant parts of Leach, *Flintlock*; Vaughan, *Frontier*; Stout, *Soul*; Jennings, *Invasion*; and Slotkin and Folsom, *Judgment.*

47. For the imperial dimensions of the war, see Webb, *1676.*

Chapter Two

The Response
to Empire

REJECTION OF EMPIRE

In the late 1680s, Connecticut became embroiled in the Anglo-French contest for North America. A state of tension had existed along the frontier with Canada for three decades, principally because the Iroquois, who had been struggling with the French for control of the fur trade, looked to New York for support. Connecticut would have preferred to let New York alone help the Iroquois, but imperial planners realized that the cheapest and most effective method of defending the frontier was to combine the military resources of the northern colonies under a professional officer and send a few regular troops from England around which the colonies could gather their own forces in time of danger. The plan was an intelligent way to protect the margin of empire, but it began a twenty-five year period during which Connecticut was forced to redefine its place in England's transatlantic empire.

The leaders divided sharply among themselves when imperial planners merged Connecticut into the Dominion of New England in mid-1685. Many deputies wanted to continue as though nothing had changed, but the rest, along with most of the senior leaders, made the best of a bad situation and surrendered the government to the new governor-general, Edmund Andros, in October 1687. While Andros could now theoretically mobilize Connecticut's resources to help New York, he faced great difficulties because the Court no longer existed to legitimize the raising of troops or taxes. The senior leaders and deputies who accepted office under the Dominion claimed that "most" people in Connecticut did not have the "wherewithall" to pay taxes and thus could not afford to help "a few mercenary-spirited" Albany merchants protect their fur trade. The leaders refused to recognize that Connecticut benefited in the long run from New York's alliance with the Iroquois, still the most powerful military force in eastern North America, and that the imperial government could reasonably expect them to help sustain it. Forced to take what he could get, Andros in November 1688 sent fifty Hartford county militiamen to winter in western Massachusetts, where they helped protect the towns that formed Connecticut's first line of defense against Canada.[1]

The Dominion collapsed when news reached New England in mid-April 1689 that its principal sponsor, King James II, had been deposed by William of Orange. Connecticut was in a muddle for two weeks before a majority of the senior leaders decided to reestablish the suspended charter government, although they lacked a clear legal right to do so. Former Governor Robert Treat, former Deputy Governor James Bishop, eight former assistants, and thirty-nine newly elected deputies reconvened the General Court at Hartford on 9 May 1689, in part to give the colony a government to guide it through the war against Canada that loomed on the horizon. Despite considerable anger against the men who had knuckled under to Andros, in May and again in October the voters confirmed the senior leaders in office; they had helped Connecticut weather King Philip's War and were best qualified to handle the new challenge. But they were also under intense scrutiny. The Court met twenty-one times between May 1689 and May 1694, twice as often as required by charter, and it denied its surrogate, the seven-member Council of War, the power to raise money or to alter the charter government in any way. While Governor Treat and the council of six Hartford county leaders could raise men in an emergency, the entire Court made all important military decisions in special sessions

---

1. The best account of imperial policy is Johnson, *Adjustment*; see also Lovejoy, *Glorious Revolution,* pp. 203–08; and Barnes, *Dominion.* Webb claims imperial planners wanted to impose a "garrison government" on New England, but they never sent the soldiers to do so; as he himself says, "there are no empires without armies" (*Governors-General,* pp. xvii–xviii). Connecticut's charter government was suspended and supplanted, but the charter itself was neither revoked nor surrendered. On the split among the leaders, see CPR:III/212–13, 382; MHC:5,VIII/301; and MHC:6,III/479. On Albany, see SPC:VII/1548, 1684; and MHC:3,III/167–69 (quotation). Connecticut had accused Albany merchants of selling arms to enemy Indians during King Philip's War (CPR:II/396, 404). On poverty, see MHC:6,V/19 (quotation). On the company, see CPR:III/451, 453–54; MHC:5,VIII/487, 489–90; SPC:VIII/879, 912; CHS-WY:II/42; and Lovejoy, *Glorious Revolution,* pp. 218–19.

where senior leaders had to convince their colleagues of the wisdom and propriety of their policies.[2]

There was little disagreement about the need to preserve maximum self-government within the empire. The senior leaders, chastened by the swift collapse of the Dominion, worked to achieve this goal along with the opponents of imperial control, who reluctantly acknowledged that Connecticut was still a colony, not a sovereign state. During wartime, the leaders suppressed their deep differences about how to reach the desired end, but after the war the simmering antagonism and resentment prompted the Court to divide itself in October 1698 into an upper house of the governor, the deputy governor, and the twelve assistants and a lower house of the deputies, usually two from each town. Thereafter, the senior leaders, who were generally willing to take a more pragmatic and concil-iatory approach to imperial relations because they could expect to prosper under any reorganization, had to negotiate agreements with deputies who generally espoused a more provincial desire to keep the empire beyond arm's length and so keep expenses down and imperially appointed officials out of their backyards.[3]

The Dominion interlude permanently soured Connecticut's leaders on the idea of an imperially imposed military union of the northern colonies, and increased the time it took them to mobilize their military forces. However, the abrupt recovery of responsibility for their own defense brought new clarity to their assessment of the military situation. They now accepted the need to support Albany, and the trade that kept the Iroquois allied with the English, and in early May 1689 sent an agent to

2. On the collapse of the Dominion, see CHC:III/144–45, 156–57; Lovejoy, *Glorious Revolution,* pp. 220–70; and Johnson, *Adjustment,* pp. 71–135. On re-suming the charter government, see CPR:III/250–53; Johnson, *Adjustment,* pp. 110–13; Dunn, *Puritans and Yankees,,* pp. 287–89; Andrews, *Colonial Pe-riod,* IV/373; and Barnes, *Dominion,* p. 249. Treat had succeeded the late Gov-ernor Leete in 1683. On the Council, see CPR:IV/6, 18, 62, 84–86, 205, 262–63, 320. Gershom Bulkeley, a physician from Wethersfield and the most vocal opponent of the charter, unfairly claimed that the reinstalled leaders invented "bugbear stories . . . to fright the people into conformity and compliance with them" (CHC:III/173, 195; also CPR:III/455–60). John Allyn of Hartford, senior assistant until his death in November 1696, directed the response to frontier emergencies and relayed information to Treat at Milford, who rode north for Council meetings. On cooperation among the leaders, see MHC:6,V/111.

3. On dividing the General Court, thereafter called the General Assembly, see CPR:IV/267.

join New York and Massachusetts in renewing the alliance with the tribes. Their concern did not extend to Manhattan, however, where in late May the last remnants of the Dominion fell to a mob led by Jacob Leisler, a local merchant and militia captain; they sent little aid because the town was not in immediate danger. By late June 1689, Connecticut had solved its military problems for the moment with a minimum of effort, but new threats from Canada over the summer forced it to consider other ways of helping its neighbors. Although cooperation in meeting the new dangers would demonstrate to London that the colonies did not need imperial supervision, they squabbled constantly about what to do, principally because Connecticut was less exposed to French raiders than were New York and Massachusetts.[4]

The Court was willing to bear its fair share of the burden once it decided that military action was necessary. In early September 1689 it was willing to raise two hundred volunteers to help prevent the Indian war in Maine from spilling into the upper Connecticut valley, but it shelved this project a few weeks later when it learned that Albany was in danger again. Because Massachusetts claimed it was too deeply committed in Maine to spare any aid, and despite an "epidemical sickness" that "disabled and impoverished" the colony, the Court sent sixty-three men to Albany in mid-November after the town agreed to pay part of the cost. (Twenty-four men from western Massachusetts joined the Connecticut company, for a total of eighty-seven men.) The Court's investment was not large (only 2 percent of the thirty-one hundred militiamen) because Connecticut was not directly threatened. Few men volunteered to spend the winter on the frontier, and the Court reluctantly had to invoke impressment the first time it sent soldiers beyond the upper Connecticut valley. The men themselves lacked military skills. They were farmers and laborers, not woodsmen or Indian-fighters. Indeed, the "bulk" of them had never been "far from home" before.[5]

4. On helping Albany and Manhattan, see DNY:I/179–80, 183; DNY:II/ 5, 13, 16, 147; CPR:II/492–93; CPR:III/255, 460–63, 466–67; and Trelease, *Indian Affairs*, pp. 296–97. The Court also feared that helping Leisler's illegal government might provoke imperial anger against Connecticut.

5. On Maine, see CA-War:II/10–13, 16; CHC:XXI/311–12; DNY:II/51; CPR:IV/2–5; and Colden, *History*, p. 88. On helping Albany, see Colden, *History*, pp. 92–93; CA-War:II/22, 24–26, 29–30, 45; DNY:II/40, 43–46 (quotation), 53, 55–58, 67, 74–76, 83, 86, 89, 95–96, 103, 127–28; CHC:XXI/ 317–18; SPC:VIII/524; Pynchon, *Papers*, I/217; and Leder, *Livingston*, p. 61.

As in King Philip's War, prominent political and militia leaders did not go to war. Instead, the Court gave command of the company to a forty-year-old, one-term Hartford selectman and militia ensign, Jonathan Bull. The son of a former active service officer and son-in-law of Hartford's influential minister, Bull was the sort of well-connected, second-rank leader on whom the colony relied in wartime. His experience actually made him the best choice: he had led the company Andros sent to western Massachusetts in 1688–89 and had been the colony's agent to Albany in May and August 1689. The Court trusted him and, more importantly, so did the soldiers, the bond which lay at the heart of military leadership in Connecticut. The need to appoint officers who were acceptable to the men in the ranks was underscored when the company's lieutenant was killed in the French raid on Schenectady on 9 February 1690. In accordance with long-established custom, the Council promoted the ensign to replace the lieutenant. However, the Connecticut men in the company did not want the first sergeant, the leader of the men from western Massachusetts, to succeed the ensign, and they demanded that the second sergeant, whom they claimed was more capable, become ensign. The Council agreed to violate seniority to placate its soldiers: it thought they would be more obedient if they chose their own officers as they did in the militia.[6]

The Schenectady raid shocked Connecticut into paying more attention to its own defenses and less to the New York frontier. Bull's men had been "in hopes of returning home" even before the attack, and the Council allowed them to come home in early March, as soon as it was clear the raid did not herald a full-scale invasion; the leaders understood that or-

Albany asked New England for help to avoid sharing the fur trade with Leisler. On the company, see CPR:IV/13; CA-War:II/29 (quotation); and Pynchon, *Papers*, pp. 218–20. On the number of militiamen, see SPC:VIII/879. On men from western Massachusetts, see Pynchon, *Papers*, I/219, 225. A Massachusetts man illustrated the fragility of the impressment system when he "ran away, to the great discontent of some and to the emboldening of others, so that some of the soldiers told me [Pynchon] if he were let escape . . . they would also run away" (Pynchon, *Papers*, I/220).

6. On Bull, see CPR:II/285, 306, 497, 573; CPR:III/215; and CHC:VI/193, 215, 225. He went to Albany in August to join in renewing, yet again, the English alliance with the Iroquois (Pynchon, *Papers*, I/213–16). The company lost ten men at Schenectady (DNY:I/189–92; and CA-War:II/30). On the promotions, see CA-War:II/29; and Jacobus, *New Haven*, pp. 1715–16. The Massachusetts soldiers were "troubled they had not a commissioned officer of their own" (Pynchon, *Papers*, I/219, 225).

dering the company to remain at Albany would only provoke a mutiny and make it harder to raise soldiers in the future. The Council directed the towns to erect fortifications to protect themselves against a surprise attack, and the Court followed in early April with measures to rejuvenate local defenses without straining its resources. Harking back to the model of King Philip's War, it did not hesitate to draft every seventh militiaman into "a flying army" of dragoons ready to ride to any threatened town. It gave command of these ad hoc units to veterans of King Philip's War and appointed prominent subordinate officers to ensure local support. At the least possible cost and inconvenience, the dragoons filled the slot in the defense system between the militia and the active service troops on the frontier; they cost nothing until called into service and were not intended to remain away from home for extended periods. The dragoon companies saw little service before they were disbanded in October 1690, although a few men were drafted from the Hartford county company to serve on foot against Canada during the summer of 1690. Rather than call out the dragoons, for two years after mid-1690 the Council used the Hartford county militia troop (about fifty-five men) as its mobile reserve, a burden it was willing to impose because the troopers had volunteered to serve in this elite unit.[7]

The Schenectady disaster greatly complicated intercolonial relations because it changed the strategic situation on the New York frontier. Arguing that the English now had to "root out" the French or risk losing Iroquois support, Albany wanted the New England colonies to attack Canada in the spring. It claimed that an invasion down the Champlain valley to

---

7. On bringing home the company, see CA-War:II/29 (quotation), 46–48; CHC:XXI/318; DNY:II/95–99, 105–07; and SPC:VIII/805, 2763. To replace the company, the Council gave New York permission "to beat the drum for volunteers" in Connecticut, but few men enlisted (DNY:II/117, 130–31). On the dragoons, see CPR:IV/19, 38; and SPC:VIII/879. The Court exempted five frontier towns from raising dragoons. John Miles, a veteran of King Philip's War, became the New Haven county dragoon captain (NHT:II/352; and NHT:III/46, 73–75, 78–79, 82–86, 92–93, 108, 144, 181, 190). He retired in May 1690 when he was elected to the committee to manage New Haven town's military affairs (CPR:IV/27). On the troop, see SPC:VIII/879; CPR:IV/15; and CA-War:II/84, 87, 108. It went to western Massachusetts in June and to New London in July, when French privateers threatened islands off the coast. Four hundred militiamen could not stop French privateers from ravaging Block Island; ships from Rhode Island later destroyed the seaborne raiders (MHC:6,III/3–11; and MHC:5,VIII/493).

Montreal would not be difficult, and suggested that a concurrent attack up the St. Lawrence River against Quebec might be decisive; the principal problem would be coordinating the two attacks to divide French resources. Albany's idea was the source of the strategy which led to the conquest of Canada in 1758–60, but New England did not immediately adopt this bold plan in 1690. As the situation rapidly developed beyond Connecticut's ability to meet it alone, the Council waited to hear what Massachusetts would do. Although Massachusetts claimed to understand the importance of Albany, it decided to attack Port Royal in Nova Scotia with all the forces it could spare from its own frontiers. Connecticut was left to do what it could to defend Albany, and in mid-April the Court ordered one hundred men (sixty colonists and forty Indians) to march immediately to the town, and sent another hundred men in early June to guard farmers as they planted their crops. By then, delegates from New York and New England, meeting at Manhattan, had agreed to launch an overland invasion of Canada, an attack which by itself, however, did not promise decisive results. Connecticut agreed to contribute two hundred soldiers (6.5 percent of thirty-one hundred militiamen), plus forty Indian scouts, a force to be built around the men already at Albany.[8]

The Court wanted men to volunteer to serve against Canada, and to encourage them to enlist it increased a private's wages to 9 shillings a week, a shilling more than in King Philip's War, although less than the rise in food prices since 1675. It also granted them all the plunder they could find, a no-cost way of stirring up enthusiasm it would repeat every time it raised men for an invasion of Canada, but one which soldiers found nearly meaningless on a barren frontier. Twenty years later, it would offer bounty money to attract volunteers, but it refused to strain its resources to do so now. Connecticut spent over 3,600 pounds sterling in 1690, over half its total military expenditure of 6,000 pounds sterling between 1688

8. On Albany's ideas, see CA-War:II/29 (quotation), 41–42, 46, 55, 61, 74; and SPC:VIII/805, 836, 865, 955, 2763–64. On French strategy, see Eccles, "Frontenac's Military Policies." Albany had first suggested a two-pronged invasion during the Second Dutch War. To get additional help, it submitted to Leisler's government in March 1690. On the companies, see CPR:IV/15–16, 21–22. Albany wanted Connecticut to train its men in woodscraft (CA-War:II/ 55), but only Albany's own bushlopers came close to matching the French *coureurs de bois*. On the conference, see CPR:IV/21, 26; DNY:II/134–35; CA-War:II/80, 82; and MHC:5,VIII/307. New York raised half the four hundred men it promised.

and 1695; it could not have afforded more. Instead of offering bounty money, the Court tried to attract recruits by appointing popular and experienced officers, including two men who had proven their worth over the past winter at Albany. These incentives drew few volunteers, however, and most soldiers were draftees. Some young men thought that being drafted meant they could rely on the colony for their support, but four Hartford county bachelors learned differently when the Court refused to pay them between the time they were drafted on 20 April and when they marched on 2 June. Still, the Court did not want to antagonize the draftees or compromise future efforts to raise soldiers. For example, it refused to punish desertion strictly; while a deserter from the contemporary English regular army would face savage physical punishment if caught, a Connecticut deserter would only forfeit half his wages.[9]

The chances of conquering Canada improved dramatically in late June 1690 when Massachusetts augmented the force that had sacked Port Royal and sent it to attack Quebec by sea; the plan thus finally achieved the shape recommended by Albany. The Court realized that a seaborne attack would divert French attention from the overland invasion, but it was itself distracted by French raiders in the upper valley and along the seacoast, and refused to raise troops to join the Massachusetts fleet. Even worse, it squabbled with New York over who would command the attack on Montreal. Connecticut soldiers refused to serve under Jacob Leisler's nominee, and the Court insisted that he name a new commander. It wanted, and Leisler eventually agreed, to appoint fifty-two-year-old Fitz-John Winthrop of New London, the popular scion of the most famous family in New England, but a man who had not served in King Philip's War and who thus had limited understanding of war in the wilderness. He showed little confidence in the invasion plan, and lacked the determination to overcome the serious logistical obstacles his army faced. After dysentery and smallpox broke out among the troops, Winthrop was reduced to sending a few raiders to alarm Montreal. His inability to divert French attention from the fleet contributed to the failure to take Quebec; defeat

9. On the companies, see CPR:IV/15–16, 19, 21–22. On food prices, see CPR:IV/13. On costs, see CA-War:III/10; CSL-RW/191; and CA-FC:I/13. Sixty years later, Jonathan Trumbull believed that Connecticut spent 7,000 pounds sterling in 1690, 5,000 for Albany and 2,000 for western Massachusetts (CSL-JT:XXI/10). On the officers, see Jacobus, *Fairfield*, 1/302, 340–42, 611. On the bachelors, see CA-War:II/152. On deserters, see CPR:IV/41.

turned into disaster when storms and disease decimated the fleet on its way home.[10]

The northern colonies had the right plan to conquer Canada, but they lacked the resources to do so without help from England. Because their economies could not generate vast sums of money on short notice, they did not have the financial strength to organize and supply a campaign over distances unprecedented in colonial experience and which taxed their logistical expertise beyond the breaking point. Nor, despite a ten-to-one advantage in population, did they have the surplus manpower to keep large numbers of men in service all summer. Fundamental weaknesses forced them to defer offensive action until London decided to send the men, money, and ships that would give another invasion a better chance of success. The colonies were willing to live with the chronic danger of French and Indian raiders rather than strain their resources again. Apart from the cost (which, however, was less than during King Philip's War), this way of meeting the French threat was not a burden on Connecticut.

The failure of the 1690 expedition drew attention to intercolonial disputes, and convinced imperial officials to try again to supervise the defense of the northern frontier. They sent a royal governor with a few regular troops to New York in the spring of 1691, a step which renewed Connecticut's fears for its charter. The Court refused to relinquish control of its military resources to imperial officials, and its partnership with New York deteriorated into a confrontation with imperial authority. Benjamin Fletcher, New York governor for most of the 1690s, underestimated how much Connecticut hated anything that resembled the Dominion, and he

10. On the expedition, see CA-War:II/64, 69, 72, 79, 86–87, 96, 98–99, 104, 108–14; MHC:5,VIII/305–06; CHC:XXI/321–24; CHC:XXIV/35–36; SPC:VIII/875; DNY:II/142, 149; MHC:6,III/508–10; Johnson, *Adjustment*, pp. 190–204; and Leach, *Arms*, pp. 89–99. One ensign deserted and spread rumors that Connecticut soldiers were so ill treated that they were about to fight Leisler's men (CA-War:II/97, 106). On Winthrop, see CA-War:II/102; MHC:5,VIII/303–10; CHC:XXIV/32–33; and Leder, *Livingston*, pp. 71–73. He did not understand how thoroughly Iroquois warriors terrorized Canada (CA-War:II/102). Connecticut Indians were drunk much of the time (CA-War:II/75, 107). On conditions in camp, see CA-War:II/64–66, 70, 89–90; DNY:II/143; and CHC:XXI/321–22. Better sanitation and provisions might have curbed dysentery, but smallpox was harder to stop. On the failure of the expedition, see CA-War:II/114–17, 125; SPC:VIII/1157, 1239, 1282, 1313; SPC:X/229; MHC:5,VIII/308–24; MHC:6,III/12–13; and DNY:II/169. The Court retroactively approved Winthrop's conduct in October 1690 (CPR:IV/38).

antagonized his neighbors even more by denigrating their previous efforts to help Albany and by encouraging a recalcitrant few to complain against the charter. The Court responded by petitioning King William III to confirm its right to control the militia, and in February 1693 he gave Connecticut most of what it wanted. While he ordered Connecticut to support New York, and gave the New York governor control of its militia in an emergency, he did not reestablish the Dominion; Fletcher never received the "absolute government" of Connecticut he said he needed.[11]

Geography allowed Connecticut to treat principles of intercolonial parity and local control as every bit as urgent and important as defense of the frontier. The fact that the colony was not directly threatened by the French gave the leaders freedom to wrangle about costs and to mobilize their resources only when they were convinced a disaster was about to overwhelm the frontier: "In case of invasion we should be ready to grant all assistance in our power, but we do not see our way to incur such expense upon every report of an enemy." Like their predecessors in 1666, they wanted Albany and the Iroquois to bear the burden of their defense, and failed to see that the tribes would not continue to fight without tangible evidence of English support. Even when the French raided the Mohawks in February 1693, the Court took the time to meet in special session before sending 150 dragoons to Albany; the French had retired long before the first soldier left Connecticut. Although the leaders admitted that raiders could attack and withdraw "before we can possibly get thither," they refused to support a permanent force ranging the frontier because disease and floods were ravaging Connecticut's own food-growing regions. When Fletcher went to Hartford in October to demand aid for the "staggering" Iroquois, the leaders gave him little beyond assurances

11. On relations with New York, see CA-War:II/135, 170, 172; CHC:XXIV/49–54; SPC:VIII/1374, 1463, 1628, 1638, 1691, 1987, 2462, 2477; and SPC:IX/84, 86, 185, 245, 499–500, 557, 603. The defense of Albany cost 10,000 pounds sterling a year (two-thirds more than Connecticut spent in seven years of war), and New York's revenues were down because people were emigrating to escape taxation and military service (SPC:IX/178–79, 414, 611, 829, 991; and SPC:VIII/2247). On petitioning the king, see CA-War:II/ 160–63; SPC:IX/75–78, 93, 96, 499, 500 (quotation); and CSL-RW/214–16. In June 1692, the imperial government gave command of the Connecticut militia in an emergency to Massachusetts governor Sir William Phips, but the leaders deflected his attempts to enforce his commission before it was transferred to the New York governor (Pynchon, *Papers*, I/259, 265).

that they would help "according to our ability, and in proportion with our neighboring colonies," the formula to which Connecticut adhered for the rest of the colonial period. They were unresponsive to genuine threats because they wished to remain free from imperial control, but they were fortunate that the Iroquois survived all attacks launched by the increasingly weary French.[12]

Connecticut avoided imperial wrath because New York withstood French raiders, and because the Court sent Fitz-John Winthrop to London in August 1693 to convince the king it was doing its utmost to defend the frontier. Winthrop exaggerated the help Connecticut sent to Albany, emphasized the debilitating effects of disease and floods, and blackened Fletcher as a tyrant who called the colony's men into service without the slightest hint of a French invasion and who illegally demanded full power over the Connecticut militia. Winthrop won confirmation of self-government in internal matters, including control of the militia except in case of an actual invasion of New York, because the king wished to uphold the rights of the charter colonies, mainly to show domestic critics that he exercised royal authority within legal limits. By December 1696 imperial officials, responding to domestic political needs, had resolved to recall Fletcher and were asking Winthrop for proof of his misconduct. Con-

12. On Connecticut's attitude, see SPC:VIII/1647 (quotation), 1671; DNY:II/219–20; and Allyn and Pitkin, *Connecticut Vindicated.* The Council rejected New London's request for help to build a harbor-defense fort, even though it knew "it is next to impossible after the enemy is discovered upon the coasts to send for and receive relief" (CA-War:II/134; and CSL-RW/156). The Council garrisoned the existing Saybrook fort in late 1693 to help protect towns upriver (CA-War:II/184–94). On the attack on the Mohawks, see CA-War:II/165–66, 168–69, 177, 212 (quotation); CSL-RW/229; CPR:IV/87–88, 159–60, 168; SPC:IX/82, 1918, 1961, 2054; SPC:X/27; CHS-WY:II/44; and Pynchon, *Papers,* I/263. The same thing happened when the French attacked the Oneidas and Onondagas in July 1696 (CA-War:III/12–16; and CPR:IV/171–73). On Fletcher at Hartford, see CPR:IV/111–18 (quotation 113); and SPC:IX/500 (quotation), 590, 606, 610, 613, 649, 667, 672. The Council later promised to help him apprehend deserters from the regular companies at Albany and to punish those who hindered his legal right to recover his men (CA-War:III/6, 9; SPC:IX/1987, 2054; CPR:IV/156–57; and CSL-RW/207–08). Opponents of imperial control convinced the Court in October 1696 to free a Farmington man caught hiding deserters, in effect revoking the Council's pledge (CPR:IV/163–64). Desertion was still a problem in Queen Anne's War (SPC:XIV/358; SPC:XVI/861; SPC:XVII/184, 410; CSL-RW/209; and MHC:6,III/267–68).

necticut voters showed how highly they valued Winthrop's services by electing him governor when he returned home in May 1698.[13]

As King William's War turned into the longest conflict Connecticut had yet encountered, the colony expended most of its effort to guard the frontier in western Massachusetts, where long periods of tedious garrison service alternated with short bursts of deadly danger. The leaders sent Hartford county dragoons to chase French raiders, and occasionally dispatched men from New Haven and Fairfield counties to garrison the most exposed upper valley towns. The amount of aid was always small (thirty to sixty men), and service was so arduous that soldiers seem to have been younger and poorer than previously. Raids on frontier towns were serious business, but they did not generate the kind of public interest seen in King Philip's War. Because no disaster galvanized the population, Connecticut had great difficulty finding soldiers, and instead relied on Indian allies, whose importance increased as the war dragged on. The longer the war lasted, the harder it became to find soldiers. Most men were impressed, while the few volunteers seem to have been poor men in search of employment. By the spring of 1697, the Council thought "the most likely method" of protecting the frontier was to arm, provision, and pay thirty Indian and colonial rangers and, like Massachusetts, offer them a 10-pound bounty for every enemy scalp they took. But bounty hunters were no substitute for regular patrols. King William's War demonstrated that a military system based on popular consent and participation could be mobilized only when the threat animated and energized the entire colony.[14]

13. Winthrop's connections in England made him the best agent (CPR:IV/ 102–03; CA-For:I/42; CHC:XXIV/57–97; and SPC:IX/861, 999, 1015, 1107). No colony contributed to the defense of Albany (CA-War:II/208–09; SPC:IX/ 1176, 1247–51, 1253). On Connecticut's exaggerations, see CHC:XXIV/111–16; and CSL-RW/219, 227, 235. According to Fletcher, squabbling among the colonies demoralized the Iroquois, who "plainly see we are not united; . . . the stronger these colonies grow in parts, the weaker we are in the whole" (SPC:X/ 14). On confirmation of militia privileges, see MHC:5,IX/176–78. On Winthrop's election, see CPR:IV/244; Governor Treat was relegated to deputy governor.

14. On helping the frontier, see CPR:IV/47, 67–69, 90, 106, 149, 152, 179–80, 216–18; CA-War:II/85, 153, 156, 177, 180, 240, 243–44; CA-War:III/1–5, 7, 10, 33–34, 39, 42; CHC:XXIV/74–75, 109–10, 113; CSL-RW/191; CHS-WY:II/33, 54; and Pynchon, *Papers,* I/242, 252, 254–55, 266, 286, 288–90. On 1 October 1691, a draftee complained that he had been

Recruiting for the regular company at Albany in November 1696 illustrates the difficulty of keeping men in the field. To begin with, the recruits were not the ablest men available; the sergeant, thirty-seven-year-old Jonathan Colefax of Wethersfield, had been so "much disenabled in one of his arms" during King Philip's War that he had been excused from militia training. Although men like Colefax may have had few prospects at home, like all Connecticut men they viewed soldiering as only temporary employment; Fletcher had earlier learned that "no man here will be a soldier for life." When he tried to keep them past the expiration of their enlistment on 11 May 1697, they began to return home. The governor called them deserters, but in their own eyes they had fulfilled their obligations. In the absence of a direct threat, the leaders could not require a soldier to serve longer than the time for which he had originally contracted: if they "should not hold to their word," it "may discourage our soldiers from going out when they are prest." Fletcher was the first imperial official to complain about how Connecticut men viewed military service, although strict adherence to the contract between soldiers and government had always been part of the way the colony made war.[15]

Lack of popular involvement made good leadership vital: "If our soldiers have officers whom they know and love, they will be more free to attend the service and more courageous against the enemy." The length of the war meant that the colony had to rely constantly on the same cadre of second-rank leaders; unlike in King Philip's War, turnover was low. In early 1692 the distinction of being the most active officer on the frontier passed from Captain Jonathan Bull to thirty-three-year-old William Whiting of Hartford, who owed his initial appointment to the fact that he was the son of the local minister, nephew of the colony treasurer, and

---

impressed illegally because "the constable neither read nor showed any warrant." The Court backed the constable, whereupon the man replied that then the constable "had a license to lie" (CA-CM:I/184a). Connecticut thought western Massachusetts exaggerated the danger at least once, in January 1692 (Pynchon, *Papers*, I/245–47). On scalp bounties, see CA-War:III/29 (quotation); and CPR:IV/196. The best study of the war is Hanna, "New England Military Institutions."

15. On the recruits, see CA-War:III/22–23, 31–35, 39–42; CPR:IV/170, 190, 204, 216–20; and SPC:X/14 (quotation), 521–22, 526, 823, 852. On Colefax, see CPR:III/99–100; Stiles, *Wethersfield*, II/246; and Jacobus, *Hale*, p. 467. Six months after he married in May 1696, he left his pregnant wife to serve on the frontier. On the Council, see CA-War:III/41 (quotation).

Bull's brother-in-law. During his twenty-year military career, he demonstrated considerable ability and played the most important role in making the military system work. He led the companies to western Massachusetts, sent back to Connecticut the information on which the Court and Council based their decisions, and wisely advocated an active defense with scouts in constant motion to reduce the chance that locally superior enemy forces might overwhelm an isolated town. Although his relations with other Hartford county leaders were sometimes strained, he did a good job under circumstances so difficult that no one could be persuaded to replace him.[16]

Like Bull before him, Whiting never became an important elected leader. Failure to win a decisive victory over French raiders denied him the chance to bask in public acclaim, and his protracted absences on the frontier diminished his appeal with the voters. When the Hartford county troop elected him captain in May 1696, he gave "considerable offense" by always leaving it "destitute of an officer." He fared no better with political office. Hartford voters waited until December 1697, after the end of the war, to elect him tax assessor, and did not elect him a deputy for the first time until May 1712, after major service in Queen Anne's War. Whiting received more recognition and reward than his subordinates, some of whom were never elected to commissioned rank in the militia because they were always away defending the frontier. While thirty-four-year-old Stephen Hollister of Wethersfield was appointed initially in 1693 because he was Governor Treat's nephew, his skill as a leader of scouts and rangers turned him into the Connecticut equivalent of a professional officer. But because he never won militia rank, he remained a junior captain in Whiting's command. He led a company to Deerfield in 1703 only because the original captain's pregnant wife demanded that her husband stay home.[17]

16. On officers, see SPC:X/27 (quotation). On Whiting, see Goodwin, *Genealogical Notes,* pp. 330–31; MHC:6,III/176–77, 281, 368–69; CPR:IV/133, 190n, 274, 284; CA-TL:IV/69; and Pynchon, *Papers,* I/252. He was wounded in September 1697 (Pynchon, *Papers,* I/304).

17. The Court named Whiting colony marshal from 1693 to 1701 (CPR:IV/87, 303) and appointed him an agent to Massachusetts in March 1693 (CPR:IV/90; SPC:IX/191). Hartford voters elected him a tax assessor between and after the wars (CHC:VI/250, 252, 256, 258, 262, 265, 271, 303), and the Lower House chose him as its first clerk in October 1698. He was nominated to be an assistant in 1714, but was never elected. Part of his difficulty in winning elective

All in all, Connecticut could be satisfied with the way it had managed its military affairs during King William's War. By contributing to the defense of western Massachusetts, it helped divert French raiders from its own towns. Equally important, it thwarted the efforts of imperial officials to control its militia, and kept to a minimum the men and money it had to send to the New York frontier. This success was the crowning achievement of Connecticut's desire to remain free from imperial supervision, an attitude pushed to the extreme by vivid memories of how the colony had lost its independent identity during the Dominion debacle. Unfortunately for Connecticut, its efforts to keep control of its military resources were too successful. Around the turn of the eighteenth century, the imperial government became increasingly angry about Connecticut's attempts to hold it at arm's length and began to consider ways of curbing the colony's truculent behavior. Successful isolationism in the 1690s misled some leaders into thinking that Connecticut could avoid the empire indefinitely.

ACCOMMODATION TO EMPIRE

Connecticut faced two major problems when the second round of the Anglo-French conflict (known in North America as Queen Anne's War) began in February 1703. The first was a radically different military situation along the frontier. The Iroquois, unhappy with the lack of English support, had signed a treaty of neutrality with Canada in 1701, leaving New England to defend itself without their help. Initially, the Assembly responded in traditional ways to the new danger. It gave direction of military affairs between its sessions to Governor Winthrop and a Council of seven leaders who lived near his home at New London. But New London was so far from the frontier in western Massachusetts that in October it created a seven-member Committee of War at Hartford to coordinate aid for the upper valley. Winthrop tried to exercise greater control over the Hartford leaders than Treat had in the 1690s, until the devastating French

---

office in Hartford town was the fact that men only a few years older filled most offices for twenty years after 1690. He had been a captain on active service for more than two years when he was elected a militia ensign in October 1694. No other post was available: Bull was captain, and Ciprian Nichols, a deputy who had led dragoons to Albany in 1690, was lieutenant (CPR:IV/133). On the troop, see CPR:IV/258; and MHC:6,III/56 (quotation). On Hollister, see Jacobus, *Hale,* pp. 615–22; MHC:6,III/140, 145, 148, 247; CSL-RW/177; and Pynchon, *Papers,* I/288–90, 298. He died in the 1709 expedition.

raid on Deerfield on 29 February 1704 convinced him to let them manage the details of helping the frontier.[18]

The second problem concerned the poor state of Connecticut's reputation in London. Complaints against the charter had reached such an intensity that Winthrop feared the imperial government might revoke the colony's privileges of internal self-government. He wanted to use the help Connecticut sent to the upper valley to deflect imperial anger and convince London to let it keep its charter. He was incensed when Governor Joseph Dudley of Massachusetts complained that Connecticut was not doing enough to help defend the frontier. Like the New York governors in the 1690s, Dudley refused to treat Connecticut as a sovereign state, and antagonized it by claiming authority to command its troops in western Massachusetts and by recruiting Mohegan warriors for service in Maine without its permission. The colony eventually found a solution to both problems: by participating in the expeditions against Canada in 1709–11, it simultaneously helped to eliminate the menace to the frontier and demonstrated its loyalty to the empire.[19]

Some familiar weaknesses in Connecticut's military system were evident at the start of the war. In October 1703 the Assembly ordered parties of

18. Connecticut seems to have been unaware of Iroquois neutrality (MHC:6,III/219–20, 223–25, 247, 262–63, 282). On Winthrop's relations with the Hartford leaders, see CPR:IV/442–43, 462, 483, 497, 535; CPR:V/29, 32–33, 87; CSL-RW/171; CHC:XXIV/172–73, 177–78; and MHC:6,III/193. Committees of war were created in the seacoast counties in May 1704; as always, senior leaders served with deputies and militia officers (CPR:IV/462, 483). Because only two assistants lived near the governor, the Assembly included four "able and judicious freemen" in his council (CPR:IV/320, 407–08, 442, 488–89, 519; and CPR:V/22 et seq.). The Council played a major role in organizing Connecticut's part in the three expeditions against the French, especially in 1710 when the troops sailed from New London for Port Royal.

19. On the charges against Connecticut, see CA-For:II/73, 87, 93, 99, 101; MHC:6,III/302; CPR:IV/219–20; SPC:XVII/701, 976; and SPC:XVIII/18. The imperial government eventually forced it to repeal its ban on Quakers, enforce the Navigation Acts, and allow appeals from its courts to the Crown. On Dudley, see MHC:6,III/190–91, 195–99, 216–17, 229–30, 273–79, 337–45. He complained that Connecticut harbored men who were trying to escape taxation and military service (SPC:XVI/1094; SPC:XVII/109–10, 205, 455, 659, 947; SPC:XVIII/70, 85; SPC:XIX/391; MHC:6,III/330–31, 337–39; and Great Britain, *Proceedings,* III/26, 148) and lied about the help Connecticut did send to the upper valley (SPC:XVII/1274, 1422; SPC:XVIII/69).

Indians and colonial soldiers to patrol the frontier, but when the warriors refused to serve, the colonists stayed home, claiming that they knew neither "the woods nor the manner of that work." The colony was unprepared to respond quickly to French raids because the Assembly refused to pay dragoons to be ready to march on receipt of an alarm. Towns in western Massachusetts reacted by asking for help at the first hint of danger, thereby angering the men who rushed to their aid when no attack materialized. Hartford county leaders knew the best solution was to garrison Connecticut men in the upper valley, but they shrank from forcing men to undertake such unpopular service because "the people" now construed the power to raise soldiers "to be for the defense" of Connecticut and "not [to] extend to other provinces." The arguments the colony had used to avoid sending men to Albany during King William's War now kept it from doing more to defend western Massachusetts.[20]

The destruction of Deerfield grabbed Connecticut's attention by showing how unexpected, devastating, and uncomfortably close a raid could be. Dragoons were dispatched immediately, and in March and May the Assembly enacted measures that greatly improved home defenses. For the first time since March 1690, it ordered towns to fortify to reduce their vulnerability to surprise attack. It established a system of scouts, reinforced the more exposed western towns, paid residents to guard themselves (which it had refused to do during King Philip's War), and even restricted the movements of Indians within the colony. These measures assuaged Connecticut's fears for its safety, and cleared the way for the unprecedented help the Assembly sent to western Massachusetts in 1704. For a year it made demands on manpower and resources that had been unthinkable during King William's War, and brought Connecticut's frontier military system to a peak of effectiveness. By making impressment more stringent and creating a commissary system, it was able to keep unprecedented numbers in the field, "not less than eight hundred men" in July, costing "more than 100 pounds per day." Perhaps fifteen hundred men (35 percent of forty-two hundred militiamen) served at some point during the year. Pay was the largest single expense, but costs for horse hire, provisions, and ammunition were also substantial. Connecticut spent almost 10,000 pounds sterling in the year after March 1704, a third more than during all of King William's War.[21]

20. On the military system, see CPR:IV/444; CSL-RW/164, 201; CHC: XXIV/163–64 (quotation); and MHC:6,III/140–41, 147–52 (quotation 148), 159–60, 169–70, 173–76.

21. On the dragoons, see MHC:6,III/176–77, 182–83, 186–88; CHC:

As had been the case whenever it sent reinforcements to western Massachusetts, the Hartford Committee of War drafted men from several militia companies into temporary dragoon units. For example, the 150 dragoons it sent to Deerfield on 1 March 1704 were drawn from the five companies in Hartford, Windsor, and Wethersfield. It built the dragoons around a core of men who served again and again, and filled out the ranks with young bachelors impressed from a wide range of social and economic backgrounds, as in King Philip's War. Some towns drafted any able-bodied man. Even before the sack of Deerfield increased the numbers required, Greenwich militia officers impressed the younger brother of one of the town's deputies as one of its six dragoons. After March, the sheer size of the effort disrupted economic activity. In Hartford county, shoes were scarce by July because "most of the shoemakers" had been drafted. The dragoons were almost always led by officers of the militia companies from which they were drafted, including many captains who were also political leaders. These men were not the perennial deputies—such men rarely served—but they were the most prominent men to go on active service since King Philip's War.[22]

XXIV/172–77; and SPC:XVII/260. On defensive measures, see CPR:IV/455–56, 462–66, 472; CHC:VI/271–72; CPR:V/15–16, 32, 39, 83, 86–87; CSL-RW/165, 180; MHC:6,III/209, 366–67; CSL-LH/27–28 Oct 1708; and CHS-RW/26 Jun 1704. On costs, see CPR:IV/457–59, 483–84, 504; MHC:6,III/235–36 (quotation), 276, 281; CA-War:III/67; and MHC:6,V/128–30. Trumbull thought seventeen hundred men and nine hundred horses served between 1703 and 1706, costing 11,000 pounds sterling (CSL-JT:XXI/10), most of it in 1704. Connecticut reported that it had thirty-five hundred militiamen in 1709 (CA-For:I/126), only 10 percent of the population; forty-five hundred is more likely. The colony was doing its utmost to attract more recruits, as the increase in a private's wages from the 9 shillings a week of 1690 to 10 shillings, 6 pence demonstrates; in October 1704 pay was lowered to the previous level, with 12 shillings a week reserved for men who turned out fully equipped during the winter (CPR:IV/440, 483–84, 506; and CA-War:III/62). Connecticut paid Indians a shilling a day (CPR:IV/456–57, 463–64; and CHC:XXIV/172–73). Wages, as always, were calculated in country pay, not sterling.

22. On Deerfield, see CA-War:III/67. On Greenwich, see CSL-RW/202; and Jacobus, *Fairfield,* I/385. No militia company served as a complete unit, not even the Hartford county troop. Troopers received higher pay and tax advantages not shared by the dragoons (CPR:V/12, 83, 301). The conclusion about who served is based on lists of one-third of Fairfield and New Haven county militiamen

The principal virtue of the dragoons was speed of response. When news arrived at Hartford on 13 May 1704 that raiders had attacked Northampton that day, Major Whiting and 192 men rode north immediately, some on horses impressed from deputies attending the Assembly. "All the brisk able men as far as Wethersfield, being then in the fields, left their plows . . . and marched away immediately, and were followed by more from as far as Middletown and Farmington in three or four hours . . . when we could hardly have thought they had yet [had] notice." Although the response was "as expeditious as was rationally to be expected," it could not catch a hit-and-run enemy. Whiting knew that dragoons based in Hartford county could never overtake raiders who had withdrawn even before he received news of their attack. He recommended keeping dragoons in the upper valley, but the Assembly would not keep men "away longer from their business than necessity requires" because "it may discourage them from the like readiness another time."[23]

Long weeks of patrolling and standing watch diluted the sense of urgency that induced men to serve temporarily in an emergency, and made it difficult for Connecticut to sustain popular enthusiasm for the scouting and garrison service needed to counter French raiders. The Council quickly spread the burden beyond Hartford county. The three seacoast counties supplied 45 of the 60 men (75 percent) who spent twenty-seven weeks at Deerfield over the summer and 206 of the 343 men (60 percent) sent to other towns for up to seventeen weeks. Protracted service eroded morale. By mid-July the company at Deerfield was "out of order" because, according to the Hartford Committee, the men were "without the enjoyment of the public worship." Inability to come to grips with the enemy probably did more to dishearten the soldiers, who wanted to find the raiders, destroy them, and go home. This strategy still required the help

---

ready to serve as dragoons in the summer of 1706 (CSL-RW/186, 205–06). On the shoemakers, see MHC:6,III/237 (quotation).

23. On the response to the Northampton raid, see MHC:6,III/199, 206–07; and MHC:6,V/128 (quotation). On inability to catch raiders, see MHC:6,III/203–05 (quotations), 241–43, 247–49, 275; and CSL-RW/177–78, 181. Leaders in western Massachusetts understood the problem: "If we look back for twenty-eight years past [to King Philip's War] of war with this sort of enemy, our losses . . . hath been by their sudden surprizals and immediate drawing off . . . , all our successes having been when they have been surprized so as the English could come at them, and such opportunities rare" (CHS-WY:III/1).

of Indian allies; when they were drunk, colonial soldiers could not safely move through the woods. As always, the raiders never fought when they could slip away, and the pursuers never assembled fast enough to trap them and make them fight.[24]

The unprecedented demand for soldiers sharpened the distinction between the short-service dragoons and the troops who stayed to patrol the frontier. The garrison companies drew on a narrower segment of the population and contained more of society's outsiders than did the dragoons. Norwalk initially drafted the twenty-year-old eldest son of a deputy for garrison service, but then replaced him with an older man not so well connected. A majority of garrison soldiers drafted from Hartford county in 1706 were young men from the lower end of the economic spectrum, although not all were permanently poor; thirty years later, three of eight from Hartford would pay the tax to build a new meetinghouse. Garrison officers were also less prominent than their dragoon counterparts. Like Bull in 1690, the Council relied on family connections to find men who were both trustworthy and popular with the soldiers. It named thirty-five-year-old Ensign Benjamin Newberry of Windsor as captain of the Deerfield garrison in 1704 largely because his father had been a political leader in the 1670s and 1680s. Officers from all units worked well together, although one dragoon captain did object that Major Whiting had not been elected to his command.[25]

Connecticut was exhausted by early 1705, and slid into a period of relative inactivity. Fortunately for the colony, frontier towns in the upper valley managed for the rest of the war to resist the small raids that Canada was able to mount. Success was due to vigilance along the frontier, plus the decision by Massachusetts to send rangers between towns (on horseback in summer, on snowshoes in winter) and to attack the homes of the raiders in Maine. While the Assembly agreed that taking the war to the enemy was a good idea, no major expedition was launched up the Connecticut

24. On service along the frontier, see MHC:6,III/186, 195, 202, 236 (quotation), 240, 242, 259, 275, 280; CPR:IV/458, 496–97; CA-War:III/67; and CSL-RW/167.

25. On Fairfield county, see CSL-RW/203; and Jacobus, *Fairfield,* I/14, 357, 373, 699. On Hartford county, see CA-War:III/66, 70; and CHC:XXI/418. Newberry died from disease contracted on the 1709 expedition (Bartlett, *Newberry,* pp. 55–58). Militia sergeants were commissioned as officers in garrison companies (CPR:IV/465). On objections to Whiting, see MHC:6,III/240, 250–51.

valley. Connecticut concentrated on defending its frontier, and still fielded substantial numbers when necessary. In three days in the summer of 1708, it sent a thousand dragoons into the upper valley. But it could not duplicate its efforts of 1704. Desertion was such a problem that the Assembly in October reminded soldiers they would be penalized for neglect of duty and prohibited militia officers from resigning their commissions to avoid active service. The average soldier's patriotism held up well over a long war, although it clearly had taken a beating by October 1714, when the Assembly made it harder for men to avoid service. Too many militiamen were submitting certificates from two physicians asserting that they were physically incapable of "training, watching and warding, and the like."[26]

Left to itself, Connecticut would not have participated in expeditions against the French. However, for three years after May 1709, it did not have a choice, largely because Samuel Vetch, a well-connected Scots immigrant to New York, painted such an appealing picture of the benefits and ease of adding Canada to the empire that imperial officials could not resist the attempt. Connecticut found good reasons to participate. The chance to crush the French and end the border war at its source generated substantial enthusiasm. (The Assembly did not foment a crusading mentality, however. For example, in an address to Queen Anne in June 1711 it complained about the barbarous way the French made war, but showed

26. On attacking Indians in the upper valley, see CPR:IV/464, 517; MHC:6,III/207–09, 211, 217, 226–28, 233–34, 239–40, 282; and CSL-RW/ 172, 181, 183. Snowshoes were the most important Indian invention adapted to military use by the colonists (CPR:IV/484, 497; CPR:XV/556; and CPR:V/ 295–98). One draftee prosecuted for dereliction in March 1707 complained that his captain had told him he would not have to serve "if there were the number without him" (CHS-WY:III/9). For 1708, see MHC:6,V/207–08; and CPR:V/ 81; according to Saltonstall, although the alarm "did not last very long, yet it cost us several thousand pounds." Connecticut sent troops into the upper valley during all three years of expeditions against the French (CPR:XV/564–65; SPC:XX/337; and CPR:V/213). Finding enough men was not easy. In August 1710 the Assembly offered a ten-pound scalp bounty for the first time since 1697 (CPR:V/167). In May 1711 it paid fully-equipped volunteers on the frontier a third more than expeditionary soldiers, and raised pay again in December (CPR:V/213, 295). On frontier defenses after mid-1711, see CPR:V/295, 300, 325–26, 339, 347–48, 359. On the Massachusetts frontier system at its maximum in 1712, see SPC:XXI/375. "Two companies" were sent out in February 1712 (CPR:V/297–98, 300), Connecticut's last major operation in Queen Anne's War. On avoiding service, see CPR:V/454 (quotation).

no anti-Catholic animus.) In addition, joining the expedition showed that Connecticut was a loyal colony and helped to persuade London not to inquire too closely into how it managed its internal affairs. Meeting imperial military demands was the cornerstone of the way the colony dealt with the imperial government until Canada was conquered in 1760.[27]

The man who led Connecticut into the new imperial age was Gurdon Saltonstall, who had been the forty-one-year-old minister at New London when the Assembly chose him to succeed the late Governor Winthrop in December 1707; he was the first minister in New England to leave his congregation to accept high public office. A scion of a distinguished Massachusetts family and a Harvard College graduate, Saltonstall had been called to the New London church in May 1688, where he quickly became a confidant of Winthrop, his parishioner. He had a traditional view of the political order, as he showed in May 1697 when he asserted in the annual election sermon to the Court that people should obey the leaders God put over them, an argument that pleased men who deplored how popular deference to political leaders had declined in the ten years since the Dominion debacle. After the start of Queen Anne's War he became Winthrop's secretary and alter ego, and acquired an unmatched knowledge of the military situation, a large part of the reason he was elected as Winthrop's successor. The choice proved to be inspired, for he soon revealed an excellent sense of how to accommodate imperial military demands without compromising Connecticut's local autonomy.

Saltonstall paid particular attention to the protocols of Connecticut politics. He refused to leave Assembly sessions to attend imperial conferences and apologized when imperial business kept him away from its meetings, courtesies that showed he was the servant of the Assembly, not the toady of outsiders. He reported regularly to the Assembly, which met fifteen times between May 1708 and May 1713, only four more than required by law, and almost always received approval for the agreements he negotiated with imperial officials. His colleagues rebuffed him only in October 1709, when he carelessly demanded that they agree to another

27. In April 1707 the Assembly refused to help Massachusetts attack Port Royal because it was heavily committed in the upper valley and because it had not been consulted in planning the attack (CPR:V/17; and MHC:6,III/371, 387–92). On Vetch, see SPC:XIX/60, 196; and Waller, *Vetch,* pp. 94–157. On imperial demands, see CA-For:I/128; DNY:V/72–74; SPC:XIX/387, 475–76; and CPR:V/91–93. On the address, see CPR:V/245.

expedition after a year of unprecedented expense and loss; he got his way when he turned his demand into a suggestion. Saltonstall put considerable effort into consulting with other leaders, and traveled regularly to hold council meetings at Hartford and New Haven to brief his senior colleagues and impress upon them his own activity and indispensability. He was Connecticut's principal intermediary with the empire from 1709 through 1711, and acted as more of a chief executive than the colony had yet seen.[28]

The plan for the invasion of Canada in 1709 was based on the two-pronged scheme of 1690. A British fleet would carry five thousand regulars to Quebec, while an army of fifteen hundred colonial soldiers moved north down the Champlain valley to Montreal. Logistical obstacles stacked the odds against the overland expedition, as they had in 1690. Forty miles of portaging around low water in the Hudson exhausted men and beasts, as well as doubled the cost of feeding the army. Disease in the swampy ground around Wood Creek drained the army of all offensive power long before news arrived in early September that the fleet had been diverted to Portugal. Still, the colonies were bitterly disappointed that England put marginal operations in Europe ahead of helping them remove a deadly menace; Vetch reported that they were "much more miserable than if . . . [an expedition] had never been projected or undertaken." Connecticut troops suffered severely. "Between eighty and ninety men" (16 percent of the roughly five hundred soldiers, including Indians) died in camp, on the return, or at home before the end of the year; many more were exhausted beyond hope of immediate recovery. Although Saltonstall claimed that the troops behaved well, morale had collapsed and desertion had been

28. On Saltonstall's career, see MHC:6,III/3–12, 411; CPR:IV/105; CPR:V/ 488–89; and Sibley, *Harvard Graduates*, III/277–86. He declined the Court's invitation to accompany Winthrop to London in October 1693. His election sermon is *A Sermon Preached before the General Assembly*. The Assembly explicitly named him to the Council only in October 1704 (CPR:IV/488–89). On his relations with other leaders, see CSL-UH/19 May 1708, 13 May, 8 Jun and 19 Oct 1709, 26 May 1711; CSL-LH/9 Oct 1712; CPR:V/108, 122; and CHS-WY:III/31. Twenty men attended the eighty Council meetings Saltonstall held at New London (forty-five sessions), Hartford (twenty-one), and New Haven (fourteen) between 30 October 1710 and 26 August 1713, the only period for which records survive. Three assistants attended most frequently at Hartford, two others at New Haven. Only one assistant lived at New London.

rampant; the military system had crumbled before his eyes. Connecticut lost so many of the officers and men on whom it had relied since 1704 that it had to scramble to raise troops in 1710 and 1711.[29]

When the Assembly learned in early August 1710 that Vetch had convinced imperial planners to attack Port Royal by the end of the month, it "unanimously," if reluctantly, agreed to participate. It had good reasons to do so: Port Royal was home for privateers off the New England coast and raiders along the inland frontier. But it had ignored those reasons before, and could now legitimately claim that Connecticut needed time to recuperate from the disaster of 1709. The summons from the imperial government was the deciding factor; the continuing need to defend the colony against accusations of misconduct forced the Assembly to abandon its uncooperative attitude of the 1690s and strain its resources to raise troops on short notice. It turned out to be worth the effort: Royal Navy ships controlled the waters around Nova Scotia while the colonial army isolated and overwhelmed Port Royal. The attack itself was a siege, which made the best use of the colonists' talents. They dug siege lines under the direction of a British engineer, dragged cannon into the entrenchments, and captured the town in less than a week. It was a triumph of logistics and the spade, symbolic of how Connecticut's military activity was changing: the campaign resembled a minor operation in Europe far more than an Indian-style conflict on the frontier.[30]

The imperial government tried the next year for an even bigger prize when it revived and augmented its 1709 plan for the conquest of Canada. The 1711 expedition was the most complex and powerful yet seen in North America, the first time that large numbers of British soldiers and sailors—nearly ten thousand men—set foot in the northern colonies. De-

29. On the expedition, see SPC:XIX/387, 604, 666; SPC:XX/503 (quotation); MHC:6,V/186–88, 218; CA-War:III/81, 83, 90; CPR:V/139, 163; CHC:XXIV/184–85; CHS-RW/1 Jul, 7 and 27 Sep 1709; Livingston, "Wood Creek," pp. 455–56; Waller, *Vetch*, pp. 121–57; and Leach, *Arms*, pp. 139–42. Disease at Wood Creek left men "incapable of labor" (CA-War:III/92), some for the rest of their lives (CA-War:V/53). The colonies could not maintain their base at Wood Creek over the winter. On Saltonstall, see CA-War:III/84, 87. Vetch claimed that only the absence of the fleet had denied victory, but this was wishful thinking (SPC:XIX/666 (quotation); and CA-War:III/79, 82).

30. On the expedition, see CPR:V/163–64 (quotation); SPC:XX/503; [Watkins], "Expeditions," pp. 81–112; Waller, *Vetch*, pp. 158–87; and Rawlyk, *Nova Scotia*, pp. 117–22. London planned to invade Canada in 1710, but diverted the fleet before the colonies made any preparations (SPC:XX/302, 380).

spite extensive preparations and effective imperial-colonial cooperation, it was a complete failure. A series of shipwrecks at the mouth of the St. Lawrence panicked the irresolute Admiral Hovenden Walker into retreating to Boston, a decision that scuttled the entire project. Morale in the well-organized and disease-free overland expedition collapsed like a house of cards. Fortunately for the exhausted colonies, Britain had already decided to make peace with France. Scouting operations continued along the frontier through the summer of 1712, but Connecticut was not asked to join another expedition against Canada for thirty-five years.[31]

The three expeditions were enormously expensive. Pay and provisions were the principal costs, to which were added sizable sums for billeting and horse hire. Food was very expensive, partly because the Assembly paid more than its own stated prices (on which tax payments were based) for pork, wheat, and corn; this attempt to ameliorate the impact of the embargo it clamped on trade was another indication that Connecticut was straining to obey imperial instructions. The largest unexpected expense was the cost of transporting provisions from Albany (where they arrived by ship from Connecticut) to Lake Champlain in 1709; Saltonstall claimed that Connecticut spent at least 20,000 pounds that year, twice the cost of the frontier emergency of 1704. The Assembly met these expenses by levying taxes of over 36 pence on the pound of rateable persons and estates in 1709–11, on top of the 33 pence it had levied since May 1704. Taxes totaled 30 percent of the value of polls and property, and raised about 77,000 pounds to pay for seven years of war. Connecticut taxpayers bore this heavy burden because the economy was buoyed by the expansion of settlement in the northeast and the emission of paper money; tax rolls expanded by 15 percent from 1704 to 1711 as part of an overall pattern of growth which lasted into the 1720s.[32]

31. Even after losing a thousand regulars, Vetch was probably right in insisting that "we have as yet force enough left to reduce" Quebec (SPC:XXI/175; and Graham, *Walker Expedition*). Connecticut provided 150 horses to transport provisions and baggage from New Haven to Wood Creek (CPR:V/260–61), and sent ten carpenters to help make canoes and batteaux to carry the army across Lake Champlain (CPR:V/249). Saltonstall himself accompanied the troops to Albany (DNY:V/261, 268).

32. On the embargo, see CPR:V/161; and CPR:XV/561, 576–77. For Saltonstall's estimate, see MHC:6,V/211. Presumably he meant pounds of the new paper money, which the Assembly seems to have expected to circulate at par with sterling. Massachusetts said it spent 30,000 pounds sterling on the expe-

The unprecedented costs of the expeditions forced the colony to reorganize its financial structure. To facilitate the transactions needed to raise and support its troops, the Assembly created Connecticut's first paper money in June 1709. Through the middle of 1711, it issued 34,000 pounds in bills of credit to purchase supplies and pay bounties in a society that had outgrown the old system of crediting earnings against taxes owed. The Assembly remembered that the first colonial paper money, issued by Massachusetts to help pay for the 1690 expedition, had inflated rapidly, and it took care to devote substantial tax revenues to underwrite the value of its new currency. It always established a sinking fund to retire the bills, although the length of time it allowed for payment of these taxes grew from two years in June 1709 to twelve years by June 1711. In the long run, the introduction of fairly stable paper money into an economy almost devoid of specie helped to promote business transactions, but the transition was not easy.[33]

Between 1709 and 1711 the Assembly adapted its frontier military system to the demands of waging war further from home than ever before. It eventually found solutions that laid the foundation for the way Connecticut made war for nearly seventy years, but, like modernizing the financial system, the process did not always go smoothly. The first problem involved avoiding attempts by the imperial government to change the way it organized its troops. Vetch brought guns and ammunition to arm the colonial soldiers, and in 1709 sensibly wanted to collect them into regiments around the four New York regular companies, a plan he had to abandon when the soldiers refused to serve under regular officers. With the need for speed in 1710, Vetch managed to increase imperial control

dition and another 30,000 pounds sterling on frontier defense (SPC:XX/81). "Living in a manner wholly upon husbandry" made war more burdensome for Connecticut than for its neighbors (SPC:XX/503). On expenses, see CPR:V/109, 125–26. For accounts, see CA-FTA:I. Provisions for 360 men for four months in 1711 included 40,300 pounds of bread and 1,488 gallons of rum (CA-War:III/75). Parliament refused the colonies' requests for reimbursement (MHC:6,V/211; and SPC:XXI/448). On taxes in 1704–1711, see CPR:IV/466, 488–90, 519, 534; and CPR:V/5–6, 31, 82, 111–12, 127–29, 182–83, 228–29, 252, 277, 285–96. On patterns of growth, see Bushman, *Puritan to Yankee*, pp. 107–43, especially pp. 115–16; and Main, *Society*, pp. 115–22.

33. On bills of credit in 1709–11, see CPR:V/111–12, 127–29, 157–58, 166, 182–83, 226–29, 244, 252. From October 1709, bills were "accepted in all public payments" at a 5 percent premium (CPR:V/127). One pound in bills of credit was equal to 1 pound, 10 shillings in country pay.

over colonial manpower by organizing a few colonial companies under regular officers. In 1711 the colonies insisted on different arrangements, and Vetch compromised by providing regular lieutenants to train companies which remained under the command of colonial captains. His plans were an intelligent attempt to increase the military value of colonial soldiers, but they had little practical result because the men were short-term enlistees who resented serving under officers they did not know and trust.[34]

The biggest change from the frontier system was the reduced importance of Indian allies, the best indication that the way the colony made war now emphasized logistics over stealth, speed, and scouting. Roughly 150 warriors went out in 1709, but they were often drunk and undisciplined, and did not distinguish themselves in battle. According to a New York observer, they were "a poor, mean-spirited people, [who] have not been accustomed to war, as appeared in the skirmish . . . with the French [in early August] . . . , where they run first." In 1711 they were relegated to "managing batteaux and canoes and all other hard labor." The colony ensured that the best warriors stayed home by paying them only 6 shillings a week, a third of what it paid colonial soldiers. It was a far cry from the situation in the upper valley eight years earlier, when colonial soldiers had refused to scout between towns without a screen of loyal Indians.[35]

The most delicate problem in 1709 was finding enough soldiers to meet the imperial government's demand for 350 men (7 percent of 5,000 militiamen). The Assembly was very anxious to use the considerable popular enthusiasm for an attack on Canada to induce men to volunteer. To encourage them to enlist—and thus to postpone the day when it would have to invoke impressment—it took the unprecedented step of offering each recruit an enlistment bounty of 40 shillings, and strained its resources even further by increasing a private's wages by a shilling a day, to 17 shillings, 6 pence a week; imperial officials claimed that pay for colonial soldiers was "four times" that of Europe. (This largesse seems to have worried the fiscally conservative Upper House, which refused to reduce

34. On imperial plans for organizing colonial manpower in 1709, see SPC:XIX/387, 604; in 1710, see [Watkins], "Expeditions," pp. 95–96; and in 1711, see CPR:V/256, 291–92, 353.

35. On Indians in 1709, see CPR:XV/567; CHC:XXI/372; and Livingston, "Wood Creek," p. 453 (quotation). On Indians in 1711, see SPC:XXI/96 (quotation); and CPR:V/253. They were led by colonists from families long associated with the tribes (CA-War:III/117–18).

the tax base by abating the taxes of soldiers, as proposed by the Lower House.) The emphasis on economic incentives shows how Connecticut was reshaping its frontier military system to raise an imperial regiment: appeals to individual self-interest were replacing reliance on calls for collective self-defense. The imperial government underscored the transition, probably unintentionally, by completing the package with a powerful if less tangible inducement: priority in sharing the Canadian lands it expected the troops to win. The fact that towns did not give land to expeditionary veterans is another indication that attitudes about war were changing. Land in Connecticut was too scarce to be granted for imperial military service away from the community.[36]

Financial incentives enabled Connecticut to attract a core of frontier veterans to the new expedition, but it had to draft militiamen to fill out the regiment. The Assembly specified how many soldiers each town had to raise, either as volunteers or draftees, and logically imposed a greater burden on older, more populous communities. In 1709 (and again in 1710), Hartford and New London counties each contributed roughly a third of the soldiers, New Haven county over 20 percent, and Fairfield county about 15 percent. To prevent militia captains from drafting less-than-able-bodied men, the Assembly allowed the field officers of the regiment to impress men to replace "insufficient or unfit" recruits. The combination of enthusiasm, financial incentives, and draft quotas allowed Connecticut to exceed the planned number of soldiers; the muster rolls of the regiment contain the names of 365 colonists and mention the presence of 150 Indians. Some young men volunteered because military service offered an escape from home or work. A servant from Lyme spent the last months of his indenture as a soldier, and deserted the uninhabitable camp

---

36. On the number of militiamen, see CPR:V/71. For bounties paid in 1709, see CHC:XXI/361–72. On wages, see CPR:V/92–93. Wages in May 1709 were calculated in "pay" (credit used to discharge tax obligations). Accounting changed over the summer as part of the decision to issue paper money. Thereafter, wages were calculated in "money" at two-thirds the value in "pay" (CPR:V/93, 125). Officers' wages were raised to equal what Massachusetts paid (CPR:V/91–93; and CA-War:III/90). Vetch's comment on pay is in SPC:XIX/604. On abating taxes, see CSL-LH/10 Jun 1709. On earning rights to Canadian land, see SPC:XIX/387. The Assembly occasionally abated taxes for some veterans and gave a few as much as 40 pounds for medical care (CPR:IV/56–57, 79, 128, 252, 271, 405; CPR:V/176, 212, 320, 347, 371, 429, 432, 493, 576; CPR:VI/72, 219–20, 283, 494; and CA-War:III/96, 107, 129–30, 133, 136, 140–53).

at Wood Creek a free man. His mistress later collected his wages for the four months he had still been her servant.[37]

The need for speed in 1710 after the disaster of 1709 forced the Assembly to offer additional incentives to attract up to 300 volunteers, 6 percent of the militia, including as many veterans of 1709 as possible. The package, identical to the one offered by Massachusetts, was substantially better than in 1709: a month's wages in advance, a coat worth 30 shillings, an imperial musket worth 40 shillings (or 40 shillings if a man brought his own gun), and exemption for three years from impressment for service outside the colony, an offer which would hamper recruiting in 1711. These inducements, plus the possibility of plundering Port Royal, were the main reasons why men volunteered; the money to be earned for three months in Nova Scotia was substantially more than what a man could make for longer periods on the frontier. Despite the short time available to raise the regiment, the Assembly found nearly all the men it wanted; when it invoked impressment in late August, only "some of each county" were "yet wanting." The transports sailed from New London with 292 men, nearly all of the 300 men demanded by London.[38]

The colonies had difficulty digesting the capture of Port Royal, now renamed Annapolis Royal. Connecticut had promised to bring its soldiers home as soon as the town surrendered, a necessary inducement that ignored the problem of how to keep the conquest. Holding territory required

37. Conclusions about the composition of the regiment are based on its muster roll (CHC:XXI/361–72) and the rolls of New Haven and Fairfield county dragoons in 1706 (CSL-RW/205–06). On town quotas, see CA-War:III/74; and CHS-WY:III/30; the Assembly ordered 372 men to be drafted, of whom only 350 were to serve. On proportions drawn from towns in New Haven and New London county, see returns for 1710–11 listing the size of each militia company in CA-Mil:I/33–34, 40. On impressment, see CA-War:III/76, 78; and CPR:V/91–92, 126, 161, 236–38. The upper age limit for impressment had been lowered to fifty-five in October 1708 (CPR:V/83–4). The impressment law contained a tough penalty against taking bribes to "spare any from said service" (CPR:V/131–32). On rejecting unfit recruits, see CA-War:III/78 (quotation). On apprentices and servants, see CPR:V/159, 320; and CA-War:III/125, 133. On the servant, Benjamin Fox of Lyme, see CA-War:III/106; and CPR:V/368–69.

38. On raising the troops, see CPR:V/164–65, 181; CPR:XV/586–88 (quotation 587); SPC:XX/491; and Rawlyk, *Nova Scotia,* p. 18. There was some confusion about whether or not soldiers could keep their arms (DNY:V/261). On the number raised, see [Watkins], "Expeditions," p. 100.

troops who would do as they were told for as long as necessary; only British regulars filled the bill. The colonies found a temporary substitute by using bounties to hire 250 soldiers to join 200 Royal Marines in holding Annapolis Royal for a year until the regulars arrived. The Assembly was willing to live with the caliber of recruits attracted by low bounties, and in fact cut a private's wages by 40 percent, to 7 shillings a week, abysmally low by civilian standards. Its 53 volunteers were young (the median age was twenty-one), some were servants, and at least two were married men. They had in common the idea that serving through a hard and dangerous Nova Scotia winter for soldier's pay was better than any work they could find at home. Probably most were poor men, and looked upon a private's wages of 18 pounds for the year as the key to a brighter future. For some, it was not enough. As one man explained to the Assembly in May 1714, he was too poor to sue for his back pay "as otherwise I might, had I an estate." Still, he was lucky: half the soldiers died before April 1711. Connecticut men had served in winter garrisons before, but the soldiers at Annapolis Royal were the first the Assembly had raised by financial incentives to serve in a region of so little interest to the rest of the colony. It was the closest Connecticut had yet come to raising colonial regulars.[39]

The Assembly knew it would be an uphill fight to raise three hundred volunteers (plus sixty Indians) in May 1711. But rather than strain its financial resources for a third year in a row, it offered incentives that suggest it was willing to accept recruits who found lower bounties attractive. It gave each man a 20-shilling enlistment bounty, the same wages it had paid in 1709, a month's wages in advance, and abatement of taxes, to which the imperial government added a new suit of clothes and ownership of the gun it supplied him for the campaign. If the officers of the

39. Port Royal was renamed in honor of Queen Anne. On returning the soldiers, see CPR:V/91–92, 165. On the garrison, see Buckingham, *Roll*, p. 7. Six men deserted, 6 were captured by the French, and 1 man died shortly after returning home, a total loss of 39 men, three-quarters of the 53 (Buckingham, *Roll*, pp. 44–62). Massachusetts claimed that "scarce one of five" men from Connecticut, New Hampshire, and Rhode Island returned home (SPC:XXI/123). Muster rolls for the six Massachusetts companies show 95 men dead and 24 deserted, for a total loss of 63 percent of 188 soldiers ([Watkins], "Expeditions," pp. 113–17). On the petition of the poor veteran, Yelverton Perry of Stratford, see CA-War:III/141 (quotation), 144; and CPR:V/432. On levels of wealth in the first decade of the eighteenth century, see Main, *Society,* pp. 115–73.

regiment could not find enough volunteers, the Assembly would invoke impressment. Each militia captain received authority to draft from his company as many men as required (excluding the veterans exempt by the law of August 1710) "or of vagrant or wandering persons residing within the limits thereof," the first time the Assembly explicitly told local leaders to shift the burden of service to men at the bottom of the social and economic ladder. The demand for soldiers taxed manpower resources in new ways. So many apprentices and servants enlisted or were drafted that the Assembly ordered each soldier to add to the muster roll "his master's name if he be a servant, [and] his father's name if he be under age." These young men helped Connecticut raise its third consecutive imperial regiment; the New York governor later reported that it had fulfilled its quota "to a very few."[40]

Some of the pressure was taken off impressment in each year by allowing well-to-do draftees to hire substitutes and by using blacks and Indians, who were legally excluded from the militia, to help fill the ranks. The more names on the muster roll like Hercy Indian, Cupid Freeman, and Black John, the fewer white militiamen had to serve. The total number of black and Indian soldiers is unknown: the three names are the only identifiable names on the 1709 muster roll, the only one extant. Several Irishmen also served, including one immigrant whose experience made him a desirable recruit. Leonard Dennit had served in the British army in Flanders during King William's War and had been impressed into the local regular company when he arrived at New York in 1700. He moved to Connecticut a few years later and bore arms seven times, taking part in all three expeditions.[41]

40. On the incentives, see CPR:V/291–92, 353; and CA-FTA:I/29. Some soldiers who returned their arms had not gotten them back by May 1737 (CA-War:III/164, 167, 174). On drafting militiamen, see CPR:V/249–51 (quotation 250). The Assembly enacted heavy fines to force militiamen to appear at the impressment muster, but reduced the punishment in October 1711 to avoid alienating men who might be needed for another expedition (CA-War:III/115, 120–21, 127; and CPR:V/294–95, 332). On servants and apprentices, see CPR:V/236 (quotation). At the behest of imperial officials, the Assembly enacted a tough law against desertion, including a six-month jail term (SPC:XX/893; and CPR:V/223, 248–49). There are no precise figures on how many Connecticut men served. On New York governor Robert Hunter's report, see DNY:V/262 (quotation).

41. Substitutes were officially allowed from October 1709 (CPR:V/442–43). The three names are from CHC:XXI/365, 368, 370. On Dennit, see CA-

As always, popular officers played the central role in recruiting the soldiers. In all three years, the field officers illustrate the mix of military experience, political popularity, and family connections the Assembly thought would attract the maximum number of volunteers. In 1709, the colonel was fifty-year-old William Whiting, whose experience as the colony's chief frontier officer was unrivaled; the lieutenant colonel was forty-nine-year-old Mathew Allyn of Windsor, a deputy who had led dragoons to western Massachusetts in 1704 and who would be elected an assistant in 1710; and the major was twenty-nine-year-old John Livingston, whose principal qualification was the fact that he was the son-in-law of the late Governor Winthrop and the brother-in-law of Colonel Vetch. Whiting served again in 1710, while Allyn was replaced by sixty-five-year-old Ebenezer Johnson of Derby, a superannuated militia officer and veteran of King Philip's War; Livingston served as chief of the expedition's scouts. The major, thirty-eight-year-old John Burr of Fairfield, was a scion of a locally prominent family who had been a captain in 1709 and was already on his way to becoming the county's most important leader for two decades after 1725. Whiting and Burr continued in 1711, and were joined by Livingston, now as lieutenant colonel.[42]

The Assembly struck a similar balance when it appointed the company officers, the men directly responsible for conveying the offers of bounties and wages to potential recruits. Half the twenty-four in 1709 were frontier veterans like Captain Benjamin Newberry and Captain Stephen Hollister, or local leaders like Captain Burr. Six of ten in 1710 were veterans of

---

War:III/170–71; he served four times in western Massachusetts, twice at Wood Creek, and once at Port Royal. "Some negroes" who tried to enlist in the regular regiments at Boston were returned to their masters (SPC:XXI/61).

42. On officers in 1709, see CPR:V/91–92; and CHC:XXI/361–74. Allyn was a nephew of Assistant John Allyn and cousin-in-law of Whiting (CPR:IV/162, 256, 318, 327, 350, 406, 434, 458, 461, 465, 481, 497–99, 520, 531–32, 535; CPR:V/143; and Hinman, *Settlers*, pp. 37–38). Livingston had been twice elected a New London deputy, but he had no roots in the town (CHS-WY:III/29; CPR:V/1, 29; and Waller, *Vetch*, p. 129); Vetch asked the Assembly to find him employment. On officers in 1710, see CPR:V/167–68. Johnson had retired from the militia in May 1709 (CPR:V/95; and Jacobus, *Fairfield*, I/340–41). On Livingston, see DNY:V/259; and [Watkins], "Expeditions," p. 94. On Burr, see Jacobus, *Fairfield*, I/128–29. On officers in 1711, see CPR:V/255–56. Whiting spent the winter at Annapolis Royal and was recalled to command the regiment (Buckingham, *Roll*, p. 44). In all three years, each field officer also commanded a company.

1709, but the Assembly had to search hard among the survivors for qualified candidates, and included twenty-seven-year-old Samuel Keeler, Jr., a private who became a lieutenant thanks to his father, a Norwalk deputy. Three of the remaining four were militia officers, and the tenth was thirty-eight-year-old Richard Miles of New Haven, who like his father rose to prominence only during wartime. In 1711, the Assembly thought popularity was more important than experience, probably in an effort to boost recruiting. Three of four captains were militia officers and political leaders; British lieutenants supplied the military skill.[43]

In each year the Assembly rounded out the company officers with men new to commissioned rank, a circumstance which created problems in the field because the personal prestige of the officers was essential to maintaining order in the regiments. Connecticut officers did not so much command as persuade, and established discipline by agreement and consent as in the militia, not by imposing it from above as in the British army. Soldiers were inclined to obey officers whose prominence and recognized force of character lent substance to their position; rank alone did not confer command authority. The Assembly expected that, in addition to being good recruiters, the militia officers in the regiment could elicit obedience from many of the same men who had voted for them at home. But not enough militia officers were willing to serve, and the Assembly had to appoint men without military experience or militia rank. Their lack of prestige undercut discipline and magnified the already considerable faults of the traditional militia command structure. According to a New York observer in 1709, Connecticut soldiers "are not apt to pay that deference to their officers as could be wished, and the officers are rather too indulgent and mild, and seem to be more fond of the love of their men than the men are of the reputation of their officers. They affect . . .

43. There were nine companies in 1709, including two of Indians (CHC:XXI/361–74); six in 1710, including an elite company of grenadiers ([Watkins], "Expeditions," p. 100); and seven in 1711, including one of Indians (CPR:V/255–56). Hollister led one of the Indian companies in 1709 (CHC:XXI/371). On Keeler, see Jacobus, *Fairfield*, I/357. Miles, the son of Captain John Miles, was elected a selectman for the first time in December 1710 and a militia lieutenant in May 1712, but returned to minor offices thereafter (Jacobus, *New Haven*, p. 1183). The commissariat also operated through personal connections. In 1710 Assistant Richard Christophers, who was in charge of gathering supplies at New London, gave contracts to favored suppliers who could act quickly (CPR:V/165, 167, 188–204; and CPR:XV/586–87).

[an] equality which is not so consistent with martial discipline." This egalitarian attitude, which annoyed imperial officials accustomed to the strict discipline of British regulars, had always been a prominent feature of the way the colony made war.[44]

The three expeditions opened a new era in Connecticut's relations with the empire and marked a watershed in its military history. Beginning in 1709, the colony no longer focused on defending its frontier against French raiders. Instead, in an effort to end the menace at its source and curry favor in London, it raised troops for campaigns that were initiated and directed by the imperial government. As attention shifted from western Massachusetts to the upper Hudson valley and Nova Scotia, the leaders wanted to avoid compelling Connecticut men to serve so far from home in regions of so little interest to the colony. They began to transform their military system from a local defense force raised by impressment from the militia into an imperial army raised by voluntary enlistment from among men who viewed temporary military service as a good way to earn money. They were able to do so because Connecticut society was becoming more mature and stratified. The colony's population had reached the point where the number of men who could be tempted by offers of bounties and wages approached the number of soldiers the colony required. Moreover, the leaders were confident that Connecticut was sufficiently prosperous to be able to afford the costs of paying men to enlist. The transition was not complete by 1711: the Assembly continued to back financial incentives with the threat of impressment. Still, the militia ideal of universal service was no longer the central paradigm in the way the colony organized its resources for war. Connecticut's military system began to look more like Britain's, which had long since learned to use bounty money to induce poor men to perform dangerous military service, than like that of a frontier colony in which leaders could compel men to join together in common self-defense.[45] In the next twenty-five years, the idea of basing military service on economic self-interest became the dominant theme in the way Connecticut organized its resources for imperial war.

44. Examples of men who lent their rising prestige to the service include, in 1710, Lieutenant John Hall and Captain Roger Newton; they would be elected assistants in 1729 and 1736, respectively. Military service played little part in their advancement. On indiscipline in 1709, see Livingston, "Wood Creek," pp. 450–51 (quotation).

45. On the way Britain created its regular army, see Childs, *British Army,* pp. 102–31, esp. p. 122.

Chapter Three

Expansion and Transition

AN EXPANDING SOCIETY

Connecticut recovered quickly from the exhaustion of Queen Anne's War. Not long after the border war petered out, the colony began to grow rapidly. Population burgeoned and society became more complex as a restless and enterprising people consolidated settlement in the northeast and extended it to the northwest. The strain of this unprecedented growth, the search for new economic opportunities, and the lack of a significant threat nearby turned attention away from war. Connecticut was not involved in major military activity for a quarter-century after 1715, and was free to focus its energies on economic expansion. As the society grew and matured, its view of military affairs changed profoundly: war came to be seen primarily as an economic activity rather than as a fight for physical, political, or religious survival. The transition began to be apparent when the border war flared up in the 1720s.[1]

For four years after 1722, Connecticut maintained a scaled-down version of its frontier military system to help protect the upper valley from the war Massachusetts was waging against Indians in Maine. The maximum effort came in the summer of 1724, when eighty Hartford county dragoons spent seven weeks in western Massachusetts; at other times, as few as ten young bachelors garrisoned frontier towns, principally in northwest Connecticut. The system continued to rely on consent: the Hartford Com-

1. On the transition, see Main, *Society,* pp. 115–73; Bushman, *Puritan to Yankee,* pp. 41–143; Grant, *Democracy,* pp. 1–103; and Daniels, *Connecticut Town,* pp. 45–63.

mittee of War quickly released the draftees it sent to Litchfield in the spring of 1723 because it wanted them to be willing to serve again. The most effective elements in the system were the colonists and Indians who ranged the frontier, but the lack of a military emergency led the Assembly to treat its Indian allies with a condescension that would have been un- thinkable twenty years earlier. It restricted their hunting grounds, and even took precautions against the unlikely event that they might join the enemy. The Upper House, moreover, demanded economies it might have omitted had the danger been greater. While it agreed to raise a private's wages to 4 shillings a day in October 1723, it insisted on paying soldiers for six days a week instead of the customary seven, and only reluctantly paid frontier residents to guard themselves. It wanted to reduce the costs of defense, and refused to accept the idea that men had to be paid fair wages for nonemergency military service. The senior leaders showed a better grasp of the need for financial incentives in 1740, when Britain asked the colonies to raise troops for its war against Spain in the West Indies.[2]

Imperial planners wanted to recruit colonists to join British troops in sweeping through the poorly defended Spanish Main, and correctly fore- cast that "a very considerable number of men may be easily had, upon proper encouragement." They offered each recruit arms, clothing, and wages, and assured him he would be sent home as soon as possible with his share of the booty. They expected three sorts of men to enlist: poor men who could leave "some subsistence money with their families," debt- ors who could pay their creditors, and "many servants" who "might obtain their masters' leave to enlist, if three or four months pay were . . . paid to their . . . assigns after their embarkation." The incentives were de- signed to attract poor men with the illusion of easy wealth in the Car- ibbean. As in 1711, the planners wanted to turn colonists into disciplined soldiers by having a regular officer train each company, and tried to mit-

---

2. On the frontier system in the 1720s, see CA-War:III/191, 201–02, 213; CHC:V/9–10, 13–15, 32–35, 42–45, 384–87; CPR:VI/334–36, 407–10, 425– 27, 435–36, 464, 474, 485–86, 502–05, 511–12, 537, 552, 566; CPR:VII/ 60–61, 76; and CHS-WY:IV/29. On the soldiers sent to Litchfield, see CA- War:III/193. On the rangers, see CPR:VI/426, 479–82, 534–35, 578–79; and CA-War:III/196, 206; the Assembly offered them a 50-pound bounty for the scalp of any enemy. Indian rangers got drunk on hard cider in the fall of 1724 (CHC:V/10). On wages, see CPR:VI/428, 475, 500–501, 541–42; CA-War:III/ 194, 209, 220, 241; and CPR:VII/77, 113.

igate jealousy by promising colonial officers and soldiers that they would receive "the same rank and pay" as the regulars. The scheme was an intelligent use of manpower, even if planners incorrectly assumed that colonial soldiers would be inured to tropical diseases.[3]

The Assembly agreed in April 1740 to raise men as a way of improving its reputation in London, which had been tarnished by controversies over Indian lands, inheritance laws, and paper money. Connecticut continued to base its relations with the imperial government on the bargain of military cooperation in return for local self-government that it had struck during Queen Anne's War. As in 1709–11, raising troops showed London that Connecticut was a loyal colony and, moreover, allowed the Assembly to issue large amounts of paper money to remedy the "great scarcity of a medium of exchange" without running afoul of imperial currency restrictions. In May the Assembly began by issuing 4,000 pounds Old Tenor to pay bounties to recruits. The Lower House then wanted to splurge with an additional 100,000 pounds printed on new plates and called New Tenor currency; this was seven times the value of the Old Tenor then in circulation. The deputies earmarked 8,000 pounds to pay the costs of defense and wanted to use the rest to generate credit by lending it at interest to Connecticut inhabitants for four to eight years. The Upper House, fiscally conservative as always, agreed to issue the 8,000 pounds but reduced the value of the loans to 22,000 pounds. In July both Houses agreed to issue 15,000 pounds Old Tenor, for a total of 46,000 pounds Old Tenor for the year. To maintain the value of its bills of credit against inflation, the Assembly levied taxes to retire them over the next ten years.[4]

3. On the war, see Pares, *War and Trade,* pp. 85–97; Leach, *Arms,* pp. 216–19; and Harkness, "Americanism and Jenkins' Ear." It was the first time since 1666 that Britain asked Connecticut to send troops to the West Indies. On recruiting, see CHC:V/192–93 (quotation), 230–33 (quotation 231–32), 237–38, 241–43, 251; Kimball, *Rhode Island,* I/151 (quotation); MHC:6,VII/339; and DNY:VI/165, 167, 171.

4. On raising troops, see CHC:V/304; CA-War:IV/51b; and CPR:VIII/313–14, 326, 567–68. On issuing paper money, see CPR:VIII/295–96, 318–21, 327; CSL-UH/28 May 1740; and CA-FC:III/93–94. Rhode Island claimed that the "great expense" of the campaign required a massive increase in paper money (Kimball, *Rhode Island,* I/213). Officially, 1 shilling of New Tenor was initially equal to 2 shillings, 6 pence in the Old Tenor of Queen Anne's War (CPR:VIII/360), but ten years later it was pegged at 1 shilling New Tenor to 3 shillings, 6 pence Old Tenor (CHC:XV/435). The imperial government refused to allow the bills of credit to pass as legal tender (CPR:VIII/356–61). On the

The Assembly raised soldiers in a way that marked a new stage in the evolution of its military system. It knew it had to offer additional incentives to attract recruits because war in the Caribbean was even less important to the average colonist than frontier defense had been in the 1720s. But what was the best way to raise soldiers? The cost-conscious Upper House wanted to exempt each volunteer from impressment for three years, as in 1710, but this plan was out of step with the times. The more economically astute Lower House proposed paying 5 pounds to any man who was "actually called forth" for the service, and the Upper House eventually conceded the bounty to the first five hundred volunteers, thus explicitly shifting the burden of service onto men who needed the money. Despite the tremendous wave of religious revivals sweeping across New England, neither House used anti-Catholic rhetoric to spur enlistment. Military preparations proceeded without reference to events which were shaking the rest of the colony.[5]

The Lower House had an accurate understanding of how society had matured. In mid-May, when every militia captain read to his company Governor Joseph Talcott's proclamation "to invite and encourage men to enlist," about 450 men volunteered on the spot, although many were "not free to dispose of themselves, and some so young and others so impotent as rendered them" unfit for service. Fewer men volunteered thereafter, because the Assembly stipulated that enlistees had to be "able-bodied effective men, and free to act and dispose of themselves and their service." By mid-July, 700 men (in a population of about 90,000 people) had decided to take a chance on "a golden adventure" in the Caribbean, more men than the imperial government was prepared to accept. In mid-September, Connecticut sent only 200 of the "most effective and able men" at its own expense to the West Indies, leaving behind 500 men who were denied the opportunity to earn bounties and win plunder. Recruiting officers sent home in mid-1741 tried to maintain this enthusiasm, but

---

5,738 pounds of Old Tenor in circulation, see CHC:V/212. The Assembly raised in taxes 5 percent more than the face value of the bills because it accepted them in "all public payments at the advance of 12 pence on the pound" (CPR:VII/ 477). On Connecticut paper money in general, see Taylor, *Connecticut*, pp. 101–07.

5. On raising volunteers, see CA-War:IV/52, 54 (quotation); and Kimball, *Rhode Island*, I/151. On the revival of religion, see Bushman, *Puritan to Yankee*, pp. 147–232; and Hatch, *Sacred Cause*, pp. 21–54.

they could not overcome the news that the dream of plunder had collapsed with tremendous loss of life, principally to disease. Perhaps as few as one in ten colonial soldiers saw their homes again.[6]

Young volunteers had both need *and* ambition; they enlisted because they wanted to earn money to get ahead. The price of land was rising (it would double between 1700 and 1750), and shrinking opportunity enlarged the pool of men for whom temporary military service was an attractive option. According to Jackson T. Main, the most careful student of Connecticut society, around mid-century "young men delayed entrance into agriculture for a few extra years, remaining artisans or laborers, and some farmers' sons who normally would have stayed on the land went into a trade, a profession, or a craft." Or into the army: the monies to be earned in military service attracted young men who were unable to follow the traditional life-cycle pattern. "Clearly farm boys now had to continue as wage laborers for three or four more years, and since they did not postpone marriage that meant some additional young families with properties close to subsistence . . . . This change did not mean a universal decline in wealth or property since the young couple ultimately had as good a chance as before; but it certainly must have caused discontent and doubts about the future." These discontented young men were not permanently poor like the soldiers in European armies, but their post-service economic and social success obscures the poverty and anxiety that drove them to enlist in the first place. For some older men, plundering the Spaniards was their last chance to rescue land from foreclosure. In 1733 they had mortgaged their farms to the colony for up to 60 pounds in bills of credit, and now, as the mortgages approached maturity, they found

6. On volunteering, see CHC:V/237 (quotation), 269–70, 303–05 (quotations); CPR:VIII/324–25 (quotation); and CA-War:IV/66, 70. Talcott's proclamation is CA-War:IV/54; and CHC:V/251–52. One case of illegal impressment came to the attention of the Assembly (CA-War:IV/59–61; and CPR:VIII/316). On recruiting in 1741, see CHC:V/366–68; CHC:XI/14–18; CA-War:IV/98–9, 115; CPR:VIII/439–40, 460–61; and Kimball, *Rhode Island,* I/187–88. On population, see Daniels, *Connecticut Town,* p. 47. Recruiting officers were instructed to reject anyone over "thirty-five years of age, or any native of Ireland, unless you have undoubted proof of his being Protestant and of a good character" (CHC:V/367; and CHC:XI/17). The estimate of casualties is from Trumbull, *History,* II/268, a good barometer of the popular wisdom. The survivors came home in late 1742 (CHC:XI/60–61).

they would not be able to pay the debt. For others, volunteering was a fraud: at least two men subsisted for three months at the king's expense and absconded with their bounty before boarding the transports.[7]

The captains of the two companies were more prominent than their counterparts in Queen Anne's War. Fifty-three-year-old John Silliman of Fairfield was a militia captain, deputy, and tax collector. His colleague, thirty-four-year-old Roger Newberry of Windsor, was a Yale graduate, militia lieutenant, and merchant who had married the daughter of Roger Wolcott, the senior assistant. He had a thriving political career (an unusual string of eleven consecutive terms as a deputy) when he left his wife and seven children in September 1740, never to return. Why either man chose to serve is something of a mystery. Clearly, they wanted the wages and perquisites available in the king's service, including half-pay for life after the regiment disbanded, but neither was so poor that he needed to plunder the Spaniards; Newberry's estate would total the enormous sum of 5,600 pounds Old Tenor. Perhaps they were greedy, or perhaps they wanted an honor not in the gift of their peers. For whatever reason, unlike most Connecticut men, they sought advancement outside the traditional leadership structure, an indication that the colony's isolation from the empire was breaking down.[8]

Their lieutenants were less prominent, more typical of garrison officers in Queen Anne's War. The king's commission was a step up the social ladder, and it gave them a temporary boost in popularity. But, as always, military service did not translate easily into political prominence. While twenty-five-year-old John Slapp of Mansfield was elected a militia captain

7. On the social structure, see Main, *Society,* pp. 371 and 377–78 (quotations). On mortgages, see CPR:VIII/476; CPR:IX/249–50; CA-FC:2,II/85, 145; and CSL-AB:Box 196/12, 17. The colony had loaned out nearly 50,000 pounds Old Tenor in 1733, of which 33,600 pounds was still outstanding in January 1740 (CHC:V/213). On deserters, see CHC:V/300; and CA-War:IV/ 65, 67, 73, 75, 78. The Assembly apparently aided only one crippled veteran, paying 50 pounds Old Tenor to a man with a wife and two children (CA-War:IV/ 116, 124).

8. On the officers, see CPR:VIII/325; and DNY:VI/167. On Silliman, see Jacobus, *Fairfield,* II/868–89; and CPR:VIII/333–34. In his will, probated in 1752, he gave 100 pounds and a silver cup to his congregation. On Newberry, see Bartlett, *Newberry,* pp. 58–62; and Dexter, *Yale Graduates,* I/333. His father, Benjamin, had died of disease contracted while commanding a company in the 1709 expedition. His widow had trouble collecting money owed to him by the imperial government (CHC:XVI/95–96).

in 1751 (and became a captain and major in the expeditions of the final French war), he was never elected a deputy. The other lieutenant, thirty-eight-year-old Macock Ward of Wallingford, was elected a militia captain in 1742 and a deputy in 1743, but he faded thereafter. He was elected a deputy only once during the final French war, when turnover was high. His Assembly career revived when he opposed the Stamp Act in 1765–66, on the other side of the issue from Assistant Benjamin Hall, who favored accommodation. Ward opposed the Hall family's control of politics in Wallingford and, starting in May 1766, won fifteen elections in eight years—uncommon political strength which was grounded in the merging of the imperial conflict with a local dispute.[9]

The commissaries who supplied food and equipment to the two companies, and arranged their transportation to the West Indies, earned more than the officers and soldiers. The money to be made in commission fees and by placing contracts with favorite suppliers was so enticing that the Houses quarreled about who to appoint. The Upper House suggested three merchants, two of whom, however, were not members of the Assembly. The Lower House substituted two deputies, and showed its impartiality by reducing their 5 percent commission to a smaller flat fee. The Assembly also built, at considerable public expense, a hundred-ton sloop-of-war to cruise the coast during the summer. Since the danger from Spanish privateers was minimal, the sloop benefited mainly Middletown, where it was built, and New London, where it was based.[10]

The way Connecticut raised soldiers for the West Indies revealed a major improvement in its ability to wage war. Its military capacity had greatly increased during twenty-five years of peace: population had grown rapidly

9. On Ward, see Jacobus, *New Haven,* p. 1941; CPR:VIII/203, 489, 511; CPR:X/399; CPR:XI/173, 213, 220; and CPR:XII/453. A measure of his popularity was his overwhelming election as lieutenant of the southeast company in Wallingford in October 1738; he received eighty-three affirmative votes from the eighty-eight men in the company, a greater percentage than the captain (CA-Mil:3,III/4). He invested in western land in 1754 (Boyd, *Susquehannah,* I/108 and III/45), perhaps because he saw no future at that time in Wallingford. He was elected a deputy in October 1758, and attended special sessions in February and March 1759 as well (CPR:XI/173, 213, 220).

10. On the commissaries, see CA-War:IV/68, 79–80, 82, 121; and CPR:VIII/354. On the sloop *Defence,* see CHC:XI/47–48, 219; CA-War:IV/89, 91–93, 96–97, 142; CA-War:V/1–23; CPR:VIII/275, 314, 326, 361, 411–13, 428–29, 440–41, 461–62, 503, 516–17, 530, 567–68; and CPR:IX/33, 53–54.

and society was wealthier in aggregate and more stratified, making it easier to find and pay for soldiers. In addition, the expansion of settlement gave Connecticut even greater security behind the edge of the frontier with Canada. All of these trends made the leaders more self-assured and more willing to participate in imperial expeditions. Where the colony had struggled to find men and money for expeditions against the French in 1690 and 1709–11, in 1740 it had the resources and desire to join offensive operations in an area of no concern to its own security. When the war came closer to home a few years later, it applied its new strengths and self-confidence to some familiar military problems.

THE PINNACLE OF COLONIAL ARMS

In the middle of 1743, the imperial government warned the colonies that war against France was again on the horizon. It was not therefore a shock when Britain declared war on France in March 1744, transforming Connecticut from a bystander in a Caribbean war into a participant defending its own frontier; the conflict was known in the colonies as King George's War. At the outset, fear of French raiders rekindled some of the old sense of emergency, and allowed the Assembly to resurrect part of the frontier system of Queen Anne's War. In May it drafted young men into dragoon companies to be ready to reinforce threatened towns, and in June the Hartford Committee of War rushed thirty draftees to western towns, although it quickly replaced those who had "much business lying on their hands" with others "whose business will not suffer" if they served for an extended period. While the leaders allowed officers to fine deserters and inflict corporal punishment, they continued to be careful not to demand more of draftees than what community consensus would support. The most important change in the system was the fact that Indian allies no longer had much of a role, the best measure of how secure behind the frontier Connecticut had become since 1704. The Assembly confined them within prescribed ranges and made them wear identifying badges.[11]

11. On warnings, see CA-War:IV/129–33; and CPR:IX/30–31. The declaration of war is in CHC:XI/135–39. Only thirty-eight of two hundred Fairfield county dragoons were volunteers (CHC:XI/205–10); the dragoons were drawn from among men in their late teens to early thirties. On the six-member Hartford Committee, see CPR:IX/30; and CHC:XI/198 (quotation). A committee of three officers could punish soldiers for crimes that ranged from swearing to mutiny; offenders could be forced to run a gauntlet between two lines of club-bearing

The Assembly took no extraordinary steps to help western Massachu-setts, even though the danger was greater now than forty years earlier because in 1731 the French had built a fort at Crown Point on Lake Champlain a hundred miles closer to the upper valley. Because it was unlikely that raiders would actually reach Connecticut (the deeper they penetrated, the more likely they would be cornered and forced to fight), the leaders happily used western Massachusetts as a buffer. Despite re-minders that their help was most valuable when it was "ready upon the spot," they sent up to sixty scouts and garrison troops to the upper valley only when raiders were reported in the vicinity, and always posted them where they covered western Connecticut.[12]

The Assembly acted more aggressively in early February 1745, when Governor William Shirley of Massachusetts asked Connecticut to join an expedition against Louisbourg, the French fortress on Cape Breton Island. The request was not unwelcome. In October 1744 the Upper House had wanted the imperial government to help mount an expedition against Canada and Cape Breton, but the Lower House had thought the idea was premature. Now the deputies agreed that the colonies "can expect no safety until . . . Cape Breton and Canada be subdued." The leaders re-alized that Louisbourg was "the key of North America," and that its capture would open the way for an attack on Quebec. They agreed to raise five hundred men to join thirty-three hundred soldiers from Mas-sachusetts in the largest colonial expedition to date.[13]

Unlike the West Indies expedition in 1740, the attack on Louisbourg received enthusiastic support across Connecticut. According to Jared Eliot, the minister of Killingworth, "high and low, rich and poor con-curred. . . . If the upper orders of men had not concurred, the expedition must have failed; if the lower ranks of men had not been strongly engaged, the grand design must have come to nothing." The most potent source

---

colleagues, to ride a wooden horse, or to be put on or under guard (CPR:IX/76–77). Deserters paid a fine of 20 pounds Old Tenor (CPR:IX/77). On Indian allies, see CPR:IX/76; and CHC:XI/199.

12. On Crown Point, see CA-War:IV/45–47; and CPR:VII/352–53. On help for western Massachusetts, see CPR:IX/110–11; CHC:XI/189–91, 244, 262–64, 270–72; CHC:XIII/127; and CHC:XV/451–52.

13. On the genesis of the Louisbourg expedition, see CHC:XI/225–26, 252–56, 324; CPR:IX/83, 158–61; CA-War:IV/145h (quotations), 146–48, 219; Shirley, *Correspondence*, I/151–78; Schutz, *Shirley*, pp. 80–96; and Rawlyk, *Nova Scotia*, pp. 145–64.

of this enthusiasm was a desire to strike a blow against the people who had been gnawing at the frontier for half a century and against whom so many lives had been lost. Eliot vividly illustrated the strength of the collective memory when he compared the health of the Louisbourg army with the mortality "sorrowfully experienced" at Wood Creek in 1709 thirty-six years earlier. Old men remembered how hopes for an end to the border war had been dashed repeatedly, and everyone had grown up believing that Canada imperiled the safety and prosperity of the colonies.[14]

The Louisbourg expedition was the boldest and most successful military venture ever initiated by New England. The colonists had crucial help from the Royal Navy ships that blockaded the fortress and prevented it from being resupplied by sea, but they conducted the siege themselves. As at Port Royal in 1710, their principal weapons were the pick and shovel, and the luck to appear before the fortress when it was ill-prepared to resist. According to Eliot, the colonists did not have knowledge of "encamping, entrenching, erecting batteries, bombarding, and cannonading," but, "being used to turn their hands to many sorts of work, they soon understood what was to be done," and set about the job "with resolution and good will" because "they were able-bodied men, able to endure labor and fatigue." Massachusetts troops did most of the work, and lost ninety-five men killed and fifty-seven dead by disease; Connecticut did not lose a man to enemy action and only four to disease. More than one minister credited divine intervention with enabling a mob of laborers to capture Louisbourg on 16 June 1745, after a siege of forty-nine days. It was the pinnacle of colonial arms, and it convinced the colonists of the power of their amateur military system for a generation to come.[15]

Success in 1745 led the northern colonies to try the next year to conquer Canada, an expedition to be organized and led by the imperial government much like the 1740 expedition to the West Indies. Connecticut wanted no part of the overland invasion down the Champlain valley, and so for the first and only time its troops were to go by water up the St. Lawrence. The project collapsed when the British fleet earmarked to carry the colonial army to Quebec was sent to raid the French coast to offset French victories

14. Quotations are from Eliot, *Kindness,* pp. 10 and 17.

15. On the siege, see Eliot, *Kindness,* p. 14 (quotation); Rawlyk, *Yankees;* Rawlyk, *Nova Scotia,* pp. 165–71; and Leach, *Arms,* pp. 224–43. On losses, see CA-War:IV/277; CHC:XI/333; and CHC:XIII/43. On celebrating the surrender at Hartford, see CHS-RW/9 Jul 1745.

in the Netherlands. As in 1709, London demonstrated that a colonial campaign was a sideshow to more important events in Europe. Thereafter, the colonies turned their attention back to the frontier, where French raiders, as bold as ever, had sacked Saratoga, twenty miles north of Albany, on 17 November 1745. The Assembly supported a plan to capture Crown Point, "the pernicious fort" which "like Pandora's box is full of all mischief to us," but it also understood that an attack on what it called "the key of Canada on the land side" made sense only as part of an overall plan to conquer Canada. Even if colonial troops had taken Crown Point in the fall of 1746 (no easy task), they could not have supplied and held a post so close to Montreal until the summer of 1747. Reports in mid-September 1746 that a French fleet was on its way to attack New England turned Crown Point into "an unprofitable hole." Efforts to organize expeditions in 1747 and 1748 also failed; the Assembly refused to endorse Governor Shirley's request for a viceroy to oversee preparations because it smacked too much of the hated Dominion of the 1680s. Enthusiasm for military adventures declined rapidly after 1746, and Connecticut did nothing more than help defend the frontier until hostilities ended in October 1748.[16]

The war that began so incredibly ended in a peace no less incredible: the imperial government returned Louisbourg to the French in exchange for concessions in the Netherlands. By undoing New England's greatest victory, Britain lost a tremendous amount of trust and goodwill in the colonies. As Governor Jonathan Law explained, "Our country has never been put upon assisting the Crown on any expedition that has not by some means or other been defeated to our impoverishment and the great abatement of the growth of our country; and when any expedition has been undertaken at the mere instance of our own government, we find by unhappy experience, though attended with success, that it hath turned out much to our disadvantage." One minister later claimed it would have

16. On the expedition of 1746, see CHC:XIII/201–04, 224–25, 231–32, 242–43; CHC:XV/452–53; CPR:IX/210–13; and Buffinton, "Canada Expedition." On Saratoga, see CHC:XIII/115–17; the raiders actually came from Maine. On Crown Point, see CHC:XIII/132, 135, 149 (quotation), 268, 288–94 (quotation 289), 327–28, 336–38, 340; CPR:IX/262–64; and CHS-RW/10 Dec 1745. On later proposals, see CPR:IX/345–46; CHC:XV/53–54, 85–86, 89–95, 190, 194, 197–98, 206–07; and CHC:XVI/463–65. Because Connecticut had no ports to attract Royal Navy press gangs, it avoided anti-impressment riots like the one at Boston in November 1747 (see Lax and Pencak, "Knowles Riot").

been better to have bought Louisbourg "with millions of money, than to have given it up."[17]

Despite this bitter ending, Connecticut could be happy with the way it had managed its participation in the war. The lack of an emergency along the frontier, plus a more comfortable attitude about cooperating with its neighbors in an imperial war, led to the smooth operation of the decision-making process. Governor Law's council, composed of leaders from New Haven and Fairfield counties, met at Milford and performed the traditional function of managing military affairs between Assembly sessions. The Assembly itself met ten times between February 1745 and January 1747, a relatively heavy workload due to the difficulty of organizing two complex expeditions. An average of twelve magistrates and ninety deputies attended the four regular sessions, with an average of seventy-seven deputies present at the six special sessions. Thirty-seven men served on the twelve committees that made military policy. The thirteen who served three or more times (Deputy Governor Roger Wolcott, four assistants, and eight deputies from around the colony), along with Governor Law, were the core of the leadership. Committee recommendations were usually accepted verbatim; changes reflected differences in how the two Houses approached a problem—the Upper House usually wanted cheaper solutions—and were not major policy disagreements. Everyone agreed on the importance of striking a blow against the Roman Catholic French, despite the fact that the Great Awakening was creating deep disagreements in religion and politics. The senior leaders, most of whom distrusted the excesses that accompanied the religious revival, worked in harmony on military matters with their colleagues who believed the Awakening to be a work of God's grace.[18]

The way the Assembly organized its military resources reflected the enthusiastic acceptance of war as an economic activity, a decision made

17. On Law, see CHC:XV/292–93, 412 (quotation); and CHC:XVI/491. On buying Louisbourg, see Lockwood, *Man Mortal,* p. x (quotation).

18. On the Council, see CPR:IX/31, 212, 215, 235. Records of Assembly committees are in CA-War:IV. The assistants included Thomas Fitch of Norwalk and Jonathan Trumbull of Lebanon, major figures in the quarter century of imperial wars between 1740 and 1765. The deputies included Benjamin Hall of Wallingford, John Ledyard of Groton, Gurdon Saltonstall, Jr., of New London (the son of the late governor), and Roger Wolcott, Jr., of Windsor (the son of Deputy Governor Wolcott). On political disagreements engendered by the Awakening, see Bushman, *Puritan to Yankee,* pp. 235–66.

easier by the popularity of the Louisbourg expedition. There was even a hint of jealousy in the Assembly's charges that Albany was continuing its lucrative trade with Canada (as it had during Queen Anne's War), and that New York and Rhode Island merchants were profiting from an illicit trade with the French West Indies under "pernicious flags of truce." It was bad enough that its neighbors were supplying the common enemy, but that they were making a profit in a way denied to Connecticut was just too much. The best the Assembly could do was give Connecticut's stagnating economy a tremendous boost by issuing nearly 115,000 pounds of New Tenor paper money in 1745–46. In a society with a strong desire for economic success, the fact that war stimulated the economy reinforced the already strong desire to remove the French challenge to the security and expansion of British America.[19]

Paying for the expeditions strained, as well as stimulated, the economy: "This great and expensive undertaking," plus the costs of the 1740 expedition, have "run this colony extremely into debt, and reduced it to a very low ebb." The Assembly always created a sinking fund to retire the currency, but the fact that it stretched out the payment of those taxes for fifteen years may have contributed to the 20 percent depreciation the New Tenor suffered by the end of 1745. To help curb this inflation, the Assembly asked the imperial government in August 1746 to reimburse the cost of taking Louisbourg. Parliament took until 1749 to agree, prompting Governor Law to complain that "when our assistance is wanted we are caressed but when that is over we are neglected." Connecticut's share came to nearly 29,000 pounds sterling, plus 17,000 pounds in 1750 for expenses incurred in 1746, a total reimbursement of nearly 75,000 pounds New Tenor that helped to defuse anger about the return of Louisbourg. No specie was transported to the colony; the Assembly retired its paper money by selling bills of exchange to local merchants, thereby strengthening the 97,000 pounds of New Tenor left in circulation in October 1751. Despite its sound money policies, Connecticut was flooded by highly inflated Rhode Island paper money, which produced business instability until the next war revived the economy with a new round of procurement.[20]

19. On jealousy, see CHC:XV/212–14 (quotation). On the economy, see CHC:XVI/26, 102. On paper money, see CA-War:IV/391; CPR:IX/42, 66–67, 99–100, 151, 217–18, 234–35; and CHC:XV/435–37. The sum was equivalent to 402,500 pounds Old Tenor at official rates of exchange.

20. On costs, see CPR:IX/160 (quotation). On taxes, see CPR:IX/42, 66–

The infusion of paper money in 1745–46 helped the Assembly organize and pay for the largest and most expensive logistical apparatus it had yet created. Building on the models of 1709–11 and 1740, in February 1745 the Assembly appointed five experienced merchants, all important local political leaders, to spend 16,000 pounds Old Tenor to purchase food and supplies for four months and hire ships to transport everything to Louisbourg. Although they were permitted to impress whatever "cannot otherwise be procured upon just and reasonable terms," they had already spent over 20,000 pounds Old Tenor by 29 May. Two other merchants were empowered to spend 2,000 pounds to feed, equip, and transport the May reinforcement. The system worked well enough so that in May 1746 the Assembly named six merchants, including four veterans of 1745 and one of 1740, to prepare the new regiment for five months of service; in June, when it seemed that the imperial government might not be able to feed the troops in the field, it directed them to procure a further seven months of provisions. The efforts of the commissaries were eased in each year by the embargo the Assembly clamped on the export of foodstuffs over the summer, a measure the colony accepted because the expeditions were popular and provided a massive assured market for all sorts of commodities.[21]

67, 99–100, 151, 217–18, 234–35. The Assembly also levied a tax of one-and-a-half pence in October 1745, and two pence in October 1746 (CPR:IX/167, 256), which together generated a credit of roughly 15,000 pounds New Tenor. On inflation, see CA-War:IV/369. The Old Tenor still in circulation depreciated even faster than the New Tenor. On reimbursement, see CHC:XI/343; CHC: XIII/89 (quotation), 351–57; CHC:XV/6–7, 83, 219–20, 223, 251, 337, 367, 471–72; CA-War:IV/219, 386; CPR:IX/158–61, 183–84, 217, 264–65, 410–11, 418, 447–49, 452–54, 456, 472–73, 509–13; Great Britain, *Proceedings,* V/267, 271, 418; and Gwyn, "British Government Spending." On Law, see CHC:XV/104 (quotation). On retiring paper money, see CHC:XVI/191–95, 237; CPR:IX/474–75; and CPR:X/65. On Rhode Island currency, see CHC:XVI/60–66.

21. On the commissaries in 1745, see CPR:IX/89, 97 (quotation); and CA-War:IV/199, 200, 212. The Upper House wanted to halve their commission (CA-War:IV/212; and CPR:IX/143). On supplying the May reinforcement, see CPR:IX/144–45. Two of the seven (Assistant Hezekiah Huntington of Norwich in February and Deputy Jabez Hamlin of Middletown in May) had been commissaries in 1740; the third commissary in 1740 (Deputy Andrew Burr of Fairfield) would serve again in 1746 (CPR:VIII/324). On commissaries in 1746, see CPR:IX/213–14, 234. On the embargoes, see CPR:IX/88, 233–34. For a list of articles supplied in 1746, see CA-War:V/38, 40.

The commissaries had many opportunities for profit: the fact that they served the public interest did not prevent them from making money at the public trough. Each man earned a 2.5 percent commission on his purchases, and was free to place contracts as he saw fit. For example, by the end of May 1745 the most active commissary, thirty-seven-year-old Gurdon Saltonstall, Jr., of New London, the son of the late governor, had earned 130 pounds on purchases of 5,300 pounds Old Tenor. The next year, he was even busier because the regiment assembled at New London. In addition to providing 6,800 pounds' worth of clothing and blankets for parts of the two companies raised in New London county, he supplied nearly 20,000 pounds of sundries for the regiment, for which he was paid 640 pounds in commissions. Accounts for four of the six commissaries show expenditures for sundries of nearly 60,500 pounds Old Tenor (17,300 pounds New Tenor), including commissions of 1,475 pounds. The colony recouped some of the costs of the canceled expedition by selling off unused materiel; Saltonstall eventually sold 11,320 pounds of the sundries he had purchased (57 percent).[22]

The close connection between public office and private interest was typified by the career of thirty-five-year-old Jonathan Trumbull, a Lebanon merchant and the most important leader in Windham county, whose political prominence did not hurt his business with the colony. He had become a major political figure with astonishing speed after being graduated from Harvard College in 1727—speaker of the Lower House in May 1739 and assistant a year later—and owed his rise to a good marriage and great ability fired by intense ambition. During the war, he helped to negotiate with Massachusetts about Connecticut's part in each expedition, and sold provisions to the commissaries each year. After the war, he tried for an even greater prize—victualing the Louisbourg garrison—but Connecticut did not have the political clout to win a share of the business. Still, the fact that Trumbull aspired to expand his mercantile activity in Britain's trans-Atlantic empire was another sign that Connecticut was becoming less and less of an isolated, and overlooked, imperial outpost.[23]

22. On Saltonstall, see CA-War:IV/212, 355, 383; CHC:XIII/264–66; CHC:XV/462–63; and Dexter, *Yale Graduates,* I/316–18. The other commissary accounts are CHC:XV/457–61 and CA-War:IV/354. Sundries included such things as tents, beds, nails, wood, a storehouse frame, hogsheads, buckets, bowls, iron ware, spoons, candles, knapsacks, axes, soap, rum, medical supplies, lead, bullet moulds, flints, powder, ship hire, pilots' wages, and "a standard [flag] for the regiment."

23. On Trumbull, see Shipton, *Harvard Graduates,* VIII/267–300; and

The Assembly capitalized on economic ferment in a growing colony (almost 100,000 people by 1745) to raise 850 troops by financial incentives alone, an achievement made possible by the tremendous popular enthusiasm for the campaign against Louisbourg.[24] During Queen Anne's War, Connecticut had begun to use bounties to raise an all-volunteer force for a single campaign at a time—a temporary creation that was neither part of the militia nor the first step toward a standing army like Britain's—and had refined the idea in the West Indies campaign in 1740. Five years later, the Assembly combined enthusiasm and bounty money to create what a generation would idealize as a quintessentially American invention: a group of amateur soldiers who freely joined together to form an army capable of defeating the French. What contemporaries overlooked was the extent to which the Assembly had shifted from using financial incentives as a way of ameliorating compulsory service, as it had done in 1709–11, to openly and happily paying poor men to go to war.

Connecticut society had evolved to the point where the Assembly could rely on bounties and wages, plus the chance to plunder the French, to recruit soldiers from among men who wanted or needed to make money. The fact that it paid men to perform military service does not mean, however, that the fundamental principles of Connecticut's military experience had changed, or that the enthusiasm for the campaign was anything less than powerful and genuine. The Assembly used money to tap a reservoir of popular sentiment in favor of a particular military action, not to create a colonial version of a mercenary professional army. Money by itself would probably have attracted some men, although the numbers would have been much reduced by the losses in, and the memory of, the West Indies disaster in 1740–41. As in 1709–11 and 1740, the Assembly did not use anti-Catholic rhetoric to stir enthusiasm for a Protestant crusade against the French; none was necessary in a society already bubbling with religious fervor. For one of the very few times in Connecticut's colonial

---

Weaver, *Trumbull*, pp. 31–41. At Harvard, he ranked twenty-eighth of thirty-seven according to family prominence. He was elected a deputy in 1733, appointed to the county court in 1738, and named a militia lieutenant colonel in 1739. On his wartime service, see CA-War:IV/245, 291; CPR:IX/177–78, 214; CHC:XI/296–97; and CHC:XVI/237–39. On the desire to victual Louisbourg, see CHC:XIII/201, 213.

24. On population, see Daniels, *Connecticut Town*, p. 47. Main's estimates (*Society*, p. 14) seem too low. The initial force was 500 men in March, followed by 200 men in May and 150 garrison troops in July.

history, a surge of war-fever at the start of a conflict combined with the lure of economic self-interest to create an army that was as close to a cross-section of society as it was possible to get, even though poor men were still more inclined than their wealthier neighbors to risk their lives in military service. It remained to be seen what the Assembly would do when it had to raise troops for a less popular campaign.[25]

Because the Assembly was not yet certain of the depth of enthusiasm in February 1745, it took no chances and gave recruits "greater encouragements" than Massachusetts thought were necessary. It offered each volunteer an enlistment bounty of 3 pounds Old Tenor, 7 pounds more if he came equipped with a gun, sword, and blanket, and a month's wages "before embarkation." The Lower House wanted to advance the wages at enlistment, but the Upper House thought men might abscond if paid too soon. Pay for a private soldier was 8 pounds Old Tenor a month, not much given the inflation of the paper money, but sufficient to attract the volunteers the Assembly wanted. To enable recruits to earn the money that might allow them to get ahead economically, the Assembly gave each of them immunity from arrest for debts under 50 pounds, a sign that it wanted to enlist men of responsible character, not the chronically debt-ridden.[26]

25. On the expectations of the recruits, see DeForest, *Journals,* p. 2. On the millennial hopes of ministers, see Stout, *Soul,* pp. 233–40; and Hatch, *Sacred,* pp. 36–44. While "the apocalyptic dimensions of the conflict became even more pronounced in the minds of the clergy" (Hatch, *Sacred,* p. 41), they were not prominent factors in how the Assembly went about raising soldiers. An identifiable surge of war-fever occurred in 1745, 1755, and 1775.

26. On bounties and wages, see CA-War:IV/148; and CPR:IX/83–84 (quotation 84), 93, 156–61 (quotation 160). On immunity from arrest, see CPR:IX/87. Wages paid to draftees who served on the frontier were eventually as high as for expeditionary soldiers; these men too seem to have viewed military service largely in financial terms. Pay for a private began at 6 pounds, 6 shillings Old Tenor a month in May 1744, rose to 7 pounds in May 1745, to 8 pounds, 8 pence in October 1746, and hit the peak of 12 pounds, 12 pence in May 1748. There is no reason to believe that the three hundred militiamen sent north after the sack of Saratoga in November 1745, or the four hundred draftees sent to the upper valley in the summer of 1748, differed socially or economically from the expeditionary soldiers. While a few did desert, their principal complaint was that the Assembly took too long to pay them. On the frontier in 1745–46, see CHC:XIII/130–32, 138–39, 142–43, 148–49, 154–55, 158–63, 167–71, 195, 208, 218–20, 243–44, 300–306, 317–19; CA-War:IV/296, 300;

While most recruits combined enthusiasm and the quest for economic opportunity in varying degrees, not all of them were young bachelors who could look forward to better prospects in the future. The average age of the soldiers may have been as high as the late twenties, and at least half may have been married, indications that patriotism and financial incentives were attracting men who viewed earning money in the service with less optimism and more urgency than did their younger, less encumbered colleagues. Even young men could encounter pitfalls on the road to success: the minor son of a large New Haven family tried to use military service to make a start in the world, but when he died he left medical bills his father could not pay. Farmers who had mortgaged land to the colony grasped at the chance to pay their debts, while others sought an escape from destitution. One sailor shipped aboard the colony sloop-of-war "in order to earn clothing." A "considerable number" of poor volunteers did not own guns; after exhausting stocks left over from 1709–11, the Assembly impressed arms from militiamen, but did not draft the militiamen themselves. Blacks and Indians also enlisted to earn bounty money, although both groups were legally excluded from the militia. The total number is unknown; 25 (6 percent) of the 430 men who spent the winter at Louisbourg can be identified as blacks (4 of the 25) or Indians (21), undoubtedly less than the actual number. Unfortunately, the Indians especially disliked the tedium of siege and garrison service, and were dismissed as soon as possible because they were always "getting drunk [and] quarreling with the [other] soldiers."[27]

CPR:IX/198; and CHS-RW/Nov 1745–May 1746. On the frontier in 1748, see CHC:XV/51–52, 68–69, 96–98, 102–03, 191, 236–39, 248–49, 260–63; CHC:XVI/461, 471, 475–78; and CPR:IX/346. On wages from 1744 through 1748, see CPR:IX/30–31, 110–11, 227–29, 258, 355. Officers of the militia troop in Woodbury complained in May 1746 about low pay (CA-War:IV/280). The Upper House rejected even higher wages in June 1747 (CA-War:IV/351). On four deserters from New London county, see CHS-FIW:II/100. In May 1746 the Assembly offered bounties for enemy Indians, paying more for a captive than for a scalp alone, but suspended the scheme before it went into effect (CA-War:IV/297–99; and CPR:IX/227–29).

27. Conclusions about age and marital status are based on men who died in service. Some soldiers came from the bottom of society. John Back was born in England in 1701, immigrated to New England in 1717, spent seven years as a servant to pay his passage, and lived thereafter a wandering life. He enlisted in 1745 and reenlisted for the winter, the longest he had voluntarily stayed in one place (CA-TL:IX/29–30). On the minor, Abraham Hotchkiss of New Haven,

The best insight into the economic standing of the soldiers comes from the probate inventories of men who died in service; their circumstances are frozen in time and do not have to be separated out from success—or failure—later in life. Roughly 150 soldiers died at Louisbourg, almost all over the winter of 1745–46. Probate records are available for 33 men (over 20 percent), a sufficient sample to suggest that the soldiers may have been a more representative cross-section of Connecticut men than any army before or since. The value of their estates averaged 183 pounds Old Tenor, enough to maintain a young married man and his family at what Jackson T. Main calls a "subsistence plus" standard of living; the average of the central half, omitting the highest and lowest quarters, was 110 pounds, enough for bachelors and young marrieds to live between "subsistence" and "subsistence plus." Nineteen (58 percent) lived at or below "subsistence plus," and, as a reminder that bounties and wages also attracted very poor men, at least nine estates (27 percent) were insolvent.[28]

A few examples illustrate the range of economic backgrounds. Jonathan Fuller, a twenty-four-year-old unmarried shoemaker from Branford who owned no land, had an estate of 60 pounds, 31 pounds (52 percent) of which was in wages and possessions sold at Louisbourg. John Sparks, an insolvent married weaver from Glastonbury, had an estate of 65 pounds including his loom, cloth, clothing, books, and household goods (40 pounds), and wages (25 pounds, or 38 percent); after deducting payments to his widow and the cost of administration, 40 pounds remained to pay debts of 70 pounds. Land sharply boosted the value of an estate, but it was difficult to turn into cash; even relatively well-off men could want liquid capital. Joseph Squire, a forty-seven-year-old married man from Woodbury, earned 30 pounds in wages, 14 percent of his estate of 215

---

see CA-War:IV/366, 417. On mortgages, see CA-War:IV/275; and CA-FC:2,II/98, 146–47. On the sailor, Jeremiah Chester of Groton, see CA-War:2,I/14 (quotation). On arms, see CPR:IX/95–97 (quotation 95); and CHC:XV/448. Muster rolls of the winter companies are in CHC:XIII/68–82. On Indians, see CHC:XI/351; and CHC:XIII/60–61 (quotation).

28. Probate records at CSL are incomplete. Probate files are hereafter referred to by district, date of filing, and record number. On standards of living, see Main, *Society*, p. 163, Appendix 4J, "Eighteenth-Century Standards for Levels of Living." I have derived my conclusions from the column labelled "1700–1749: Total [Value of Estates, in Pounds]." I have assumed that the figures approximate Old Tenor values, and have raised the requirements for each standard to reflect the inflation over this fifty-year period.

pounds; he owned a house and livestock worth 173 pounds (80 percent), the rest in clothing and household goods. Aaron Church of Colchester was even more tied up in property. His estate totaled nearly 600 pounds, 493 pounds (82 percent) of it for a home lot, half a house, and nearly ten acres of land; his wages were 38 pounds (6 percent). Most leaders doubtless believed, in the words of Roger Wolcott, that "God gave us the victory, but humanly speaking it was because our soldiers were freeholders and freeholders' sons, and had a force of interest in the country and liberty." Strictly speaking, that was accurate, but it was hardly the whole truth.[29]

No soldier or sailor won the riches of which he dreamed. The hundred sailors on the colony sloop were the only Connecticut men to come close. The sack of a small French village yielded 1,200 pounds, and their share of prize money from a captured French ship was 5,000 pounds, all in Old Tenor. But Captain John Prentiss withheld three-eighths for himself, claiming he was applying Royal Navy rules for dividing plunder. Although the Assembly ordered an equal division in May 1746, Prentiss died insolvent shortly thereafter. Thirteen sailors were still trying to collect their money from Prentiss's estate in May 1749. The sailors were still luckier than the soldiers. By the terms of the capitulation, everything in Louisbourg was preserved for the garrison—a wise decision, but one which undercut morale among men who had expected to win "the riches of the city." While looting never broke out on a large scale, colonial leaders lied when they told imperial officials that the soldiers "generously acquiesced in the loss of the plunder." Because they needed cash now, some soldiers sold to speculators their rights to any future division of land or plunder. Dashed hopes of plunder prompted a quarter of a two-hundred-man reinforcement to seek and receive a discharge as they were about to embark from New London in July.[30]

29. On Fuller, see Guilford:1746/no number; on Sparks, see Hartford:1746/5049; on Squire, see Woodbury:1746/4179; and on Church, see Colchester:1746/726. Wolcott's comment is in CHC:XVI/436 (quotation).

30. On plunder earned by the sailors, see CA-War:IV/271, 367–68. On Prentiss, see CPR:IX/402–03, 471, 476, 484–85, 527–28. The sloop's chaplain eventually received 39 pounds (Bidwell, "[Journal]," pp. 154, 158, 193). On suits against Prentiss, see CPR:IX/209–10, 332, 356–57. On the sloop, see CHC:XI/257; and CPR:IX/84, 157, 212. It cruised again in 1747–48, and was later sold to a Norwich merchant (CA-War:2,I/16–17; CA-War:IV/376, 389–90, 401–03; and CPR:IX/340, 360–61, 411). Before May 1746, the wages of the colony's sailors were "in some instances, below the rates" for merchant seamen

The Louisbourg expedition was unique in the prominence of the senior Connecticut officers who went to war, a fact that emphasized to Massachusetts that the colony had voluntarily engaged in a partnership with its neighbors. The Assembly sent sixty-seven-year-old Deputy Governor Roger Wolcott of Windsor as commander of, and spokesman for, its contribution, and named forty-nine-year-old Andrew Burr of Fairfield, speaker of the Lower House and a militia major, as colonel of its regiment. As might be expected, the field officers were affluent men, especially fifty-one-year-old Major Israel Newton of Colchester, who owned three slaves and was worth 2,500 pounds Old Tenor when he died at Louisbourg on 24 May 1745. Although Connecticut soldiers remained "under the direction of their own officers," the Assembly accepted forty-eight-year-old William Pepperrell, a merchant from Maine and the president of the Massachusetts Council, as commander-in-chief, in deference to the far larger investment Massachusetts was making in the expedition. Intercolonial cooperation went smoothly because Pepperrell used the New England style of collective leadership. Important decisions were reached in conferences which, on such crucial issues as whether or not to storm Louisbourg, included the captains and lieutenants who would know if the soldiers would obey any orders the senior officers cared to give. Harmony broke down only after the city was captured, when it came time to divide spoils and apportion credit.[31]

(CA-War:IV/358). On loss of plunder, see CHC:XI/323 (quotations); and CPR:IX/158–61. On selling rights to plunder, see Wilcoxson, *Stratford,* p. 306. On reinforcements in May, see CPR:IX/128; and CHC:XI/296; and in July, see CPR:IX/148; CHC:XI/325–32; and CHC:XIII/76–79. A further three hundred men were never raised (CPR:IX/148–49, 158–61; CHC:XI/318–20, 326, 342; and CHC:XIII/7).

31. On the field officers, see CPR:IX/84–85, 93. In February the Assembly intended them also to command the first three companies as in 1709–11, but in March recognized that they would have their hands full managing the regiment and appointed eight captains for the eight companies. Burr had been a commissary in 1740 and would be again in 1746. Simon Lothrop, a fifty-six-year-old militia captain from Norwich, was the lieutenant colonel (Huntington, *Lathrop,* pp. 58–59). On Newton's estate, see Colchester:1745/2201. On working together, see CHC:XI/258–59. On the conferences, see DeForest, *Journals,* pp. 15, 26–27. The troops were theoretically subject to the death penalty for desertion because the Assembly had ordered each man to swear an "oath of fidelity" based on the British Articles of War (CPR:IX/91), but strict discipline had never been enforced in colonial armies and was not now. The October As-

As always, company officers played the most important role in raising the troops because they convinced their neighbors to accept the bounties and go to war. With "an eye to gratify" prospective volunteers, the Assembly appointed only the man who was "well-respected . . . where he dwells." Virtually all officers were married men in their late thirties to early fifties, the captain almost always being the oldest. Recruiting relied heavily on their personal connections, and it was not uncommon for their sons or younger brothers to serve in their companies. Officers drew money to pay bounties out of the treasury in Hartford, or received it directly from the local tax collector, and went to recruit in their home regions. One captain was advised to raise part of his company "near [him]self and the other part near adjacent to [his] lieutenant and ensign." Another captain, who started late because the original appointee declined to serve, had to recruit fifteen miles from his home.[32]

As in Queen Anne's War, the Assembly wanted to appoint militia officers to lead the companies because it thought they had the best chance of persuading men to enlist and then to obey orders. Seven of ten captains appointed in March and May were militia officers, and the eighth, David Wooster of Stratford, a thirty-four-year-old Yale graduate, had commanded the colony sloop in 1742; in addition, three had been deputies and six more would be elected for the first time after their return. The fact that the soldiers found them to be acceptable officers was the final ingredient in the mix of reasons why the colony was able to avoid impressment. The captains used corporal punishment sparingly, preferring to rely on consent to secure obedience from the men they had persuaded to enlist, men on whom in part rested their reputation back home. The popularity of the captains was especially important in recruiting the winter garrison and in keeping the soldiers together in the face of appalling mortality; some men made "the choice of their head officer" a condition for re-enlisting. As had been the case in 1709–11, the Assembly thought popularity was less important for subordinate officers: only one of twenty held a militia commission.[33]

---

sembly named three new field officers for the winter garrison (CA-Mil:III/484), but they were not needed. On the breakdown of harmony, see CHC:XIII/151.

32. On acceptability of officers, see CHC:XIII/236 and 248 (quotations). Privates David and James Darling, for example, served in the company of which their older brother John was ensign (CA-War:IV/329; and Jacobus, *Fairfield*, II/ 274–75). On receiving bounty money, see CPR:IX/145–46. On recruiting, see CHC:XI/310–11 (quotation); and CA-War:IV/273, 287–88, 369.

33. On officers in March and May see CPR:IX/85–87, 91, 128, 143–44;

The need to hold Louisbourg until two British regular regiments could arrive in the spring of 1746 led Connecticut to recruit poor men for the winter garrison, the same situation that had existed after the capture of Annapolis Royal in 1710. Although "many" of the original 500 volunteers were "bare foot and very poorly clothed and very uneasy of being detained so long after the expedition . . . is over," a reminder that "it was likely to be worse for them to go home being so poorly clothed than to stay" convinced 160 men (32 percent) to remain for the winter, along with 140 men of the 200-man May reinforcement. Some veterans tried to bargain for additional incentives—some would re-enlist only if they received "a bounty of 12 pounds and one month's advance pay," others if they could have "as big a bounty as will cost to transport men here"—but the Assembly did not have to offer anything extra to recruit the men it wanted.[34]

The best indication that military service was viewed as a good way to earn money is the fact that 130 men enlisted for the first time to spend the winter at Louisbourg. With farming suspended until spring, they had no better employment at home. They received the same incentives as the original volunteers, plus an additional month's advance pay, and a promise of half a pint of rum a day. The new enlistees included some substantial citizens: Abraham Thomas of Durham left a widow, six daughters, and an estate worth over 270 pounds. But the conditions of service—a cooling of enthusiasm at home, no prospects for plunder, and garrison service known to be unhealthy—must have been most attractive to men more anxious about their economic standing than the original volunteers had been. When disease killed a third of the garrison before mid-April 1746 (145 of 430 soldiers), the colony lost a large number of the men who made the military system work. The mortality had a profound effect on communities with a large number of men in service. Ellington parish in Windsor, where three-quarters of the land was owned by people who lived elsewhere, could not support a new minister because its population was "much diminished by [en]listing" into the army: "no less than eleven"

and for the winter, see CHC:XIII/49, 55–58 (quotation 56), 63, 66–67. Militia companies elected new officers to replace the men who went to Louisbourg (CA-Mil:III/25, 439).

34. A muster roll of the garrison is in CHC:XIII/68–82. On reenlisting, see CHC:XI/351; and CHC:XIII/4, 13–15 (quotation 13), 55–57 (quotations 56). The Assembly made provisions to care for sick and wounded soldiers at New London, but it did nothing for destitute veterans (CPR:IX/166).

men had died at Louisbourg. The mortality also discouraged recruiting for the two colonial regular regiments that were scheduled to join the British regulars as Louisbourg's permanent garrison. Enlisting in the regulars was anathema to some Connecticut men. Volunteers were dissuaded, sometimes forcefully detained, from enlisting, "had sham actions brought against them to keep them from their duty," and even had "the mob" rescue them from recruiting officers.[35]

The Canada expedition never fired Connecticut's imagination the way the Louisbourg campaign did, and the decline in enthusiasm led to an even greater reliance on financial incentives, the penultimate stage in the transformation of the military system. With fewer veterans available, the colony was hard pressed to raise six hundred soldiers. In May the Assembly offered each volunteer 10 pounds Old Tenor for enlisting, plus 30 pounds Old Tenor if he equipped himself with clothing and a blanket. The total was four times the level of 1745, to which was added the prospect of earning rights to land in Canada, as in 1709. The Assembly continued to exempt soldiers from imprisonment for debts under 50 pounds, the better to enable poor men to take advantage of the opportunity to volunteer. At the outset it seemed these incentives would not be enough. Recruiters from neighboring colonies were "outbidding" the Assembly to the extent that ninety Connecticut men had enlisted in Rhode Island by the end of May. The competition for volunteers shows how far New England had come from the militia ideal of universal service. Like Wolcott in 1745, the Assembly later claimed the soldiers "looked upon themselves . . . as going to fight for their country," but for some, patriotism was alloyed with a willingness to sell their services to the highest bidder in the neighborhood.[36]

35. On enlisting for the winter, see CHC:XIII/59, 79–82; and CPR:IX/156–57. On Thomas, see Guilford:1746/no number. On casualties, see CHC:XIII/68–82, 152, 204, 207. Massachusetts lost a third of its 3,000 men. Only 320 of the 365 Connecticut men at Louisbourg in mid-January 1746 were fit for duty; some companies had as few as 16 men (CHS-FIW:II/979). On Ellington, see CA-Ecc:VII/239 (quotation). On the colonial regulars, see CHC:XIII/213, 330 (quotation).

36. On bounties, see CA-War:IV/289–90; CPR:IX/210–13; and CHC:XIII/203. On immunity from arrest, see CPR:IX/214, 258–59. Some suits were started, it seems, to stop Massachusetts from recruiting in Connecticut (CHC:XIII/258–59, 278–79, 283, 330). On recruiting by other colonies, see CHC:XIII/237. On the Assembly's claims, see CPR:IX/575–76 (quotation).

The problem became acute in June, when the Assembly agreed to raise four hundred more men, to quiet complaints that Connecticut was not contributing its fair share and to convince Parliament to reimburse its expenses for 1745. It increased the total incentives for each soldier from 40 to 70 pounds Old Tenor—30 pounds for enlisting (ten times the 1745 level, although much reduced by inflation) and 40 pounds for supplying his own clothing and a blanket. The Assembly realized the colony was reaching the upper limit of its ability to raise soldiers by financial incentives alone. As it had done under similar circumstances in 1711, it voted to impress able-bodied men out of the militia or from among "vagrant or wandering persons" to ensure it met its commitments. It ameliorated impressment by offering draftees all applicable bounties if they volunteered within twenty-four hours of being impressed, but it was ready to compel them to serve if necessary. Deserters had to refund all bounties they received, in addition to being fined the standard 20 pounds; if the man was penniless, he would be sold into service to pay his debt to the colony, a harsh penalty by Connecticut standards and one that showed the Assembly meant business. Fortunately for the leaders, enough volunteers came forward so that they did not have to invoke impressment.[37]

The volunteers in 1746 were not vagrants, although a few were "very poor," and many enlisted without a blanket or a gun. In some companies as many as fifty-seven of the hundred men lacked a firearm. Few soldiers came from more prosperous towns: in Windsor only six of three hundred militiamen enlisted. Judging by names like Abner Indian, John Negro, and Prince Noguier, blacks and Indians comprised about 10 percent of the regiment (twice as many Indians as blacks), probably more than in 1709–11 and 1745. As in 1745, a majority of soldiers were young bachelors, apprentices, and farm boys who were looking for a way up economically or a grand adventure, although there were enough older married men to suggest that for some going to war was the best employment available.[38]

37. On the response to complaints by Massachusetts, see CPR:IX/214; and CHC:XIII/224, 237–39. On bounties, see CA-War:IV/313; CPR:IX/231–32; and CHC:XIII/231–34, 242, 350. The penalties for desertion had been enacted in October 1744 (CPR:IX/77). On refunding bounty money, see CPR:IX/233.

38. On firearms, see CHC:XIII/247, 258, 269–73, 276; and CA-War:V/58. On Windsor, see CHC:XIII/247. Muster rolls are in CHC:XV/114–60; and CA-War:IV/329. One master illegally kept his apprentice's bounty (CA-War:IV/333; and CPR:IX/254–55).

The field officers were less prominent in 1746 because the regiment was to serve under a British commander-in-chief. The shift from 1745 was most apparent among the field officers, where personal ambition was a more important qualification than either political prominence or military experience. Fifty-two-year-old Elisha Williams of Wethersfield, who won appointment as colonel of the regiment against stiff opposition, was a restless character perpetually seeking new opportunities; he had been a lawyer, merchant, minister, Yale College rector, speaker of the Lower House, and chaplain of the Louisbourg regiment. Although Pepperrell considered him to be "a gentleman of good council and accomplishments," he was not as prominent as the senior officers in 1745. His lieutenant colonel, thirty-five-year-old Samuel Talcott of Hartford, a relatively undistinguished son of the late governor, served primarily for financial reasons. He had such high expectations for the expedition that he "sold and disposed of his stock in trade" and left his "flourishing and profitable business" to concentrate on his duties. His only military experience had been as a militia ensign for two years in the 1730s.[39]

The 1746 captains combined popularity with experience: nine of ten were either militia officers or Louisbourg veterans. More subordinate officers held militia rank or were Louisbourg veterans (eleven of thirty) than in 1745 because the Assembly needed to recruit soldiers more quickly. There was even competition for an appointment as ensign. Captain William Whiting wanted the man who had been his ensign at Louisbourg—"he did good service there, and will be agreeable to me"—but a Pomfret man won the job because local people thought "it their right to have an officer from thence." There was enough interest in the expedition that some men offered to recruit soldiers to earn a commission. In Wallingford, Elihu Hall, a rising member of the prominent local family, recruited with two unemployed veteran lieutenants; Hall was apparently more successful than his prospective subordinates and was the only one to earn a commission. While the war did give officers a chance to display their talent, no man who was not already a local leader was elected a militia officer or deputy thereafter.[40]

39. On Williams, see Shipton, *Harvard Graduates,* V/588–98; and CHC:XI/258 (quotation). Pepperrell had wanted Williams to be an officer in 1745 (CHS-RW/8 Mar 1745). On Talcott, see CA-War:X/307 (quotation); and CHC:IV/xxx. On their appointment, see CA-War:IV/304, 308.

40. On officers, see CPR:IX/213–14, 235–37; and CHC:XV/114–60. On the ensign, see CHC:XIII/251–52 (quotation) and CHC:XV/114. On recruiting

Like the soldiers, most company officers served for the chance to plunder the French. The minister of a prospective appointee in 1746 explained that his parishioner, Captain William Whiting, would welcome an appointment now "when by repeated losses at sea, and abounding generosity to his friends, his outward substance is much diminished." (He declined appointment as a first lieutenant, evidently because he wanted to be a captain.) Officers were as ambitious as any soldier. The quest for plunder was part of a career of entrepreneurship for forty-four-year-old Second Lieutenant Timothy Bigelow of Hartford; his estate was worth over 1,750 pounds Old Tenor, mostly livestock and land, but including three slaves, when he died in June 1747. The decision to spare Louisbourg and the failure of the 1746 expedition were extreme disappointments. There were other ways of getting ahead economically, but not even speculation in western lands offered a similar prospect of instant riches. Although three Louisbourg captains and an unknown number of "associates" petitioned the Assembly in 1753 for rights to land in the Susquehannah valley, speculation in western lands was not popular with veterans.[41]

By late June 1746, Connecticut had raised a thousand men on short notice by voluntary enlistment. The irony was that the fleet was overdue; by late October it was clear that the invasion would have to be postponed. The Assembly furloughed the soldiers in early November, sold all perishables, and stored public arms and ammunition, suspending the regiment until London sent word on what to do next. It was a sensible decision, but it caused all sorts of trouble. Captain Benjamin Lee of Plainfield revealed some of the attraction of military service for poor men when he reported that the men in his company declined the furlough because they had enlisted "into His Majesty's service, . . . expecting their maintenance from the King until he discharged them, that they were ready to serve as they should be ordered and would throw themselves upon me for their bread. I told them I was not able to give them bread . . . and urged . . . them to retire home." Lee paid their billeting for ten days out of his own

for rank, see CHC:XIII/225–28, 235, 248. The lieutenants were Macock Ward, a veteran of 1740, and Nathaniel Beedle, a veteran of Louisbourg. On Hall, see CHC:XV/114; and Dexter, *Yale Graduates,* I/427.

41. On Whiting, see CHC:XIII/229–30 (quotation). He had recently overcome "temptations" to join the Anglican communion. On Bigelow, see Hartford:1747/533. On land, see Boyd, *Susquehannah,* I/88. Both Williams and Talcott were Company members (Boyd, *Susquehannah,* I/21–22).

pocket, for which he was later reimbursed by the Assembly, but otherwise the soldiers were forced to fend for themselves.[42]

The furlough also made it difficult to convince the imperial government to pay the soldiers their wages to 31 October 1747, the date when soldiers from the other colonies were formally discharged. The Assembly claimed the soldiers had been ready to "muster upon the first notice that the expedition was putting forward" and so were in service although living at home. Colonel Williams and Lieutenant Colonel Talcott went to London, and eventually won half-pay for the year spent on furlough. The soldiers saw very little of this money because most had long since sold rights to their wages to speculators like Jonathan Trumbull for a small amount of ready cash. But accounts were so complex, and reimbursement so slow, that the speculators did not make a profit.[43]

The late 1740s saw many changes in how Connecticut men viewed war, including the increasing appeal of a career in imperial military service, a sign of the colony's continuing integration into the empire. Deputy Governor Wolcott was miffed when he was not offered the lieutenant colonelcy of the colonial regular regiment that Pepperrell was allowed to raise as a reward for his success; whether he would have accepted, at age sixty-six, is another matter. Two younger ex-officers, like the captains in 1740, sought advancement outside traditional paths to political power, despite being well connected in Connecticut. Pepperrell appointed thirty-six-year-old David Wooster of Stratford, who had led a company to Louisbourg, as one of his captains. After helping escort the defeated garrison back to France, Wooster returned home to recruit his company, taking time out

42. On postponing the campaign, see CHC:XIII/244–46, 257–58, 278; CHC:XVI/461–62; and CA-War:V/50, 58. On the furlough, see CA-War:IV/321, 325–27; CPR:IX/257–58, 341–44; and CHC:XIII/306–07. The regiment gathered at New London in mid-August and was sent home in mid-September (CHC:XIII/278, 297). On Lee's company, see CA-War:IV/380 (quotation); and CPR:IX/379.

43. On the Assembly's claims, see CPR:IX/575–76 (quotation). On Williams and Talcott, see CA-War:IV/410, 414. On the half pay, see CHC:XV/348–49, 375, 383; it amounted to 6,494 pounds sterling, nearly 40 percent of the total amount Parliament reimbursed for the 1746 expedition (Great Britain, *Proceedings,* V/418). On rights to wages, see CHC:XVI/51; and CHS-FIW:I/62, 126, 128. Officers' clothing accounts were not settled until 1760 (CPR:IX/215; CPR:XI/409–10; CA-War:VIII/294; and Lockwood, *Man Mortal,* p. xi). On speculation in wages, see CA-TM:II/110–13, 116; CA-FC:V/43; and CPR:XIII/384–85.

to marry a daughter of the Yale College rector. Another Louisbourg veteran and Yale graduate, twenty-one-year-old Nathan Whiting of New Haven, received an ensign's commission, thanks largely to Wolcott's intercession; he admitted that ambition was "a reigning principle in my breast." Neither Wooster nor Whiting had an active political career after Pepperrell's regiment was disbanded when Louisbourg was returned to the French in 1748. They were not favorites with the voters, but were popular with the sort of men who might volunteer for military service, an asset the Assembly would put to good use in the next war.[44]

Another sign of change was the Assembly's eagerness to raise three companies as a winter garrison for Albany in 1747–48 so men could earn bounties and wages; similar requests in the 1690s had given rise to foot-dragging and complaints about subordination to New York. Since the men would remain under their own officers, a deep aversion to corporal punishment did not deter volunteers. They enlisted primarily for the money, despite Wolcott's claim that "the love our men bear to their country" induced them "cheerfully to enter into the service." The careers of the forty-eight men in Captain Nathaniel Farrand's company show that some enlisted whenever they had the chance. Eight were veterans of 1745–46, including one who had been "in the service of his King and country ever since the siege of Louisbourg." Twenty-six (54 percent) would serve again in 1755–56, including four veterans of 1745–46; only eighteen (38 percent) served just for the winter. Most officers were veterans, but space was found for younger men, including Wolcott's twenty-one-year-old son Oliver. He had just been graduated from Yale College, where, said his father, "arms have been his favorite study," and, by serving as captain of "the College Artillery," a militia company of his classmates, "he has in some measure learned how to use them." The economic possibilities of war were so appealing that a veteran sergeant offered to lead "forty or fifty" men to hunt French Indians above Albany and earn the scalp bounties offered by New York, an inducement the Assembly now thought was

---

44. On Wolcott, see CHC:XIII/184–85, 193. On Wooster, see Dexter, *Yale Graduates,* I/616–20. On Whiting, see Dexter, *Yale Graduates,* I/750–51; and YU-MS:Whiting/21 (quotation). Whiting was a brother of the mother of Wooster's wife. His letters to his future wife show that he did not spend a great deal of time with his company at Louisbourg (YU-MS:Whiting/13–15; also Whiting, "Letters," pp. 133–35). On Wolcott's help, see CHC:XV/283; Shirley asked him to help raise colonial regulars (CHS-RW/4 Feb 1746).

"unchristian, inhumane, and barbarous." It had used scalp bounties before, but it had been fighting to protect lives and property, not for profit.[45]

By mid-century, Connecticut had reached a comfortable and satisfying understanding of how it created and used military force, validated by a fierce pride in the pinnacle achieved at Louisbourg in 1745. That success convinced the colonists of the power and suitability of their amateur military system for decades to come. But, while the leaders smugly congratulated themselves that God had provided clear evidence of His favor, they overlooked the fact they had capitalized on thirty years of uneven growth and increasing inequality to raise soldiers through the fear and anxiety of economic compulsion. Yes, most of the soldiers were freeholders and their sons, but they were worried about staying afloat economically. The leaders would never have formulated the situation in that way; if they had, they would have thought raising expeditionary troops by free choice was much better than straining their authority by compelling men to serve. Connecticut had made the transition from basing war on collective self-defense to relying on individual self-interest to motivate men to serve. Their most important success was fielding soldiers without suffering much economic and social dislocation. Victory in 1745 was very satisfying, but raising a thousand men in 1746 was more impressive. The colony arrived at mid-century with great confidence in its ability to make war.

45. On the companies, see CHC:XV/108–11; and CHC:XVI/473. British and New York officers were said to treat soldiers "ten-fold worse than we treat our dogs" (CHC:XV/110). On Farrand's company, see CHS-FIW:I/86; and CA-War:V/32 (quotation). On the officers, see CHC:XV/161, 170, 186, 190, 192–93, 199–201, 209, 215–17. Farrand had declined to serve in 1745 and would do so again in August 1755. On Wolcott, see CHC:XV/186–87 (quotations), 190, 200, 234; and Dexter, *Yale Graduates,* II/137. He signed the Declaration of Independence in 1776 and was elected governor in 1818. On bounty hunting, see CHC:XV/247 (quotation), 249. Each man was to have "two great dogs" for tracking. On scalping, see CA-War:IV/298; CPR:IX/227–29; and CHC:XV/83 (quotation). The Assembly had rejected scalp bounties in May 1746 (CPR:IX/227).

PART TWO

The Final French and Indian War

Chapter Four

Imperial Partner

The final chapter in Connecticut's colonial military history opened in 1754, when the colony began to consider what it had to do to help its neighbors remove French encroachments on the frontier between Canada and British America. The conflict grew into the largest and most complicated military activity Connecticut had yet undertaken when Britain turned a defensive struggle into an offensive war to dismantle the French empire in North America. Connecticut's relations with the imperial government went through three stages between 1755 and 1762, corresponding to the changes in imperial strategy. Through 1757 Britain clung to the old idea of defending the colonies as cheaply as possible by sending a commander-in-chief with a few regulars around whom the colonies could gather their own forces. Between 1758 and 1760, Britain used its superior seapower to bottle up the French navy, and sent the bulk of its regular army to overwhelm Canada. Regulars played the primary role in defeating the French, and transformed the character of the war by relegating colonial forces to support functions. Britain paid the colonies handsomely for their help, and drew from them their greatest military effort before the Revolution. In 1761–62 the colonies helped consolidate and enlarge Britain's gains, but pride in the empire soon dissipated as the euphoria of victory gave way to closer imperial supervision.[1]

1. The most extensive history of the final round of the Anglo-French contest is Gipson, *British Empire,* but his account lacks the spark of Francis Parkman's. Fregault, *Canada* corrects the Anglocentric bias of Gipson and Parkman.

THE POLITICS OF WAR

Connecticut reacted to tension along the frontier during the early 1750s with a mix of understanding and cupidity that would be its hallmark throughout the decade. Shortly after succeeding the late Governor Law in November 1750, Roger Wolcott told imperial officials that the French in Canada were "threatening to drive us and all the English on the continent into the sea." He was closer to the truth three years later when he reminded London that only the conquest of Canada would end forever the French threat to the prosperity and expansion of British America. Wolcott was no fool, and he thoroughly understood that "union must be the safety of these plantations." But he crippled the value of his insight by supporting the claims of Connecticut speculators to land in northeast Pennsylvania, the quickest way to ensure that the colonies remained disunited. The same kind of self-interest that the Assembly had learned to exploit to raise expeditionary troops was now clouding the way senior leaders assessed their military problems.[2]

The Assembly had similarly mixed motives about defending the New York frontier when it sent three delegates to an intercolonial conference at Albany in May 1754. Three considerations overrode its traditional distaste for joining in "measures for the general defense." First, as in 1689–90, French raiders were so active that the colonies wanted Iroquois help to make frontier defense more effective and less costly. The Assembly wanted to keep costs to a minimum. It exaggerated the danger to induce the imperial government to pay more to protect New York, and only reluctantly acknowledged that the time-honored practice of paying to renew the alliance with the tribes was the best and cheapest way of dealing with the French threat. Second, sending delegates to Albany helped Connecticut to repair its reputation in London, which had been damaged by the relentless attempts of some of its inhabitants to acquire western lands and by the plunder of a Spanish ship driven into New London harbor by storms in November 1752. By participating in the conference, the Assembly hoped to show that Connecticut was a responsible member of the empire, one that was willing to contribute to the common defense. Finally, many leaders supported the idea of purchasing from the Iroquois rights to western lands for the immediate benefit of a group of speculators called the Susquehannah Company. While company members did not dominate the

2. Wolcott's opinions are in CHC:XVI/25 (quotation), 98, 402 (quotation), 428–29, 435.

Assembly, their goals were so popular that the delegates, all company supporters, were clearly expected to combine public service with the pursuit of private advantage.[3]

Connecticut's limited and parochial concerns were quickly overshadowed by the efforts of delegates from Massachusetts and Pennsylvania to reorganize British America under a single royal governor-general. The Assembly objected strongly to the Plan of Union developed at the Albany conference because it smacked so much of the hated Dominion of New England in the 1680s. In October a committee called the plan "subversive of the just rights and privileges" of Connecticut, and claimed that giving imperial officials power to levy taxes would undermine "the rights and privileges of Englishmen." The report echoed efforts to keep the empire at arm's length in the 1690s, but on second thought the full Assembly was more conciliatory; imperial officials were paying closer attention to Connecticut now than they had been sixty years earlier. In its address to Parliament, the Assembly emphasized Connecticut's participation in past wars and recognized the imperial government's right to call on it to help defend the New York frontier. Still, its desire to avoid an imperial viceroy, plus the thirst of many members for western lands, led it to underestimate the need for united action to meet the French threat. In a misguided effort to protect the frontier by expanding settlement, it resurrected Wolcott's idea that the imperial government should create new colonies "on such lands . . . as the Indians will readily sell, to be formed and conducted as the New England colonies have been." The suggestion had no chance of adoption: the last thing London wanted was more fractious colonies on the eve of war with Canada.[4]

The Assembly's objections to the military reorganization proposed at

---

3. On the conference, see CA-War:V/65; CHC:XVI/437–38, 441–42; CHC:XVII/15–17 (quotation 17); and CPR:X/267–68. The delegates were a distinguished group: William Pitkin of Hartford, an assistant who had just been elected deputy governor; Roger Wolcott, Jr., of Windsor, an assistant whose father the governor had just been voted out of office; and Elisha Williams of Wethersfield, a deputy who had been colonel of the 1746 regiment and speaker of the Lower House in May 1753. On the plundered ship, see Hooker, *Spanish Ship*. Voters denied Roger Wolcott, Sr., reelection in May 1754 for failing to placate imperial anger about this incident. On the Company, see Boyd, *Susquehannah*, I/Introduction; Boyd, *Susquehannah Company*; and Johnson, *Papers*, I/398–400.

4. On reaction to the Albany plan, see CA-War:V/70, 91; CHC:XVII/35–42 (quotations 35–36, 41–42), 52–55; CPR:X/292–94; and CSL-JT:XXIII/8ab.

Albany shed light on how the leaders thought their military system operated at mid-century. They objected to allowing the governor-general and
his council to nominate and commission all military officers because, in
a government as large as the proposed union, the senior leaders could not
be "well acquainted . . . with the persons who will best serve to encourage
soldiers to enlist, and who may conduct them with a prudence, and
encourage their hearts." Their description of how the Assembly raised
troops combined Connecticut's traditional desire to control its military
resources with a confidence in its military ability derived from the capture
of Louisbourg. "It hath hitherto been practised in the New England
governments to appoint officers out of their best yeomen, who live in good
circumstances on their own property in lands; and when chosen freely,
and without any application of their own for such offices, . . . they look
upon themselves obliged . . . to serve their country in the field . . . ;
and under such officers, well known and esteemed among the people,
freeholders' sons, not moved by necessity, but their country's good, generally have enlisted with cheerfulness and alacrity. Now, should officers be
sent among them from abroad, and to whom they are strangers, it is plain
such youth will not enlist; and to [im]press such generous young men
into service, must be not only hard and grievous, but very much dishearten
and dispirit them. . . ." It was an appealing vision that seemed to offer
sound reasons for allowing Connecticut to continue to control its military
resources, but it took no account of how the unique circumstances of
1745 might apply to a more difficult, less popular, and less decisive
campaign.[5]

The long-anticipated war against the French began in mid-1754 as a
skirmish over land claims in the Ohio valley. Later that year, the imperial
government sent a commander-in-chief, Major General Edward Braddock,
with two understrength regular regiments to Virginia as the core of an
expedition to drive the French out of the valley. It ordered the colonies to
gather recruits for these regiments and to help re-raise the two colonial
regular regiments disbanded at the end of King George's War. Because
the plan harked back to 1740, when colonists served under regular officers,
instead of 1745, when the colonies had organized their own regiments,
the Assembly was reluctant to comply. It eventually did so to placate
London, but it added conditions. In January 1755 it voted to raise up to
300 men to serve under American-born officers in one of the 1,145-man
colonial regular regiments on the northern frontier; even then, Governor

5. Quotations are from CHC:XVII/38.

Thomas Fitch, who had succeeded Wolcott in May 1754, warned that there might be few recruits because men would not "cheerfully enlist" under officers they did not know and trust. The Assembly may have worried too that British strategy was poorly conceived. Imperial planners naively expected that a show of force would convince the French to abandon their frontier forts without a fight. Attacking them would inevitably provoke a border war, but London was not yet willing to invest the resources needed to end the menace at its source by conquering Canada, and even failed to appreciate the logistical difficulties of campaigning in the wilderness. Braddock performed a small miracle just getting his army into the Ohio valley, but once there, his raw recruits shattered when ambushed by French-led Indians on 5 July 1755, a catastrophe that set off an avalanche of destruction across the southern frontier.[6]

Connecticut had not been idle while Braddock was marching to disaster. Hostile Indians had so alarmed the frontier that the Assembly eagerly agreed to a proposal by Governor Shirley of Massachusetts "to erect a strong fortress" near Crown Point. The leaders "very generally approved" of the idea and "were well spirited to exert themselves to the utmost." They voted in March 1755 to raise one thousand men for the five-thousand-man expedition, "beyond their due proportion" because they knew that Massachusetts was heavily committed in Nova Scotia and that New York feared a French naval attack on Manhattan. They also agreed that William Johnson of New York would lead the expedition; his connections with the Iroquois would be vital in inducing the Indians to join the expedition and protect it from ambush on the march. In May, they voted to raise five hundred more men, and gave New York permission to recruit three hundred men in Connecticut. When Braddock's defeat showed how formidable the French could be, they voted to reinforce the Crown Point expedition with a further fifteen hundred men.[7]

6. On raising men for the regulars, see CHC:XVII/48, 73–74 (quotation); CA-War:V/79; and CPR:X/327–28. On the colonial regular regiments, see Great Britain, *Proceedings,* I/24. Recruiting by a cadre of regular officers with the help of colonial half-pay officers went well; the Fiftieth Regiment mustered 979 privates on 24 April 1755 (Graham, "British Intervention," p. 242; YU-MS:Loudoun/6, folio 1; and YU-MS:Whiting/30). On strategy in 1754–55, see Pargellis, *Loudoun,* pp. 1–44, the best book on the war; Gipson, *Defeat,* pp. 3–61; and Graham, "British Intervention."

7. On the frontier, see CA-War:V/141; CPR:X/331; and CHC:XVII/65–66, 74–75. The Hartford Committee of War was revived in October 1754

The Assembly wanted to show London that "a spirit of loyalty and zeal for His Majesty's service" prevailed "universally in this colony," but it should have known that the expedition offered no chance of decisive results. Attacking Crown Point made sense only as part of a plan to conquer Canada, something not contemplated in 1755; even if the troops reached the fort, they could not have stayed there long in the face of French counterattacks. Governor Fitch understood that the best way to aid Braddock was to strike at Niagara, the fort on Lake Ontario through which French power flowed to the Ohio valley. The Assembly acted rashly because it was blinded by a desire to acquire and protect western lands: in May 1755, in the middle of organizing the expedition, it endorsed the Susquehannah Company's claims to the land its representatives had purchased from the Iroquois at Albany in June 1754.[8]

The Crown Point expedition did have some tangible benefits for Connecticut because the French were thrown on the defensive; one Hartford county leader reported that "not so much as one Indian has appeared on any of the frontiers" since the army marched north from Albany. Two thousand colonial soldiers, slowed by logistical difficulties, reached the head of Lake George in late August, where they stopped to build bateaux to carry them across the lakes. There on 8 September they defeated a French counter-expedition in a three-part, day-long battle that Governor Fitch called "the severest that has been in this country." Connecticut lost 45 men killed, 20 wounded, and 5 missing, 9 percent of its 800 men engaged and a quarter of the army's 280 casualties. Massachusetts lost much more heavily, especially in the morning ambush: 165 men killed, wounded, and missing, including 2 colonels dead, 18 percent of its 900 men engaged and nearly 60 percent of the total loss.[9]

(CPR:X/319–20). On the Crown Point expedition, see Shirley, *Correspondence*, II/133–38; CA-War:V/85, 88, 118–19; CHC:XVII/98, 133, 136–37, 146; and CPR:X/336–37 (quotations), 346, 390, 397.

8. On Connecticut's zeal, see CHC:XVII/146 (quotation); and CA-War:V/130. On Fitch's percipience, see CHC:XVII/121. On the Company, see CPR:X/378.

9. On the absence of raiders, see CHC:XVII/142 (quotation). The Hartford Committee of War sent only seventy-five men north when French raiders alarmed the upper valley in the summer and fall (MHS-IW/19 Jun, 7 Aug, 15 Sep 1755). On the battle, see CHC:XVII/143–46 (quotation 145), 150–51, 157–59; *Gazette*, 20 Sep 1755; Johnson, *Papers*, IX/235–37; and Gipson, *Defeat*, pp. 162–77. On the number of colonial soldiers, see CHC:XVII/158. The rest

Having regained the initiative (and begun immediately to quarrel about who had been responsible for the success), the army's leaders now had to decide what to do next. Connecticut officers wanted to advance, but the Assembly was more concerned that the fort Johnson was having the army build at the head of Lake George be "sufficiently defensible" and well placed for intercepting French raiders. The Assembly understood that the campaigning season was fast running out, and agreed to abandon all idea of an advance when it learned in mid-October that the logistical problems were overwhelming. The army disbanded in mid-November, without ever having advanced beyond the head of Lake George, and a winter garrison was left behind to hang on to the forts created during the summer. Back home, the people of Connecticut were enormously disappointed that the repulse of the French had not led to the capture of Crown Point, but in truth no opportunity had been lost. Logistical obstacles, the late start, and the piecemeal voting of reinforcements all prevented the expedition from reaching its goal, but that goal had been the wrong one in the first place.[10]

Shirley, who succeeded Braddock as imperial commander, had a better plan for 1756. He wanted the colonies as far south as Virginia to help dislodge the French from Lake Ontario, an intelligent way to end the danger to the southern frontier, but only the five northern colonies sent delegates to a conference at Manhattan in mid-December. Connecticut's principal aim was to retain control of how its troops were organized and employed; the last thing it wanted was an influx of regulars under a more powerful imperial commander-in-chief. An Assembly committee claimed that regulars "can't be used to equal advantage with those [troops] raised here, for want of acquaintance and discipline suited thereto." Moreover,

---

of the troops, and the remainder of the casualties, were from New York and Rhode Island. Casualty figures are in Johnson, *Papers,* IX/235–37.

10. On the end of the campaign, see CHC:XVIII/346; CA-War:V/174, 176, 190–91; CHC:XVII/151–55, 159–60, 163–69, 181–82; and CPR:X/420–21. James Parker, publisher of the *Connecticut Gazette,* the colony's only newspaper, asked: "What have we been doing all these eight months past?" (*Gazette,* 18 Oct; see also 1 Nov and 13 Dec 1755). One correspondent was astonished "that a few slaves of France, with their motley savages, should bid these powerful colonies tremble" (9 Aug). On rivalry between Johnson and Lyman, see Clark, *Lyman,* pp. 18–26; and YU-MS:Whiting/11. The Assembly suggested that the winter companies attack Crown Point by sled across the ice, but the soldiers were barely able to patrol around Fort William Henry (CPR:X/421–22; and CHC:XVII/194).

it argued that regulars and colonists "cannot be safely united, or act advantageously together" because of fundamental differences in the way they were organized and disciplined. The full Assembly toned down the language but left the committee's conclusions intact. It urged "the advantage" of raising colonial soldiers "who are well acquainted with, and have been used to" service along the frontier rather than asking Britain for more regulars. Where it would find such formidable soldiers was a question it left unanswered. Still basking in the glow of capturing Louisbourg, and to a lesser extent of turning back the French at Lake George, it claimed that all that was "wanting to enable the colonists to serve His Majesty's interests here is a supply of arms, ammunition, clothing, and money." These ideas reflected great pride and confidence in the prowess of colonial arms, but the imperial government put little trust in colonial soldiers, correctly so from a conventional military standpoint. When London asked the colonies for more troops in the next few years, it wanted them mainly as an adjunct to a vastly expanded regular army.[11]

The failure of the 1755 campaign convinced imperial officials to assert greater control over operations which were much more complex than any that had hitherto been contemplated in North America; in doing so, they took direction of the war away from the colonial legislatures. Parliament took two steps in 1756 which changed the character of the conflict. First, on 3 February it voted to reimburse the colonies for their expenses in 1755, which, it hoped, would encourage them "to continue to exert themselves with vigor." This was the first time the imperial government had subsidized colonial soldiers in wartime, and it marked the largest intrusion of imperial power into Connecticut since the first decade of the century. Reimbursement ensured that the colony did what its paymaster wanted; the Assembly did not object that accepting the money reduced its control over how its troops would be used. Second, in May 1756 Parliament radically altered the strategic situation by declaring war against France. The earl of Loudoun, the new commander-in-chief, could use the seven regular regiments recruiting in the colonies as the core of an invasion of Canada, but neither he nor the declaration arrived in time to organize an expedition in 1756. The best he could do was to follow through with Shirley's modification of the plan of 1755 that was already underway. The

11. On Shirley's plan, see CHC:XVII/183–92; Shirley, *Correspondence,* II/343–50; Schutz, *Shirley,* pp. 219–31; and Gipson, *Defeat,* pp. 176–86. On the Assembly's ideas, see CPR:X/420–21; CA-War:V/190 (quotation); and CHS-GA/Oct 1755 (quotations).

Assembly had authorized twenty-five hundred troops to take part in a secondary expedition against Crown Point that was designed to draw French attention away from the main army as it moved up the Mohawk valley to Lake Ontario. But both armies were hampered by logistical obstacles and moved forward too slowly, allowing the French time to besiege and sack Oswego, the most important British post on the lakes, in early August. Far from launching an invasion, Loudoun's first task was to stabilize the frontier.[12]

Connecticut's unwillingness to abandon legislative consultation in this emergency strengthened the imperial government's determination to secure its subordination. The Assembly fenced with Loudoun for a month about reinforcing the New York frontier. When he asked for soldiers on 20 August, Fitch "immediately gave out orders for the General Assembly to meet in order to consider what aid to afford," principally, it seems, to determine how to persuade Connecticut troops to serve so far outside the colony. The leaders convened on 11 September, and although Fitch said they showed "a very forward disposition to exert themselves," they wanted to know what Loudoun intended to do. Since it seemed the French were not going to advance down the Mohawk valley to Albany, the general calmly answered the questions. He assured the leaders that he would have "struck a material stroke" if he had had more support, and complained that consulting them had compromised his plans. "Without I can have your confidence so far as to be trusted with the operations of the campaign, without being previously obliged to lay before each Assembly the service for which the troops are destined, the enemy must always be apprized where to prepare" because too many men would know the campaign plan.[13]

The Assembly was aware of the need for secrecy and speed, but it still wanted a voice in deciding how to fight the war. Moreover, it was unwilling to act without its neighbors, none of whom, it claimed, had made

12. On Parliamentary subsidies, see CHC:XVII/198 (quotation), 300–301; and CPR:X/546. On Loudoun and the declaration of war, see CHC:I/277; and CHC:XVII/216–17, 222. The Assembly doubled its quota to twenty-five hundred men because it doubted the southern colonies would send any troops (CHC:XVII/198–99; CHC:I/301, 304; and CPR:X/458–59). On the campaign, see Pargellis, *Loudoun*, pp. 132–66; Fregault, *Canada*, pp. 112–42; Gipson, *Defeat*, pp. 186–211; and Schutz, *Shirley*, pp. 232–42.

13. On the Assembly's attitude, see CHC:XVII/251, 254–59 (quotations 254–55, 257).

"any effectual preparations" to reinforce the army, and asserted that raising men now would only reduce its ability to do "much service in some future and important crisis." It authorized Fitch to dispatch one thousand militiamen "upon notice of the approach of the enemy to attack the army" only if Loudoun certified that "reinforcements will be necessary." When Loudoun called for this help on 30 September, Fitch set a draft in motion but waited until the Assembly convened on 18 October to seek approval to send the troops to the New York frontier. By that time the French threat had evaporated entirely, and the Assembly dismissed all the men who had enlisted or been impressed. Both Fitch and the Assembly met Loudoun's urgent requests with time-consuming questions principally because they wanted to retain control over Connecticut's military resources. Their assessment of the colony's ability to respond to a frontier emergency in late October may have been accurate (although the militia did perform creditably in mid-August the next year), but it did not accord with what they had led increasingly frustrated and skeptical imperial officials to expect. [14]

Not surprisingly, Loudoun wanted to avoid dealing with the legislatures when he organized the 1757 campaign. He asked each colony to send representatives with plenipotentiary authority to confer with him at Manhattan, but the Assembly empowered its delegates only to present its position, not to negotiate on its behalf. It offered to raise 1,250 men, expected to appoint its own officers, and wanted Loudoun to reduce the friction between regulars and colonials which had surfaced in 1756. Loudoun asked Connecticut for 1,400 men (and all New England for only 4,000 men, half the number in 1756), and wanted them to be "good effective men," not the second-rate soldiers he claimed to have seen the preceding summer. The New Englanders, he reported, had been "frightened out of their senses at the name of a Frenchman, for those are not the men they used to send out, but fellows hired by other men who should have gone themselves." The Assembly agreed to the quota, and promised to supply the best soldiers possible. Despite the Assembly's promise, however, the troops did not meet Loudoun's exacting standards; he later called them "the lowest dregs of the people, on which no dependence can be had." [15]

14. On Connecticut's reaction, see CHC:XVII/261–66 (quotations 261), 277; and CPR:X/545, 554–55, 571–72. On the need for secrecy, see CPR:X/ 343, 447. In October 1756, the Assembly prohibited the *Gazette* from printing information "detrimental to His Majesty's designs" (CA-War:VI/156).

15. On the quotas, see CHC:XVIII/277–78 (quotation), 286–87, 297, 302;

Loudoun learned in early May that William Pitt, the new secretary of state in charge of managing the war, expected each colony to provide the same number of troops in 1757 as it had in 1756. Instead of having the colonies raise more expeditionary soldiers, Loudoun asked them to keep their militias "in readiness to march at an hour's warning." He was actually trying to improve the quality of the army since, according to him, the militiamen were "the real inhabitants, stout able men, and for a brush, much better than the provincial troops." Their only drawback was that they "cannot be detained any time in the field, but will return home." Loudoun's request caused a stir in the Assembly. The deputies "long and largely debated out of how many and whose regiments the forces to be in a more especial readiness should be taken. The members nearest to the exposed places were for as many as possible, the eastern for as few." After "much debate" about costs, the Assembly chose three regiments, the minimum number the westerners would accept. Such controversies were neither common nor of major military significance because Connecticut was never in real danger; the French were just too far away.[16]

Unlike in 1755 and 1756, Connecticut's expeditionary troops were on the defensive in 1757, five hundred men in western Massachusetts and nine hundred men in the largely colonial army occupying the forts north of Albany. Loudoun planned to use most of the regulars in a seaborne attack on Quebec, a strategy that held the potential for decisive results while also diverting French attention from the New York frontier. He was willing to leave Louisbourg untouched in his rear, but when Pitt ordered him to take it before proceeding up the St. Lawrence, the French had time to launch another spoiling attack on the frontier. By 4 August they

---

CA-War:VI/173, 175, 182; and CPR:X/593–94, 598. On Loudoun's opinions, see CO-5:II/403–04 and 528 (quotations) and YU-MS:Loudoun/5 (quotation). Provincial troops, according to Loudoun, "when first brought out, will undertake any rash thing, but if they do not get forward, they immediately languish and go home" (YU-MS:Loudoun/6).

16. On Pitt's demands, see CHC:I/314; and CHC:XVII/305 (quotation), 307–10. On Loudoun's request and his opinions, see CO-5:II/403–04 (quotations). On the Assembly's deliberations, see Williams, *Journal,* pp. 30–31 (quotation). Although the frontier was far from Connecticut, memories persisted of how French raiders had sacked exposed towns in 1690 and 1704. In July 1758 the town of Windham was terrorized before people discovered that "the dread inimical army was an army of thirsty frogs going to the river for a little water" (Peters, *History,* pp. 129–31 (quotation 130–31). The "Battle of the Frogs" has become a Connecticut legend.

had invested the most exposed British post, Fort William Henry at the head of Lake George. The New England militia, primed to act, responded quickly to the most dangerous threat to the frontier in fifty years. In Connecticut, militia officers organized about five thousand men, a quarter of the colony's militiamen, into composite companies and led them off to Albany between 7 and 10 August, more than half of them on horseback. This massive effort did not prevent the loss of the fort on 9 August, although the colonies claimed, erroneously, that it did help dissuade the French from advancing further. When it became clear that the French were retiring (in truth they had no place else to go), the militiamen were sent home; the Connecticut companies returned between 23 and 25 August. At a cost of nearly 15,000 pounds lawful money for about eighteen days of service, more than a third of what it cost to keep the expeditionary regiment in the field for the entire campaign, the militia showed it was still British America's last line of defense. But, while it was an asset in a crisis, as an institution it had no role to play in the conquest of Canada.[17]

Connecticut's strength had ebbed by the end of 1757. Fitch reported to London that "our treasure is exhausted, our substance consumed, [and] the number of our able-bodied men much lessened." Worse still, "the spirit, vigor, and resolution of the people" had "so much abated that . . . it appeared difficult to devise any method to raise them to their former life and activity." But things were about to change, thanks largely to the energy and vision of William Pitt. Not content with restoring the balance of power in Europe or North America, he sought total victory over France, and the failures of his predecessors gave him the political strength in Parliament to make the attempt. His program had several features: expand

17. Loudoun drew on nearly a century of sound strategic thinking when he advocated a seaborne attack up the St. Lawrence (YU-MS:Loudoun/6). He knew Major General Daniel Webb to be a poor choice to command the army above Albany, but he had no one better (YU-MS:Loudoun/7). On the campaign, see Pargellis, *Loudoun,* pp. 228–52; Gipson, *Victorious,* pp. 62–89; and Fregault, *Canada,* pp. 143–62. On the militia, see CHC:I/325; CPR:X/623; CPR:XI/ 59–60; CHC:XVII/348–49; CHC:IX/197–265; Fitch, "Diary," V/251–52, VI/ 74–75; and Pitt, *Correspondence,* I/94–98. The Assembly thought Massachusetts had not dispatched a fair share of its militiamen to the frontier, so it sent delegates to Boston to ensure that its neighbors would respond better in the future (CPR:XI/634; and CHC:XVII/321–27). It threatened to recall its troops in 1758 if "other governments should fail in exerting themselves properly" (CPR:XI/106). Loudoun in desperation proposed a winter campaign in 1757–58 (YU-MS: Loudoun/11).

the army and navy, support Prussia as a way of keeping France occupied in Europe, send the bulk of the regular army to North America (nearly twenty-five-thousand men by the spring of 1758), and subsidize more colonial soldiers than ever before. By combining naval superiority and victories in North America with parity in Europe, Pitt sought to prevent France from using victories on the continent to win the return of her colonies, the way she had regained Louisbourg at the end of King George's War.[18]

Pitt's strategy of rolling up French power from the edges was eventually successful, but he might have achieved decisive results more quickly and less expensively if he had concentrated on the Louisbourg-Quebec-Montreal axis and reduced the need for so many costly and inefficient colonial troops. He waged the war in a very expensive manner by placing great importance on massive overland campaigns against the periphery of French power, instead of using smaller numbers of better-trained and more mobile colonial and regular soldiers to terrorize Canadian farmers and thereby divert resources from the overwhelming land forces the Royal Navy could bring up the St. Lawrence. He spent lavishly for colonial regiments that did little more than build and guard supply lines while the regulars advanced slowly overland to Canada. In the short term, his strategy shrewdly asked the colonies to do more of what they had done in 1745, albeit a great deal more and now under imperial direction. He did not try to change the way they made war by asking them to enlist for extended periods the few colonists who knew how to fight Indian-style in the wilderness. Pitt used the tools he had at hand, however inefficient they might have been, rather than have the colonies spend time training men in a way of war that was alien to most North American experience. Still, the longer-term costs of his strategy were significant. Fewer troops would have been less expensive, and fewer subsidies would not have led the colonies to think that imperial largesse was the norm in their relations with Britain.[19]

18. On Connecticut's state of mind, see CHC:XVII/335 (quotation); and CHC:I/329. On Pitt's strategy, see Pitt, *Correspondence,* I/Introduction; Gipson, *Victorious,* pp. 174–79; Paregellis, *Military Affairs,* pp. xiv-xxi; and Fregault, *Canada,* pp. 202–211. On the size of the regular army in North America, see YU-MS:Loudoun/folio 2; and CO-5:II/860–62

19. My analysis owes much to Pargellis, *Military Affairs,* pp. xiv-xxi, who generally agreed with Loudoun's ideas. In a letter to London on 2 October 1756 (YU-MS:Loudoun/6), the general pointed to the biggest problem facing conven-

The Assembly was not concerned with long-term consequences when it considered Pitt's plans for 1758. It was stunned that he had asked the northern colonies to raise twenty thousand men for operations across the frontier; Connecticut's troops were to join a force of regulars in an attack on Crown Point. The leaders agreed to try to meet Connecticut's share of the quota principally because Pitt assured them he would make "strong recommendations" to Parliament to reimburse the colony for the cost of raising, clothing, and paying its soldiers. Britain thus offered to assume most of the costs of creating massive new colonial armies to help the regulars conquer Canada. Pitt's commitments revived Connecticut's "almost desponding spirits" because people hoped the campaign "might be a finishing stroke." In March the Assembly voted to raise five thousand men, nearly double the number in any preceding year.[20]

The Assembly realized it no longer had a voice in the direction of the war, but it kept up appearances by insisting that its troops, directly under the command of officers it appointed, were "to cooperate with and second a body of His Majesty's forces." It was following the policy begun in 1709 of complying with imperial military demands to win a favorable hearing in London on challenges to the charter. Two months after endorsing Pitt's plans, the leaders sent an agent to London to "set us in a favorable light" about boundary disputes with Massachusetts, the case of the Spanish ship, and the security of land tenure in northeast Connecticut. The agent also carried accounts to obtain reimbursement "as our vigorous exertions in the service may appear to merit." Although the risk of over-

---

tional operations in North America. Success would be more likely if colonial troops "could be brought to cross the country in small bodies, for great ones cannot be maintained that way, and break up all their [the Canadians'] settlements, they would strike a terror into the enemy." His principal lament was that "the enemy are so superior in irregulars, for in reality we have none but our rangers." His analysis was intelligent, but it took little account of colonial military and political traditions. American rangers, led chiefly by the redoubtable fighter and self-publicist Robert Rogers, were never more than a small fraction of the colonial war effort.

20. On Pitt's request, see Pitt, *Correspondence*, I/137, 139. Colonial troops already received ammunition and provisions at imperial expense (CHC:XVII/ 276–77, 280, 284–85). On the Assembly's response to Pitt's request, see CHC:XVII/335 (quotations), 349–50; CA-War:VII/147, 150; and CPR:XI/93. On the finishing stroke, see CSL-JT:XXI/10 (quotation).

extending the colony's resources was great, the rewards in credit and specie were impossible to resist in a society short of both.[21]

Pitt designed the campaign of 1758 to breach Canada's outer defenses, and at Louisbourg and in the Ohio valley he succeeded. The enormous size of the Crown Point expedition (6,300 regulars and over 9,000 colonials) caused many delays, but its failure was not due to logistical insufficiency. The army's staff work showed the benefit of three years of practice; Connecticut even appointed three commissioners to expedite the flow of provisions and equipment to its troops. For the first time, the army embarked in its bateaux on Lake George, and on 6 July landed near the new French fort at Ticonderoga, where Lake George flows into Lake Champlain. It had to take the fort before it could proceed, but, once ashore, things began to go wrong. The army's second-in-command, Lord George Howe, was killed in the first skirmish, bad luck that deprived timorous Major General James Abercromby of his most trusted, competent, and daring subordinate at the most crucial moment. Poor intelligence stampeded Abercromby into making a frontal assault against French breastworks 350 yards west of the fort. The regulars lost 1,610 men killed and wounded, a quarter of their number, and Abercromby could see no alternative but to retreat back to the head of Lake George. Defeat did not demoralize the Connecticut men, who wanted to stay and construct a fort near Ticonderoga, something they had set out to do near Crown Point in 1755. Their aggressiveness owed something to "the mortification of returning . . . without a conquest over the enemy," but they failed to take into account the insurmountable obstacles facing such a project. If Abercromby did not want to fight again, he had to retire to a more defensible position: his army did not have enough rangers to stay so close to a victorious, woods-wise foe who could wreck havoc on its communication and supply lines. The largest force Connecticut had ever raised came home in failure, and the disappointment was only partly assuaged by news of victories elsewhere.[22]

21. On cooperating with the regulars, see CPR:XI/93–94 (quotation). On the colony's reputation in London, see CPR:XI/127–28 (quotation); and CHC:XVII/358–61. A "narrative of Connecticut's part in the war" to 1758 is in CHC:XVII/344–50.

22. On the commissioners, see CPR:XI/103–05. On the size of the expedition, see CO-5:II/860–62, 977–78. On the late arrival of colonial troops, see CO-5:II/961–62, 991–93; and CO-5:III/27. On the battle, see Pitt, *Correspon-*

The burst of enthusiasm that carried Connecticut through 1758 had evaporated when it came time to raise troops in 1759. According to Fitch, Abercromby's retreat had "abated the vigor and spirit of the people." Connecticut had strained itself in 1758, and the Assembly was wary of asking for another massive effort the following year. Moreover, it was not happy with the way Major General Jeffrey Amherst, the new commander-in-chief, was trying to change its military system to get the most for Pitt's money. Amherst displayed a basic misunderstanding of how Connecticut made war when he asked Fitch in mid-December to keep the 1758 regiments in pay and "ready to take the field as early as the season will admit" in 1759. The soldiers had already gone home because neither they nor the Assembly thought that military service was a year-round occupation; enlisting for a single campaign at a time had always been the way Connecticut organized its expeditionary troops, and the Assembly was not about to break its contract with the soldiers, especially when it needed every ounce of goodwill to raise troops in 1759. It was content to raise men anew each spring because the danger was not so great that it had to keep men under arms twelve months a year. Amherst had to settle for Fitch's assurances that the regiments would be ready to start campaigning by early May.[23]

Fitch tried to preserve Connecticut's right to know, and agree to, the campaign plan by appealing to Amherst's desire for military efficiency. He informed the general on 22 December "that in order to induce the Assembly vigorously to engage in raising and providing for men, it will be necessary I should be able to inform them of the general plan of operations, . . . something more particular than that it is designed against the French to the northward; this also will be of very great importance for facilitating the levies as the people have been used to enlist

---

dence, I/297–302; Fregault, *Canada,* pp. 220–22; and Gipson, *Victorious,* pp. 208–36. The colonists lost 334 men killed and wounded (4 percent), most of them from Massachusetts (CO-5:II/981). Gipson blamed failure on logistical delays (p. 218), but Abercromby could have won despite such problems. Gipson also criticized Howe for being too far forward (pp. 223, 225), but he had to be there to understand what was going on. On the attitudes of the Connecticut soldiers, see Gipson, *Victorious,* pp. 224, 232–34; and CHC:XVII/350–53 (quotation 350).

23. On Connecticut's spirit, see CHC:XVIII/14 (quotation). On keeping troops under arms, see CHC:XVII/366–67 (quotation 366). Amherst asked again in late 1759, with similar results (CHC:XVIII/43, 46–47).

for some particular service and unless they are acquainted with the general intentions and designs of that kind it will be to little purpose to invite them to enter into the service." Amherst, like Loudoun, thought the colonies should trust the commander-in-chief, and said only that the troops would again march against Crown Point, not enough to induce the Assembly to strain its resources in 1759.[24]

The Assembly was unwilling to do more than what it thought was its fair share, and believed that in past years it had raised more than its proportion of troops "compared with the other provinces." In March it voted to raise only four thousand men, and refused to guarantee by impressment the presence of more than thirty-six hundred. Amherst learned that raising volunteers was a slow process when he arrived at Albany in early May to find that the Connecticut regiments had not yet arrived. The Assembly continued to eschew impressment even when it agreed in May to raise a thousand more volunteers to meet Pitt's demands that it provide "at least as large a body of men" as in 1758. It was doubtless relieved to know that Fitch was able to report to Pitt on 14 July that the "levies were made up with uncommon dispatch and beyond the expectation of many," a phrase the governor used to hide the fact that Connecticut had failed to meet Pitt's demand. Fitch knew that men had not flocked to enlist, but, given the massive buildup of regulars in and around Albany, he also realized that the colony's failure did not jeopardize the expedition's chances of success. He decided that protecting Connecticut's reputation in London was more important than asking the Assembly to strain its resources to meet demands which reflected Pitt's obsession with numerical superiority at every point of contact more than actual military necessity.[25]

Amherst's generalship in 1759 did nothing to reinvigorate Connecticut. Although his army overwhelmingly outnumbered the French in the Champlain valley, he moved with the deliberate speed of a general intent

24. The correspondence is in CHC:XVII/366–68 (quotation 366–67); and CHC:XVIII/1–2.

25. On parity in raising troops, see CPR:XI/92–93, 221–22 (quotation). On the numbers raised, see CHC:XVIII/10; and CA-War:VIII/145; the Upper House was willing to impress three thousand men. On the late arrival, see CHC:XVIII/19–24; and CO-5:IV/149, 153. An outbreak of measles delayed some companies (CHC:XVIII/21–22). Fitch's correspondence with Pitt is in CHC:XVII/363 (quotation); CHC:XVIII/12–13, 15, 21–25 (quotation 25); CA-War:VIII/190; and CPR:XI/251–52.

on avoiding mistakes rather than taking advantage of opportunities. The French withdrew before his careful advance; they were more worried about the Royal Navy squadron ascending the St. Lawrence to Quebec with an army under Major General James Wolfe than about Amherst's army. A few small ships gave the French command of Lake Champlain and forced Amherst to stop at Crown Point to build a fleet to assure British dominance, a halt that effectively ended the campaign. Connecticut rejoiced that Wolfe's army had captured Quebec on 13 September (and mourned his death at the moment of victory), but it knew it had done little to achieve the goal for which it had been striving since 1690.[26]

The skillful French retreat in the Champlain valley and the length of time it had taken Wolfe to capture Quebec meant that there had to be a campaign in 1760 to complete the conquest of Canada. For the third year in a row, Pitt asked Connecticut for five thousand soldiers. The Assembly smoothly agreed and even voted additional bounties to encourage volunteers, but as in 1759 it refused to strain its authority by using impressment to fill the quota, and thus fell almost two thousand men short of the number it promised. Moreover, as in 1759, they arrived at Albany later than Amherst desired. Logistical obstacles proved to be the most formidable foes in 1760, as all three armies converging on Montreal met little opposition from the enemy. The Connecticut regiments were part of the expedition from Oswego across Lake Ontario and down the St. Lawrence to Montreal. The trip acquired a near legendary reputation for the exhausting work required to manhandle equipment, provisions, and batteaux around portages, across the lake, and down the river; the regiments lost more men running rapids above Montreal than fighting the French. One senior Connecticut officer resented the fact that Amherst used the regiments only as labor battalions, "confined to . . . promoting and forwarding such things . . . as the principal action may depend upon." Still, when Montreal surrendered on 8 September, Connecticut men were on hand to watch the French empire in North America pass into history.[27]

The conquest of Canada did not end Britain's worldwide imperial war,

26. On the 1759 campaign, see Amherst's letters in CO-5:IV; Gipson, *Victorious,* pp. 349–427; and Fregault, *Canada,* pp. 233–67. On raising troops, see CPR:XI/221–34; and CHC:XVIII/5–25.

27. On the 1760 campaign, see CHC:XVIII/47–54; Gipson, *Victorious,* pp. 428–67; and Fregault, *Canada,* pp. 268–94. On raising troops, see CPR:XI/349–51; and CHC:XVIII/57–75. Whiting's opinions are in YU-MS:Whiting/19 (quotation).

and for two years the colonies helped London maintain and expand the advantages it had already won. In 1761 Pitt asked each colony to raise two-thirds the number of soldiers it had supplied in 1760, and indicated he would use them to garrison forts in North America so the regulars could be sent to capture the French islands in the West Indies. The Assembly voted to raise twenty-three hundred volunteers, about a thousand fewer than Pitt intended. In a brilliant piece of casuistry, Fitch told Amherst that Pitt had asked for two-thirds the number raised in 1760, "not two-thirds of the number voted." Since Connecticut had failed to meet its 1760 quota, its 1761 commitment was therefore reduced. Fitch insisted that "though in every instance the colony has not been able fully to accomplish what was intended to be done, yet that was not for want of zeal or good intention . . . , but for want of ability to perform what the Assembly . . . was willing and hoped to be able to effect." The good news was that he expected Connecticut to meet its reduced quota. To help attract volunteers, he wanted Amherst to employ Connecticut troops in the Champlain valley; some veterans had refused to reenlist if they were again to be sent to Oswego. Fitch insisted that his request was an outgrowth of the days when New Englanders served close to their own frontiers, but he could not have been unaware that many soldiers wanted to examine lands in the Champlain and Connecticut valleys that were then being opened for settlement. Amherst disliked having a colonial governor dictate his dispositions, but he needed the troops and went along with the suggestion.[28]

Connecticut reached the climax of its participation in Britain's imperial wars in 1762, and the way the Assembly responded to London's request for troops shows how far its conception of its military system had come in seven years. In March it agreed to raise twenty-three hundred men, to be employed by Amherst "in such manner as he shall judge most conducive to the King's service." Major General Phineas Lyman, Connecticut's senior officer, claimed that "good able-bodied men" were enlisting "very freely," and assured Amherst that the regiments "shall choose to be appointed to such service as your Excellency shall judge most for His Majesty's service, without consulting the humor of the soldiery." Lyman was obsequious

28. On raising troops, see CHC:XVIII/89–91, 99–111, 117 (quotations); and CA-War:IX/480–82. On refusing to serve at Oswego, see CHC:XVIII/103, 105–10, 119. The Assembly had asked that its troops serve in the Champlain valley in 1754 and 1757 (CHC:XVII/16, 280, 285, 287). On new lands being opened for settlement, see CHC:XVIII/29–32.

and over-optimistic in part because he hoped for a postwar land grant for himself and his soldiers. In truth, recruiting began slowly because the soldiers did not know where they would serve, but eventually Connecticut met its quota. One of the two regiments was sent to help an expedition from Britain capture Havana from Spain, against which Parliament had declared war on 7 January. Connecticut men had volunteered enthusiastically on the only prior occasion when the imperial government sent them to the West Indies, and although the 1740 expedition had failed amid appalling mortality, the promise of plunder now overcame the serious misgivings the soldiers had about service in the disease-riddled Caribbean. Havana fell in late July, only a few days after regular and colonial troops began arriving from New York. Connecticut soldiers earned rights to a small part of the loot, but half of them died of disease during the two and a half months they lingered in Cuba. It was fortunate that the 1762 campaign was the last of the war, for it crippled both the Connecticut military system and the British regular army in North America.[29]

Connecticut raised soldiers for imperial campaigns in 1761 and 1762 to maintain a good reputation in London and to earn the reimbursement the imperial government continued to offer. The Assembly was also reluctant to eliminate a source of employment for several thousand men for eight months a year. But the colony paid a price for these benefits. After 1760 British money pushed its military system as close as it would ever come to a colonial version of a professional army, an aberration that Connecticut society was neither wealthy nor stratified enough to have developed on its own. Parliamentary subsidies paid for more soldiers than Connecticut could have raised by itself, and allowed the Assembly to follow the path of least resistance and increase financial incentives to a level specifically intended to induce poor men to volunteer for military service, a development which would have been impossible without British assistance.

Connecticut mobilized its military system once more, in March 1764, when Major General Thomas Gage, who had succeeded Amherst as imperial commander on 17 November 1763, asked for 500 men to help fight Indians on the western frontier. Although an Assembly committee

29. On raising troops, see CPR:IX/613–15 (quotation); and CHC:XVIII/ 191–94, 198–99. On Lyman's opinions, see WO-34:XLIII/431–32 (quotations). On the Havana campaign, see Syrett, *Havana,* pp. xiii–xxxv; Syrett, "Provincials," pp. 375–90; Bates, *Two Putnams,* p. 8; and Gipson, *Culmination,* pp. 260–68. On the regulars, see Shy, *Lexington,* pp. 106–09, 114–17.

insisted that the colony was only "remotely interested" in the war, the full Assembly voted to raise 265 men, 10 percent of the number the colony had supplied in 1762, to be drawn from among veterans who had lacked their customary employment in 1763. The Assembly agreed to provide only half the number Gage requested partly because the imperial government did not offer to reimburse its expenses and partly because it knew that raising the battalion would not be easy without giving veteran soldiers substantial incentives. Raising troops was a good piece of imperial politics because it helped to defuse imperial anger at the way Connecticut was grumbling about increased supervision from London, but the process took so long that Gage complained that the battalion came "straggling along as usual," and finally he lost his temper: "I am out of all patience with those cursed people." The battalion traveled to Detroit during the summer, but saw no action because the war had been nearly won even before it left Connecticut. Its return went unnoticed in a colony in turmoil over new imperial regulations.[30]

Pitt's willingness to spare no expense won for Britain a worldwide empire, but it also sowed the seeds of a constitutional crisis that would lead to rebellion in 1775. The imperial government increased taxes in Britain and borrowed heavily to pay wartime expenses; by the end of the war, the national debt had doubled to 130 million pounds sterling, with annual interest of 4.5 million pounds sterling. The imperial government reasonably expected the colonies to help reduce the burden on British taxpayers, if only by paying part of the administrative costs of the vastly enlarged empire. But this expectation came into conflict with what the colonies perceived as their place in the imperial relationship. The Indian uprising in 1763–64 convinced imperial planners that they needed regular troops to deter Indian wars on the new frontier, but the colonies refused to help pay for soldiers who could also be used to overawe colonial dissent. The decision to keep regular troops in North America to help meet frontier contingencies hastened the day when British regulars would face American armies on the field of battle.[31]

---

30. On the battalion, see CA-War:X/194; CPR:XII/230, 232–33; and CHC:XVIII/256–57, 274–75 (quotation), 279–80. Gage's opinions are in MHS-FP:XXVI/282–83 and 313 (quotations). On the Indian war, see Gipson, *New Responsibilities,* pp. 88–126.

31. On Britain's debts, see Beer, *Policy,* p. 272. On keeping regulars in the colonies after the conquest of Canada, see Great Britain, *Proceedings,* I/440; Shy, *Lexington,* pp. 45–83; and Bullion, "'Ten Thousand,'" pp. 646–47. The *Sum-*

THE PROCESS OF GOVERNMENT

The final French and Indian war was Connecticut's largest and longest conflict before the Revolution, and it forced the leaders to cope with unprecedented problems in organizing their military resources. They were flexible and adaptable within the limits of what they thought their society could endure, and generally found workable solutions, especially about financing the war. They applied to each new problem all the experience they had gained in projecting force beyond Connecticut's borders since 1690, but the issues were so complex that decision making continued to be deliberate and time-consuming.

Change in the rate of turnover in the Lower House is the best measure of how the war affected the process of politics. Each town customarily elected two deputies to attend regular Assembly sessions in May and October, and it was more common for voters to rotate the office among several men than to elect one man to a string of consecutive terms. Even the most active deputies would not normally have been elected all seventeen times between October 1754 and October 1762; in the decade before the war, turnover between elections had averaged between 40 and 50 percent. Managing military affairs during the first four years of the war radically increased the demands on a deputy's time; ten special sessions were held between January 1755 and May 1758 in addition to the seven regular sessions. The heavy work load sharply boosted turnover, especially after Governor Fitch reconvened the October 1755 Assembly three times (in January, February, and March 1756) to plan the new expedition. Attendance in May 1756 sank to a ten-year low, seventy-nine deputies instead of an average of one hundred. Turnover reached a forty-five-year high; sixty-five deputies (71 percent) had not served in October 1755, a rate that would not be matched even during the American Revolution twenty years later. Between 1755 and 1758, war accelerated the recruitment of the next generation of leaders. More men participated in making decisions: as the number of deputies elected to consecutive terms declined, so did the number of consecutive terms they served.[32]

---

mary reported on 4 March 1763 that "it is said ten regiments of provincials will be kept in the pay of the colonies in America besides the fifteen regiments of regulars in the pay of Great Britain." That did not happen because imperial officials seem not to have wanted to use colonial troops: "a rotation was intended of these American regiments, that though residing in America, they might still be a British army" (Great Britain, *Proceedings,* I/456).

32. Twenty-one men were elected for the first time in May 1756, higher than average but not a record.

The winnowing of the Lower House ended after 1758, principally because the Assembly had learned how to organize an expedition. For four years, it smoothly applied the lessons learned in previous years, always with some small adjustments, but essentially using time-tested methods to recreate its military forces annually. There was at least one special session each year, usually in March to prepare the campaign, but this was not a burdensome work load by recent standards. With less to do, and with most decisions about strategy and the number of troops now in the hands of the imperial government, there seems to have been less interest in serving in the Assembly. Between 1759 and 1762 the leadership contracted. Turnover dropped below prewar levels as fewer men served more often. Many men undoubtedly wanted to attend to their own affairs, especially at a time when they could make money feeding and supplying colonial and regular troops. After 1762, rates of turnover returned to prewar levels as the colony entered the postwar era of increased imperial regulation. During the war, noticeable changes took place in the patterns of participation in the Lower House, but these fluctuations all proved to be temporary. War did not permanently alter the underlying stability of politics in Connecticut.

Turnover among deputies was largely unforced. Men more often declined reelection than lost a genuine political fight, although prewar disputes occasionally did intrude into wartime decision making. Some of the increase in turnover in 1756 and 1757, for example, was the product of electioneering among groups that had their roots in differing reactions to the Great Awakening. The entrenched Old Lights, suspicious of upstart New Light enthusiasm for revived religion and speculation in western lands, dominated the Upper House, and tried to regain control of the Lower House by convincing each town to elect only one deputy. Their attempt to concentrate votes on the more widely popular Old Light candidates won some support because it could save money and speed decision making at a time when expenses were increasing and Assembly sessions were reaching unprecedented lengths. It failed because towns refused to reduce their representation when "such weighty affairs" as the conduct of the war were before the House.[33]

The heart of the decision-making process was the committee system in

33. On electioneering, see *Gazette,* 20 Mar, 15 May, 28 Aug 1756, 19 and 26 Mar 1757; and Williams, *Journal,* p. 30 (quotation), the only known journal kept by a deputy during the war. On tensions between Old and New Lights, see Bushman, *Puritan to Yankee,* pp. 235–88.

the Assembly. Whenever the leaders had to make a decision, they created a committee of members from both Houses to recommend a course of action. Several informal rules guided the selection of committee members. On local issues, like petitions from veterans for special compensation, the Lower House appointed the deputies most likely to be familiar with the needs of their constituents. On matters of colony-wide significance, it named a geographically balanced committee. One or two deputies from each of the six counties conferred with up to three assistants—the more important the issue, the larger the committee. The largest committees were appointed in March 1758 and March 1761: fifteen assistants and deputies to consider a demand from the imperial government for more troops. Even Deputy Governor William Pitkin served on major committees early in the war, but Governor Fitch, as chief executive, remained outside the Assembly's decision-making system. Each House considered the committee's report separately, and generally accepted its conclusions. Not infrequently, however, a house voted to disagree, whereupon the whole process began again.[34]

Records have survived of the membership of 141 committees that dealt with military affairs during the war. Most committees were appointed between 1755 and 1758 when the Assembly was learning to raise, organize, and pay for its troops. No one dominated what continued to be a collective leadership, although a few men were appointed again and again to important committees. Of 136 deputies appointed to these committees, the sixteen in table 4.1 were the core of the oligarchy in the Lower House. Each county organized committee service in a slightly different way. For example, Ebenezer Marsh represented Litchfield county on most major committees, a role David Rowland filled for Fairfield county. In Hartford county, Jabez Hamlin and John Ledyard split the most important assignments in the early years; in 1755 alone, Ledyard served on thirteen major committees, more than any other deputy in any one year. Thereafter, committee service was spread among more Hartford county deputies. Timothy Stone and John Hubbard represented New Haven county most frequently, Stone over a longer period, Hubbard more intensively while he was present. Joseph Fowler and Obadiah Johnson looked after the interests of Windham county, as did Christopher Avery and Simeon Minor for New London county; both were fairly far down the list,

34. On the largest committees, see CHS-GA/Mar 1758; CA-War:IX/115; and Williams, *Journal,* p. 26.

Table 4.1
Committee Service of Deputies, 1754–62

Name	Town	Terms as Deputy		Wartime Committees	
		Before War	Wartime	Number	Per Term
Ebenezer Marsh	Litchfield	19	15	37	2.5
John Ledyard	Hartford	14*	10	36	3.6
Jabez Hamlin†	Middletown	42	7	31	4.4
Timothy Stone	Guilford	23	14	26	1.9
David Rowland	Fairfield	11	14	23	1.6
John Hubbard	New Haven	9	7	22	3.1
Joseph Fowler	Lebanon	6	7	21	3.0
Obadiah Johnson	Canterbury	5	13	21	1.6
Christopher Avery	Groton	27	11	18	1.7
Elihu Hall	Wallingford	3	6	16	2.7
Simeon Minor	Stonington	14	10	16	1.6
Elisha Sheldon‡	Litchfield	0	8	15	1.9
Seth Wetmore	Middletown	20	15	15	1.0
Isaac Tracy	Norwich	10	8	14	1.7
Joseph Pitkin	Hartford	16	11	14	1.3
Robert Dixon	Voluntown	18	15	14	0.9

Note: 120 other deputies served on from one to thirteen committees.
*Elected twelve times as a deputy from Groton (1742–49), twice from Hartford (1753–54).
†Elected an assistant in 1758 and served on nine more committees.
‡Elected an assistant in 1761 and served on one more committee.

indicating that New London county leaders rotated committee assignments more frequently than did their peers in the other counties.[35]

The patterns of service of these men show that most of them made military decisions as an extension of prewar political careers. A few were members of the rising generation (Johnson, Elihu Hall, and Elisha Sheldon), but most were leaders of ten years' standing or more; Hamlin was the most experienced, having been elected a deputy for the first time in October 1731 at age twenty-two. Deputies generally did not have colony-wide popularity, although wartime service did give a few men new prominence. Ledyard's experience as a merchant made him an important member of committees that dealt with raising money, paying debts, and auditing accounts, and led to a modest rise in his popularity; he received

35. Committee records are scattered through CA-War:V to X.

501 votes for nomination as an assistant in 1761. (Assistant Hezekiah Huntington led with 3,205 votes.) Rowland, a member of the governor's council, rose more spectacularly, from 268 votes in 1755 to 1,403 in 1762. However, neither man turned a wartime boost into a postwar political career. Ledyard returned to his mercantile pursuits, and Rowland was not reelected to the Lower House after October 1765. The timing suggests that Rowland may have run afoul of voter discontent about how best to oppose increased imperial control. Although the Assembly sent him as one of its three delegates to the intercolonial conference called to oppose Parliament's attempt to levy a stamp tax in the colonies, he may not have opposed the Stamp Act vigorously enough to suit his neighbors.[36]

The political structure in the Upper House was similar to that in the Lower, although membership was more stable because the electorate was broader and elections were a two-step process; the governor, the deputy governor, and the twelve assistants were elected annually in April by all voters in the colony, not semiannually by voters in each town, as were the deputies (table 4.2). Senior leaders tended to be reelected until they died or retired, although occasionally an assistant could be bumped off the list by a more popular man; a strong regional following was sufficient to win election as an assistant or even as governor. As in the Lower House, no one assistant dominated his colleagues. Jonathan Trumbull served on thirty-two important military committees, but he was not substantially more influential than, say, Ebenezer Silliman, who was a close colleague of Governor Fitch and a member of his council. Other assistants were active in other roles—Hezekiah Huntington, for example, was the prin-

36. On politics in the Lower House, see Selesky, "Patterns," pp. 177–93. On Sheldon, see Dexter, *Yale Graduates,* I/418. On Hamlin, see Dexter, *Yale Graduates,* I/371–72. On Ledyard, see CHC:XVI/191–92, 194–95. He had been a prominent deputy from Groton in the 1740s before moving his business and his political career to Hartford in the early 1750s. It was not common for a leader from one town to become a powerful figure in another community because he would displace incumbents and disappoint the expectations of the rising generation. In September, voters nominated twenty men to stand for election as assistants in April. The top twelve vote-getters were sworn in at the May Assembly. Tallies of the nominating ballots survive in CHS-GA for 1755, 1756, 1758, 1761, and 1762. On Rowland, see Jacobus, *Fairfield,* II/796–97; and Dexter, *Yale Graduates,* I/463. The Assembly continued to appoint him to the top judicial posts in Fairfield county until he died in 1768; political disputes were never grounds for replacing an experienced judge.

Table 4.2
Committee Service of Assistants, 1754–62

Name	Town	First Elected	Committees
Jonathan Trumbull	Lebanon	1740	32
Hezekiah Huntington	Norwich	1740	22
Ebenezer Silliman	Fairfield	1739	21
Roger Wolcott, Jr.	Windsor	1754	20
Daniel Edwards*	Hartford	1755	18
Benjamin Hall	Wallingford	1751	18
Andrew Burr	Fairfield	1746	16
John Chester	Wethersfield	1747	15
Phineas Lyman	Suffield	1752	13
Roger Newton	Milford	1736	12

Note: Five other assistants served on from one to nine committees.
*A noted attorney and judge, he was the only assistant who had never been a deputy.

cipal commissary in eastern Connecticut. Trumbull, Silliman, and Phineas Lyman, an assistant until 1758 and the colony's senior field commander, were the most active assistants in negotiations with neighboring colonies and the imperial government about Connecticut's role in each campaign.[37]

Once the Assembly agreed on a policy, it appointed executive agents to carry out its wishes. The principal executive was Governor Thomas Fitch, a well-regarded attorney and highly experienced political leader from Norwalk who was fifty-five years old in 1755. He kept the government operating smoothly by corresponding with neighboring governments and imperial officials, and by deciding in consultation with his council whether or not to call a special Assembly session. The Assembly often gave him specific tasks, like issuing a proclamation announcing an embargo on provisions and appointing new officers when the original nominees declined to serve, and always named him where appropriate to lead its delegation to conferences with neighboring colonies and imperial commanders. In 1755–56 his authority approached that wielded by Governor Saltonstall during Queen Anne's War. He was the colony's chief intermediary with the imperial government, in which role he followed the

37. On politics in the Upper House, see Selesky, "Patterns," pp. 168–77; and Stark, "Upper House." On Roger Wolcott, Jr., see *Summary*, 30 Nov 1759. On Daniel Edwards, see Dexter, *Yale Graduates*, I/216–17.

traditional policy of complying with military demands as a way of protecting the charter. He always acted within his authority and referred all
major issues to the Assembly, as in February 1758 when he offered to
meet with Loudoun "to settle so far as I am able . . . what may concern
this colony, and then forthwith to call the Assembly and lay the whole
before it for consideration." He took his responsibilities very seriously and
worked hard to make sure that the military system could bear the strain.
He was helped by the fact that he shepherded a popular cause—everybody
agreed that conquering Canada was a good idea—and he exercised more
authority between 1755 and 1762 than before or after the war.[38]

Fitch did not dominate the leadership as Saltonstall had in 1709–11
because he succeeded the first governor who had been ousted for what the
voters thought was incompetence in office. Roger Wolcott, Sr., had failed
to protect the colony from imperial anger over the Spanish ship plundered
at New London in 1752, and the threat to the charter had ended his
political career in May 1754, even though he had done his best in an
impossible situation. Defense of the charter had been a major theme in
Connecticut politics for eighty years, but the antagonisms generated by
the revival of religion in the 1740s made voters much more willing to
criticize their elected leaders; sacking Wolcott marked a major step toward
creating a political culture in which voters expected to hold leaders responsible for their actions. Fitch successfully managed Connecticut's war
effort while under close scrutiny from voters who no longer believed that
his authority to rule them was God-given.

Fitch worked hard to keep Connecticut free from imperial intrusion
into its internal affairs. He made a good impression on the earl of Loudoun, who thought the governor "seems well disposed and has great

38. On Fitch, see Dexter, *Yale Graduates,* I/248; and CHC:XVII/xxxvii-xlix.
He had a lasting good reputation. In 1811 President Timothy Dwight of Yale
termed him "probably the most learned lawyer who had ever been an inhabitant
of the colony," and remembered that "in his various public stations . . . he was
considered as not surpassed in wisdom and integrity" (Dwight, *Travels,* III/354).
Examples of proclamations issued by Fitch are in CPR:X/350, 550–51; CPR:XI/
22; and *Gazette,* 12 Apr 1755. On filling vacancies, see CPR:X/348; CA-War:V/
153; and CA-War:VI/48. On his service as a delegate, see CPR:X/421–22, 593–
94. The Assembly gave him authority to help re-raise the colonial regulars
(CPR:X/327–28), and, in 1755–56, to do everything to forward the expeditions
(CPR:X/348, 483–84). On referring issues to the Assembly, see CHC:XVII/321
(quotation).

influence" with his colleagues, and although the general concluded that "Connecticut is a strange government," he thought it had "at present . . . a good man at their [*sic*] head." Subsequent imperial commanders learned to work with Fitch, although Amherst did not like him. After the governor "made disputes" about supplying wood for a regular regiment quartered in the colony over the winter of 1758–59, Amherst claimed he had never "heard any pettyfogging lawyer more equivocating or half so silly on any subject as he was on this." It was Fitch's misfortune to be caught in an age of increased imperial control, when striking a balance between Connecticut voters and the imperial government was more difficult than at any time since the 1680s. He held the empire at arm's length during wartime, thus allowing the Assembly to manage Connecticut's military affairs without direct imperial supervision.[39]

Experience gained in prior wars was always the most important element in determining how the Assembly organized its military resources. In 1755–56 it based the army's logistical apparatus on the model that had operated so well during King George's War. It gave the job of purchasing provisions and supplies to six experienced merchants from around the colony who were also important local leaders (four were veterans of 1745–46), and embargoed the export of foodstuffs to make their job easier. Each man spent roughly 3,000 pounds lawful money each year to feed, clothe, and transport the troops (table 4.3). They bought, among other things, guns, cartridge boxes, hatchets, swords, ammunition, blankets, and knapsacks for men who did not equip themselves, and bread, pork, beef, peas, and rum for everybody; foodstuffs were transported by water to Albany, and livestock was driven overland. Each commissary earned a 2.5 percent commission on his purchases in 1755 (as in King George's War), reduced to 1.5 percent in 1756 because the Assembly thought the job was easier the second time. Opportunities for profit were substantial: in 1755–56 Theophilus Nichols of Stratford earned 118 pounds lawful money. The power to determine who got contracts gave the commissaries great influence. Generally they bought from favorite suppliers, men who were occasionally also prominent leaders. For example, both Ledyard and Trumbull sold provisions and equipment to Gurdon Saltonstall, Jr., in 1756. The commissaries retained their power until the imperial government took over provisions contracting in September 1756.[40]

39. On Loudoun's opinions, see CO-5:II/243 and 527 (quotations). On Amherst's, see his *Journal,* p. 104 (quotation).

40. The four veterans of King George's War were Thomas Wells of Glaston-

Table 4.3
Expenditures by Commissaries, 1755–62, 1764
(In Pounds of Lawful Money)

Year	Commissaries	Total Expenditure	Average
1755	Six	18,000	3,000
1756	Six	19,200	3,200
1757	Three	3,400	1,134
1758	Four	6,700	1,675
1759	Four	8,000	2,000
1760	Four	6,000	1,500
1761	Four	2,900	725
1762	Four	4,800	1,200
1764	Two	400	200
Total		69,400 pounds	

Sources: CA-War:V/248–71; CA-War:VI/315–44; CA-War:VII/137–45; CA-War:VIII/110–21, 338–41; CA-War:IX/94–100, 261–63; and CA-War:X/86–89, 234, 240.

Note: 3,000 pounds of lawful money was equivalent to 7,500 pounds New Tenor.

The expansion of British military and naval forces in North America put great pressure on the agricultural resources of the colonies. In mid-August 1758 Trumbull reported that "our people have had such a great

---

bury (assistant), Hezekiah Huntington of Norwich (assistant), Gurdon Saltonstall, Jr., of New London (deputy and former assistant), and Jabez Hamlin of Middletown (deputy). The two new commissaries, Theophilus Nichols of Stratford (deputy) and John Hubbard of New Haven (deputy), replaced men who had died since the colony had last been at war. On commissary accounts from 1755 through 1764, see the source note for table 4.3. On embargoing provisions, see CPR:X/350, 485; and CPR:XI/22. The Assembly agreed to sell provisions to its partners in 1756, provided they joined in embargoing provisions east of Halifax and south of New York (CHC:XVII/236–38). On articles provided in 1755–56, see CA-War:V/252, 257; CA-War:VI/322; CA-War:VIII/114; and CA-War:IX/97. In 1756, each soldier was to receive each day one pound of bread, fourteen ounces of pork or a pound of beef, a half-pint of rum, and a half-pint of peas or beans, plus two ounces of ginger a week (CPR:X/478). On Nichols, see CA-War:V/256; and CA-War:VI/327. Cronyism was allowed if the supplier sold at a competitive price (CA-War:VI/330 and CA-War:IX/100, 261). On the transfer of contracting, see CA-War:VI/132, 150, 210, 213; CHC:XVII/253–54; MHS-IW/1 Feb 1757; and Great Britain, *Proceedings*, I/213–19, 456.

demand for their fat cattle" that prices had skyrocketed. By March 1759 the chief imperial contractor reported that "the whole produce of the country" would not meet his demands. Connecticut merchants did not profit greatly from these new markets. The *Gazette* reported that most of them lost "the best opportunity of enriching themselves" by pricing provisions "higher than they were in neighboring colonies, or could be imported from Europe." Shortfalls in domestic supply were covered by imports from Ireland.[41]

After 1756, the Assembly maintained a much reduced commissary system, principally to provide soldiers with blankets, cloth, tents, hatchets, kettles, knapsacks, ginger, sugar, and rum; it generally split contracting among four commissaries who drew their goods from different regions of the colony (table 4.3). Starting in 1758 the Assembly also allowed contractors to sell supplemental provisions and clothing to soldiers in the field. In 1758–59 these sutlers supplied shoes, shirts, blankets, rum, tobacco, sugar, chocolate, coffee, and soap, at up to 50 percent over the price in Connecticut. The soldiers thought the prices were "exorbitant," and although the Assembly understood the difficulty of transporting goods north and west of Albany, in 1758 it reduced the accounts of three sutlers by one-seventh to placate the troops. In 1761 two assistants, Trumbull and Huntington, charged such high prices—a former sutler said he could supply food a third cheaper and clothing 45 percent cheaper—that their contract was not renewed.[42]

Wartime economic activity required a radical expansion of the colony's financial system. Agents were appointed to print and issue paper bills of

41. On Trumbull, see CHS-JT/21 Aug 1758 (quotation). On imperial contracting, see CO-5:IV/31 (quotation); and Pargellis, *Loudoun*, pp. 291–96. On prices, see *Gazette,* 2 Apr 1757 (quotation).

42. The commissaries after 1758 were Huntington for New London and Windham counties, Hamlin for Hartford county, Hubbard for New Haven county, and Nichols for Fairfield county. On the variety of articles, see CA-War:VIII/112, 115; and CA-War:X/262. For their accounts, see the footnote to table 4:3. On the sutlers, see CPR:X/124–25, 231–33; and CA-War:VIII/101, 199. On their prices, see CA-War:VIII/185, 187; CA-War:IX/126; CPR:XI/216 (quotation), 488–89; *Gazette,* 11 Apr 1761; and *Summary,* 10 Apr 1760. On Trumbull and Huntington, see CA-War:IX/127, 152; CHS-FIW:II/1007; and CHS-JT/6 Jun, 23 Jul, 3 Aug 1761. They supplied clothing at 80–85 percent over cost, and food at 110 percent; John Ledyard was an associate. On Trumbull's earlier activities, see CA-War:V/217; and CPR:XI/136. For stated prices in 1761–62, see CA-War:IX/139; and CA-War:X/209.

Table 4.4
Agents for Financial Matters, 1755–64

Name	Town	Rank	Appointed as Agent
			(Maximum of 48)
John Chester*	Wethersfield	Assistant	25 (52%)
William Pitkin*	Hartford	Deputy Gov.	22 (46%)
George Wyllys	Hartford	Secretary	20 (42%)
Joseph Buckingham*	Hartford	Deputy	17 (35%)
John Ledyard*	Hartford	Deputy	17 (35%)
Daniel Edwards*	Hartford	Assistant	11 (23%)
Jonathan Trumbull	Lebanon	Assistant	10 (21%)

Note: Twenty-nine other assistants and deputies were appointed from one to six times.
*Members of the Committee of the Pay-Table; Buckingham died in November 1760 and was replaced by Edwards.

credit, to borrow money from wealthy inhabitants, to audit the treasurer, to settle commissary accounts, to receive the reimbursement voted by Parliament, to sell specie and bills of exchange, and to run a public lottery. Most of the work was done by a half-dozen Hartford county leaders (table 4.4), five of whom also served on the Committee of the Pay-Table, a standing committee of the Assembly that handled most wartime financial administration. At the start of each campaign, the Committee advanced specie and paper money to enable captains to pay bounties to volunteers. At the end of the campaign, it audited the accounts of company paymasters and of anyone else who had performed public service for the colony. After 1758 it also sent to the colony's agents in London an account of the expenses the imperial government had agreed to reimburse.[43]

After their accounts were approved, creditors went to the treasurer, Joseph Talcott of Hartford (fifty-four years old in 1755), to receive payment. The bulk of the colony's debts (which, after 1758, consisted mainly of wages) was met by credits generated through direct taxation on prop-

43. Public notices to bring accounts to the Committee are in *Gazette,* 9 Dec 1758, 3 Mar and 15 Dec 1759, and 8 Mar 1760; and *Summary,* 29 Dec 1758, 26 Jan 1759, and 7 Mar 1760. Two members were a quorum (CPR:X/367). Paymasters were required to post a bond to assure that they performed their duty. Colonel Whiting's bond for 2,000 pounds in 1757 is in YU-MS:Whiting/ 29. For an example of a captain's "book of settlement," see CHS-Whitney.

erty. Taxes, as always, were assessed by local officials according to rates set by the Assembly, and each town then sent to the treasurer an account of what it owed. Talcott paid the colony's debts by ordering local tax collectors to pay receipts to men who had earned the money. Taxes collected in a town were generally used to pay soldiers who were recruited there. In like manner, commissaries were paid by orders on the collectors of the towns where they filled their contracts. In June 1756, for example, John Hubbard of New Haven received a mix of paper money, orders on Boston merchants from whom the colony had borrowed money, and orders on the New Haven, Milford, and Wallingford tax collectors. Talcott was the colony's hardest-working public official, and his duties sometimes overwhelmed him. One captain who thought he had been shortchanged complained that on 10 June 1756 "it was very observable that his [Talcott's] mind was confused, being overborne with the fatigue and business of the day, and he was not able to cast accounts, and . . . was obliged to send for the help of his son."[44]

Despite the burden on Talcott, the two-step process of Committee authorization and treasurer payment effectively supervised expenditures. Such a system was perhaps inevitable in a colony that began the war with a massive investment of its own resources, and it persisted after 1757 because the Assembly wanted every penny of reimbursement to which it was entitled. But it was a cumbersome way of managing money. Seven senior officers complained in May 1759 that the "method of paying the troops takes up the greater part of . . . three or four months after the campaign," a burden on paymasters who had "to travel from one town and place to another in order to accomplish that service."[45]

Connecticut used this complex administrative system to manage the most expensive war in its colonial history. Taxation per capita was less than during the Pequot War or King Philip's War, but the total tax levied in ten years far surpassed anything attempted earlier. In 1755 alone, the Assembly imposed taxes totaling 24.5 pence (over 10 percent) on the

44. On payments by the Treasurer, see CPR:XI/63 (quotation), 235–37, 351–53, 482–84; CPR:XII/222; CPR:XIII/59; and CA-War:X/158–59, 273. Hubbard got 1,200 pounds in paper money, 850 pounds in borrowed funds, and 1,100 pounds in tax receipts (CA-War:VI/316). Nichols received money from four collectors (CA-War:VI/327). On Talcott, a son of the late Governor Joseph Talcott, see CA-War:X/287 (quotation), 310; CA-War,2:I/30–31; and Williams, *Journal,* pp. 48, 54. His predecessor, Nathaniel Stanley, had died on 17 August 1755 (CHC:XIX/263).

45. On the paymasters, see CA-War:VIII/170 (quotation).

Table 4.5
Rates and Yields of Taxes, 1755–66*
(In Lawful Money)

	Rates (in Pence)		Yields (in Pounds)	
Year to Be Paid	Scheduled to Be Paid	Actually Paid	Sum Raised	One-Penny Raises
1755	4.00	4.00 (100%)	22,325	5,581
1756	5.00	5.00 (100%)	29,567	5,913
1757	9.50	9.50 (100%)	56,601	5,958
1758	14.00	12.50 (89%)	76,895	6,408
1759	14.50	13.00 (90%)	77,082	5,929
1760	19.00	10.00 (53%)	59,494	5,949
1761	18.00	10.00 (56%)	61,043	6,104
1762	10.00	5.75 (58%)	35,921†	6,247
1763	16.00	6.00 (38%)	38,244†	6,374
1764	17.00	8.00 (47%)	50,895	6,362
1765	8.00	1.00 (12%)	6,401	6,401
1766	8.00	none		
Total	143.00	84.75 (60%)	514,468 pounds	

Source: CSL-TAL/19–41.
*Taxes levied between 1755 and 1762 were to be paid through 1766.
†Sums were later reduced 5 percent by abatements.

pound of rateable estates and persons, an amount six times the rate in any of the preceding five years and the best measure of the enthusiasm with which the colony went to war. Connecticut bore the burden because the Assembly postponed collecting most of these taxes in hopes of receiving reimbursement from Parliament before the taxes were due. Payment of 84 percent of the taxes levied in 1755 (20.5 of 24.5 pence) was deferred for up to five years (table 4.5), including most of the taxes earmarked to retire the 62,000 pounds of paper money, bearing 5 percent interest per annum, issued that year (table 4.6). As early as May 1755, the Assembly petitioned the king to repay its military expenses. It counted on a favorable response as the foundation of its financial system, and acted as though it had received a guarantee of such assistance, when in fact it had not. The gamble paid off when Parliament agreed to repay the colonies for their efforts.[46]

46. Taxes in 1751–54 are in CPR:X/65, 129, 157, 197, 318. In and after May 1753, taxes were calculated in lawful money, 1 shilling of which was equal

Table 4.6
Bills of Credit Issued, 1755–64
(In Pounds of Lawful Money)

Date Issued	Amount	Date Due
1755 January	7,500	1758 May
1755 March	12,500	1759 May
1755 August	30,000	1760 August
1755 October	12,000	1760 April
Subtotal, 1755	62,000	
1758 March	30,000	1762 May
1759 February	20,000	1763 May
1759 March	40,000	1764 March
1759 May	10,000	1763 May
Subtotal, 1759	70,000	
1760 March	70,000	1765 March
1761 March	45,000	1766 March
1762 March	65,000	1767 March
Subtotal, 1758–62	280,000	
1763 May	10,000	1765 May
1764 March	7,000	1768 March
Total	359,000 pounds	

Source: CPR:XII/339, which omits March 1755.
Note: The total is equal to 897,500 pounds New Tenor (1 pound of lawful money equals 2 pounds, 10 shillings New Tenor) or 269,250 pounds sterling at the official exchange rate of 1 pound lawful money for 15 shillings sterling (Gipson, *Taxation*, pp. 31–32).

The two houses divided sharply over how to raise credit. The Upper House was inclined to pay as it went, and was more worried than the deputies about the short-term strain of funding an imperial war. The Lower House wanted to stretch out the payment of taxes for as long as possible, and was more willing to rely on paper money backed largely by the promise of reimbursement. These differences came to a head in October 1755, when the Assembly learned that the colony was running out

---

to 2 shillings, 5 pence New Tenor (CPR:X/328–30, 338–39). Four pounds lawful money was officially equal to 3 pounds sterling or 10 pounds New Tenor. On the petition for reimbursement, see CA-War:V/130. Three petitions were sent, in August and October 1755, and in April 1756 (CHC:I/268, 271, 294; and CPR:X/484–85), each one begging harder than the last.

of money; the Treasury had only 12,200 pounds of lawful money on hand to pay debts of 32,000 pounds. The Upper House wanted to appoint men in each county to "excite and quicken" the collection of the taxes already levied, and to borrow money from private citizens. The Lower House vetoed both ideas, and proposed to print 20,000 pounds in paper money to cover the deficit, with payment of the tax needed to retire the paper extended to 1 April 1760. They compromised on 12,000 pounds of new paper money, and a new tax to be paid by 20 August 1759.[47]

The 1755 campaign so exhausted Connecticut that it barely had the financial resources to create an army in 1756. By January the colony was said to be "wholly destitute of cash," and the Assembly refused to issue any more bills of credit for fear "of sinking the value of those already emitted and stretching the credit of this government beyond what it can well bear." Connecticut fielded soldiers only by finding a new financial expedient, one which also relied on the expectation of reimbursement. In March the Assembly asked Governor Shirley, as commander-in-chief, for a loan of 10,000 pounds sterling, along with two thousand stand of arms from imperial stocks. It promised to repay the loan out of the monies it expected to receive from Parliament as reimbursement for 1755, a way of paying for this year's campaign with last year's promises that further postponed the burden on the Connecticut taxpayer.[48]

In the absence of immediate reimbursement, the Assembly continued to impose heavy taxes to float the paper money needed to meet current expenses. These taxes caused considerable discontent and unrest, feelings that were compounded when it became clear that the 1756 campaign was moving no faster or farther than the one the year before. An anonymous correspondent in the *Gazette* for 7 August 1756 noted that the war had "increased our taxes beyond what is usual," and warned that "heavy taxes have a tendency to produce inquietudes in the minds of people." A week later, another correspondent tried to mollify people who had been "murmuring against those who sustain sway in the government, for putting us under heavy taxes," by reminding them that "otherwise all our estates would be taken from us" by the French. The *Gazette* printed several

47. On raising credit, see CA-War:V/178 (quotation), 194. Debts included 24,200 pounds for wages and 7,800 pounds for provisions.

48. On generating credit in 1756, see CA-War:VI/1 (quotations); CPR:X/448–49, 459–60; and CHC:XVII/199, 207. On the loan of money, equal to 13,333 pounds lawful money, see CPR:X/476–78; and CHC:XVII/207. On the loan of arms, see CPR:X/494.

schemes to take the burden off the "middling livers," who paid the bulk of their taxes according to the amount, not the value, of their land. One correspondent wanted the Assembly to build ships with tax money and trade with the West Indies for the profit of the government, while another suggested replacing property taxes with an excise on liquor, but the Assembly adopted neither idea.[49]

The Assembly searched hard for new ways of raising money. In May 1756 a blue-ribbon committee suggested that it issue 20,000 pounds in unsecured paper money, levy a tax of 5 pence on the pound of the October 1759 list (with collection deferred until May 1761), and tax public officeholders on a scale from 15 pounds for Governor Fitch down to 1 pound for each militia captain. The Upper House rejected all three ideas. Instead, it proposed that the tax already due in December 1756 be increased from 4 to 6 pence, and that the colony borrow up to 10,000 pounds from its own inhabitants. The Lower House rejected any increase in the tax rate, but agreed to borrow 7,100 pounds, despite its reluctance to pay interest to men who were wealthy enough to loan money to the government. The debate over how to generate credit continued for the rest of the war, but without the hard edge it had in 1755–56. The deputies never again implied that public office was a taxable source of income for the well-to-do, and the prospect of reimbursement eventually made issuing paper money more attractive to both Houses than quarreling about how to raise loans.[50]

The 1757 campaign was the last to be funded by Connecticut from its own resources: after two years of war, it had reached the limits of its ability to finance war in conventional ways. Because the colony did not have enough money in the treasury to recruit the 1,400 soldiers the earl of Loudoun wanted, the Assembly searched in February for unconventional ways of raising money. The Upper House appealed to popular enthusiasm and fear of the French by asking all congregations to contribute voluntarily

49. On the schemes, see *Gazette,* 24 Jul, 7 Aug (quotation), and 14 Aug 1756 (quotation).

50. On Lower House plans, see CA-FC:IV/103–04. The deputy governor and the imperial customs collector were assessed 12 pounds, 10 pence each, the Yale College president 12 pounds, and ten named attorneys 10 pounds each, reflecting more about opportunities to profit from fees than a social hierarchy. The deputies rejected borrowing 5,000 pounds at 6 percent interest in August 1755 (CA-FC:IV/64), and increasing tax rates by 2 pence in October 1756 (CA-War:VI/162). On Upper House ideas, see CA-FC:IV/109. Approval for the loans is in CPR:X/495–96, 530–31, 536–38.

to support the war. It wanted "the rich and wealthy . . . freely and liberally" to donate "five or six thousand pounds," and expected "many rich and wealthy persons" to pay the 2-pence tax levied in January before it was due. It was willing to ask constables to collect this tax ahead of time "by distress of so many and such persons as they shall judge best able to pay the same," but the Lower House vetoed the idea. The treasurer was reduced to writing to "gentlemen" in several towns, asking them to "procure by your influence" enough money to enable the companies to march. And, finally, both houses supported a public lottery to raise 8,000 pounds.[51]

The search for new taxes intensified in May because the Lower House did not want to increase the property tax until it had canvased all other ways of paying the projected 24,000 pounds in military costs. Both Houses agreed to a series of taxes on trade, including 3 pence per ton every time a Connecticut-owned ship cleared port on a local voyage, 6 pence if it was going farther (say to the West Indies), and a shilling more in each case if it was not Connecticut-owned. In addition, they agreed to charge every peddler 5 pounds for an annual license, to add a 6-pence duty on each pound of imported tea, and to levy a 5 percent duty on all goods imported by noninhabitants. All of these discriminatory measures, which were sure to antagonize Connecticut's neighbors and the imperial government, were expected to net a mere 1,600 pounds. The deputies turned down several ideas that would have been unpopular with voters. They rejected a tax on unimproved lands because it "would lay the burden on the middling sort of men and not on the richest" where they thought it belonged. They also voted down a tax on "all houses in proportion to their number of lights" because it would affect "the poor more than the rich." Relieving the burden on the poor was, they agreed, "the principal design of going out of the common method of taxing."[52]

The Lower House favored using interest-bearing paper money to fund the war, despite angry objections from the Upper House about "the folly of paying interest for money that we had in our pockets" and which could

51. On the contribution, see CPR:X/604–05; it raised less than 1,400 pounds (CSL-AB:Box 196/11; and CSL-TA/5). On paying taxes early, see CA-FC:IV/156 (quotation); and CPR:X/603–04. On writing to the gentlemen, see CSL-Talcott to Trumbull/9 Apr 1757 (quotation). On the lottery, see CPR:X/605–06; CHS-JT/22 Mar 1757; and *Gazette,* 5 Mar, 12 Mar, 4 Jun 1757.

52. On new methods of taxation, see CPR:XI/10–14; CA-War:VI/239; Williams, *Journal,* pp. 31–41 (quotations 41 and 36); and CHS-GA/[Mar 1757].

be raised by a direct tax on property. The deputies had "no desire to make any money if it was possible to do without" because they realized that issuing more bills would accelerate depreciation and drive specie out of the colony. Nonetheless, they thought the risk of inflation was preferable to more direct taxation. The Upper House was less willing to print money, and it harped on "the difficulties and disadvantages" of issuing bills of credit, which it said were "many and obvious." It had reason to be cautious. Although Connecticut bills were reputed to be the best paper money in North America, already by August 1756 "many persons had been obliged to be large purchasers of lands uncultivated, to avoid the mischiefs of a vile depreciating medium." By April 1757, inflation was reported to be 6 percent a year, and farmers were forced to sell their wheat and flour at a discount to draw in specie. These circumstances convinced the Lower House to forgo issuing more paper money in 1757. In the end, the deputies accepted an increase in the property tax, but only after being reminded of the sacrifices their predecessors had made during the Pequot War 140 years before, a striking instance of the strength and durability of the collective memory. They raised the tax rate by 3 pence (to 7 pence) and doubled (to 5 percent) the duty on goods imported by noninhabitants. Since a tax of 1 penny on the pound generated a credit of roughly 6,000 pounds (table 4.5), the combination of taxes, duties, lottery, and contributions paid for one more year of war.[53]

Thanks to the failure of successive expeditions, which made people reluctant to bear heavy taxation, and to the difficulty of converting property into liquid capital, by late 1757 Connecticut had reached the politically feasible limits of its financial ability to project military force beyond its borders. The French never came closer than during the attack on Fort William Henry in August 1757, and while that emergency generated a massive—and enormously expensive—popular response, it did not galvanize the people in the way the attack on Deerfield in February 1704 had led to heroic exertions for a year during Queen Anne's War. The danger was too far away for that kind of sacrifice.

William Pitt's promise to reimburse most of the costs of creating new colonial armies rescued Connecticut's war effort from collapse, and made

53. On awareness of the danger of paper money, see Williams, *Journal,* p. 40 (quotation). On Upper House opinion, see CA-FC:IV/192 (quotation). On economic conditions, see *Gazette,* 7 Aug 1756 (quotation), 2 Apr and 8 Oct 1757. On the memory of the Pequot War, see Williams, *Journal,* p. 41. The final measures are in CA-War:VI/239; and *Gazette,* 9 Jul 1757.

it possible for the colony to raise an unprecedented number of soldiers in the years from 1758 through 1762. The leaders paid for most of this effort by issuing bills of credit, rather than using direct taxation to generate credit. In the four years after March 1758, the colony issued 280,000 pounds in lawful paper money (table 4.6), an extraordinary sum which, while legally backed by massive taxation, was in reality guaranteed against hyperinflation by the promise of specie payments from the imperial government. Paying interest of 5 percent per annum added 67,500 pounds in debt to the face value of the bills, and allowed them to pass at reasonably close to par. The Lower House wanted to issue even more money, but was restrained by the need to compromise with the Upper House.[54]

Subsidy payments from Parliament were the vital element in backing Connecticut's paper money, even though the colony did not receive all the reimbursement it requested. The Assembly asked the imperial government to pay over 527,000 pounds in lawful money for raising, equipping, and paying its troops (table 4.7), and was eventually granted 61 percent of that total (323,866 pounds; table 4.9). The colony's London agents periodically received payments from the British Treasury, and had shipped 48,475 pounds sterling in specie across the Atlantic by late 1759. They deposited the rest in London banks because the Assembly had decided to retire its paper money by using the safer and more lucrative method of selling bills of exchange in Connecticut. It appointed committees to sell the bills, redeemable in sterling in London, for the maximum amount of paper money local merchants were willing to pay. By late July 1765, Governor Fitch had written orders paying 173,467 pounds sterling (230,700 pounds lawful money) to purchasers.[55]

54. The Upper House wanted to issue 15,000 pounds in March 1758, but eventually agreed to the Lower House's 30,000 pounds (CA-War:VII/147, 149). It proposed 60,000 pounds in March 1760, the Lower House 75,000 pounds, and they compromised on 70,000 pounds (CA-War:VIII/252). It proposed 35,000 pounds in March 1761, the Lower House 55,000 pounds, and they compromised on 45,000 pounds (CA-War:IX/116). On interest, see CPR:XII/339. See also Gipson, *Taxation*, p. 18, although I disagree with his conclusion that Connecticut did not exert itself financially during the war.

55. The reimbursement requested was equal to over 395,000 pounds sterling. On reimbursement granted by Parliament, see Great Britain, *Proceedings*, I/128, 205, 259, 293, 337, 358, 389. On receiving specie from imperial bankers, see CPR:XI/128–29, 257–58, 437–38, 489—91, 574; CPR:XII/78–79, 135–36, 192; and CHC:XVIII/137–42. On shipping specie to Connecticut, see CPR:X/546–48; CPR:XI/238, 345–46; CHC:XVII/205; and CHC:XVIII/3. On selling

Table 4.7
Reimbursement Requested, 1755–62
(In Pounds of Lawful Money)

Year	Total Cost	For Wages
1755	31,400	62%
1756	42,700	70%
1757	25,500	79%
1758	81,300	75%
1759	114,700	Not known
1760	95,800	64%
1761	70,250	59%
1762	65,900	66%
Total	527,550 pounds	

Sources: CA-War:V/205–46; CA-War:VI/282–314; CA-War:VII/75–88, 140; CA-War:VIII/6–55, 93, 102, 327; CA-War:IX/1–49, 193–214; and CA-War:X/2–53.

Reimbursement allowed the Assembly to reduce the tax burden on Connecticut inhabitants. After 1758 it required them to pay 20 pence on the pound to support the paper money, while at the same time lifting 46.25 pence off their backs. A total of 51.25 pence in taxes levied between 1758 and 1762 was canceled (table 4.8). Using the reimbursement to retire bills of credit kept Connecticut's paper money relatively secure and stable; virtually all the bills issued before March 1762 had been redeemed by October 1764. The leaders showed great responsibility in handling their paper money after 1758, but their success raised unrealistic expectations when the next generation faced the far more complex task of financing a revolutionary war without British subsidies.[56]

While the promise of reimbursement allowed Connecticut to rely more heavily on paper money than otherwise would have been the case, the colony did not shift all—or even most—of the burden of paying for the war to British taxpayers. Direct taxes on property during the four years after March 1758 totaled 32.75 pence, which generated nearly 200,000

bills of exchange, see CPR:X/566–67; CPR:XI/128–29, 345–46, 437–38, 489–91, 502; CPR:XII/61, 78–79, 135–36, 256, 467–68; *Gazette*, 5 Jul 1760; CHC:XVIII/353; CSL-AB:Box 196/8; and CSL-TA/4.

56. On redeeming the bills, see CPR:XI/615–18; and CPR:XII/339. On the sinking fund, see CA-War:VII/148; CPR:XI/100–103; and CHC:XVIII/298–99.

Table 4.8
Summary of Taxation, 1755–66
(In Pence of Lawful Money)

Purpose	Levied	Paid	Canceled
1758–62			
Redeem currency	66.25	20.00 (30%)	46.25 (70%)
Supply treasury	32.75	32.75 (100%)	None
Repay loans	5.00	None	5.00 (100%)
Total	104.00	52.75 (51%)	51.25 (49%)
1755–66			
Redeem currency	85.50	35.25 (41%)	50.25 (59%)
Supply treasury	49.50	49.50 (100%)	None
Repay loans	8.00	None	8.00 (100%)
Total	143.00	84.75 (60%)	58.25 (40%)

pounds in credits for the treasury. Of 143.00 pence levied during the war, Connecticut taxpayers were assessed 84.75 pence, or 60 percent, to generate 514,468 pounds in credits; by comparison, the canceled 58.25 pence would have brought in 350,000 pounds (table 4.8). The sums illustrate an important point about the way the people of Connecticut viewed the war. To them, it was a partnership between the imperial government and the colony, with each partner working hard to meet Pitt's demands for superiority over the French at every point of contact; Connecticut spent over 1.2 million pounds on the war, only a quarter of which was paid by the imperial government (table 4.9). As Governor William Pitkin explained in June 1768, "We . . . doubtless have borne more than our proportion of expense, in treasure as well as blood, in every war the nation has been engaged in since the first settlements in America; and in the last war especially . . . have gone much beyond our ability to pay. Witness the credit we were always obliged to betake ourselves to, particularly in the last war, and the vast sums that still remain unpaid, notwithstanding the reimbursement of the Parliament of Great Britain." After the war, when imperial officials sought ways to have the colonists pay more for administering the empire, they prejudiced their case in Connecticut by implying that the colony had not done its fair share to help win the war.[57]

57. On Pitkin's assessment, see MHC:5,IX/281 (quotation). He was elected governor in May 1766. Jonathan Trumbull claimed that Connecticut's expenses

Table 4.9
Balance Sheet, 1755–66
(In Pounds of Lawful Money)

Income		
Taxes (projected yield)	514,468	(42%)
Paper money	338,996*	(28%)
Reimbursement	323,866†	(26%)
Miscellaneous income	45,699‡	(4%)
Total	1,223,029	(100%)
Payments	1,153,363	(94%)

Source: CSL-TAL/1–48.
*Of 359,000 pounds printed (94%).
†Of 527,550 pounds requested (61%).
‡Includes voluntary contributions, excise payments, import duties, interest income, and sale of surplus equipment.

Part of Connecticut's sensitivity to imperial taxation after 1762 arose from the fact that taxpayers were having difficulty paying their property taxes. Imposing a tax created an obligation to pay, but it was not always discharged as quickly as the leaders might have hoped. In 1765, taxpayers were 80,000 pounds in arrears because, according to Jared Ingersoll, the colony's London agent, they were too poor to pay. Warrants requiring the payment of taxes "have been long out," and "many of the people" who could not pay the tax had been "committed to gaol." On 8 December 1768, taxpayers still owed over 48,000 pounds in taxes levied up to twenty years earlier (table 4.10). Towns in all regions were delinquent: for example, Suffield in the Connecticut valley owed 84 percent from 1760, Norwich in the east owed 75 percent from 1763, and Fairfield in the west owed 65 percent from 1764. The Assembly never tried hard to collect these taxes (some were paid as late as 1780) because there was no point in bankrupting people just to retire the bills of credit that gave the colony its best currency.[58]

from 1755 through 1762, "over and above the Parliamentary grants, exceeds 400,000 pounds," probably in lawful money (CSL-JT:XXI/10).

58. On Ingersoll, see his *Letters*, pp. 44 and 50 (quotations). Between 1763 and 1765, the Assembly restructured the bankruptcy laws to help debtors meet the demands of their creditors (CPR:XII/127–33, 228, 357–66; and *Gazette*, Jul–Dec 1763). On delinquent towns, see CSL-AB:Box 196/19–20; and Gipson, *Taxation*, p. 11. Over 45,000 pounds were still unpaid on 23 March 1769 (CSL-

Table 4.10
Amounts Due from Towns, December 1768
(In Lawful Money, Except in New Tenor as Noted)

Year	Rate (Pence)	Towns (Number)	Amount (Pounds)
1749	2.00 NT	15	72
1750	2.00 NT	13	57
1751	1.00 NT	4	5
1752	1.00 NT	7	101
1753	0.75	9	158
1754	0.50	13	35
Subtotal, 1749–54			428
1755	4.00	19	103
1756	5.00	21	315
1757	8.00	21	235
	1.50	13	426
1758	12.50	19	1,379
1759	13.00	28	2,146
1760	10.00	29	2,813
1761	10.00	43	5,606
1762	5.75	48	4,675
1763	6.00	49	8,816
1764	8.00	64	18,959
1765	1.00	62	2,265
Subtotal, 1755–65			47,738
Total			48,166

Source: CSL-TAB:Box 196/19.

Connecticut handled the extraordinarily complex financial side of the war with great skill and success. The strain was not great by comparison with the financial chaos of the Revolution twenty years later, but it was far more than the colony had ever experienced, so traumatic indeed that it made the leaders fear unrestrained Parliamentary taxation. As Ingersoll explained, "If Parliament once interpose and lay a tax, tho' it may be a very modest one, and the Crown appoint officers of its own to collect such tax, . . . what consequences may, or rather, may not follow? The people

---

TA/50). Connecticut was relatively successful in managing its debt: on 15 April 1769 William Samuel Johnson, in London as the colony's agent to Parliament, was "glad to find the colony is so nearly out of debt; though . . . [the towns] will still be in arrear" (MHC:5,IX/333).

think if the precedent is once established, larger sums may be exacted
. . . and that in short, you [the imperial government] will have it in your
power to keep us just as poor as you please. . . . 'Tis difficult to say how
many ways could be invented to avoid the payment of a tax laid upon a
country without the consent of the legislature of that country; and in the
opinion of most of the people, contrary to the fundamental principles of
their natural and constitutional rights and liberties."[59] In this case, concern for "rights and liberties" had a sound practical foundation.

59. Ingersoll, *Letters,* p. 9 (quotation). The leading authority on Connecticut
taxation, Lawrence H. Gipson, thought that the colony was ungrateful for the
reimbursement. "The full extent of the benefit is so extraordinary as to make
almost incredible the furious anti-ministerial agitation" after 1765 (Gipson,
Taxation, pp. 32–33). He was correct regarding taxes levied to retire paper
money, but he overlooked the unprecedented sums needed to supply the treasury
with credit. An appreciation of that fact makes the reaction to the prospect of
imperial taxation a natural response.

Chapter Five

The Structure of
a Colonial Army

CREATING THE ARMY

Connecticut participated in an expedition against Canada for the first time in 1690, sixty-five years before the start of the final French and Indian war. It had accumulated vast experience in the five expeditions since then, knowledge that the Assembly used to create its armies for the longest and most complex war the colony had yet encountered. The Assembly's most important decision was to apply the methods that had worked so well in King George's War to raise troops by financial incentive; the leaders rejected any attempt to use the militia ideal of universal service as a model for the expeditionary regiments long before they received the imperial subsidies that allowed them to come close to creating a colonial version of a professional army by 1762. The regiments became a source of employment for men who viewed military service as a way to get ahead financially—just the sort of men the Assembly wanted to attract—and had a continuity in personnel unlike any previous Connecticut military force. But they were still not a standing force like the British regular army. The regiments were raised each year for one campaign at a time—eight times in eight years—and retained many of the characteristics of the militia, including rudimentary training, poor discipline, and officers chosen primarily for their popularity with the soldiers.

Understanding how Connecticut raised soldiers in 1755 is complicated by the fact that many contemporaries idealized the army that had captured Louisbourg in 1745. Former Governor Wolcott believed that an army of "freeholders and freeholders' sons," one that was "well appointed and disciplined" like the men he had led to Cape Breton, would be "more than a match for a multitude" of Frenchmen who "have no thing to fight for of their own." Wolcott realized that the soldiers were motivated by self-interest—each man would fight "for his country according to his interest in it"—but his understanding of why they served in 1745 and especially 1746 was too sentimental, and his prediction of their military ability in 1755 was too optimistic. The idea of the citizen-soldiers who fight willingly and effectively to defend their liberty and property because they have "a force of interest in their country" is an appealing myth, but the reality had been different during King George's War—the Assembly had drawn soldiers disproportionately from men at the bottom of society, the more so as enthusiasm cooled in 1746—and it continued to be so in and after 1755 on a scale unprecedented in Connecticut's history.[1]

As in 1745, the Assembly's rejection of universal service was camouflaged by the enthusiasm with which men volunteered at the start of the conflict. The colony welcomed the war in 1755 as the decisive encounter in the long struggle against Canada. The *Gazette* reported that men were enlisting with "alacrity and spirit" because they wanted to fight "the enemies of the British Constitution." While the mortality Connecticut men suffered in the West Indies in 1740–41 "frightens them from enlisting . . . , tis neither danger nor difficulty they dread when they are satisfied their King calls for them. . . . Tis plain tis not the lucre of their pay or reward that tempts them . . . but only what is dear to Englishmen." By 26 April "most of the companies" were "quite full." The company in New Haven, said the *Gazette*'s publisher, James Parker, "entirely consists of healthy, able-bodied men, in the vigor of life; their behavior was decent, resolute, and cheerful." He was especially pleased "to see so many of the flower of our youth inspired with so noble an ardor."[2]

In many towns, the send-off included a sermon by the local minister, who roused enthusiasm by preaching a Protestant crusade against the Roman Catholic French. In Lebanon, Solomon Williams encouraged the soldiers to fight well "against the enemies of Christ." In New Haven,

1. Wolcott's opinions are in CHC:XVI/436–37 (quotation). Shy emphasized that New England's expeditionary soldiers were not a cross-section of its militiamen in "New Look."

2. "War was very much discoursed upon" in the spring of 1755 (Fitch, "Diary," I/38). On motivation, see *Gazette*, 3 May and 9 Aug 1755 (quotations); and CHC:XVII/146. On the companies, see *Gazette*, 26 Apr, 14 May, and Jun 1755 (quotations).

Isaac Stiles asserted that "our lives and properties, our religion and liberty of conscience" were at stake: "The prejudices of their religion, prompt . . . [the French] mortally to hate us, and seek our overthrow." Ministers had used similar rhetoric to promote the Louisbourg campaign, but now, as in 1745, most of it was directed at the men and women who stayed behind. The sermons reflected a climate of opinion, seen also in the Assembly's invocation of God's favor and "the Protestant cause," but although religious enthusiasm made recruiting easier, it was probably not the main reason why most men enlisted.[3]

Morale remained high at home because people were unaware of the logistical problems the army faced. Men who had volunteered to fight Frenchmen were disheartened by the difficulty of building roads and hauling supplies, but they found no sympathy in Connecticut. A rash of desertions in mid-August prompted the *Gazette* to charge that the deserters were "robbing the public, who are daily laboring to support them." The Assembly bolstered the army's sagging morale by voting reinforcements in late August; according to one senior officer, this news "very much animated the spirits of our men who had begun to flag and to have some discontents unworthy [of] New England men." When the colony learned that, after the repulse of the French on 8 September, the army needed even more help, "in less than six hours above eighty able-bodied men" volunteered in New Haven. In towns along the shore, the post-rider "observed multitudes" of men "preparing for a march." (Enthusiasm was not universal, however. A Middletown leader reported that "some persons have endeavored to disengage the minds of many that were warmly engaged." The Assembly, reluctantly taking no chances in an emergency, decided to invoke impressment.) When the army did not proceed to attack Crown Point, publisher Parker predicted that the wives of the soldiers would "fling their p-s-pots" at their husbands, "as unworthy the name of New England men." The memory of Louisbourg was so fresh that anything less than total victory now was a bitter disappointment; Major General Phineas Lyman, the Connecticut commander, could not "bear that the French should hold Crown Point this winter." Failure prompted recri-

3. Ministers emphasized that the war was just and lawful (Stiles, *Character,* p. 5; Dickinson, *Sermon,* pp. 13–15; Beckwith, *People*; Estabrook, *Praying,* p. 7; and Bird, *Importance,* pp. 3–4, 16–19). On Williams, see *Duty,* p. 13 (quotation). On Stiles, see *Character,* p. 4–5, 13 (quotation). He rejoiced to see so many "who make so good a figure" enlisted into "the service of your King and country" (p. 13). On "the Protestant cause," see CHC:XVII/343 (quotation).

minations. On 3 January 1756 the *Gazette* noted with great understatement that representing "some of the principal managers of our military affairs as a set of criminals certainly has a tendency to make our men dislike the service."[4]

Connecticut men never again went to war as eagerly as they had in 1755. The Assembly tried to rekindle enthusiasm in 1756 by asking Massachusetts to appoint Sir William Pepperrell, the hero of Louisbourg, to lead the colonial army. But Pepperrell was not physically able to undertake the new challenge, and Massachusetts instead appointed John Winslow, an experienced commander but one who lacked the prestige to motivate men in Connecticut. Lack of enthusiasm led to the recruiting of what some imperial officials thought were soldiers "not equal to those. . . [New England] had employed on former occasions." Connecticut met the 1757 quota largely because it was half that of 1756. The disaster at Fort William Henry shook the colony, but General Lyman, for one, was not dismayed: the French would be "in our power if we would . . . enter their country . . . [and not stop] on our own frontier building forts and thereby exhausting the treasures of our country."[5]

Connecticut was "considerably roused" in 1758 when it seemed the full weight of imperial power would bring the long-sought victory. Enthusiasm was highest in April, when General Abercromby claimed that the "levies meet with no difficulties." A month later, he reported that recruiting "went on but slow" and could not be completed without a draft. Morale plummeted when his army retreated after the defeat at Ticonderoga in July. Lyman could not "bear the thought of coming home til we have done something," and another officer bitterly asked, "Are our

4. The logistical problems were said to be greater than anyone in Connecticut imagined. News of Braddock's defeat "did not seem to dispirit" the troops, but "animated them with a due thirst for revenge" (*Gazette,* 9 Aug 1755). On deserters, see *Gazette,* 16 Aug 1755 (quotation). On flagging morale, see YU-MS:Whiting/16 (quotation). On reinforcements, see *Gazette,* 6 and 20 Sep 1755 (quotation); CA-War:VI/112–5; CHC:XVII/143, 146; and CHC:XIX/265–66. On the post-rider, see *Boston Weekly News-Letter,* 25 Sep 1755 (quotation). On Middletown, see CHC:XIX/267–68 (quotation). On wives, see *Gazette,* 11 Oct 1755 (quotation). On Lyman, see CHS-WY:IV/352 (quotation). On recriminations, see *Gazette,* 9 Aug, 13 Dec 1755, 3 Jan 1756 (quotation).

5. On Pepperrell, see CA-War:VI/17; and Fairchild, "Pepperrell," p. 105. On the quality of troops in 1756, see CHC:XVII/277. On Lyman, see CHS-JT/10 Dec 1757 (quotation); the response to the alarm was based on the old frontier system and did not reflect enthusiasm for expeditionary service.

armies never to effect anything?" The last four campaigns generated only occasional excitement. Connecticut celebrated the fall of Quebec on 13 September 1759, but the need for a campaign in 1760 muted the joy. A "sore and distressing sickness" in the fall and winter of 1760–61 killed "multitudes both at home and in our army" and capped a year of increasing war-weariness. Enthusiasm in 1761 and 1762 focused on how to acquire some of the land now being opened for settlement. Drought was the principal news in the summer of 1761, and only the high mortality suffered by the army at Havana in July and August 1762 attracted interest in the last year of the war.[6]

Connecticut raised soldiers after 1755 principally because some men had come to depend on the bounties and wages they could earn in military service. Some ministers still preached a crusade against the French, but pious words were no substitute for adequate wages. In 1757 James Cogswell told Pomfret soldiers that "your country would be ungrateful" if it did not pay them adequately for their "labor and danger." Some ministers were unhappy about the decline in altruism. In 1759 Samuel Bird of New Haven doubtless antagonized the soldiers in his audience when he accused them of having "no higher or nobler views than to waste away a summer in ease, idleness, and vice at the public expense." He was closer to the truth when he said there were soldiers "who, instead of serving their country, mean nothing but to serve themselves."[7]

A clearer understanding of who served, and why, begins by examining how Connecticut raised its soldiers. The Assembly had begun to use financial incentives to attract volunteers in 1709, and in 1755 it applied on an unprecedented scale the methods that had worked so well in 1746. It designed the military system to draw in the maximum number of volunteers for the lowest possible cost, and used enlistment bounties as the principal way of inducing men to undertake nonemergency service

6. On reinvigorating in 1758, see CHC:XVII/335–36 (quotation); and Throop, *Religion,* p. 29. Abercromby's opinions are in CO-5:II/807 and 866 (quotations). On Lyman, see CHS-JT/29 Aug 1758 (quotation). On frustration, see *Summary,* 29 Sep 1758 (quotation). On sickness, see *Summary,* 3 Apr 1761 (quotation); Ingersol, *Sermon,* p. 35 (quotation); and Stiles, *Itineraries,* pp. 104–15, 111. On Havana, see *Summary,* 8 Oct, 26 Nov, 17 Dec 1762, 7 Jan, 8 Jul 1763; and *Gazette,* 30 Oct, 18 Dec 1762.

7. Cogswell exhorted soldiers to fight "as men inspired with an unconquerable aversion to popery and slavery, and an ardent love to religion and liberty" (*Pious Soldier,* p. 26). On Bird, see *Importance,* pp. 6 and 21 (quotations).

Table 5.1
Enlistment Bounties, 1755–62
(In Pounds, Shillings, and Pence of Lawful Money)

Date	Amount
1755 March	1.10.0 (UH = 1.4.0, LH = 2.2.0), plus 1.10.0 for arms and blanket.
1756 March	1.16.0, plus half-pay for veteran from 17 Dec. 1755 (5.0.0 for private).
1756 Oct.	0.18.0.
1757 Feb.	2.2.0 (UH = 1.16.0), plus 1.10.0 for veteran.
1758 March	4.0.0 (UH = 3.10.0, LH = 3.12.0).
1758 May	4.0.0 for volunteer; 2.0.0 for draftee.
1759 March	Full pay for veteran, 1 Dec. 1758–5 April 1759 (8.2.0 for private); 4.0.0 for new enlistee (LH = 4.10.0).
1759 May	Full pay for veteran, 1 Dec. 1758–25 May 1759 (11.7.0 for private); 7.0.0 for new enlistee (LH = 8.0.0).
1760 March	Full pay for veteran, 15 Dec. 1759–4 April 1760 (7.4.0 for private); 4.0.0 for new enlistee (LH = 6.0.0).
1760 May	Full pay for veteran, plus 2.0.0 bounty and 0.4.0 more a month in wages.
1761 March	11.0.0 for veteran; 7.0.0 for new enlistee.
1762 March	7.0.0 for all recruits.

Sources: CPR:X/344, 397–98, 475, 554–56, 599–600; CPR:XI/93–94, 121–22, 222–23, 251–53, 349–51, 387, 480–82, 613–15; CA-War:V/99; CA-War:VI/73, 186; CA-War:VII/147; CA-War:VIII/146, 190, 252; CA-War:IX/116, 268.
Note: UH = Upper House proposal; LH = Lower House proposal.

outside the colony. In March the Assembly offered each volunteer 1 pound, 10 shillings of lawful money to enlist, plus 1 pound, 10 shillings more if he brought his own musket and blanket, for a total of 3 pounds per man (table 5.1). Each soldier received his bounty, along with a month's advance wages, when he was mustered in at the start of the campaign, but he was not paid the rest until the campaign was over. The sums were not large when compared with what had been offered in 1746, but they were sufficient to tap the desire to fight the French in 1755.

Bounties rose thereafter, an increase made necessary by the decline in enthusiasm, but made possible largely by the imperial government's promise to reimburse such expenses. (A similar increase in enlistment bounties was occurring at the same time in Britain.) The Assembly was happy to recruit soldiers annually from among men who wanted the money; until bounties reached unprecedented levels in and after 1759, it was actually cheaper to raise troops each year than to keep them in pay over the winter. The fiscally conservative Upper House tried to hold down costs by increasing the amounts paid to recruiting officers rather than to the soldiers themselves. The recruiting bounty rose from 2 shillings in 1755 to a peak of 10 shillings in May 1759 (when the colony was desperate for soldiers) before dropping to 5 shillings in 1760–62. The Lower House, on the other hand, wanted to increase the bounty paid directly to recruits, and convinced the Upper House to do so in 1755, 1757, and 1758.[8]

The Assembly agreed to pay higher bounties to attract veteran soldiers. It gave a veteran private 5 pounds in 1756 (a total of 6 pounds, 16 shillings), but dropped the bounty to 1 pound, 10 shillings (a total of 3 pounds, 12 shillings) in 1757 because it needed only fourteen hundred soldiers, the fewest of the war. The idea of recruiting five thousand soldiers in 1758 was so daunting that the leaders offered more than they originally anticipated, 4 pounds for a veteran private, half paid when he enlisted and half before he marched out of the colony. In March 1759 the bounty reached 8 pounds, 2 shillings, and in May it peaked at 11 pounds, 7 shillings, nearly twice the total in 1756 and seven-and-a-half times the enlistment bounty of 1755. Of course, bounties did not ensure able-bodied recruits. One man tried to enlist for a third time in 1757 despite having been "sick and unfit for duty immediately" after leaving home the past two years. Recruiters were warned to reject him because he was "defective in one of his arms, if his age is not sufficient hinderance to his passing muster." High bounties also provoked some bounty jumping. A man enlisted twice in the same company in 1760 and deserted both times after receiving his bounty.[9]

While the Assembly was forced to increase bounties to attract soldiers, it tried to reduce costs by keeping wages low, a decision which reflected a recognition that soldiers would be content with rates of pay and pro-

8. "By 1759 the bounty for an able seaman had risen to 5 pounds sterling, so that one who volunteered [for the Royal Navy] could expect over 7 pounds sterling in cash when he joined his ship" (Rodger, *Wooden World,* p. 127). Each Connecticut recruit signed a printed certificate attesting to his enlistment. Examples from 1756, 1757, 1758, and 1759 are in YU-MS:Whiting/30.

9. On bounties for expeditionary soldiers during the war, see the source note for table 5:1. On the unfit recruit, see CHS-JT/25 Apr 1757 (quotation). On bounty jumping, see *Gazette,* 14 Jun 1760.

Table 5.2
Wages, 1755–62
(In Pounds, Shillings, and Pence of Lawful Money, Per Month of 28 Days)

Rank	1755	1756	1757	1758	1759	1760–62
Colonel	12.16.0	12.16.0	20. 0.0	15. 0.0	25. 0.0	25. 0.0
Lieutenant colonel	9.12.0	10.13.4	13. 0.0	10.15.0	15. 0.0	16. 0.0
Major	6. 8.0	9. 1.4	10.15.0	9. 1.4	12. 0.0	12. 0.0
Captain	4.16.0	5. 8.0	6. 0.0	6. 0.0	8. 0.0	8. 0.0
Lieutenant	3. 4.0	3.12.0	4. 0.0	4. 0.0	5. 0.0	6. 0.0
Ensign	2. 8.0	3.12.0	3. 5.0	3.10.0	4. 0.0	5. 0.0
Sergeant	1.15.6	1.18.4	1.18.4	2. 0.0	2. 0.0	2. 4.0
Corporal	1. 8.0	1.13.6	1.13.6	1.18.0	1.18.0	2. 2.0
Private	1. 6.8	1.12.0	1.12.0	1.16.0	1.16.0	2. 0.0
Private as % of colonel	10.4%	12.5%	8.0%	12.0%	7.2%	8.0%

Sources: CPR:X/349, 474–75, 600; CPR:IX/94, 223–24, 350–51, 387, 482, 615; CA-War:VI/37, 187; CA-War:VII/147, 205; CHS-GAP/[Mar 1758].

visioning equal to the lowest level in Connecticut society (table 5.2). In March 1755 the Assembly agreed to pay each private 1 pound, 6 shillings, 8 pence for a month of twenty-eight days. This was less than what a man could earn as a civilian, and also less than what the Assembly had paid in October 1754 to a private for service on the frontier: he received 1 pound, 16 shillings if he came equipped with a gun and "all other accoutrements." The 3-pound enlistment and equipment bounties the Assembly gave to expeditionary soldiers made up most of the difference, but the frontier soldier still received 2 shillings a month more. General Lyman could not convince his colleagues in the Upper House to raise wages to the level of "common laborers at home in the field," but he did prevent them from reducing billeting money from the barely adequate level of 4 shillings a week.[10]

As with enlistment bounties, the two houses quarreled over the pay scale. The Lower House wanted to reduce wages for field officers in 1757 and 1758; the Upper House tried to reduce wages for noncommissioned

10. On wages for expeditionary soldiers during the war, see the source note for table 5:2. On wages on the frontier, see CPR:X/317. On Lyman, see CA-War:V/106, 137 (quotations).

Table 5.3
Comparison of Bounties and Wages, 1755–62
(In Pounds, Shillings, and Pence of Lawful Money,
for a Veteran Private)

Year	Wages for Eight Months	Bounty	Bounty as Percentage of Wages
1755	10.13.4	3. 0.0	28%
1756	12.16.0	5. 0.0	39%
1757	12.16.0	3.12.0	28%
1758	14. 8.0	4. 0.0	28%
Average, 1755–58			31%
1759	14. 8.0	9.17.0	68%
1760	16. 0.0	8.19.0	56%
1761	16. 0.0	12.15.0	80%
1762	16. 0.0	8.15.0	55%
Average, 1759–62			65%

officers and privates in 1758. Although the Upper House refused to pay a private 2 pounds per month in 1759, it agreed to the higher pay two years later when volunteers were harder to find. Even with an increase in wages, the Assembly paid proportionally more to raise the troops than to keep them in service. Before 1759 the total bounty for a private averaged 31 percent of his wages for eight months of service; average bounty as a percentage of wages doubled during the last four years, to 65 percent, peaking at 80 percent in the difficult recruiting year of 1761 (table 5.3). The smallest number of troops, 1,400 men in 1757, received the largest fraction of expenditures as pay, 79 percent (table 4.7), because fewer troops took fewer bounties to raise. In 1761 wages were just 59 percent of total costs, while 41 percent went to raising the soldiers and supplying them with coats, blankets, and knapsacks.

The Assembly offered several other incentives to attract volunteers. Each year it gave a recruit extra money if he came equipped with a musket. (Because there were never enough weapons available from imperial stocks, it continued to impress guns of good manufacture, and offered bounties for firearms in 1758 when it had to arm a force of unprecedented size.) Beginning in March 1759, it also gave each volunteer 1 pound, 15 shillings for a coat; recruits in new blue coats of roughly uniform cut, generally faced with red, looked more like soldiers, but they never approached the smartness of the redcoated regulars. To enable soldiers to use their earnings to get out of debt, the Assembly each year gave them immunity from arrest for debts under 10 pounds, as in 1745–46; this also followed British practice. Eastern deputies wanted to exempt them from taxation, as in 1711, but the Upper House was reluctant to reduce the tax base. It acceded to the proposal in 1755, and again in 1758 and 1759 after being assured of a steady flow of reimbursement income. Aware that land would attract men in a land-hungry colony, the Lower House in 1758 wanted to give soldiers rights to any Canadian lands Connecticut might earn in the campaign. The imperial government had made a similar offer in 1709 and 1746, but the Upper House vetoed it now; land, even in Canada, was too valuable to be doled out just for military service. Hope of plunder was less important than in 1745 because the Champlain valley contained no city of fabled wealth like Louisbourg. Connecticut soldiers won plunder only at Havana in 1762, less than 3 pounds for each private who risked his life to the diseases that killed half the army.[11]

Connecticut's willingness to raise troops by financial incentives was the

11. The Upper House rejected arms bounties in 1756 (CA-War:VI/71). On arms bounties in 1758, see CPR:XI/122–24; less than two thousand muskets were on hand for five thousand men: sixteen hundred (80 percent) from imperial stocks, ninety (5 percent) owned by the colony, and the rest (15 percent) previously impressed (CA-War:VII/213). In one company, five guns were government-owned and seventy-three were impressed; only seven men carried their own gun (CSL-Charles Whiting). By 1760, deserters were commonly described as wearing "an old regimental coat" (*Gazette*, 21 Jun 1760). Two deserters were mentioned as wearing blue soldier's coats with red lapels (*Summary*, 11 Jul 1760). A few militia units wore blue coats, for example, the troop in the Eleventh Regiment in 1758 (CA-Mil:2,I/122) and the "Artillery Company" at the New London fort in 1762 (*Summary*, 14 May 1762). On immunity from arrest, see CPR:X/342–33, 469; and CPR:XI/230–31, 385, 487–48, 621–22. By the Navy Act of 1728 "seamen in men-of-war could not be arrested or imprisoned for debts of less than 20 pounds sterling (Rodger, *Wooden World*, p. 131). On wages paid to a third party (1755), see CHS-FIW:II/266–75. On exemption from taxes, see CPR:X/424; CPR:XI/182, 344; and CA-War:VI/158, 174. On the offer of Canadian land, see CA-War:VII/208. The Upper House rejected the Lower House's idea of a bonus of 10 pounds per soldier if Canada were conquered in 1759 (CA-War:VII/208). On plunder earned at Havana, see *Summary*, 26 Nov 1762, 4 Mar 1763; and *Gazette*, 30 Oct, 18 Dec 1762. Getting the prize money took up to nine years, by which time nearly all the soldiers had sold their rights to plunder. On powers of attorney, see *Summary*, 4 Mar 1763; and CHS-JT:3 Nov 1763. The final distribution of prize money began in London in November 1771 (*Courant*, 22–29 Oct 1771).

culmination of a change in attitude about military service. The idea that soldiers were members of the community temporarily bearing arms in time of danger gave way to the assumption that men could be hired to perform dangerous and disagreeable work. The professionalization of military service had begun to be evident in 1740 and 1746, but it had been camouflaged by popular enthusiasm for the campaigns in 1745 and 1755. In and after 1756, it blossomed. The leaders fully understood that bounties appealed principally to men who wanted or needed the money, especially the roughly half of the men in the colony who owned less than 50 pounds in personal property, an amount that was "about rock-bottom for a decent standard of living." Recruits were not abjectly or permanently poor; half the poor men were young, "and most of them would become self-supporting" in later life. The economic character of recruiting did cause some disquiet in 1758, however, when Parker refused to print a letter to his *Gazette* because it complained about "the unequal share of the public service borne by the poor and the rich." Still, the fact remains that the leaders had decided that the most efficient and least disruptive way to fill the regiments was to use money to induce men to volunteer.[12]

There also seems to have been a new popular attitude about the men who accepted financial incentives to go to war. When ministers tried to explain why a war against "our anti-Christian foes" had had so little success before 1758, they blamed "profaneness, wickedness, and indolence in the army." An East Haddam minister told soldiers from his congregation that God would withdraw His help if they should "profane His holy name, which," he emphasized, "is the too common but infamous character of soldiers." Ministers returned frequently to the theme of morally weak soldiers swearing, profaning the Sabbath, neglecting prayer and public worship, and trusting in numbers rather than in God, any one of which corruptions would bring disaster to British arms. Some people thought that men who became soldiers were especially improvident. A correspondent suggested in the *Gazette* of 5 February 1757 that the colony buy clothes for recruits because "it is well known that all soldiers are not the most prudent men when they get money into their hands." (The Assembly rejected the idea because it was easier to pay volunteers to find their own coats.) Even when dressed in a semblance of a uniform, soldiers faced the prejudice that their "regimentals" might cover a weak or corrupt character, an attitude about soldiers that was new in Connecticut.[13]

12. On levels of wealth, see Main, *Connecticut Society,* pp. 13 and 16 (quotations). On unequal shares, see *Gazette,* 13 May 1758 (quotation).

13. On "anti-Christian foes," see Bird, *Importance,* p. 3. Bird thought "a

Paying poor men to perform military service diverged sharply from the image of free men fighting for their liberty and property which Connecticut and its neighbors cultivated in the years before the American Revolution. But no one complained about raising troops by bounty during the final French and Indian war because it replaced raising them by impressment. While both financial incentives and compulsory service drew soldiers disproportionately from the bottom of society, the Assembly preferred bounties because it did not wish to strain its authority to force men into service. Connecticut did not avoid impressment entirely, but it certainly relied more heavily than ever before on the fact that many men thought military service offered a better source of ready cash than any other employment they could find between April and November of each year.

The Assembly was never comfortable with compelling men to serve, and it always tried to coax them into volunteering. Because the war was popular in 1755, it managed to avoid impressment until 8 September. Even then it tried to ameliorate its action by giving draftees all applicable bounties if they volunteered within twenty-four hours of being impressed, the same incentive it had granted each time it drafted men for an expedition since 1709. The offer curbed discontent—but did not stop draft dodging—and was part of the impressment law until the Assembly abandoned compulsory service entirely in 1760. The Assembly also tried to ensure that impressment was applied fairly across the colony. After May 1756 it instructed each militia colonel to take into account the number of volunteers already in service when drafting more men from a company. It specified each militia regiment's quota in October 1756 and again in 1758–59, when the demand for soldiers was at its peak.[14]

thorough reformation in persons of every rank would do more towards recovering our invaded rights . . . than all our military strength" (pp. 12–13). On reasons for the lack of success, see Throop, *Religion,* pp. 23, 30, 31 (quotation). On East Haddam, see Estabrook, *Praying,* pp. 15, 18. On reforming the conduct of soldiers, see CHC:XVII/343–44; Russell, *Duty,* pp. 9–20; *Gazette,* 13 May, 24 Jun 1758; Bird, *Importance,* pp. 19, 23; Fish, *Christ Jesus,* p. 54; and Taylor, *Praise,* p. 27. On what ministers thought about the war, see Hatch, *Sacred,* pp. 21–54; and Stout, *Soul,* pp. 244–47. On improvident soldiers, see *Gazette,* 5 Feb 1757 (quotation). On attitudes about soldiers, see Martin and Lender, *Respectable Army,* pp. 11–15.

14. On impressment in 1755, see CPR:X/398. For examples of draftees who volunteered, see CA-War:VI/37; CA-War:VIII/248; CA-War:IX/145, 299, 304; CA-War:X/132; CPR:X/602–03; and CPR:XI/122, 224–26. For an example of draft dodging, see Fitch, "Diary," I/39. For examples of draftees who served,

The Assembly relied on the officers of the thirteen militia regiments to make impressment work. Each colonel apportioned his regiment's quota among his companies and left the captains to consult with their lieutenants and ensigns about which men to choose. The officers generally tried to draft men who might serve willingly, but the choice was never simple. In Gilead parish in Hebron in June 1756, for example, they picked one man because he "could be better spared than any else" and another who "could not well be spared but it is so with all our young men." A call to impress sent captains scurrying to find able-bodied men they might have overlooked. One master complained in May 1758 that his servant "was never called into the train band but yesterday, and to be prest immediately after seems hard." The same year a captain in East Haddam claimed as part of his quota a young man who had lived with his father over the winter, within the limits of his company, but who had gone to the next town to enlist for the 1758 campaign. In March 1757 a captain in Lebanon had tried a different approach. To reduce his company's quota he shrank the size of his company by illegally omitting from his muster roll men who had served the previous year.[15]

To its great dismay, the Assembly encountered a few occasions when militia officers themselves flouted the law. The most serious case occurred in 1755 in the Seventh Regiment, where by 8 September only 12 men had enlisted. Colonel Samuel Willard instructed his militia captains to impress 150 men, and most obeyed "with utmost care and dispatch."

see CA-War:VIII/105; CA-War:X/253; and CHC:X/96, 202. The Lower House wanted to impress militia troopers in 1755, but the Upper House vetoed the idea (CA-War:V/154); it later agreed to limited eligibility for the troopers, every sixth man in 1758 and every ninth man in 1759 (CPR:XI/121–22, 224–26). On the quotas, broken down into regiments by the Assembly, see CA-War:VI/37; CPR:X/494–95, 554–55, 602–03; and CPR:XI/121–22, 224–26. On drafting in 1757, see Fitch, "Diary," I/179.

15. The best information on impressment comes from Colonel Jonathan Trumbull's records of the Twelfth Regiment (which included the towns of Colchester, East Haddam, Hebron, and Lebanon) in CHS-FIW. On dividing the quota, see CHS-FIW:II/407, 573, 579, 593. On Captain Samuel Gilbert of Hebron, see CHS-FIW:I/44 (quotation). On the servant, Daniel Lamphear, described by his master as both a "very good hand" and very infirm, see CHS-JT/23 May 1758 (quotation). On Captain Jared Spencer of East Haddam, see CHS-FIW:I/70. On Captain Nathaniel Cushman's attempt to omit veterans, see CHS-FIW:I/50. An account of Colonel John Chester's activities in the Sixth Regiment in the Connecticut valley from October 1756 to February 1759 is in CA-War:VIII/98.

But captains James Wells and Abraham Brooks of Haddam appealed for a reduction in their quotas of 13 men each. When Willard refused, they impressed invalids. According to the colonel, Wells drafted one man who had "a lame, dislocuted [*sic*] ankle" and another who had "never enlisted in any company nor [been] called to muster or bear arms" because his right eye had been "blind from his childhood." The Assembly did not want to punish the captains severely, especially since the expeditionary companies ended up only 6 men short of their authorized strength of 81 men each. When Wells presented affidavits that he had used "his utmost endeavors" to impress his quota, the Assembly dismissed Willard's complaint. It clearly believed the colonel was being too strict when it was important to secure cooperation over a distasteful but necessary use of power. On the other hand, the Assembly did discipline militia officers when appropriate. In October 1757 it dismissed Lieutenant Isaac How of East Haven because it was convinced he had obstructed impressment during the Fort William Henry alarm in August.[16]

A few militia officers abused their power when it came time to decide which of their neighbors they would compel to serve. While most tried to spread the burden among as many men as possible, in Goshen parish in Lebanon the officers drafted the same four men in October 1756 and, along with twenty-one others, again for the August 1757 alarm. Many of the August draftees enlisted for the first time the following year (for example, ten of twenty-two draftees from Hebron volunteered in 1758), which may indicate that they were enlisting moments ahead of a draft their officers had modeled on the past summer's experience. Impressment was clearly tainted in Northington parish of Farmington in 1756. Captain Jonathan Miller's subordinates advised him to impress one of his sons and his nephew as part of a four-man quota, but instead he drafted "sundry poor men"; his neighbors still condemned his partiality a dozen years later. Other captains also drafted poor men. In May 1759, a Colchester captain impressed an only son whose father was dead, whose mother was insane, whose sister was infirm, and whose family owned only a cow. Even prominent citizens could be impressed in an emergency. Daniel Brainard, Jr., of East Haddam was chosen in August 1757, possibly the only As-

16. On the Seventh Regiment, see CA-War:V/198 (quotations). The quota was sixteen men of every one hundred in the 950-man regiment. Wells's affidavits, sworn before his brother, the local justice of the peace, are in CA-War:V/201–03; the Assembly's decision is in CPR:X/443. The Assembly allowed Willard to retire in October 1757. On How, see CA-Mil:2,I/81–85.

sembly deputy ever drafted. Also a selectman and town treasurer, he had a sick wife, three small children, a "negro wench" with a small child, a fourteen-year-old "negro boy," and a Frenchman deported from Nova Scotia all living under his roof. The local captain refused to release him, and he appealed to Colonel Jonathan Trumbull to win his freedom. Why Brainard was impressed is unknown, but it may have been the result of a personal dispute with the captain.[17]

Impressment was used at least once to settle a personal grudge. Cyprian Dudley was "the head of a family of small children," Saybrook's only clothier, and one of its selectmen when he was drafted in April 1757. He told the Assembly that drafting him would hurt the town, and claimed that Captain Gideon Leet should impress some "single able-bodied effective men" who "might be spared without any great inconveniency either to themselves or the public." Dudley did not mention that he had recently tried to have Leet ousted from his captaincy by painting him as "a hard drinker of strong drink" who obstructed impressment. Leet impressed Dudley out of revenge, and the Assembly refused to interfere because it had to demonstrate that it would enforce impressment. "A considerable number" of draftees had already refused to serve, and they had not been deterred by the 10-pound fine. They were not interested in bounties and wages: if brought to court, they probably would have paid the fine rather than leave their businesses. By refusing to release Dudley, the Assembly sought to coerce men into compliance with the impressment law.[18]

Draftees tried all sorts of excuses to avoid service. Most involved some claim of physical disability. Lemuel Storrs of Colchester succeeded in May 1756 because his minister certified that he was "an infirm and weakly man, unable to endure any hard service, or to go through wet or cold without injury." The fact that Storrs also collected the tax that paid the minister's salary undoubtedly had "its due consideration." Mental incapacity seems to have been treated less sympathetically. In April 1757, for example, a draftee who claimed to be "in a proper delerium and not

17. On Goshen, see CHC:IX/162, 257. On Hebron, see CHC:IX/257–58; and CHC:X/95. One East Haddam draftee in 1756 volunteered for the next four years (CPR:XIII/64). On Miller, see CA-Mil:2,I/960; and CPR:XII/586–87. On Moses Fuller of Colchester, see CHS-FIW:II/744; he apparently did not serve in 1759, but seems to have enlisted in 1762 (CHC:X/340). On Brainard, see CHS-FIW:I/66.

18. Dudley's story is in CA-War:VI/237 (quotations), 277; CA-Mil:V/523 (quotations), 525–36; and CHC:IX/266.

capable of acting for himself" failed to win release. One man tried to avoid service in a way that raised a fundamental question about the proper use of the Assembly's authority. In June 1758 a father in Colchester asked to have his only son freed from impressment because he thought it unjust for the Assembly to make "only sons and heirs . . . engage in a foreign war without the free consent of the parent or the child." It was fear of just this sort of question that induced the leaders to strain their resources to raise soldiers by voluntary enlistment and avoid, at great cost, a recourse to impressment.[19]

Several circumstances reduced the pool of draftees and made it harder for the Assembly to risk invoking impressment, even when the need for soldiers was great. Each campaign saw a few more men dead or incapacitated. Some enlisted in the regulars, while others worked on the army's logistical lifelines. In East Haddam in 1757, one captain reported that "several of the likeliest to be impressed" had enlisted as teamsters, which left "scarcely one man above nineteen years old but what has the care of a family . . . , except such as were impressed or enlisted last year." To make matters worse in 1758–59, the Assembly charged that, as in 1746, neighboring colonies were offering large bounties to attract Connecticut men to serve in place of their own citizens. Despite the need for soldiers, the Assembly in May 1758 specifically excluded "free Negroes, Molattoes, and Indians" from impressment. This policy seems to have been racially motivated, but it did not prevent blacks and Indians from volunteering, as they always had; indeed, the Assembly specifically encouraged Indians to volunteer. Black and Indians were also among the men hired as substitute soldiers by well-off draftees who chose not to go to war themselves.[20]

19. On Storrs, see CHC:XVII/239 (quotations). On the man in the delirium, Obadiah Dunham, see CHS-FIW:I/58 (quotation). On the only son, Jabez Chapman, Jr., of Colchester, see CHS-FIW:I/552 (quotation); he probably did not serve.

20. On the size of the pool of draftees, see CPR:XI/221–23, 251–53; CA-War:VII/209; and CHC:XVIII/14. On a former soldier as teamster, see Fitch, "Diary," VIII/46. On Captain Jared Spencer of East Haddam, see CHS-FIW:I/48 (quotation). Poaching by other colonies was not a problem until 1758 (CHC:XVII/336). The Upper House vetoed the Lower House's idea to ban Connecticut men from enlisting in neighboring colonies, or at least to have them count toward each company's quota (CA-War:VII/239, 207). It seems that few men from other colonies enlisted in Connecticut companies. On excluding blacks and Indians from impressment, see CA-War:VII/207; they had been excluded

As it had for each expedition since 1709, the Assembly tacitly sanctioned the hiring of substitutes to reduce the challenge impressment made to its authority. Governor Shirley condoned the practice in 1756, but Loudoun complained that it produced an inferior army. "In place of sending out the inhabitants of the country, which they always did before, . . . [now they] hire any man they could get; . . . the New England men are almost all of those hirelings who are dying daily from a languishing to go home." Hiring substitutes could even interfere with impressment. A Hebron captain complained in 1758 that allowing a draftee to hire himself to the highest bidder would always prevent the company from meeting its quota. The next year the Assembly regulated the traffic in substitutes by allowing a draftee to free himself by paying a fine of 10 pounds, money to be used to hire a replacement. The relatively well-to-do members of the militia troops—notorious for being "uncertain and disaffected" draftees—regularly hired substitutes. In 1757 the Assembly had worried that a 10-pound fine might not hold draftees to their duty; two years later, it made the payment a legal way to escape service and shift the burden to men who wanted the money.[21]

The unprecedented demand for five thousand soldiers in 1758 and 1759 revealed serious weaknesses in the impressment system: the draft created the most problems when it was most necessary. The Assembly had to balance its need for soldiers against its extreme reluctance to strain its authority or to antagonize men who might, with proper encouragement, be induced to volunteer. It had reason to suspect there might be difficulty with impressment in 1758. An East Haddam captain had reported in September 1757 that many of the militiamen he had drafted for the August alarm had refused to serve, and he had insisted that if violators were not "dealt with according to law and justice," men would "take the same liberty" the next time and impressment would collapse. In 1758 and again in 1759, the Assembly resurrected a method it had first used

---

from training with the militia since 1660. On recruiting Indians, see CA-Ind:II/102.

21. On substitutes, see CA-War:VIII/105, 201; CPR:XII/224–26; and CSL-Giles Wolcott. On Loudoun's opinion, see CO-5:I/981 (quotation). On Captain Samuel Gilbert's complaint in Hebron, see CHS-JT/29 May 1758. On militia troopers, see CHS-FIW:II/555, 742; and CHS-JT/4 Jun 1758 (quotation). Despite complaints about the erosion of the troopers' privileges, the Lower House rejected an Upper House attempt to prevent them from being drafted for service on foot (CA-Mil:2,I/477–8).

in 1711, which had also been a year of heavy demand after several years of great exertion. It ordered all militiamen between the ages of sixteen and seventy to attend a special company muster where anyone present, or who was "found within the limits" of the company, could be impressed; veterans were to be drafted first because they were "likely to be the most serviceable." It enacted no special penalties to compel men to attend the muster, and hoped that popular enthusiasm for the campaign would ensure compliance. But so many men failed to attend that in October 1758 it passed a law directing the king's attorney in each county to apprehend and prosecute delinquents as well as the draftees who refused to serve. It did not impose any additional fines or threaten them with jail terms because it wanted to induce them to volunteer.[22]

The patchwork of volunteers, draftees, and substitutes created an army between 1758 and 1760 with many different kinds of soldiers, especially since there seem to have been more substitutes in the ranks, as well as more men who remained draftees, than in prior years. Of six draftees from Hebron in May 1758, three volunteered, one hired a substitute, and two went to war as draftees. In April 1759 a company in Lebanon supplied eighteen volunteers, six draftees, and two "pairs," that is, two men who each served half the campaign. Men were so scarce in Windsor in 1759 that forty-six members of the First Militia Company offered additional money to attract volunteers on condition that their sons and servants were not drafted. The offer was not wholly effective: ten men volunteered, but six were impressed.[23]

The most difficult year for impressment seems to have been 1759. Just as the draft was starting in April, Governor Fitch reported to imperial officials that compulsory service was "extremely distressing to many and is so disagreeable to all." The following May he told Amherst that, "considering the many difficulties and very great inquietudes" that had attended impressment in 1759, "and the ill success of former attempts of

22. On the need to enforce the draft, in the words of Captain Daniel Cone, see CHS-FIW:I/64 (quotation). On the impressment musters in 1758–59, see CA-War:VII/147 (quotation); CA-War:VIII/136; and CPR:XI/121–22, 224–26 (quotations). The upper age limit for militia eligibility had been lowered to fifty in 1736 (CPR:VIII/36). On laws against delinquents, see CPR:XI/174–75, 256–57. On draftees who did not serve, see CHC:IX/185; and CHC:X/39–40. On prosecutions, see CHS-FIW:II/564, 750; and CHS-JT/9 and 12 Jan 1760.

23. On Hebron, see CHS-JT/29 May 1758. On Lebanon, see CHS-FIW:II/737. On Windsor, see Stiles, *Windsor,* p. 346.

that kind, [the Assembly] judged that some further [financial] encouragements would not only better attain the end proposed, but prevent the difficulties consequent thereon, and also better promote His Majesty's service." Bitter experience confirmed the leaders in their belief that financial incentives were "likely to effect as much as could possibly be done by all the exertions of authority and compulsion last year for the King's service."[24]

The Assembly knew that impressment had to be grounded in a community consensus that men should be forced to serve: a government based on popular consent had to shape its military commitments to what its constituents would bear. After the fall of Quebec, it no longer had the moral authority to force its constituents into the service. A military system that had begun as a way of protecting settlers on an exposed frontier completed its final transformation in March 1760 when the Assembly renounced impressment, a position to which it would adhere for the rest of the war. Although there was a "considerable deficiency in the levies" in May, it did not authorize a draft. It dismissed all pretense of using impressment to approximate the militia ideal of universal service, and gladly paid poor men to join the army. The Assembly stuck to its position in 1762 when it refused to draft 575 men for the regulars because doing so "may be attended with many great difficulties." The leaders left it to Governor Fitch to explain to Amherst "in some most inoffensive and unexceptionable manner" why they rejected an idea "so reluctant to our genius and constitution as well as unpromising in its consequences."[25]

The inefficiency of raising troops anew each year was so apparent by late 1758 that the idea of "keeping up a standing army" became "a matter of some dispute among the people." This was a new notion in Connecticut, and at odds with both the ideal of a universal-service militia and the tradition of raising expeditionary troops annually by bounty. A standing army was more than a problem in military organization, since it also provided the terms in which people tried to understand whether their

---

24. On problems with impressment in 1759, see CHC:XVIII/14, 66, 75 (quotations from all three).

25. On the refusal to impress, see CHC:XVIII/14, 62–68, 73–76; and CPR:XI/121–22, 224–26. On deficiencies in 1760, see CPR:XI/387 (quotation). On drafting for the regulars in 1762, see CHC:XVIII/190–91, 199; WO-34:XXVIII/87, 181, 187; CA-War:IX/289; CPR:XI/622–24 (quotation); and CPR:XII/17. Without a draft, all Amherst could do was ask Colonel Whiting to encourage Connecticut men to enlist in the regulars (YU-MS:Whiting/1).

society was becoming more like Britain's, and whether or not that was a good thing. The fullest public debate about the issue of a standing army appeared in the *New London Summary* during the winter of 1758–59.[26]

There were good arguments in favor of a standing army. An author who signed himself "A. P." insisted on 29 December that keeping troops under arms through the winter would enable them to take the field sooner in the spring. An earlier start would give the French less time to reinforce the Champlain valley and thus make a British advance easier. More time to train would make the "raw, undisciplined" colonial soldiers "more like regular troops, and so more fit for duty." The longer the recruits practiced "at their calling," the better soldiers they would be. (General Lyman would complain in September 1759 that "it is a mean farce to pretend to make a soldier in the way we are in in constituting our troops.") "A. P." even claimed that the expense of maintaining the troops for four months between campaigns could be turned to profit. Although he admitted that half-pay for the soldiers over the winter of 1758–59 cost more than it had to raise the regiments that spring (a situation which would change as bounties rose in and after 1759), he insisted that the money "only changes hands, and so is no loss to the community in general." If the imperial government paid to billet the troops during the winter, the colony would earn 8,000 pounds sterling, money which "we very much want."[27]

The response offered by "Rank and File" on 2 February 1759 ignored the many practical objections to this scheme in favor of tendentious arguments clearly influenced by his admiration for the colonial success at Louisbourg in 1745. He denied that there was any "deficiency in the colonies, or their troops," certainly none which could be corrected by maintaining a standing army. He acknowledged "that practice . . . makes perfect," but contended that a lengthy term of enlistment (up to four years had been suggested) would not produce a trained army. Neither would training over the winter: "as to the great advantages . . . to be had in winter quarters, . . . it is what I never heard of before, except it

26. Quotations are from *Summary,* 29 Dec 1758 ("A. P.") and 2 Feb 1759 ("Rank and File"). Imperial commanders accepted the fact that New England raised troops for a year at a time. Loudoun also knew he could not march them "out of the limits . . . they will willingly go to" (MHS-IW/1 Feb 1757).

27. General Winslow had wanted to keep the best soldiers of 1756 in service through 1757 (MHS:IW/28 Aug 1756). On Lyman, see CHC:XVIII/27 (quotation).

were for service amongst the ladies." He claimed that recruiting officers could never find enough men willing to enlist for four years, "not even if they should take old and young and such as would be fit for no good purpose at all," and that those who did enlist would lack the enthusiasm of "those brave youths of good families" who enlisted for a summer's campaign. Instead of a standing army, he suggested that "our militia ought to be better taken care of, and our levies completed sooner," but he proposed no way of doing so.

Better objections to a standing army derived from the character of Connecticut society. Although five thousand men might be spared during the winter, agriculture would suffer what "Rank and File" termed "the greatest distress imaginable" if so many men were absent during the early spring planting season. A standing army, moreover, would strain the fragile fabric of authority in society. If most of the men refused to stay in the field (and there was every indication they would not serve for more than a summer at a time), what would the Assembly do? It had no institutional means of punishing such massive disobedience. Rather than risk the consensus that made government work, it accepted the inefficiency of raising troops each year. As long as the imperial government subsidized raising troops by bounty, it would continue to raise its regiments each year, albeit from among many, if not most, of the same men who had served the previous year. There was no incentive to change the military system. The argument against a colonial standing army was clinched by the presence of large numbers of British regulars, which eliminated the need for any colony to keep its own men constantly under arms. Although a colonial standing army would presumably have been underwritten by Britain, opponents do not seem to have worried that these subsidies might erode civil liberties; that ideological debate blossomed only after the war.[28]

28. From the start, the Assembly had worried about how raising troops might disrupt agriculture (CHC:XVII/146). In late June 1763, Governor Fitch gave General Amherst the best explanation of how Connecticut men understood military service. Two winter companies had been enlisted to serve until 1 July, and Amherst now argued that military necessity required him to keep them beyond their time. Fitch responded that "such an unexpected disappointment will excite considerable uneasiness among them [the soldiers], especially as they will apt to view it as an infraction made of the public faith, and to consider themselves as not further holden by their contracts, which were understood, if not expressed, to be limited to the 1st July" (CHC:XVIII/244). On anxiety to return home, see CHC:XVIII/147–48. On the understanding of enlistment in general, see

Arguing against a standing army distorted Connecticut's understanding of how the war was won. "Rank and File" contended that the length of enlistment had nothing to do with military success. Although he claimed to have "a high esteem" for British regulars, and to "look upon them in their proper place, as second to none," he insisted "that in some cases in our American wars, their brethren of New England are as good as they." As evidence of colonial prowess, he cited the capture of Louisbourg in 1745 and the defeat of the French at Lake George in 1755. In contrast, the slaughter of the regulars under Braddock in 1755, the capture of Oswego in 1756, and the sack of Fort William Henry in 1757 were embarrassing failures. But "Rank and File" did not mention that the colonial victories owed as much to luck as to skill, and that short-service colonial troops rarely had the endurance to consolidate and expand the advantages they won. Nor did he realize that a military system based on annual enlistments could not have developed and maintained the logistical apparatus that was the key to William Pitt's strategy against Canada. Smaller numbers of longer-service colonial soldiers, trained to move quickly and powerfully over long distances, would have been a more effective and less costly way of waging war. But because Connecticut's military heritage was based on limited service by citizen soldiers, the leaders chose to raise troops in ways they thought placed the least strain on their society. They endured the inefficiency of annual recruiting because it was socially acceptable. They wanted, and got, poor men to serve willingly in their army.

Their success in raising troops annually by bounty deluded the leaders into applying that experience the next time they created an army, in 1775, although they momentarily forgot the crucial role British subsidies had played in that success. Their achievements during the final French and Indian war reinforced strong political reasons for not invoking impressment or requiring long-term enlistments. Theoretically, free men did not have to be compelled to fight to preserve their liberties, and the inherent abilities of American soldiers would bring a quick victory over a mercenary standing army. The leaders realized that patriots might need financial incentives to see clearly where their duty lay, but they did not understand that they would have to raise their own American standing army to win a conflict of a scope, cost, and complexity they could not begin to imagine. They did not readily abandon the system that had carried them through

Anderson, "Contractual Principles." On the ideology of military service, see Cress, *Citizens in Arms*.

the final French war, and it did help them survive the first year of the Revolution. But the shortcomings of a voluntary system almost proved fatal to the cause of American independence.

THE SOLDIERS

The final French and Indian war imposed an unprecedented strain on Connecticut society. While the war, far away on the New York frontier, was not as traumatic as the earlier conflicts with local Indians or the emergencies in western Massachusetts, the demand for troops was the largest the colony had yet encountered. The leaders worked hard each year to find enormous numbers of expeditionary troops, and succeeded in raising "a greater proportion of our inhabitants than is voted by any other government." The maximum commitment came in 1758–60, when the 5,000 expeditionary soldiers the Assembly authorized each year amounted to a quarter of the colony's 20,000 militiamen. Only Massachusetts reached this level, in 1758, when it voted to raise 7,000 expeditionary soldiers and employed 2,500 more men to defend its trade, its settlements in Nova Scotia, and its inland frontier, a total of 25 percent of its 37,500 militiamen. By doing more than its share to help conquer Canada, Connecticut earned what the historian Lawrence H. Gipson termed "the most highly creditable record" of any of the colonies. But it had not been easy.[29]

Raising its own regiments was not the full extent of the burden. In addition to 3,000 of its own expeditionary troops in 1755, the Assembly allowed Massachusetts and New York to recruit 600 men in Connecticut, sent 75 men to guard western Massachusetts, and pledged another 300 men for a colonial regular regiment, the start of a small but steady contribution to the regulars. In 1757, although the number of expeditionary troops was the lowest of the war (1,400 men), calling out 5,000 militiamen for two weeks in August turned more Connecticut men into temporary soldiers at one time than ever before. Last but not least were the

29. The comment about Connecticut's proportion was made by Governor Fitch in March 1759 (CHC:XVII/210; CHC:XVIII/10 (quotation); CPR:X/623; and CPR:XI/630). Returns of the thirteen militia regiments totaled 20,043 men in 1756 and 20,264 men in 1762 (YU-ES:Misc/299). On Massachusetts in 1758, see Anderson, *People's Army,* pp. 59–60n82; and Pitt, *Correspondence,* I/164. The best summary of imperial attitudes about Connecticut is Gipson, *Victorious,* pp. 156–57, 213, 233–34, 310–13, 328 (quotation).

men who ran the army's logistical lifelines. The number employed is not known, but it is clear that collecting and transporting supplies each summer between 1755 and 1762 was the largest such task Connecticut had ever undertaken. Governor Fitch reported to London in April 1759 that the demands were almost insupportable: "Considerable numbers of effective men had enlisted into His Majesty's regular troops; numbers also were engaged and engaging as battoe men, drivers of teams, and others by large bounties were drawing off into the pay of the neighboring governments, which would yet further weaken this colony with respect to men fit and proper for the service."[30]

The Assembly displayed considerable confidence in voting to raise so many expeditionary troops. In 1746 it had raised 1,000 soldiers in a colony of 100,000 people. Twelve years later, it wanted five times that number from a population that had grown to roughly 135,000 people. It did so for two reasons. First, it knew the colony's real military potential was greater than the number of militiamen because muster rolls undercounted the number of men who might serve, especially apprentices, servants, blacks, Indians, and transients. More importantly, it realized that a substantial number of men could be induced to enlist for a relatively small financial incentive. Expanding on its experience in 1745–46, the Assembly gambled that a military system based on raising troops by bounty could meet the larger demands. Its forecast proved correct, and it came very close to raising the number of troops it wanted in each year before 1760, when the demand was too high in a year when the war was winding down. Connecticut could raise a maximum of about 4,500 men (1758) through a combination of enthusiasm, bounties, and impressment, about 2,200 men (1761–62) by bounties alone (table 5.4). Company officers commonly recruited in adjacent towns, and usually managed to find 85 percent or more of their quotas. Company strength could vary considerably, depending upon the skill of the recruiters. In 1760, for example, it ranged from 34 to 97 men; no company reached the desired level of 105 men. The Assembly generally gathered the companies recruited in one region into a single regiment, although it did combine companies raised up to sixty miles apart to complete a regiment.[31]

30. On the 3,975 men in 1755, see CHC:IX/88; CHC:XVII/161; and *Gazette,* 14 Jun 1755. On the effort in 1757, see CHC:I/325; CHC:XVII/348–49; and CPR:X/623. Fitch's comment is in CHC:XVIII/14 (quotation). The Royal Navy also wanted to recruit in Connecticut (CHC:XVII/15; and *Gazette,* 7 Apr 1759).

31. On the number and organization of the troops, see the source note for

Table 5.4
Number and Organization of Troops, 1755–62

Year	Authorized	Raised	Regiments/ Companies	Average per Company		
				Desired	Actual	Range
1755	3,000	3,028 (101%)	4/36	83	84	59–93
1756	2,500	2,339 (94%)	4/32	78	73	63–78
1757	1,400	1,340 (96%)	1/14	100	96	92–98
1758	5,000	4,309 (86%)	4/48	105	90	58–101
1759	5,000	4,183 (84%)	4/50	100	Not known	
1760	5,000	3,229 (65%)	4/48	105	67	34–97
1761	2,300	2,221 (97%)	2/24	95	93	84–98
1762	2,300	2,209 (96%)	2/24	95	92	59–134
Total		22,858 enlistments				

Sources: CPR:X/344–45, 469–70, 598–99; CPR:XI/92–93, 221–23, 349–51, 480–82, 613–15; CA-War:V/205–46; CA-War:VI/282–314; CA-War:VII/75–88, 140; CA-War:VIII/6–55, 93, 102, 327; CA-War:IX/1–49, 193–214; and CA-War:X/2–53.

The proportion of veterans also varied widely, despite additional bounties for experienced soldiers (table 5.5). The recruiting of veterans began poorly: only 43 percent of the soldiers in 1756 had served in 1755. It was not much better the next year (55 percent), even though the numbers required were much reduced. The range of experience subsumed under the term "veteran" can be seen in Captain Benadam Gallop's company in 1757. Fifty-two of its 91 men had served before (57 percent), 6 in King George's War, and 46 in 1755 and 1756 (19 in both years). The proportion of veterans was probably lowest in the greatly expanded army of 1758, but only fragmentary information has survived. Captain David

---

table 5.4. The census counted 130,612 people in 1756 (CPR:X/617–18), 146,519 people in 1762 (Bickford, "Census"). Muster rolls are within 1 percent of the number of men reported to London, except in 1755 when they contain 4 percent fewer men. Amherst reported 3,397 men in 1760, a 5 percent increase (Beer, *Policy*, p. 65). For enlistment documents, see CHC:XVII/302–03. On recruiting, see CHC:IX/188–89; CHC:X/39–40, 48–49, 155–56, 160–62; and CHC:XVIII/160–89. The Lower House wanted five regiments in 1756 and 1758 (CA-War:VI/37; CA-War:VII/147, 149), presumably to increase the number of officers it could appoint. In 1759, the Upper House wanted three regiments to reduce costs (CA-War:VIII/145).

Table 5.5
Veterans, 1756–57, 1760–61

Year	Total Number	Total Veterans	Percent
1756	2,339	1,011	43%
1757	1,340	740	55%
1760	3,229	2,384	74%
1761	2,221	1,883	85%

Sources: See table 5.4.

Waterbury's company from Fairfield county may have been typical: only a third of its 100 men had been in the service in previous years. In 1759 the Assembly hoped that extra bounties for "the old troops" would induce most able-bodied veterans to reenlist; apparently they did so, although evidence is again fragmentary. While the percentage of veterans increased in subsequent years, the companies were also undergoing constant replenishment. Three-quarters of the soldiers in 1760 were veterans, but the remaining quarter (850 men) enlisted for the first time. The next year, 15 percent (340 men) were first-time soldiers. By 1762, according to Colonel Nathan Whiting, there was "no want of men" and he thought it a "pity" that "new young lads should go." Connecticut was very fortunate that the number of men who wanted to earn bounties and wages always rose fast enough to fill the companies to an acceptable level.[32]

About 16,000 men filled the 23,000 enlistments in the expeditionary regiments, an average of about one-and-a-half enlistments per man, an estimate based on the experience of the 1,100 from the Twelfth Militia Regiment who served in the army. The total was roughly 12 percent of the colony's population, the highest level of military participation since the frontier emergencies of Queen Anne's War fifty years earlier, and well

32. On veterans in 1756, see CHC:IX/104, 123–24. Percentages are averages: in 1756, companies were from 21 percent to 65 percent veteran. The descriptive roll of Gallop's company in 1757 is apparently the only surviving one for men in Connecticut service. On Waterbury's company, see YU-MS:Waterbury/7 Oct 1758. Figures from his company show the wisdom of enlisting veterans who might be enured to camp diseases. Of thirty-three men who had been in service, one had died and none were sick. Of sixty-seven men who were new to the army, five had died and eighteen were sick. On veterans in 1759, see CHC:XVIII/10 (quotation). In 1761 Whiting incorrectly thought that "one third per annum were new raised troops" (Stiles, *Itineraries,* p. 104). On his comments in 1762, see CHS-JT/5 May and 14 Jul 1762 (quotations).

over the modern standard of 10 percent for a people's war. If eligible men were 20 percent of the population, then 60 percent of them served in the army at least once during the war; the total burden was actually greater since these percentages do not take into account the men who enlisted in the regulars, supplied the logistical support, or served only in the 1757 alarm. The investment of manpower over eight years was enormous, the largest of the colonial period; only the trauma of eight years of a revolutionary war would make the burden seem light in retrospect. Because muster rolls are incomplete (less than 40 percent for 1760, for example; table 5.8 [p. 190]), patterns of service must be estimated. Conservatively, three-quarters of the 16,000 men served once, while a quarter served from two to nine times; the true situation probably included more men who served two or three times, perhaps as many as 45 percent of the total. Most men who served several times did so in 1755–56 or 1758–60, but a few enlisted every chance they got.[33]

Patterns of service can be examined more closely in several ways. Jonathan Trumbull, who was colonel of the Twelfth Regiment in addition to his other duties and activities, preserved records that cast light on the experience of men from the four towns in his regiment, especially in 1755. Colchester, East Haddam, Hebron, and Lebanon stretched east from the Connecticut River into Windham county, and were average in population and wealth for Connecticut towns. They seem to have raised soldiers in ways that were more typical of the colony's rural, agricultural society than did larger, more economically diversified, and more prosperous towns like Hartford, New Haven, and New London. In 1755, the four Colchester companies sent seventy-seven men into the service of three colonies, including eighteen into the original Connecticut regiments in March and a total of forty into the two reinforcements in May and August (table 5.6). The number of volunteers from each company varied greatly, due more it

33. On soldiers from the Twelfth Regiment, see CHC:IX/81–82, 86–87, 122–23, 147–49, 160–62, 188–89, 255–59; and CHC:X/176–78, 355. The percentage of the population that went to war varied among the towns in the regiment, from 8 percent in East Haddam to 13 percent in Lebanon. The number of militiamen was about 15 percent of the population, or fifteen hundred men, the number reported in 1756 and 1762 (YU-ES:Misc/299). The average for the thirteen regiments was 1,559 men if the oversize First Regiment (3,216 men) is included, 1,421 men if it is omitted. For examples of long-service veterans, see CA-War:VIII/312; CA-War:IX/187; CA-War:X/153, 251; and *Gazette*, 20 June 1761.

Table 5.6
Soldiers from Colchester, 1755

Colony	Militia Companies				Total
	North	*South*	*Westchester*	*New Salem*	
Connecticut					
March	2*	9†	1	6*	18
May	4	1	9	0	14
August	7	9‡	1	9	26
Subtotals	13	19	11	15	58 (75%)
Massachusetts	1*	8	3	2	14 (18%)
New York	3	0	1	1	5 (6%)
Total	17	27	15	18	77

Sources: CHS:IX/86–87; and CPR:X/617–18.
Note: The population of Colchester in 1756 included 2,228 whites and 84 blacks, for a total of 2,312 people. The 77 soldiers were 22 percent of the towns's roughly 350 militiamen.
*Includes one Indian.
†Plus Ensign James Jones.
‡Includes two blacks.

seems to personal connections than to any other factor. When Ensign James Jones of the South Company went to war in March 1755, nine neighbors went with him. Of the nine men from the Westchester Company who enlisted in May, three came from one family and two from another. All across the colony, it was common for relatives to enlist together. For example, among sixty-four privates in Captain David Lacey's company from Fairfield company in 1756 were three pairs of brothers, two sets of three brothers, and one father-son pair. Captain Robert Durkee's company from Windham county in 1762 contained three father-son pairs; two sons deserted before the troops embarked for Havana, but the three fathers and the third son died in Cuba.[34]

The surviving muster rolls also make it possible to track patterns of service in one company through several years, and show that officers who

34. On the soldiers from Colchester, see CHC:IX/86–87; and CPR:X/617–18. On relatives serving together, see CHC:IX/154–55, CHC:X/313–15; and CPR:XI/312–13. Eliakim Perry, a resident of Norwich who had served at Louisbourg in 1745, sent two of his seven sons into the final French war; his youngest son, who had only been five years old in 1755, was by 1772 a convicted counterfeiter (CA-CM:V/360–61).

served for several years generated a following among the soldiers. For example, John Durkee of Norwich, a lieutenant in 1756 and 1757, commanded a company for five years (1758–62), the first year as a captain and then as a major with responsibilities for both his own company and the entire regiment. A total of 336 men filled the 468 enlistments in the five incarnations of his company, for an average of 1.4 enlistments per man. Over half the soldiers (182 men) came from the sixty-five families that sent at least two of its members to war under Durkee. Seventy-three percent (247 men) served once, 17 percent (57 men) twice, and 10 percent (32 men, the core of Durkee's following) three or more times. A few examples show the patterns of service that were at the core of his companies. Both Samuel Anderson, one of three Andersons, and Lebbeus Armstrong, one of six Armstrongs, enlisted for four consecutive years (1758–1761); Samuel wound up as a sergeant and Lebbeus as a drummer. James Williams, one of four Williams, enlisted in 1758 and was joined the next year by his brother Isaac; they reenlisted as privates each year through 1762, when both died at Havana. James Strange was even more of a professional colonial soldier. He had been a private at Louisbourg in 1745 and served in five campaigns (1755–56, 1758–60), the last three with Durkee, before being killed by a cannon shot on the St. Lawrence in 1760; he left a pregnant widow and two children.[35]

The evidence indicates that soldiers came from the same mix of social and economic backgrounds as in prior wars, with the preponderance of young unmarried men of limited economic means typical of recent expeditions. The soldiers ranged in age and marital status from young bachelors to middle-aged family men, with most being unmarried men in their mid-twenties. The median age of 27 Fairfield county soldiers in 1756, for example, was twenty-three years; they included two fifteen-year-olds and one fifty-year-old. The soldiers from New Haven between 1755 and 1757 (a total of 342 men) had a median age of twenty-four years; over 40 percent were already married, while another 50 percent were still bachelors but would marry one day. The evidence is limited, but it seems that the ages of the soldiers remained roughly constant as the war continued. In Captain Benadam Gallop's company from New London county in 1757, the median age of the 91 soldiers was twenty-one years. In Captain Timothy Northam's company of 57 Connecticut men in New York pay in

35. Durkee's muster rolls are in CHC:X/65–66, 163–64, 216, 241–43, 301–03. Anderson, Armstrong, and James Williams first served in the Fort William Henry alarm in August 1757. On Strange, see CA-War:VIII/312.

1762, it was twenty-three years. (The median height in both companies was five feet, eight inches.) The soldiers were overwhelmingly born in Connecticut, 93 percent in Gallop's company (including 24 Indians and 2 blacks) and 81 percent in Northam's company; the rest were from England, Ireland, and the other colonies. Newspaper advertisements for deserters indicate that a few Irishmen, Englishmen, and men identified only as "transients" were present as early as 1756. A few more foreign-born served in later years, but never in the numbers found in New York companies, where it was not uncommon for a majority of soldiers in a company to be foreign-born. Foreign-born Connecticut soldiers were no less faithful than their native-born colleagues; desertion rates were generally in proportion to the total number of each group in the army.[36]

Connecticut soldiers depended on their labor to support themselves and their families, and viewed military service as an alternate form of employment. Most were farmers, husbandmen, and laborers (the terms overlapped and were not used with precision). The rest were artisans who helped run a rural, agricultural economy, including blacksmiths, wheelwrights, joiners, coopers, carpenters, masons, shoemakers, tailors, ropemakers, and distillers; sailors enlisted in companies raised along the seacoast. While masters could refuse to allow their servants to go to war, many servants and apprentices apparently did volunteer; the total number is not known because they did not have to record their status on the muster roll. Minors (men under the age of twenty-one) also volunteered, and at least one was drafted, in 1757.[37]

36. On the Fairfield soldiers, see CHC:IX/154–55; and Jacobus, *Fairfield.* The average age of the New Haven men was between twenty-five and twenty-seven years; a lower average for the middle half, roughly twenty-four years, indicates a disproportionate number of older men (Jacobus, *New Haven,* pp. 242–48, 485–97). On Northam's company, see CHC:X/349–50. Deserters in 1761 ranged from nineteen to forty-five years old (*Gazette,* 21 Jun and 16 May 1761). The most difficult moment for a married soldier was learning his wife was dead at home. Robert Webster called it "the worst news that I ever heard in all my life" (Webster, "Journal," II/140). For descriptions of deserters, see *Gazette,* 29 May, 19 Jun, 3 Jul 1756, 12 Feb 1757, 17 May, 21 Jun, 12 Jul 1760, 4 Apr, 16 May, 12 Sep 1761, 29 May 1762; *Summary,* 11 Jul 1760; 12 Jun 1761; and CHC:X/222, 351. In Northam's company, forty-six men were born in Connecticut, four elsewhere in New England, four in England, and three in Ireland. On the New York companies, see New-York Historical Society, *Rolls,* XXIV/60ff.

37. Men who petitioned the Assembly for relief often said they had only

Military service was always open to members of the two ethnic groups on the bottom of society. Indians were important in some companies from southeast Connecticut, not because of any special military skills, but because they volunteered in large numbers. Ten of 63 men (16 percent) in a company raised in Norwich in 1756 had recognizably Indian names; 24 of 91 men (26 percent) in Gallop's company in 1757 were Indians. They were not good soldiers. They continually got drunk, behavior that doubtless contributed to their high mortality rate. Black men, both slave and free, also enlisted, but their numbers are difficult to determine. In 1756, the year the census counted 3,019 black people in the colony, there were 25 soldiers with names like Prince Negro, Jupiter Negro, and Solomon Scipio in the regiments, roughly 1 percent of the total. More black men undoubtedly served, but they are impossible to distinguish by name alone. An advertisement for deserters, for example, described twenty-three-year-old Hezekiah Wright of Norwich as a "molatto," but the fact that he was a black man is evident nowhere else in the record. Blacks actually ran more risks than did whites or Indians. Prince Goodin, a free black who was captured while serving as a sailor on Lake George in 1757, was sold as a slave and labored for three years until the fall of Montreal allowed him to return home.[38]

There were many reasons why men volunteered for military service. In the first years, patriotism played an important role. Twenty-one-year-old Abijah Ives, Jr., of Wallingford enlisted in 1756 "with the same good

"their own labor to depend on" (CA-War:VI/105; CA-War:VIII/178, 307; CA-War:IX/168; and CA-War:X/157, 253). For the variety of occupations, see CA-War:IX/160; CA-War:X/270, 279, 284; and *Gazette,* 5 and 20 Jun 1761. On apprentices, see CA-War:X/268; and CHC:IX/19–20. On refusing to allow a servant to enlist in 1758, see CHC:X/40. In 1760 a master collected the wages of his two apprentice soldiers (CSL-Hitchcock). On minors, see CA-War:VIII/175; CA-War:IX/156, 307; CA-War:X/150, 243, 270; Israel Webster, Windham:1756/4059; and Samuel Edwards, Windham:1760/1273. For the drafted minor, Lucius Allis of Somers, see CA-War:VIII/248.

38. On the Indians, see CHC:IX/113–14; CPR:XI/60–61; and CSL-Gallop. On indiscipline when "the devil got into our Indians," see Fitch, "Diary," I/240–41, 181, III/44, VII/93. Mortality could devastate a small tribe: the Western Niantics lost seven of its eighteen men during the war (Conkey, Boissevain, and Goddard, "Indians," in Trigger, *Handbook,* p. 185). The three black men were from Colchester, and served together in Captain Noah Grant's company (CHC:IX/122–23). On Wright, see *Summary,* 11 Jul 1760. On Goodin, see CA-War:IX/147.

and generous views for his country that . . . his fellow soldiers had, and proceeded on his march with the same zeal and resolution." Sometimes the reasons were personal. Lucius Allis, a minor from Somers, volunteered in 1757 because his relatives on the frontier were "being destroyed by the enemy and carried into a long captivity." Negro Ben, an African-born slave, volunteered "under an expectation of thereby obtaining his freedom, of which however by some means he was disappointed." Military service offered disgruntled or adventuresome young men in their teens a way to widen their world and escape from burdensome surroundings. Nineteen-year-old Joshua Hatch of New London, for example, had been apprenticed to Amos Robinson of Lebanon to learn to be a tailor. He had enlisted in 1762 and had not returned to his master as of 4 March 1763. Some men enlisted to escape punishment. James Thomas of New Haven, who was fined 10 pounds for refusing to serve when drafted in 1758, enlisted in 1759 because town leaders offered to forgive the fine if he volunteered. Zephaniah Spicer enlisted in 1756 to win release from the New London county jail, where he was serving a life sentence for counterfeiting bills of credit. Efforts to escape punishment could also work against the colony. A veteran of six campaigns enlisted in New York in 1761 rather than face two years of servitude for nonpayment of a debt in Connecticut.[39]

Most men had some economic motive for enlisting, but not all soldiers were permanently poor men. Poverty was a relative term in Connecticut, where poor men who sought to improve their economic circumstances had many options and opportunities. Many soldiers were young men waiting for a chance; war gave them one such opportunity. John Porter, Jr., the youngest son of a Stratford militia ensign, enlisted in 1758 to earn money before inheriting land and property from his father. Wolsey Scott of Wa-

39. On Ives, see CA-War:VI/117. On Allis, see CA-War:VIII/248. On Negro Ben, also known as Ben Dawson, see CA-Mis:2,I/80. He had been imported from Africa, been sold several times in Connecticut, served as a soldier in the war, been sold to a man named Dawson who moved to Philadelphia, and been manumitted by Dawson's widow; he was living in Lebanon in May 1803. On Hatch, see *Summary,* 4 Mar 1763. On Thomas, see NHT:III/747. On Spicer, see CA-CM:IV/278, 281; and CPR:X/520. On the absconding veteran, Daniel Wording, see *Gazette,* 20 Jun 1761; CHC:IX/68–69, 106, 220; and New-York Historical Society, *Rolls,* XXIV/388–89. The Assembly freed Hugh Gallespie, a transient Irishmen and counterfeiter, from the Hartford county jail, but required him to enlist in the regulars or the Royal Navy because he had no family in Connecticut to guarantee his good behavior (CA-CM:V/36–37; and CPR:X/535–36).

terbury volunteered in 1760 to earn cash "to make some beginning on a small farm left him" by his dead father. Other men volunteered for later campaigns so they could march through northern New York and southern Vermont, regions which were being opened for settlement and to which many wanted to emigrate after the war. Some soldiers used every opportunity to make money; a few even spent rare days of rest working for the contractors who built the forts along the line of march in the upper Hudson and Lake Champlain valleys.[40]

Military service was not the easiest way to earn money, and many men found pitfalls on the road to getting ahead. Porter did not live to collect his patrimony; he reenlisted in 1760 and died at Albany. Like many others, Scott contracted smallpox and incurred debts for medical treatment "which he sees no way to pay but by selling some part of his said small patrimony." Twenty-six men, "mostly of the younger sort," from Eastbury, an outlying parish in Glastonbury, died in the war and never got the chance to emigrate; their deaths were an enormous loss for a town of only eleven hundred people. Three soldiers who were falsely accused of arson on the way home in 1756 were bankrupted by court costs. Even men who worked for the army were sometimes disappointed. Teamsters were angered in 1758 when they were paid for only five days a week instead of the usual seven; they claimed they were "generally poor men . . . in debt, and took that method to get out of debt."[41]

Men who were willing to serve as substitutes always found a ready market among more affluent draftees. In 1759, for example, four veterans were hired by members of the Second Troop of Horse in the Twelfth Regiment who had no intention of going to war themselves. Finding a substitute sometimes involved coercion. One master, "being a trooper,"

40. On Porter, see CA-CM:V/286. On Scott, see CA-War:IX/160. On the desire to examine lands in 1761, see CHC:XVIII/103, 105–08. On working as a laborer on the forts, see Fitch, "Diary," II/174; Israel Webster, Windham:1756/4059; and Samuel Edwards, Windham:1760/1273.

41. On the deaths in Eastbury, where half the land was owned by residents of the First Parish, see CA-Ecc:XII/291 (quotation). On the population of Glastonbury in 1756, see CPR:XIV/492. On accusations of arson, see CA-War:VI/280; and CA-War:X/290. A farmer who had a "comfortable living" enlisted in 1758, became an invalid, and ended up indigent (CA-War:X/284). On the teamsters, see *Gazette,* 30 Dec 1758 (quotation); of the thirteen, four had served in the expeditionary regiments in 1755 and two in the militia in the alarm in 1757. On veterans as teamsters, see also Fitch, "Diary," VIII/46.

insisted in 1758 that his sixteen-year-old servant enlist as a substitute for a member of the troop, even though the servant had already volunteered to join another company. The careers of six men who were hired as privates in Captain Henry Champion's company in 1758 show how a man might make a career of military service. Three were veterans. Jacob Strong of Colchester had been a corporal in 1756, Arthur Ackley of Colchester had been a draftee in 1757, and Orlando Mack of Hebron had been a sergeant, also in 1757. The fourth man, Lazarus Waters of Colchester, had been a teamster in 1757, the fifth, Prince Freeman of Colchester, was "a free negro" who had never served before, and the sixth, Jeremiah Congdon of Norwich was "a seafaring man, newly come home" from the sea. Only Congdon the sailor served for a single year, apparently finding life at sea more to his liking. Strong served twice (in 1756 and 1758, as well as in the 1757 alarm), Waters three times (1758–60), Ackley four times (1757–60), Freeman five times (1758–62), and Mack seven times (1756–1762), ending up as an ensign in 1762. Substitutes were even hired at the end of a campaign so a man could go home before his enlistment officially expired.[42]

Probate inventories of the men who died in service contain the most detailed information about the economic status of the soldiers. The number of probates (a total of 410, or 28 percent of the known dead) is sufficient to construct an economic profile of the soldiers (table 5.7), which clearly shows that most were, when they enlisted, near the economic bottom in Connecticut society, lower than their counterparts at Louisbourg in 1745. Nearly nine of ten had assets at or below the "subsistence-plus" level, with 60 percent at or below "subsistence." The ambitious and the destitute had found military service increasingly attractive since 1740, but there was after 1755 a greater proportion of poor and very poor men among those who thought that the regiments offered the best employment available, a reality that differed from both the militia ideal of universal service and the idealization of an army of free men who joined together to protect their liberty and property.[43]

42. On two substitutes in Fairfield in 1757, see CHC:IX/179. On the Second Troop, see CHC:X/178. On a substitute hired by a deserter, see CA-War:IX/254. On the servant, Nathaniel Taylor of Colchester, see CHS-FIW:II/597. On the six substitutes, see CHS-FIW:II/597 (quotations). On 14 October 1759 a soldier went home after hiring "a man to take his place" (Webster, "Journal," p. 145).

43. On categories of wealth in table 5.7 are from Main, *Society*, p. 163; they

Table 5.7
Economic Status of Soldiers, 1755–62

Year	Known Dead	Probates Found	Standard of Living			
			Subsistence	Subsistence-Plus	Comfort-able	Well-off
1755	113	31 (27%)	11 (35%)	15 (48%)	4	1
1756	189	48 (25%)	34 (71%)	10 (21%)	3	1
1757	66	10 (15%)	8 (80%)	1 (10%)	1	0
1758	222	66 (30%)	37 (56%)	17 (26%)	8	4
1759	144	38 (26%)	21 (55%)	14 (37%)	0	3
1760	241	48 (20%)	22 (46%)	20 (42%)	5	1
1761	43	10 (23%)	8 (80%)	2 (20%)	0	0
1762	427	159 (37%)	106 (67%)	40 (25%)	11	2
Totals	1,445	410 (28%)	247 (60%)	119 (29%)	32	12

Source: Probate inventories in CSL.
Note: Categories are from Main, *Society,* Appendix 4J, "Eighteenth-Century Standards for Levels of Living," p. 163.

The probate records allow a few generalizations about economic status. Monies earned in service—wages, bounties, and the small amount of prize money from Havana in 1762—were major components of many estates, in a few cases the entire estate. Rights to part of the plunder won in 1762 increased the estates of some men by more than 40 percent, although few heirs ever saw any hard cash; the wages and prize money earned by twenty-two-year-old John Norton, for example, amounted to nearly 20 pounds, or 80 percent of his estate. Almost all married and unmarried soldiers with estates under the "subsistence-plus" level owned no land; their inventories contained mainly clothing and household goods, and occasionally

take age and marital status into account. Thus, an unmarried soldier with an estate of 90 pounds lawful money fell above "subsistence-plus." The same estate placed a young married man above "subsistence." For an older married man, it meant poverty.

tools and livestock. How a man supported a wife and family on such a small estate is hard to imagine. Insolvency was most common in and after 1760, especially among married soldiers in 1762. David Case of Symsbury, for example, left his wife of twenty years and their daughter an estate of less than 6 pounds (90 percent in wages and billeting money) and debts of nearly 8 pounds. Even married men with some movable goods could be insolvent. Thomas Fox of Glastonbury left an estate of nearly 77 pounds, but after the costs of administration and payments to his wife, less than 30 pounds remained to pay debts of 73 pounds. Land significantly increased the value of an estate. Joshua Matson, a twenty-six-year-old married shoemaker from Simsbury, owned eighteen acres of meadow worth 72 pounds, and twelve acres of "plain" land worth 9 pounds, together comprising 90 percent of his estate. Some soldiers also owned rights to land in new townships in other colonies, typically in New Hampshire, but these were of nominal value.[44]

The probate records also allow speculation about some of the economic reasons that induced men to volunteer. Some unmarried young men with considerable estates were land poor, without substantial movable wealth, and probably enlisted to earn liquid assets. In 1760, twenty-year-old Benjamin Bissel of Lebanon left 150 acres of land worth 750 pounds, but

44. On soldiers whose earnings were their entire estate, see Michael Malony, Middletown:1763/2397 (18 pounds); David Morgan, New Haven:1756/7310 (7 pounds); Eliphalet Poshetous, an Indian, New London:1764/4161 (10 pounds); and Antipas Putnam, Windham:1763/3105 (10 pounds). On plunder as a large component of a soldier's estate, see Norton, Hartford:1763/3965; Benjamin Baning, New London:1763/288; John Brown, New London:1763/786; Aaron Hays, Hartford:1763/2652; Patrick Howlett, Middletown:1763/1805; and Gideon Parker, New London:1763/3972. On insolvent estates, see Case, Hartford:1763/1113; Fox, Hartford:1762/2054; Hezekiah Deming, Hartford:1757/1597; Samuel Gains, Hartford:1762/2100; Jacob Huntley, Stafford:1763/1140; Benoni Loomis, Hartford:1763/3403; Nathaniel Reddington, Stafford:1763/1772; Lemuel Vose, Norwich:1763/1111; and Ralf Wardwell, Stafford:1763/2265. On land as part of an estate, see Matson, Hartford:1762/3631; and Robert Hollister, Hartford:1763/2802. The Assembly occasionally allowed the sale of land to pay the debts of an estate (Nathan Allyn, Plainfield:1763/51; Aaron Eaton, Stafford:1763/678; Abraham Jacobs, New Haven:1760/5862; and Samuel Wardwell, Sr., Stafford:1763/2266). On land rights, see John Dorman, New Haven:1760/3579; John Johnson, Stafford:1764/1235; John Norton, Hartford:1763/3965; and Lemuel Whitmon, Hartford:1763/5959.

only 82 pounds were in movables (he boarded with a family in Lebanon during the six months he was out of service over the winter of 1759–60). Twenty-six-year-old Elnathan Smith of Killingworth was worse off in 1762: he had real estate worth 128 pounds and movables worth 137 pounds, but debts of 135 pounds. Poverty was the principal motivation driving older men into the army; unlike their younger colleagues, they had little chance of inheriting wealth to enhance their economic standing. In 1759, fifty-four-year-old John Dorman of New Haven owned 43 pounds worth of land, mostly in the new town of Sharon, but his wages (5 pounds) were his total movable estate. Thirty-year-old Jonathan Ward (1757), thirty-nine-year-old Reuben Cook (1762), and forty-nine-year-old Moses Scott (1762) each had an estate worth less than 30 pounds, pitifully low for an older married man; all were insolvent. Information from veterans who asked the Assembly to compensate them for injuries they had suffered on active service completes the picture: poverty was the principal fact of life for many soldiers. Thirty of seventy-seven petitioners specifically stated they "had very little or no estate."[45]

There are no apparent economic reasons to explain why married men with substantial wealth enlisted in the regiments. Perhaps enthusiasm to end the war induced twenty-eight-year-old Peter Ayres of Norwich to leave his wife and two daughters in 1758; his estate totaled the enormous sum of 894 pounds, 794 pounds for 171 acres, house, and barn, but more than 100 pounds in personal estate, including over 11 pounds in wages. When forty-six-year-old Daniel Harris died the same year, he left his widow a home lot and buildings worth 150 pounds, movables worth 80 pounds, and a "molatto printis boy" valued at 10 pounds; his wages and clothing sold at camp were worth less than 9 pounds. The war was effectively over when thirty-two-year-old Jehiel Peet, a shoemaker from Woodbury, volunteered in 1762. He left his wife an estate of over 140 pounds consisting of 66 pounds in movables (including 20 pounds in

45. On earning cash, see Bissel, Windham:1761/401; and Smith, see Guilford:1763/no number. On older married soldiers, see Dorman, New Haven:1760/3579; Ward, Hartford:1758/5631; Cook, Hartford:1763/1389; and Scott, Hartford:1762/4739. The petitioners doubtless accentuated their need, but the facts could be ascertained too readily for any man to exaggerate his condition. On men who said they had no estate, see CA-War:VI/105, 117, 217, 240 (quotation), 280; CA-War:VII/257; CA-War:VIII/173, 178, 235, 251, 287, 297, 307; CA-War:IX/132, 168, 187, 301, 307; CA-War:X/157, 219, 251, 253, 270–71, 276, 290, 311; and CPR:XI/189–90, 312–13.

wages) and 74 pounds in home lot, house, barn, and shop. These were men who had a substantial stake in society, the freeholders and freeholders' sons of legend; some of them did serve, but they were not in the majority.[46]

Recruiting was just the first step in creating an army each year. The next problem was getting the volunteers and draftees to join their companies. The Lower House wanted to fine and jail men who did not report, but the Upper House convinced the deputies to treat the problem more realistically by promising not to punish recruits if they reported for duty right away. British generals always complained that colonial regiments were slow to take the field in the spring, and Governor Fitch, while exhorting the men to join their companies, always explained that colonial soldiers never gathered quickly. As the war wound down in 1760–62, notices proliferated in the newspapers urging men to report. In June 1761 Colonel Whiting complained that many soldiers who "make trifling excuses" for being absent "must now march to Albany or [they] will be considered as deserters." Some men had legitimate reasons for not reporting. In 1759 an outbreak of measles delayed many. In one company in 1762, two men were "stopt by law," probably for debt, four were "in gaol," and two were "claimed by New York officers." The exhortations worked well enough so that the regiments never listed more than 5 percent of their strength as "not joined," and then only in the last four years of the war, when enthusiasm had ebb.[47]

The process of turning recruits into soldiers began as soon as the troops reached the forts in the upper Hudson valley in early June each year. (The

46. On more affluent soldiers, see Ayres, Norwich:1759/504; Harris, Plainfield:1758/1009 (quotation); and Peet, Woodbury:1763/3478.

47. On pardoning deserters who rejoined their companies in September 1755, see CHC:XVII/139–40; and *Gazette,* 6 Sep 1755. On imperial complaints about late arrivals in 1758, see CO-5:II/991–93. On the Lower House's failed attempt in September and October 1756 to enact fines of up to 15 pounds for delinquency, see CA-War:VI/142, 148. In April 1759 Amherst agreed to pardon deserters who returned (CHC:XVIII/16). On pleas and warnings to report for service, see CA-War:X/98; *Summary,* 6 and 13 Jun 1760, 17 Jul and 24 Jul 1761, 13 Aug 1762; and *Gazette,* 6 Jun 1761 (quotation), 6 Feb, 17 Jul, 7 Aug 1762. In 1757 absentees were considered deserters on 6 July, well into the campaign (Fitch, "Diary," IV/148). On measles, see CHC:XVIII/21; and Webster, "Journal," p. 123. On being stopped for debt, see CHC:X/159, 241, 307. On men in jail, see CHC:X/307–08, 320. On men claimed by New York, see CHC:X/308–09. For lists of men who did not join in 1759, 1760, and 1762, see CHC:X/173, 222, 351–52.

companies generally marched across northwest Connecticut to the Hudson, and then north to Albany, reversing the route to return home.)[48] Military camps were among the largest temporary gatherings in colonial America, and the neophyte soldiers had to learn everything about living together, including such basics as keeping tents clean and digging proper sanitary facilities. The normal frictions of life were exacerbated by the constant danger of the rough-and-tumble camps. The soldiers spent most of their time in the exhausting work of building forts and transporting supplies, and had to endure the tedium of guard duty punctuated by unpredictable moments of deadly peril. The camps were not without their lighter, more social side, however: soldiers found time to play cards, listen to fiddle music, and visit with friends in other units, including the regulars after 1756.[49]

Religion played an important role in holding the men together, due more to the presence in the ranks of many men of sincere religious convictions than to the Assembly's exhortation "carefully and religiously to . . . avoid all profane swearing, cursing, and other evil speaking, intemperance, unrighteousness, and other immoral and dissolute practices (too frequent in camps)." Many soldiers spent considerable time reading the Bible and other devotional literature, and on Sundays gathered to hear the regimental chaplain preach and to join in the singing of hymns. Especially pious officers promoted religion, even going as far as denying the rum ration to any soldier who did not attend morning prayer. The presence of

48. On the routes, see Fitch, "Diary," I/180–81, XIII/80–81; and Lyon, *Journals,* pp. 11–13, 43–45. Soldiers received provisions or, more often, money to purchase food (CA-War:VI/358; CHC:XVII/297–300; CPR:X/567–68; and CPR:XI/178–80, 232–33). The Assembly began to improve the road in May 1758 (CPR:XI/136–37, 381–82), too late to make a difference. On traveling by ship, see Fitch, "Diary," VIII/47; CHC:XVIII/11; CHS-Sizer:12–29 May 1759; and *Gazette,* 9 Jun 1759. Although the water route was less fatiguing, it was also slow and expensive.

49. On camp sanitation, see Fitch, "Diary," IV/234, V/101; Gridley, *Diary,* p. 39; Ford, *Orders,* pp. 34, 46–47, 62, 83, 91; and CHS-Payson/4 Aug 1758. On recreations in camp, see Fitch, "Diary," I/182, 241, 243, II/48–49, 110, 174–75, IV/237, VI/76, 220–23, VII/91. On visiting other camps, see Fitch, "Diary," II/109, 175, III/244, IV/235–37, VI/223, 225, VIII/251, IX/212–13, X/187, XI/145, 223. On card playing, see Fitch, "Diary," VIII/44, 187–88, 252–53, IX/72, 74, 211–13, 222. Colonial officers played ball and went sledding in the winter; British officers played cricket (Fitch, "Diary," VI/222, XI/222).

women with New York and Rhode Island troops in the summer of 1755 troubled many Connecticut men. General Lyman reported "a very great uneasiness" among his soldiers and thought the women would inhibit more New Englanders from enlisting. When he suggested that some soldiers might "either mob or privately destroy" the women, he got the Council of War to send them back to Albany. Imperial commanders were generally less sensitive to New England morals. They were interested in efficiency and order, and although they held "a general review of the women" at least once in 1757, it was principally "to examine whether they had the etcetera [*sic*] or not."[50]

Many soldiers tried to make camp more bearable by supplementing regular-issue clothing and rations with purchases from the sutlers. Items included cheese, chocolate, sugar, coffee, tobacco, soap, thread, shirts, stockings, candles, paper, and even a pocket compass. In the early campaigns the company officers were generally the sutlers, a perquisite that allowed them to supply the soldiers "with everything they want, by which means," charged the earl of Loudoun, they could claim a large share of

50. On the Assembly's expectations, see CHC:XVII/344 (quotation). On indiscipline in 1755, see Johnson, *Papers,* I/717, 857, 870, IX/273. Some soldiers "imagine that swearing makes them look big among their companions" (CHS-FIW:I/314). On Bible reading, see Dibble, "Diary," p. 316; and Fitch, "Diary," II/174, III/43, 243, IX/73, XII/160. Ability to sign one's name was high: 86 percent of the men in one company in 1755, 88 percent in another company in 1758 (CSL-Pitkin; and Champion, "Journal," pp. 436–37). Of thirty-two names on Captain Waterbury's half-pay roll on 27 April 1759, only two were marks, although a half-dozen were illegible scrawls; the roll of the twenty-seven nonveterans contained one mark and a half-dozen more scrawls (YU-MS:Waterbury/27 Apr 1759). On sermons and singing, see Fitch, "Diary," II/174, III/243, IV/148, 234–35, V/251, VI/75, 222–23; Lyon, *Journals,* pp. 19, 24, 26–27, 30, 32, 34–36, 38; and CSL-Meacham. Jabez Fitch thought that military music was "a little improper" on Sunday and that fiddle playing was "very uncommon" on Sunday evening ("Diary," VII/91, VIII/187). On officers promoting religion, see Ford, *Orders,* p. 79; Hawks, *Orderly Book,* p. 27; CHC:XVIII/208–09; CHS-Payson/22 Jun 1758; and CSL-Nathan Whiting/11 and 18 Jul 1758. On women in camp in 1755, see Johnson, *Papers,* I/861, IX/210 (quotation); Johnson wanted "men's wives" to remain, "while they behave decently," so they could "wash and mend" the mens' clothing (*Papers,* I/783). On women in 1757, see Fitch, "Diary," IV/234–35 (quotation); and Ford, *Orders,* pp. 41, 120. On women drummed out of camp, see Fitch, "Diary," X/186; and Gridley, *Diary,* p. 35.

many soldiers' wages by the end of the campaign. After 1756, outside contractors supplied the soldiers, but under either system debts could mount up quickly; a sergeant spent over 8 pounds on sundries in five months in 1760 (80 percent of his wages). Sutlers who extended credit did so at their own risk. In 1760 many of their customers died insolvent or reenlisted before paying their debts; in 1762 some soldiers ran up bills that exceeded their wages by more than 10 pounds. Many soldiers thought that the sutlers in the last campaigns were profiteers, and the sutlers, for their part, realized that an "unreasonable prejudice" against them was "deeply rooted in the minds of offices and soldiers."[51]

The sutlers' most disruptive activity was providing a source of additional alcohol, complicating the problem of keeping the troops sober. Soldiers consumed great quantities of liquor, sometimes as an official incentive to work harder, but much of it during periods of inactivity. In less than five months in 1760, for example, a sergeant supplemented his regular ration with five gallons of liquor from the sutler. Although General Amherst claimed that "drinking rum . . . is too often the way the soldiers employ their idle time," Connecticut officers objected only when alcohol interfered with the performance of duty. Soldiers occasionally drank too much near the end of an unsuccessful campaign, as in 1756, but drunkenness was a chronic problem mainly among Indian soldiers and among men who served through the winter with little to do but guard supplies.[52]

Some efforts were made to train the soldiers, but the process was hampered by a lack of experienced noncommissioned officers. In 1757, a regular officer taught sergeants and corporals the rudiments of military

51. On the variety of articles, see CSL-Gallop. Loudoun's opinions are in YU-MS:Loudoun/6 (quotation). On Sergeant John Stevens in 1760, see CA-War:IX/85. On debtors in 1760, see CA-War:IX/142; soldiers accused the sutlers of overcharging them (CHC:XVIII/108). The Upper House did not want minors to get into debt (CA-War:IX/127). On "overrunners" in 1762, see CHS-FIW:II/884. An example of a printed sutler's receipt in 1762 is in YU-MS:Whiting/30. On soldiers' attitudes about sutlers in 1761, see CHS-FIW:II/760 (quotation).

52. For orders against sutlers supplying rum in 1757, see Gridley, *Diary,* pp. 14, 54. The normal ration in 1755 was half a pint a day (Johnson, *Papers,* I/782). On the promise of alcohol for constructing a road, up to half a pint a day, see Gridley, *Diary,* p. 32. On Sergeant Stevens, see CA-War:IX/85. Amherst's opinions are in CHC:XVIII/209 (quotation); and Hawks, *Orderly Book,* p. 65. On drunkenness in 1756 and 1757, see MHS-JW/19 Sep 1756; and Fitch, "Diary," III/44, VII/93, IX/213, XI/145, 221, XII/159.

drill, information which they were expected to pass on to their companies, but training short-service troops was always inefficient. An attempt to recruit skilled soldiers that year went awry when two sergeants turned out to be deserters from the regulars. Concern for military deportment and display began to increase late in the 1756 campaign when the colonials came into contact with the spit-and-polish British regulars. Thereafter, General Lyman wanted his men to "make the most decent and soldier-like appearance that is possible," but they never became good parade-ground soldiers because they spent their time constructing forts, trans-porting supplies, and standing guard. Even fundamental training was neglected. While whole companies occasionally shot at marks, marks-manship never had a high priority. Later in the war, Connecticut troops were taught "to fire platoons" like the regulars, but this skill was of limited value for a war in the wilderness.[53]

Connecticut did not produce good soldiers. They were brave and, within the limits of their training, effective if too much was not expected of them on the few occasions when they actually went into battle. But they were not adept at war in the wilderness because the colony did not have an active frontier to nurture the skills needed for scouting and skir-mishing. The most important colonial victory of the war, the defeat of the French at Lake George on 8 September 1755, showed the strengths and weaknesses of a New England army. The soldiers lost heavily in a morning ambush, demonstrating once again their lack of skill at Indian-style war, but in the afternoon they repulsed every French attack from behind the breastwork around their main camp. As at Louisbourg ten years earlier, they won their victory with the axe, pick, and shovel, and consolidated their defensive success by building a string of forts to advance

53. On training, see Fitch, "Diary," I/182, 240, 244, II/47, 49, 108, 110, 174–75, IV/234–35, 237, VI/223, VII/91–92; Gridley, *Diary*, pp. 25, 28–30, 33; Ford, *Orders*, pp. 5, 12, 15, 27–28, 103; Lyon, *Journals*, p. 20; Champion, "Journal," p. 424; Dibble, "Diary," p. 313; Webster, "Journal," pp. 123, 125, 128, 131–32; and Booth, "Journal," p. 142. On the regular deserters, see Fitch, "Diary," IV/149, V/101. For Lyman's general orders promoting military de-portment, see Ford, *Orders*, pp. 2–3, 25, 29, 47, 106 (quotation). Regulars were also poor marksmen (Fitch, "Diary," II/110) because standard European linear tactics generally required only unaimed rapid volley fire. On practicing drilling and volleying in 1758, see YU-MS:Waterbury/6 Aug 1758. On firing by platoons in 1759, see Webster, "Journal," p. 131; and Hawks, *Orderly Book*, pp. 15, 17, 31, 33. Amherst thought some colonial soldiers had "never fired a gun in their lives" (Hawks, *Orderly Book*, p. 15).

the frontier to Lake George. In later years, colonial soldiers provided garrison and construction service without which the methodical conquest of Canada would have been impossible. British generals were in part forced to use them this way, since they generally had difficulty recruiting batteau men and teamsters; in 1759 Amherst was "obliged to furnish them from the troops of the provinces." Most Connecticut soldiers never came into contact with the enemy after 1755, although perhaps as many as three hundred rangers saw some hard scouting and skirmishing between major troop movements.[54]

Even garrison and construction troops had to live under some sort of military discipline. In 1755–56 the colonies created their own rules, based on experience in prior wars but as always more an adaptation of civilian judicial codes than a set of martial laws. They employed corporal punishment, but never with the frequency and severity thought necessary in the British army. In and after 1756, colonial soldiers were subject to British discipline when operating with regular troops. The infractions punished by the Articles of War were serious; no army could operate effectively if privates disobeyed orders, stole from each other, slept on guard duty, or got drunk on a scout. One Massachusetts soldier in 1758 thought his fellows were "very vicious" and claimed that "although the punishment is very severe, yet there is always some or other offending."[55]

Connecticut soldiers were not notably undisciplined, but the articles enforced order and subordination on them with an often brutal corporal punishment that was a cruel departure for men accustomed to militia indiscipline and prior expeditionary practice. A soldier in 1758 received 10 lashes for alarming the camp by firing his gun without order. In 1759,

54. On building forts, see CA-War:V/285; CA-War:VIII/268; CA-War:X/290; and Webster, "Journal," pp. 128, 130. On building batteaux, see CA-War:VI/337. On Amherst's comment, see CO-5:IV/149 (quotation). Many men joined the rangers at Fort Edward in July 1757 after seeing how French and Indian raiders mutilated sentries caught unawares (Fitch, "Diary," II/175–76, III/244–45, IV/148). On the rangers, see also Fitch, "Diary," III/43, VI/76, 221, XI/222, XII/161; CHS-JT/5 Jun 1757; and Champion, "Journal," pp. 422–30. Connecticut Indians also served as rangers (CA-Ind:2,I/66; and Ford, *Orders,* p. 12). Waterbury's company sent an ensign and twelve men into the rangers in early October 1758 (YU-MS:Waterbury/8 Oct 1758). Three Connecticut men were drafted for Major Robert Rogers's attack on the St. Francis Indians in 1759 (CA-War:VIII/313; and CA-War:IX/155, 159).

55. On rules in 1755–56, see Anderson, *People's Army,* pp. 121–41. On the vicious soldiers, see Henderson, "Journal," p. 203 (quotation).

a private received 15 lashes for neglect of duty on the Sabbath. The punishment for being an "unfaithful" sentry was as much as 120 lashes that year, up from 50 in 1757. Stealing from government stores or one's comrades could bring up to 200 lashes. In 1757 a habitual offender received 500 lashes, administered at intervals, and was drummed out of camp. Another, caught sleeping on guard, was forced to "run the gauntlet through thirty men . . . [and] cried 'Lord God have mercy on me,' the blood flying every stroke." An observer reported with understatement that "this was a sorrowful sight."[56]

The contractual nature of colonial military service helped to maintain order and to reduce the severity of punishment because the soldiers remained under the direct command of their own officers, men from the same towns who often had close personal connections with the soldiers they had recruited. An example illustrates how close those ties could be. Colonel Nathan Whiting deplored the fact that the son-in-law of a friend had deserted in August 1761, but if he returned, "I will try to prevent his punishment." The fact that disciplinary regulations were intended to keep order among short-service amateur soldiers, not to intimidate long-service regulars, did not eliminate entirely the need for officers to wield their power. Senior Connecticut officers, like some imperial commanders, used clemency to demonstrate their authority and to frighten their men into obeying orders, without physically brutalizing anyone. On 19 May 1757, for example, General Lyman, "with good advice and strict direction

56. On British discipline, see CHC:XVII/81–82; CPR:XI/106–08; Ford, *Orders,* pp. 9, 20, 81; and Leach, *Roots,* pp. 110–13, 127, 187. In 1757 Loudoun threatened to execute any sentry caught sleeping at his post and to punish the unnecessary discharge of a gun with five hundred lashes (Gridley, *Diary,* pp. 67, 76). On flogging, see Fitch, "Diary," III/243, IV/150, 235–39, VI/76, 224, VII/92–93; and Gridley, *Diary,* pp. 28, 33–35, 49–51, 54, 56, 58. Noncommissioned officers were generally confined to quarters or reduced to the ranks for similar offenses (Fitch, "Diary," II/108, IV/149, 237, VI/223, 225, VII/91–93; Ford, *Orders,* pp. 49, 87, 89—90, 112–13; Lyon, *Journals,* p. 37; and CHS-Payson/11 Sep 1758). In 1757 a clerk received one hundred lashes plus reduction to the ranks (Gridley, *Diary,* p. 37). On alarming the camp, see Lyon, *Journals,* p. 24. On neglect of duty on Sunday, see Dibble, "Diary," p. 320. On dereliction, see Fitch, "Diary," III/243, IV/150, 235–38, VI/76, VII/92–93, XII/160; and Lyon, *Journals,* pp. 24, 40. On stealing, see Dibble, "Diary," pp. 317, 320; and Fitch, "Diary," VII/93. The habitual offenders are in Fitch, "Diary," IV/149–50, VI/224–25. On the gauntlet, see Gridley, *Diary,* p. 30 (quotation).

to us all," reprieved a man sentenced to receive 20 lashes "upon his begging favor and promising reformation." Officers pardoned convicted offenders at least three times in 1759. On 10 June two men were "brought to the pine tree to be whipped, one for leaving his post when on sentry and the other for getting drunk when on sentry but they were both forgiven." On 16 June General Amherst used an even crueler piece of political theater to impress upon the troops the enormous power in his hands. A Connecticut man who had been "sentenced to be shot to death for desertion was brought out in the front of . . . [his] regiment for the execution and a platoon made ready for that purpose but . . . he was reprieved."[57]

Desertion was the most serious offense with which the officers had to deal. On the one hand, they had to be strict enough so that the regiments did not crumble under adversity. For example, in late August 1758, less than two months after the defeat at Ticonderoga, three regular deserters received 1,000 lashes, 250 at a time, to remind all soldiers that leaving camp was illegal. Yet, even imperial commanders realized that because Connecticut had to raise troops each year, discipline could not be so severe that it discouraged men from reenlisting. At the same time he approved the punishment of the deserters, Abercromby reprieved eight men found guilty of leaving their scouting party and "returning to camp without leave." In the early campaigns, Connecticut officers were lenient with men

57. On Whiting's offer to use his influence, see YUMS:Whiting/20 (quotation). On the reprieves in 1757 and 1759, see Gridley, *Diary,* p. 29 (quotation), 31; and Webster, "Journal," II/124 (quotation), 128, 135. On regimental courts martial in 1757, see Ford, *Orders,* pp. 3–4, 9, 12–13, 16–17, 47–48. The Assembly wanted its soldiers to be subject to courts martial "constituted of proper officers of the provincial forces" (CHC:XVII/237), but that was not always the case. The court martial that sentenced the deserter to be shot had thirteen members: seven regular officers, three from Massachusetts, and three from Connecticut (Hawks, *Orderly Book,* p. 13). On the reprieve on 16 June, see CHS-Sizer:16 Jun 1759 (quotation); Hawks, *Orderly Book,* pp. 13–15; and Webster, "Journal," p. 125. Abercromby had done the same thing the previous year (Henderson, "Journal," p. 203). The sentence was not always commuted. A Rhode Islander was executed in 1759 (Webster, "Journal," p. 121; Hawks, *Orderly Book,* p. 5; CO-5:IV/148; and Leach, *Roots,* p. 113) and a New Yorker in 1760 (Booth, "Journal," p. 142). On imperial attitudes about discipline, see Anderson, *People's Army,* pp. 121–23. Both Abercromby and Amherst remitted death sentences imposed on regulars for desertion (Henderson, "Journal," p. 199; and Hawks, *Orderly Book,* p. 54).

who left camp after they had fulfilled the obligations for which they had contracted, an attitude clearly evident in late 1755, when the military situation required the soldiers to remain at their posts beyond the expiration of their enlistments on 1 November. On 10 November, "five or seven hundred" men who wanted to go home were "stayed and appeased with a promise of a dismission in a few days." The situation reached a climax ten days later when the men got "as far as the breastwork" and were dissuaded by General Lyman from going any further. They were dismissed shortly thereafter. Officers took a harder line in late February 1758, when men who had enlisted to serve until 1 March were told they would have to remain until the new regiments arrived in late May. The news created "a most dreadful rage" among the soldiers. One man who set out for home was brought back and received 70 lashes to discourage other men from trying the same thing; it was not a token amount but not the capital sentence the court martial could have imposed.[58]

In general, desertion did not cripple the regiments. In 1756, for example, they lost about 4 percent of their strength to desertion, not much higher than in the regulars. The rate rose to about 6 percent in 1760–62, when all the main goals of the war had been achieved. Desertion was worst in 1761, when the troops had nothing to do but garrison forts in the Champlain valley. Colonel Whiting reported that "the men most shamefully desert," despite the fact that they "were never better off and have no reason of complaint." He warned that "if men desert and live peaceably at home, it will destroy all government of the army and discourage any officer from serving." He sent officers back to Connecticut to recover the deserters and ran advertisements in the local newspapers to publicize the names of the unfaithful. Even when deserters were apprehended, they could be hard to hold; a deserter was among three men who escaped from the New Haven jail in May 1761.[59]

58. On flogging in August 1758, see Lyon, *Journals,* p. 31. On remitting punishment, see YU-MS:Waterbury/28 Aug 1758. On returning home in November 1755, see Dwight, "Journal," pp. 67–68 (quotations). On February 1758, see Fitch, "Diary," XI/147 (quotation), 221–22, XII/159–60. A regular received one hundred lashes at the same time for getting drunk on guard (Fitch, "Diary," XII/160). On the contractual nature of service, see CHC:XVIII/135; and Anderson, "Contractual Principles."

59. Desertion rates are from muster rolls in CHC:IX and X. For deserters in 1761–62, see CHC:X/283–84, 359. On the rate for regulars, roughly 3 percent, see Pargellis, *Loudoun,* p. 108*n*7. On Whiting, see CHS-JT/23 Jul 1761

Table 5.8
Number of Soldiers Dead, 1755–62

Year	Soldiers Raised	Extant Company Rolls	Known Dead
1755	3,028	31 of 36 (86%)	113 (4%)
1756	2,339	27 of 32 (84%)	189 (8%)
1757	1,340	12 of 14 (86%)	66 (5%)
1758	4,309	39 of 48 (81%)	222 (5%)
1759	4,183	37 of 50 (74%)	144 (3%)
1760	3,229	18 of 48 (37%)	241 (7%)
1761	2,221	23 of 24 (96%)	43 (2%)
1762	2,209	22 of 24 (92%)	427 (19%)
Total			1,445 men

Source: Muster rolls in CHS:IX and X.

Disease caused the most serious losses, with many soldiers falling prey to the rigors of the "camp way of living." They dreaded smallpox in particular, and despite an effort to inoculate both officers and men, they always gave contaminated areas a wide berth. Other diseases, including dysentery, pneumonia, measles, and the inclusive "camp distemper," were more common and equally debilitating. By the end of the 1756 campaign, more than three-quarters of the men in some companies were unfit for duty. The percentage of healthy men increased in later years, but by mid-November each year the regiments were much reduced in strength and filled with men anxious to get home before winter weather made travel too arduous. By 23 November 1761, for example, only 1,002 men of the 2,221 mustered in May remained on duty (45 percent), 300 more were in military hospitals, and most of the rest had already gone home. Mortality varied, 1756 and 1760 being the deadliest years before the catastrophe of 1762, when the First Regiment was destroyed at Havana (table 5.8). The experience of its Fifth Company was typical: it lost half of its 84 men between 26 August and 10 December. Of 18 soldiers from Hebron, by mid-December 15 had died at Havana, 2 remained in hospital at Manhattan, and only 1 had returned home. Although records are incomplete (especially for 1760), it seems that roughly 1,600 men died

(quotation). For an example of an advertisement, see *Gazette,* 29 Aug 1761. On escaping from jail, see *Gazette,* 12 Feb 1757, 16 May and 21 Nov 1761.

in service, 10 percent of the 16,000 who served. If 1762 is omitted, the rate falls to roughly 6 percent, or about twice that of the town of Boston in 1756–60. Military camps were clearly the deadliest places in colonial America.[60]

An unknown number of soldiers were disabled in service, most of whom were undoubtedly cared for by their families or by private and public charity at the local level. A few (seventy-seven petitioners) managed to bring their plight to the Assembly, and its response gives a glimpse of what the leaders thought they owed to men crippled in the public service. Several veterans reminded the leaders that showing "kindness and compassion towards distressed soldiers" would "animate others to venture their lives in defense of their King and country." The Assembly was not unsympathetic to the problems an invalid would have making a living, but it offered no relief if a man had any estate, a criterion it used to deny twenty-three petitions (30 percent). It was most generous to men who had been wounded fighting the enemy in 1755 and 1758. Grants increased with inflation, and varied according to the social standing of the petitioner. In May 1758 the Assembly gave 10 pounds to Abijah Ives, Jr., of Wallingford for the loss of his right arm. Three years later, Osborn Stevens received 50 pounds for the same injury, in part because his father was a deputy from Killingworth. Captain Jedidiah Fay of Ashford got 88 pounds for a broken ankle suffered in action on 8 August 1758; he was a deputy

60. On seasoning, see Champion, "Journal," p. 438 (quotation). On smallpox, see Champion, "Journal," p. 424; CA-War:VII/112–13; CA-War:X/251, 271; Fitch, "Diary," I/100, 244, II/48; and Gridley, *Diary*, pp. 24, 32, 36, 38, 40–42, 44–46, 49, 51, 55. Governor Fitch knew smallpox would "greatly terrify our people" (CHC:XVII/266). On inoculation, see YU-MS:Whiting/19. On other diseases, see Gridley, *Diary*, pp. 34, 42, 44–46, 48, 57; and Webster, "Journal," pp. 123, 131. The companies in 1756 were from 30 percent to 54 percent fit (CHC:IX/104–06, 112–14, 138–39, 154–57; and CSL-Adams). One company in 1759 had 51 percent fit on 17 June (thirty-one of sixty-one), 58 percent on 7 July, and 45 percent on 6 October (CSL-Crary). On going home, see CHC:XVIII/147–48. On 1761, see CHC:XVIII/160–89. On invalids, see CHC:XVIII/149–59. Colonel Whiting thought mortality was "one-sixth per annum," but that was highly exaggerated (Stiles, *Itineraries*, pp. 104–05). Trumbull thought Connecticut lost "several thousands of the hardiest and most able young men" (CSL-JT:XXI/10). On the Fifth Company, see CHC:X/306–07. On Hebron, see *Summary*, 17 Dec 1762. For a similar situation in Somers, see CHC:X/354–55. On death rates in Boston and among Massachusetts troops, see Anderson, *People's Army*, pp. 99–101.

on both occasions he received money from the Assembly. Private Peter Wooster of Derby, who was shot six times in the same engagement, had his left arm shattered, received nine blows to the head, and was scalped and left for dead, received half that amount.[61]

Grants of money were small compensation to men who could no longer labor to support themselves and their families. Joseph Green, an eighteen-year-old Indian apprentice, contracted an infection in 1758 which left his right hip, thigh, and leg a "putrifying sore." His master, Ebenezer Leach, spent 40 pounds treating his injury (and was reimbursed for it by the Assembly), but his care did not outlast Green's apprenticeship. When Green turned twenty-one in April 1761, Leach "cast him upon the charity of Coventry as one of the town poor." A clever and well-connected cripple could survive if he refused to give up. Osborn Stevens, a blacksmith who lost his right arm in August 1758, used a grant of 50 pounds to become a small-time merchant, and in the late 1760s managed to invest 400 pounds in a vessel and cargo. The loss of the ship reduced him to penury, and he asked the Assembly for a license to peddle because he was "loath in the prime of life to lie as a dead weight on my father and friends." He soon became a schoolteacher and clerk in a retail store. He never married and had no estate when he disappeared from the records in 1801.[62]

61. On animating the soldiers, see CA-War:VI/119 (quotation); CA-War:VIII/178; and CPR:XI/241–42. Petitions rejected because the soldier had some estate are CA-War:IX/160 and CA-War:X/253. The Assembly gave nothing to a man drafted for the St. Francis expedition in 1759 (CA-War:IX/149), or to soldiers who infected their families with smallpox (CA-War:VII/247; CA-War:IX/151; CA-War:X/271). It never gave money to men who had served in the regulars or for other colonies (CA-War:IX/311; CA-War:X/264, 266), and in May 1805 refused to help a veteran of Braddock's defeat (CA-Mis:2,II/57). On Ives, see CA-War:VI/117. On Stevens, see CA-War:VIII/218. In May 1760, three men received from 30 to 50 pounds each for a shattered arm (CA-War:VIII/251, 297, 307). On Fay and Wooster, see CA-War:VIII/182, 223, 293.

62. On Green, see CA-War:IX/164; CA-War:X/128; and CPR:XI/522. On Stevens, see CA-War:VIII/218; CA-War:X/279; and CA-War, 2:I/41; he also joined the Delaware Land Company (Boyd, *Susquehannah*, I/263, 268). On licenses to peddle, see CA-War:VII/257; CA-War:IX/182; CA-War:X/269–70, 276, 279, 286; and CPR:XI/189—90. Between 1758 and 1769, the Assembly gave eight veterans a free license, in one case because the man claimed the 5 pound fee would "consume all his profits" (CA-War:X/269). Crippled veterans lost a good way of earning a living in October 1770, when peddling got caught up in the imperial politics of nonimportation. Merchants who opposed London's

The vast majority of veterans came home in one piece. The fact that Connecticut society reabsorbed them without major instability was as important as raising the troops in the first place. The strain was lessened by continuous turnover—veterans of earlier campaigns had already returned to civilian life—and by the disaster at Havana, which brutally reduced the number of veterans returning in 1762. The war had given employment for as long as three years to perhaps as many as two thousand men, but now they faced again the economic problems that had prompted them to enlist in the first place or to remain in service. It seems that for most soldiers—certainly for most bachelors under thirty—the war was a grand adventure that turned out right. They survived, got the financial boost they sought, and had better prospects than before the war. They got on with their lives, and their success or failure did not hinge on temporary wartime employment. Ex-soldiers were politically active, under ex-officers, only once, during the opposition to the Stamp Act in the summer of 1765.[63]

Many veterans continued to exhibit the restlessness that had earlier attracted them to military service. Before the war, roughly 10 percent of the men who would serve as soldiers invested in the Susquehannah and Delaware land companies. After the war, many joined in the mania of land speculation sweeping through Connecticut. Most hoped to share in an imperial land grant as a reward for their service; those who had survived Havana in 1762 were particularly incensed about the minuscule amount of plunder, and felt the imperial government owed them a share of the land they had helped to win. Others joined the Company of Military Adventurers, organized by fifty ex-officers in June 1763 to lobby for land in Nova Scotia. But the company's efforts were unsuccessful and veterans emigrated as individuals to western Massachusetts, southern New Hampshire, southern Vermont, and even Nova Scotia. Land companies never attracted the poorest veterans, who did not have the money either to subscribe or to emigrate. But the hope that they might one day improve their economic condition helped them survive in a society suffering through a postwar depression.[64]

---

attempts to tax imports promoted a law "to suppress hawkers, peddlers, and petty chapmen" (CPR:XIII/364–65; and Taylor, *Connecticut,* p. 234).

63. The diary of Jabez Fitch, Jr., shows how one ex-soldier got back to the routine of making a living.

64. The percentage of investors is based on a sample from the Twelfth Regiment. On land fever, see advertisements after 1760 in *Gazette* and *Summary.* The

Connecticut's involvement in the final French war did not rend the fabric of its society. The colony managed to raise troops and reabsorb them without changing its traditional military system of temporary and amateur soldiers, and remained a civilian society with a suspicion of a professional military, a tradition it would carry into the far more difficult military adventure of the Revolution.

THE OFFICERS

Connecticut's military system worked smoothly and effectively during the final French and Indian war thanks mostly to the efforts of the officers who recruited soldiers for the expeditionary regiments. Officers conveyed news of the Assembly's financial incentives to their neighbors, convinced them to enlist, and then paid them their bounty money and advance wages. As had been the case since 1690, their primary qualification was popularity with potential recruits. The Assembly adhered to the traditional maxim that only "officers known and approved among our people" would induce "the best and most courageous soldiers" to volunteer. The ability to organize and lead a company through a campaign that might include hard fighting and high mortality was of secondary importance. Popularity might seem an odd way to pick officers, especially given the rigorous selection and training of officers in modern armies. But war in North America in the eighteenth century was largely a matter of logistics, the ability to concentrate more power at a particular point than the enemy could muster. Because both colonial commanders and imperial generals needed large numbers of colonial soldiers to build and maintain the army's logistical lifelines, a colonial officer's most important talent was the persuasiveness of the recruiter.[65]

All expeditionary officers were appointed annually by the Assembly. (Company officers in the militia were elected by the militiamen, commissioned by the Assembly, and served until they resigned or died; the Assembly appointed the field officers.) The deputies and assistants relied

Susquehannah Company met six months after the fall of Quebec to discuss winning confirmation of its claims (*Gazette*, 8 Mar 1760). On the Havana veterans, see Bates, *Two Putnams*, pp. 8–9. On the Adventurers, see *Summary*, 24 Jun, 2 Sep 1763; and *Gazette*, 19 Nov 1763. One veteran used an Assembly grant to move to the Susquehannah (CA-War:2,I/32).

65. On the need for acceptable officers, see CHS-GA/Oct 1755 (quotation); and CA-War:V/190.

on local connections to find suitable nominees, and they had considerable scope to appoint relatives and clients. In the early years of the war, patronage promoted recruiting because it gave important men an incentive to ensure that the companies were as full as possible. The selection process generally began in the Lower House, where the deputies (most of whom were themselves militia officers) drew up lists of nominees by county in 1755–57 and by militia regiments thereafter. While most deputies gave pro forma assent to the men nominated by their colleagues, last-minute bargaining was not uncommon. For example, of fifty men nominated as ensigns in 1758, fourteen were eventually replaced (28 percent) and four promoted. A committee arranged the nominees into companies, a captain and two lieutenants for each company in 1755–56, plus an ensign when the size of the companies was increased in and after 1757. Occasionally the Upper House replaced an individual or reorganized the combinations, presumably to find the best mix of personality, recruiting ability, and military skill.[66]

The surviving evidence shows that candidates for senior positions were reshuffled for a variety of personal reasons. Most men who refused an appointment did so because they had a genuine need to meet other commitments. John Pitkin of Hartford, for example, served as a lieutenant colonel in 1758 (at age fifty) with what he called "a great deal of self-denial," and declined to serve in 1759 because he had to support his family. Others toyed with refusing, it seems, to win a higher rank. In 1755 Andrew Ward, a militia officer and Louisbourg veteran, declined four times to serve as a major before the Assembly took the hint and made him a lieutenant colonel. If a nominee declined the appointment after the Assembly had adjourned, Governor Fitch had standing permission to name a replacement. Reluctant candidates were not allowed to hinder recruiting.[67]

66. Each year, the field officers commanded the first three companies in each regiment. The Upper House wanted to reappoint the 1755 officers as a body in 1756, but the deputies demanded the entire approval process each year (CA-War:VI/17). Even the local minister recommended candidates to Jonathan Trumbull in 1755 (CHS-FIW:II/280). On nominees, see CA-War:V/152–53, 155; CA-War:VII/165, 167–68, 170–74, 177–80; CHS-FIW:II/957–78; and CA-War:VIII/254–64. On the ensigns, see CHS-FIW:II/957. On division into companies, see CHS-GA/Mar 1756 and Mar 1758. On reshuffling, see CA-War:V/93; CA-War:VII/165, 174, 179–80; and CA-War:IX/120.

67. On Pitkin, see CHC:XVII/202. On Ward, see CA-War:V/92, 94, 120, 149. On replacements, see CHC:XVII/215.

Table 5.9
Militia Officers in Expeditions, 1755–62

Year	Number	Percent of New Officers	Percent of Total Officers
1755	41*	38% of 108	34% of 119
1756	9	26% of 34	9% of 100
1757	2	12% of 17	4% of 56
1758	34	42% of 81	18% of 192
1759	8	29% of 28	4% of 200
1760	3	27% of 11	2% of 189
1761	None	—	—
1762	None	—	—
Total	97 officers		

*Five officers were also veterans of King George's War.

The field officers and captains were the senior members of the regiments, both in responsibility and age. They bore the principal burden of recruiting, and were older—presumably more mature, better known, and therefore better recruiters—than their subordinates. Over the war, the field officers averaged forty-two years of age, three years older than the captains and a dozen years older than the second lieutenants. Captains, at an average age of thirty-nine, were generally the oldest officers in each company, nine years older than second lieutenants, who got a bit younger by 1762 (twenty-nine years old) because the rank was the entry-level position for young outsiders. Ensigns got slightly older (thirty years old in 1762) as men were promoted from noncommissioned rank. All the rest got younger, as older men declined to serve another summer.

As always, expeditionary officers were not drawn from among the colony's most prominent leaders. Of 541 officers appointed between 1755 and 1762, only 97 (18 percent) held a militia commission at the time of their appointment (table 5.9); most of them (51 of 97) served as field officers or captains, while the rest were subordinate officers. Militia officers were most numerous in 1755, a full third (41) of the 119 expeditionary officers that year. Thereafter, they were eclipsed by active-service veterans. Only when the army doubled in size in 1758 were militia officers as much as a fifth of the officer corps. Even fewer officers were deputies and justices of the peace. Only 19 of 541 officers (4 percent) had been deputies, of whom 12 had also been justices. Like militia officers, deputies and justices were concentrated in 1758, when enthusiasm was high.

Table 5.10
Sources of Officers, 1755–64

Year	New	Promoted	Nonveteran (New + Promoted)	Veteran	Total
1755	108 (91%)	—	108 (91%)	11 (9%)*	119
1756	34 (34%)	20 (20%)	54 (54%)	46 (46%)	100
1757	17 (30%)	15 (27%)	32 (57%)	24 (43%)	56
1758	81 (42%)	54 (28%)	135 (70%)	57 (30%)	192
1759	28 (14%)	51 (25%)	79 (39%)	121 (61%)	200
1760	11 (6%)	41 (22%)	52 (28%)	137 (72%)	189
1761	7 (7%)	27 (28%)	34 (35%)	63 (65%)	97
1762	3 (3%)	13 (14%)	16 (17%)	80 (83%)	96
1764	0	1 (7%)	1 (7%)	14 (93%)	15

*Veterans of King George's War.

The Assembly always tried to appoint as many veteran officers as possible, on the theory that they combined military experience with recruiting ability and were therefore more likely to attract veteran soldiers than some untested newcomers. In 1755 the Assembly appointed as many Louisbourg veterans as wished to serve again (a total of 11, less than 10 percent of the 119 officers; table 5.10), even though their knowledge of war, the most possessed by any Connecticut man, was limited to the pick-and-shovel operations that had forced the fortress to surrender in 1745. For one veteran, thirty-year-old Nathan Whiting of New Haven, the Assembly's offer of a lieutenant colonelcy in one of its regiments was a substantial promotion. An ensign who had been reduced to half-pay when the colonial regulars at Louisbourg were disbanded in 1748, Whiting had accepted an appointment in January 1755 as a lieutenant in one of the colonial regular regiments being re-raised for the new war. He had already begun recruiting for the regulars (part of the 300 men voted by the Assembly) when he jumped at the chance for higher rank, gambling that another colonial success might again open the door to preferment in the imperial military establishment for the most able colonial officers.[68]

68. On Whiting's recruiting activity, see YU-MS:Whiting/30. Some veteran officers did not serve in 1755, including Macock Ward of Wallingford, a lieutenant in the West Indies expedition of 1740, and James Grant of Norwich, a lieutenant in the colonial regulars at Louisbourg (CHS-FIW:II/571, 880).

Table 5.11
Experience of Officers, 1755–64

Year Began	Years Served									Total
---	1	2	3	4	5	6	7	8	9	
1755	62	30	9	9	4	6	3	3	1	127 (23%)
1756	33	13	5	6	3	0	3	0		63 (12%)
1757	14	5	2	6	2	4	1			34 (6%)
1758	68	20	25	7	5	4				129 (24%)
1759	32	37	2	10	2					83 (15%)
1760	35	8	9	1						53 (10%)
1761	14	17	1							32 (6%)
1762	19	1								20 (4%)
1764	0									0
Totals	277 (51%)	131 (24%)	53	39	16	14	7	3	1	541

Not every appointee found the military life as congenial as did Phineas Lyman and Nathan Whiting. The Assembly had a hard time convincing veteran officers to serve more than once. Of 541 officers, roughly half (277 men) served only once (table 5.11). A quarter (131 men) served twice, usually in 1755–56 or 1758–59, and the other quarter (133 men) served three or more times. There was substantial turnover early in the war; in 1756 and 1757, nearly 60 percent of the officers had not served before in commissioned rank (table 5.10). The number of newly commissioned officers peaked at 135 in 1758 (70 percent of 192 officers), when the army doubled in size. The figures reversed after 1758, and for four years the officer corps was never less than 61 percent veteran. In 1762, for example, 80 of 96 officers (83 percent) were veterans, and only 16 (17 percent) were new to commissioned rank.

The Assembly increased the level of experience in the officer corps by promoting the ablest noncommissioned officers, company clerks, and privates to commissioned rank. Over 40 percent of all officers (228 men) served at least once before their abilities brought them to the attention of senior officers and the Assembly (table 5.12). In 1762, for example, 13 of 16 newly commissioned officers were promoted from noncommissioned rank. The need for officers with some experience was so great in the years of greatest demand, 1758–60, that the Assembly became desperate to find men with appropriate credentials. For example, Alexander Chalker of Saybrook had been a sergeant in 1758 and 1759, and in 1760 had already enlisted as a private when the Assembly made him an ensign (at age

Table 5.12
Experience of Officers, 1755–64

	Served Once	Served Twice or More	Total
Only as officer	186	127	313 (58%)
As officer plus as noncommissioned officer	91	137	228 (42%)
Totals	277 (51%)	264 (49%)	541

twenty-seven) under his former captain. It was probably men like this who caused one veteran to remark in 1758 that he "found many [officers] . . . that I knew and some very much unexpected."[69]

As the war continued, veteran senior officers had a greater voice in the selection process, principally because they had firsthand knowledge of who was a good leader; indeed, senior officers had always had the power to commission new officers to fill vacancies created by death or disablement on campaign. Their advice was generally heeded by Governor Fitch and the Assembly. In November 1757, for example, Colonel Whiting recommended twenty-two-year-old First Lieutenant Reuben Ferris as captain of a winter company ("If the Governor approves of him, I think he will excel") and suggested twenty-eight-year-old Second Lieutenant Thomas Pierce (who "has done well in scouting this season") as first lieutenant. Fitch followed Whiting's suggestions, but the next spring the Assembly dropped the younger Ferris back to first lieutenant while keeping the older Pierce at the higher rank. The men suggested by veteran captains did not always have the right credentials. Captain Edmund Welles failed to get the son of a friend named as his lieutenant in 1757 because he was honest about the young man's recruiting skills: "As to what influence he would have to draw in soldiers I cannot say." Field officers had more latitude in appointing regimental staff, where recruiting was not a priority. Jonathan Trumbull suggested several men in 1759, but Whiting named his own company's first lieutenant, thirty-two-year-old Jabez Thompson, as adjutant because he had been "kept from promotion, having several advanced above him that were below him last year."[70]

69. On Chalker, see CA-War:IX/77. On unexpected officers, see Fitch, "Diary," XIII/81 (quotation).

70. On filling vacancies on campaign, see CHC:IX/5; CHC:X/115; and Booth, "Journal," p. 140. On Whiting's recommendations, see CHS-JT/4 Nov 1757 (quotations). On Welles, see CHS-FIW:I/54 (quotation). On Thompson, see CHS-JT/4 Apr 1759 (quotation).

Recruiting relied heavily on the rapport and reputation officers had with men who might be persuaded to enlist. A captain's success was measured in large part by the size of his following, that is, the number of men he could attract as a core of noncommissioned officers and privates around which he could build his company. There were variations in the following of any captain who served for several years, but Captain John Durkee's experience seems to have been typical. Of the total of 336 men who enlisted in his companies between 1758 and 1762, 89 men (26 percent) served twice or more, and 10 served four times. The fact that only 1 man, James Williams, served with him in all five campaigns is a reminder that each captain had to pay constant attention to the need to renew his following.[71]

To win the kind of loyalty he needed, a captain might court individual soldiers, who of course were free to choose whether or not to enlist under a particular officer. It seems to have been an established principle to win recruits with liberality, although few potential volunteers were entertained as lavishly as Jabez Fitch. In January 1756 Fitch "had some discourse" with Lieutenant Colonel William Whiting about "going with him in the intended expedition." He served as Whiting's clerk that year, and, when he took his accounts to Whiting on Christmas Day 1756, he "had a very good dinner and was treated vastly handsome." Fitch served again in 1757, as a sergeant in the company of which John Durkee was first lieutenant, and in November enlisted as a ranger for the winter under now-Captain Durkee, who "gave me a strong invitation to tarry with him." An officer's reputation was critical, and it could be fragile. A militia captain in Hebron reported in March 1757 that Captain Edmund Welles had recruited more men than had been expected "considering the unjust reports spread about him." A British observer claimed later that year that officers recruited soldiers with "no other design than to fill their own pockets with the public treasure." Officers did make money for every man they enlisted, but their profit was built into the system, put there by the elected leaders of the colony. Some officers may have abused the system by recruiting unsuitable soldiers just to fill their companies, but the Assembly did not object as long as the system did what it was designed it to do: raise the number of men the colony needed.[72]

71. On Durkee's following, see CHC:X/65–66, 163–64, 216, 241–43, 301–02. On the idea of a following, see Rodger, *Wooden World*, pp. 119–24.

72. On the courting of Jabez Fitch, see Fitch, "Diary," I/41, 102, VII/244 (quotations). On Welles, see CHS-FIW:I/52 (quotation). On the British observer, see *Lloyd's Evening Post and British Chronicle,* Oct 1757 (quotation).

The desire for military rank was so great that the Assembly relied on it to promote recruiting. In March 1757 Captain Welles gave Mason Wattles of Hebron, who had been a sergeant in 1755, more than 11 pounds to pay bounties to any men he could persuade to enlist, money that Wattles agreed to repay "in case I am not appointed a lieutenant under said Welles." The captain failed to get Wattles a commission, but he undoubtedly tried to convince the men he had recruited to remain in his company. The Assembly regularized recruiting for rank in May 1759, when it had to raise a thousand men on short notice, by commissioning only those nominees who recruited a specified number of men, in this instance twenty-five soldiers for a captain's commission. Promotion could be a powerful incentive to remain in the service. John Durkee of Norwich was a twenty-nine-year-old first lieutenant about to go home in late 1757 when he was offered a captain's commission if he would stay the winter. Despite the fact that his wife had given birth to a son a week earlier, he thought higher rank was worth sacrificing time at home. Durkee had ambition and military ability, as well as the popularity he needed to capitalize on both. It doubtless came as no surprise to his wife that he served again as a captain in 1758, accepted a promotion to major in 1759, and served for the rest of the war.[73]

There was considerable upward mobility in the regiments over the years because most officers came from the same social and economic backgrounds as the soldiers, in sharp contrast to the social chasm that separated officers and men in the British regular regiments. The career of Seth King of Suffield illustrates how a man could rise through the ranks. He began as a twenty-year-old drummer in 1755, and was promoted a rank a year for the next six campaigns, reaching captain in 1761, an advance helped by the patronage of General Lyman, a fellow Suffield resident. His career was unusual only in that he served for eight consecutive years; others rose faster in rank. King tried to prosper economically as well as socially, but he did not live to enjoy it. A captain again in 1762, he died on 23 December (at age twenty-eight) of diseases contracted at Havana. His estate totaled 361 pounds, 321 pounds in cash, but with debts, including medical treatment, of 313 pounds.[74]

It seems that, like most of the soldiers in their companies, many officers were laboring men who were hard pressed to make a living. Second Lieu-

73. On Wattles, see CHS-FIW:II/409 (quotation). On recruiting for rank, see CA-War:VIII/190; and CPR:XI/252–53. On Durkee, see CHC:IX/262.

74. On King's estate, see Hartford:1763/3284.

tenant Nathaniel Griffin of Symsbury (who served in 1758 at age twenty-six) "always was a husbandman and by hard labor got his livelihood," and First Lieutenant Adam Hinman of Woodbury (who served four times, the last in 1759 at age forty-one) claimed that his labor was the only means he had to support himself and his family. Some officers worked alongside their men building forts and repairing bateaux. During the winter of 1755–56, Captain Noah Grant spent forty-one days hewing timber and setting chimney stones for the barracks at Fort Edward. When he died on 20 September 1756 at age thirty-seven, he left a "poor widow with a number of small children" and an estate "so small and so deeply insolvent" that no one would agree to administer it. Protracted service probably did nothing to help an officer's economic situation. Although Samuel Gaylord of Middletown rose from second lieutenant in 1755 to captain in 1760, he was bankrupt in October 1762 at age thirty-nine. Even field officers were not immune to financial troubles. Major John Slapp of Mansfield served for six consecutive years and was bankrupt in August 1763, at age forty-eight.[75]

Other officers were economically well-to-do but had a considerable portion of their wealth tied up in land, a situation that made the prospect of earning bounties and wages an attractive inducement. First Lieutenant Amos Stiles of Hebron (who served in 1758 at age fifty-four) left his wife and two sons an estate of 840 pounds, 80 percent of it in land. Bachelor Matthew Smith of Pomfret (a clerk in 1755 and an ensign in 1759) left an estate of nearly 1,100 pounds, also 80 percent in land. In 1762 Captain John Stanton of Groton (who served four times as a captain, 1758–62) left his wife, three sons, and three daughters an estate of nearly 1,400 pounds, 70 percent in land. In his will, the forty-eight-year-old Stanton allowed his slaves—a man, a woman, three boys, and a girl, presumably a family, valued at 15 percent of his estate—to choose with which of his sons they would live. And, finally, a few officers had enormous wealth. Major Isaac Foot of Branford left an estate of over 7,600 pounds when he died in 1755 at age forty-eight; 82 percent was in land, but with

75. On Griffin, see CA-War:IX/154. On Hinman, see CA-War:VI/253. On working on Fort Edward, see CA-War:V/285, 290. On Grant, see CA-War:X/314. For other impoverished officers, see the estates of Lieutenant John Lay, Guilford:1757/no number (55 pounds); Lieutenant Jabez Howland, Middletown:1759/1804 (20 pounds); Captain Caleb Sheldon, Hartford:1759/4824 (insolvent); and Lieutenant David Andrus, Hartford:1763/154 (insolvent). On Gaylord, see CA-War:IX/329. On Slapp, see *Summary,* 26 Aug 1763.

1,280 pounds in movables easily covering his 520 pounds in debts. He had no evident economic reason for risking his life in military service.[76]

Some idea of the character and personality of the officers can be gleaned from two examples. The Assembly appointed fifty-year-old Ebenezer Leach of Coventry a captain in September 1755, sixteen months after it had commissioned him as a militia captain over bitter objections about his character. One deponent had heard a church member say Leach was "very debaucht [*sic*] in his language respecting women," and had seen "no reformation in him but rather [he] grows worse and worse." Seven others had testified that he was "vain, prophane, and of unclean conversation." But his supporters had contended he was "a gentleman and a Christian." A petition signed by seventy-four militiamen had described him as a good church member and militia lieutenant, a man of a "jesting disposition" who kept "a generous house" and treated "all with freedom and civility." Leach was not a model citizen (he had already been fined for threatening another man), but he was clearly the sort of ebullient, boisterous, and generous man who would be expected to attract recruits quickly, even for such unpromising service as reinforcing the army at Lake George. Once was apparently enough, however; the Assembly did not appoint him again. A glimpse of Major John Slap's behavior on the way to war in 1757 shows that he too was not an abstemious role model. At Farmington on 29 April, Jabez Fitch recorded in his diary that Slap "complained of being dry because he did not drink enough yesterday" and acknowledged he had been drunk the day before. His conduct was high-spirited, and therefore attractive to recruits, but God-fearing members of the Assembly could not have condoned it. Not all behavior was just boisterous and compara- tively innocent. Especially in the early years before the regiments stabi- lized under a cadre of long-serving captains, junior officers were confined for disobeying orders, a most serious offense in any army. Theft by an officer was especially corrosive of trust and authority: a lieutenant was

76. On Stiles, see Colchester:1758/2896. On Smith, see Fairfield:1760/ 5961. Other ex-officers did not prosper after the war. Captain Benjamin Ruggles of New Milford, who served four times, died in May 1769 at age forty-four and left "no movable estate" (CA-War:X/283). On Stanton, see New London:1762/ 5044. On other officers who were tied up in land, see Lieutenant Solomon Grant, Windham:1757/1651 (77 percent land); and Lieutenant Thomas Foster, New Haven:1757/4043 (65 percent land), also a slave owner. "Spanish Negroes" were part of the plunder brought back from Havana in 1762 (WO-34:XLIII/443–44). On Foot, see Guilford:1758/no number.

court martialed in 1759 for stealing an ensign's shirt, conduct a court of inquiry called "very unbecoming an officer."[77]

The lack of large numbers of politically prominent company officers was balanced in part by the few major political leaders who served in field rank. Joseph Spencer of East Haddam was an important local figure—a major in the militia, justice of the peace, probate judge, and former deputy—when he accepted an appointment as a major in 1758 (at age forty-four) and a lieutenant colonel in 1759–60. But the Assembly exacted a price from him that helps explain why most local leaders stayed home. In 1759–60 it appointed a substitute probate judge because it did not want the district to "remain destitute" while Spencer went to war. When the size of the force was reduced in 1761, Spencer abandoned the lure of military glory for the steady income of his judicial positions. He had no reason to serve: Canada had been conquered in 1760, and he had no interest in an imperial military commission. His three-summer absence did not harm his political career back home since he was elected an assistant in 1766.[78]

The most prominent political leader to go to war was Phineas Lyman of Suffield, who was the ninth-ranking assistant, forty years old, when the Assembly named him to command all Connecticut forces in 1755. Unlike Spencer, he was unable to balance military service with political office, especially since he chose to serve for all eight years. He failed to win reelection as an assistant in May 1759. Some voters undoubtedly took out on him their frustration about the lack of success in 1758, but many voters must have realized that one man could not organize and lead an army each summer and still remain an effective political leader. Lyman took the rebuff in stride: "My disposition to serve . . . to the extent of my power is not lessened by any frown I have met with from . . . [the voters]; but I conceit I am better able to serve 'em in the field than in the cabinet at present." Although he remained on the list of nominees through October 1764, he never regained his political prominence.[79]

77. On Leach, see CA-Mil:V/196–207 (quotations 197, 200, 203, 205–06). On Slap, see Fitch, "Diary," I/242–43 (quotation). Ensign Ezekiel Lewis disobeyed orders in 1757 (Gridley, *Diary,* p. 28). On the lieutenant, John Chick, see CHS-FIW:I/293 (quotation).

78. On Spencer's replacement as probate judge, see CPR:XI/248, 433–44.

79. On Lyman, a Yale College graduate in 1738, see Dexter, *Yale Graduates,* I/603–06; CHC:XVIII/27 (quotation); and Clark, *Lyman.* Holding two public offices was disastrous financially for thirty-year-old Timothy Seymour, a Hartford

The fact that colonial soldiers enlisted to serve under specific officers, from captain up to major general, meant that colonial officers were not interchangeable. Replacing dead or disabled company officers on campaign was only a partial exception since senior officers paid attention to choosing new officers who were acceptable to the soldiers. The weakness of this personalized command structure was most evident in 1755, when the colonies were acting as partners. The Assembly insisted that its contribution entitled it to have its chief officer appointed and paid by its neighbors as second-in-command of the army. Massachusetts and New York eventually agreed, but not before Lyman had threatened to resign, a prospect that led "many of his officers" and "many also of the soldiery" to refuse to continue because they had enlisted "in the most explicit manner to serve" under his command. On this issue, expeditionary soldiers were adhering to militia practice, where respect was accorded to individuals rather than to ranks. By contrast, Britain had instituted over a half-century earlier the more flexible system in which rank was respected and men enlisted to serve the king, not the colonel.[80]

Many Connecticut officers were touchy about proper respect for their rank and precedence in their regiments. In 1755–56 precedence was established "by the priority of the date of commissions of equal rank in former service or in the militia command." Seniority continued to be determined according to this rule, which was modified to exclude prior imperial service in July 1756, when one of the colony's very few ex-imperial officers tried to usurp Lyman's command. David Wooster, who had been a Connecticut captain in 1745, a captain in the colonial regular regiment at Louisbourg until 1748, and was now the forty-five-year-old colonel of the Second Regiment, jealously demanded "rank of General Lyman on [the basis of] his commission of ancient date in the King's service." A council of the senior colonial officers turned down his appeal by ruling "in favor of the commissions of elder date for the present service." In March 1759 the Assembly specified that the sequence in which it appointed officers did not establish their precedence, something which

---

tax collector when he was appointed a first lieutenant in 1759. He turned over his responsibilities to a previous year's collector, who died insolvent immediately thereafter and created a financial tangle that nearly ruined Seymour (CA-FC:V/18).

80. On serving under Lyman, see CHC:XVIi/101, 104, 106–07 (quotations), 123–24. On the British army, see Childs, *British Army*; and Scouller, *Armies*.

could only be done by the "rules and customs of the army," that is, by amount of prior service in the colonial army.[81]

The junction of colonial and regular troops in July 1756 raised some tough questions about the place of colonial officers in the imperial military system. According to British rules then in force, all colonial general and field officers ranked below captains in the regular army. A council of the senior colonial officers asserted that if a junction led to their loss of command and rank, "the effect will be a dissolution of the greater part of the army and have a direct tendency to prevent the raising [of] any provincial troops . . . in the future." The senior officers claimed that "privates universally hold it as one part of their terms, on which they enlisted, that they were to be commanded by their own officers, and this is a principle so strongly imbibed that it is not in the power of man to remove it." In August, the earl of Loudoun promulgated a small concession: colonial general and field officers would rank as <u>eldest captains</u>. This was not enough to assuage wounded pride, however, and to promote cooperation William Pitt in 1757 ordered all colonial officers to "take rank with the officers of the regulars according to the date of their respective commissions," thus placing them just below British officers of the same rank.[82]

However distasteful to the British sense of an appropriate command structure, enlisting soldiers under specific officers was nothing new in colonial America; the Assembly had always wanted its soldiers to remain under their own officers and not serve directly under regular officers. It was therefore highly unusual when ten senior officers dissented from the council majority in July 1756 and agreed to serve under British regular officers. The minority was led by Lyman, Wooster, and Whiting, and included six of the twelve Connecticut field officers. These men, described

81. On precedence in 1755–56, see CHC:XVII/101 (quotation), 104–07. On Wooster, who was also jealous of Whiting, see MHS-IW/26 Jul 1756 (quotations); and Whiting, "Letters," p. 140. The Assembly's views on precedence in 1759 are in CPR:XI/234 (quotation).

82. On the junction, see MHS-FP:XLI/244–46a (quotation); MHS-IW/26 Jul 1756; Johnson, *Papers,* IX/484–85; Shirley, *Correspondence,* II/492–519 (quotation 497–98); and CO-5:I/586–87, 815. On colonial general and field officers ranking as eldest captains, see Ford, *Orders,* pp. 77–78. On Pitt's alteration, promulgated at Fort Edward on 9 March 1758, see Fitch, "Diary," XII/159 (quotation). On the entire matter, see Pargellis, *Loudoun,* pp. 92–93; and Leach, *Roots,* pp. 118–21. At Fort Edward in July 1757, colonial officers were ordered to wear their swords to ensure that the regulars would recognize them (Ford, *Orders,* p. 44).

by a Massachusetts colonel as former colonial regular officers plus "two or three others," presumably wished to ingratiate themselves with imperial commanders. Whiting claimed most of his colleagues were being over-sensitive: he did not "think there need be any difficulty provided the [colonial] officers use their endeavors to make things easy." Connecticut men had been tempted by the imperial military service since 1740, but these officers displayed a greater interest in such opportunities, and less in a career as a leader back home, than had any of their predecessors. Lyman in particular worked hard to make himself acceptable—British officers considered him to be more intelligent than the other colonial officers—and he held some untraditional notions about how to organize colonial forces. He favored a standing army and in September 1758 saw "no difficulty" in raising long-service colonial troops if imperial officials would commission "some New England gentlemen" like him to do the job.[83]

Lyman was correct in implying that leadership was the prerequisite for managing military forces in colonial America. Although they were the most important element in turning farmers into soldiers each spring, Connecticut officers generally lacked the social rank and prestige required to command respect automatically, and maintained order by force of personality and example. They had to balance discipline with the need to prevent soldiers from deserting, without compromising their ability to persuade men to reenlist if necessary. While courts martial could impose severe corporal punishment, officers generally treated soldiers with considerable indulgence. Whiting in particular earned a reputation for promoting sobriety, good order, and true religion without being overly strict. According to his chaplain, he gave "universal satisfaction" by his "judiciously mild method of treating human nature."[84]

The fact that the soldiers clung firmly to a contractual view of military

83. On the Assembly's attitude, see CHC:XVII/254. On the minority, which included three colonels, two lieutenant colonels, and one major from Connecticut, see MHS-FP:XLI/244–46a; and MHS-IW/26 Jul 1756 (quotation). On Whiting, see YU-MS:Whiting/9 (quotation). On Lyman, see MHS-FP:XLII/1; and MHS-IW/15 Sep 1758 (quotation). He joined regular officers in their entertainments, especially drinking, to the disgust of one Connecticut chaplain. Lyman privately said he disliked hearing British officers swearing, but he did not reprove them (Graham, "Journal," VIII/212).

84. On Whiting, see Taylor, *Praise,* p. 25 (quotation); and CSL-Nathan Whiting.

service always made it difficult for the officers to maintain strict discipline, but nowhere was the problem as acute as when the soldiers believed they had completed their enlistment contract. Connecticut rangers nearly mutinied on 20 February 1758 when they were told that they could not "go home as soon as the time which they had enlisted for was expired." Governor Fitch made matters worse by siding with the rangers. By telling Abercromby that "the government can't without an infraction of their contract hold them for future service," Fitch chose to protect Connecticut against imperial meddling in the way it made war rather than make enforcing discipline easier for the officers. In his opinion, the rangers were not obliged to remain in the field "without they had entered again into the service." A few years later, some officers showed that they shared a contractual attitude when they tried to influence where they would serve in 1761. They did not want to go to Oswego again, and refused to accept their commissions until Amherst revealed where he was going to send them. The general told Fitch that men who declined "by reason of an aversion to the Oswego Road are not fit persons to be officers." That was true by British standards, but complaining about it did not help integrate two forces with such contrasting views of leadership.[85]

Connecticut officers behaved well on the few occasions when they saw battle, especially considering their lack of combat experience. The *Gazette* praised Whiting's conduct in extricating the rear of the scouting column from the early morning ambush on 8 September 1755, and later reported that he had "behaved exceedingly well," although a Massachusetts physician claimed that, "upon the first fire of the enemy, [Whiting] gave express command [to] retreat," and argued that "had they stood the ground . . . they would easily have drove" off the French. Lyman took command of the base camp after the commander-in-chief, William Johnson, was wounded, and he acted with what the *Gazette* thought was "undaunted courage and the greatest presence of mind" in directing its defense against a frontal assault by French regulars. Lyman's principal contribution was to remain calm and concentrate on what he had to do: steady raw troops so they could win, from behind a barricade, a defensive victory over a numerically inferior opponent.[86]

85. On the rangers, see Fitch, "Diary," XI/147, 221–22; XII/159–60; and WO-34:XVIII/2, 3b (quotation), 12b (quotation). On where to serve in 1761, CHC:XVIII/109–10 (quotation).

86. On Whiting, see *Gazette,* 20 Sep, 27 Sep 1755 (quotation); and CHC:XVII/195. On the physician, Perez Marsh, see MHS-IW/26 Sep 1755

The hardest service thereafter was the skirmishing that went on constantly in the months between major operations. Even Lyman participated in this war of scout and ambush. On 14 June 1757 he marched out of Fort Edward at the head of three hundred men, "painted like a Mohog [*sic*] as many other officers of the scout were." Captain Israel Putnam of Pomfret (age thirty-seven in 1755) was the most active Connecticut ranger as a colleague of the more famous Robert Rogers. Scouting imposed considerable wear and tear on officers because they were invariably up front directing the action. Putnam himself was overpowered and captured on 8 August 1758, and his principal lieutenant, twenty-five-year-old Robert Durkee of Windham (the younger brother of Captain John Durkee), suffered severe wounds. Durkee "was in the front and hottest of the battle, and amidst the fire of the enemy until they were repelled and forced to give way." He was shot in the wrist and groin, and still walked with crutches when he went home in October. The capture of Putnam and the wounding of Durkee disheartened the Connecticut rangers that day, and they could not be gathered to pursue the beaten enemy.[87]

Given the danger and fatigue of military service, why did men accept commissions in the regiments? Although the pay and bounties did not attract men to the senior ranks (Lyman's wages in 1755, over 140 pounds, were said to be not "a quarter equal to his business" as a lawyer in Suffield), many officers went to war to earn money, and were not happy when the Assembly's parsimony and wartime inflation made service a money-losing proposition. In May 1758 field officers and senior captains complained that their pay was "not a meet recompense . . . and is in no measure sufficient to support them in any decent manner in their respective ranks in the army." Despite the ominous mention of "a general uneasiness among the officers," the Lower House refused to increase their wages. The Assembly did increase pay in 1759 and 1760, but officers still claimed they could not compete in the splendor of their uniforms and accoutrements

---

(quotation); he lost many friends in the ambush. On Lyman, see *Gazette,* 13 Dec 1755 (quotation).

87. On Lyman, see Fitch, "Diary," III/43 (quotation); and CSL-Welles/10 Jun 1757. On Putnam, see Humphreys, *Putnam,* pp. 14–65; and Niven, *Hero,* pp. 19–37. The service was so hard that the Assembly gave the principal rangers bonuses in 1755 and 1756 (CA-War:VI/14, 98; and CA-War:VII/221). On scouting in 1756, see Graham, "Journal," pp. 210–11. On Robert Durkee, see CA-War:VIII/237 (quotation). On the scattering of the rangers, see Pitt, *Correspondence,* I/322.

with their peers in other colonies or the regulars. Long-serving officers were especially sensitive to the erosion of their earnings in the last years of the war. In May 1761 they complained that the proposed contract with the sutlers would send prices so high that "their hard-earned wages" would be taken from them to enrich men who "have not ventured where there was danger to life and property."[88]

Interest in earning rights to new lands was a powerful and pervasive motive for serving in the army. Lyman was among the 114 officers-to-be (21 percent of the total of 541) who had invested in western land before the war by joining the Susquehannah and Delaware land companies. Pre-war land speculation had even created some hard feelings. Lyman did not trust Hugh Ledlie of Windham, a captain in 1761–62, because he had tried to buy land out from under Lyman and his partners in 1754. In November 1759 six senior officers from Connecticut and Massachusetts petitioned Amherst for a grant of land along the road running from Crown Point to the Connecticut valley. The French had been "entirely dispossessed" of the area, and the officers wanted to create new settlements there to act as a buffer for the towns behind the frontier. Amherst endorsed the plan, but the conquest of Canada a year later removed the danger it was designed to meet. Lyman continued to importune imperial officials for a land grant, first in what is now northern Vermont, later in the Ohio valley. His prestige made him the principal spokesman for ex-soldiers who desired land; the *Gazette* said that five thousand veterans were ready to accompany him to Ohio.[89]

For a few years, the Company of Military Adventurers, organized by fifty ex-officers at Hartford in mid-June 1763, appeared to be the ex-soldiers' best chance for a land grant. Although the cost of joining the company rose from two to three dollars in November, two thousand men had subscribed by mid-1764, vivid testimony to the mania for land speculation. With the monies thus raised, the company sent Lyman to London

88. On Lyman, see CA-War:V/288; and *Gazette,* 13 Dec 1755 (quotation). On wages in 1758, see CHC:XVII/339–40 (quotations); also see table 5.2. On the sutlers, see CA-War:IX/137.

89. On membership in land companies, see Boyd, *Susquehannah.* Lyman also invested in New Hampshire land before, during, and after the war (New Hampshire, *Town Charters,* XXVI/560, XXV/282, 245). On Ledlie, see Johnson, *Papers,* I/400; and CHS-JT/13 Feb 1764. On requesting a land grant, see CHC:XVIII/29–32. On importuning Amherst for land, see WO-34:XLIII/427–32, 441–42, 543, 565. On respect for Lyman, see *Gazette,* 23 Jan 1768.

to solicit a grant in Nova Scotia, but his efforts were unsuccessful. Even when Lyman returned empty-handed in the summer of 1772, he revived hope that individual company members might receive land in the Mississippi valley. But men calling themselves "disbanded and discarded provincial officers and soldiers" objected that, because the "greater part" of the company members were not veterans, such an offer did not reward ex-soldiers, especially since they had to pay to join the company to get the grants. Lyman himself settled near Natchez in the summer of 1774, but he died soon after arriving and the project collapsed. Despite high hopes and Lyman's considerable efforts, no organized group of veterans ever received land from the imperial government as a reward for military service.[90]

Most officers had intangible reasons for serving, ranging from local patriotism to the chance to win favor with the imperial government. An article in the *Gazette* for 13 December 1755 described Lyman as "a gentleman of an established reputation" who left his family and his business "at his country's call" because he was "a true patriot, fir'd with a zeal for the public good." While such motives were undoubtedly present, along with substantial sentiment to defeat the French, officers like Lyman served again and again principally to earn rank and prestige, which might pay off in imperial preferment some day. It meant a great deal to some men to be known by the highest rank they had held on active service, even long after the regiments were disbanded. Lyman, for example, was referred to as "general" for the rest of his life.[91]

Connecticut officers did not succeed in using military service as a springboard to careers in the imperial service because they did not have very good connections. Nathan Whiting tried harder than anyone except Lyman, and even accepted the captaincy of one of the South Carolina independent companies to get on the imperial military establishment. When Parliament disbanded all the independent companies in the summer of 1764, he returned to Connecticut and began a campaign to win the imperial customs collectorship at New Haven. He told one prospective benefactor that he "should be glad to get it in conjunction" with his half

90. On the Adventurers, see *Summary*, 24 Jun, 2 and 23 Sep 1763; *Gazette*, 19 Nov 1763; Clark, *Lyman*, p. 60; and Bates, *Two Putnams*, pp. 9–16. Colonel Whiting, Major Durkee, and Captain Ledlie were all directors. On disgruntled veterans, see *Courant*, 22–29 Dec 1772 (quotation).

91. On Lyman, see *Gazette*, 13 Dec 1755 (quotation). On religious motives, see Hatch, *Sacred*, pp. 36–44.

pay as an unemployed ex-imperial officer; if he could not get both stipends, he would gladly accept the collectorship "if I can make it a little better than half pay." Former Governor Roger Wolcott thought that his good showing at Lake George on 8 September 1755 would win him the job, but he was wrong. Whiting never got the collectorship, a circumstance that helped to persuade him to focus his political ambitions closer to home. He was elected a deputy from New Haven for the first time in May 1769, and was nominated as an assistant in the following October. He was still on the nominating list when he died on 4 April 1771, at age forty-seven. Although the *Journal* eulogized him as a man who might have become governor one day, in fact he had devoted all but his last two years to seeking imperial favor. Failure to gain recognition in London had led him, like many other colonists, to rethink where his loyalties lay.[92]

Connecticut's senior officers did not have an easy time transferring wartime prestige into peacetime political careers. As had been the case since King Philip's War, if the men who led their neighbors to war were not already politically prominent, war service was not the way to postwar political power. Ex-officers were respectable citizens—the field officers and captains were roughly as old and as wealthy as men elected to the Assembly—but the vast majority were not on the road to elective office. Only 33 ex-officers (6 percent of the 541) were elected to militia rank before the Revolution; 7 became deputies and 4 who had been deputies before the war added judicial appointments thereafter. Some highly respected individuals never got the chance. Lieutenant Colonel Nathan Payson of Hartford wore himself out serving for six consecutive years, and was preparing to go to war a seventh time when he died on 17 April 1761, at age forty. His funeral included a procession of militiamen and Masons, and attracted the "greatest concourse of people" for such an occasion in living memory.[93]

---

92. On Whiting, see CHC:XVII/108, 195; *Journal*, 19 Apr 1771; YU-MS:Whiting/32; and Dexter, *Yale Graduates*, I/750–51. On the captaincy of the South Carolina company, see YU-MS:Whiting/20. On soliciting the collectorship, see YU-MS:Whiting/10 (quotation). His estate totaled 1,322 pounds, not enormous but certainly making him well-off; his inventory was filled with the goods of a man with pretentions to elegant living (YU-MS:Whiting/31). In May 1758 Lyman had procured for his son a commission as ensign in the regulars (WO-34:XXVIII/196).

93. On Payson, see *Gazette*, 9 May 1761 (quotation); and *Summary*, 1 May 1761.

The senior officers might have been more popular politically if the war had been successful sooner. Popular disenchantment with slow progress was a major reason why expeditionary officers did not move into the political leadership after the war. The defeat of the French in September 1755 raised expectations that went unfulfilled for three years. Lack of success in 1756 was particularly hard to stomach. The anonymous author of "A Brief Address" in the *Gazette* for 14 August asked the people to be patient. "What can have a greater tendency to induce us to enmity, than railing at the officers of the army because they don't execute things which in the nature of them are impossible? . . . If it was as small a matter to bring Crown Point into our hands, as it is to tell how easily it might be done, the business would have been long ago dispatched. And it has been too much the practice of the people . . . to seek flaws in the characters of our rulers. . . . [I] desire you not to harbor any angry thoughts" against them or the officers of the army.[94]

Several circumstances—including the lack of politically prominent officers, the shared hardships of service, the promotion of veteran noncommissioned officers, and the sting of public criticism—forged ex-officers, especially those who served for three years or more, into a self-conscious group with interests and concerns different from those of the colony's traditional political leaders. Their most important collective action was to oppose accommodation with the Stamp Act in 1765–66. Ex-officers were among those who were unhappy about Parliament's attempt to generate a revenue through a tax on paper because it seemed to open the door to more imperial supervision and taxation. They had had close contact with imperial officials during the war, and it seems that the high-handed contempt of British regular officers for their bumpkin cousins radicalized them. At Fort Edward on a Sunday in August 1756, regular officers made a bad impression by "drinking, talking, and laughing during the whole of the [religious] service, to the disturbance and disaffection of most present. This was not only a bare neglect but an open contempt of the worship of God," in which, it must be added, Lyman also participated. Callousness even alienated officers seeking imperial favor. Whiting found the British commander at Crown Point in 1761 to be "high in his notion of command and not very sensible nor [*sic*] obliging." Having seen British officers in action, ex-officers had a vivid idea of what imperial administration might mean.[95]

94. The "Address" is in *Gazette,* 14 Aug 1756 (quotation).
95. On the religious service, see Graham, "Journal," VIII/212 (quotation);

Veteran officers and soldiers emerged as a political force on 18 September 1765, when between five hundred and a thousand men stopped Connecticut's stamp distributor, Jared Ingersoll, at Wethersfield as he was riding to Hartford to attend a special Assembly session that had been called to consider the colony's response to the new tax. Ingersoll described the mob in ways that make it sound like a military operation, and remarked that "some of those people . . . , I supposed, were militia officers." That John Durkee led the mob, and Israel Putnam was said to have been instrumental in raising it, make it clear that former expeditionary officers, not militia officers, organized and controlled this display of force. And who more logical for them to call upon for help than their former comrades in arms? While the mob did not physically harm Ingersoll, he got the impression it would have done so if he had not resigned his office, an impression that even the more cautious opponents of the Stamp Act did nothing to dispel. No further mob action was needed because a single use of force was enough to intimidate anyone who might have wanted to use stamped paper. The incumbent leaders used the excuse that no stamped paper was available in Connecticut (it was being held at New York) to suspend all government functions until word arrived in the spring of 1766 that Parliament had repealed the Act. This outcome precluded any further need to call upon veterans for extralegal action, which was undoubtedly a great relief to the incumbents.[96]

Opponents of the Stamp Act, including many incumbents who did not want to provoke the imperial government into revoking the charter, were not happy to see violence become the cornerstone of the colony's resistance. However, by abdicating leadership in a crisis, the incumbents temporarily lost some of their influence. Because ex-officers controlled the muscle that molded discontent into a political weapon, their principal leaders won some political power: both Putnam and Durkee were elected to the Assembly for the first time in May 1766. However, the upheaval was not a revolution. Traditional leaders quickly learned to be less conciliatory to an imperial government that was not yet ready to compel obedience to its edicts by force of arms. Men with extensive political experience, often the previous incumbents, were returned to office as soon as the crisis had passed, while ex-officers were retired from politics. Durkee never again

---

he seems to have been perpetually disgruntled. On Whiting, who was less sensitive than other officers, see CHC:XVIII/135 (quotation).

96. On mobbing Ingersoll, see Ingersoll, *Letters,* pp. 61ff., 47n (quotation); and Maier, *Resistance,* pp. 304–07.

won election to the Lower House, and Putnam remained there only through October 1767. The next time Pomfret sent Putnam to the Assembly was in May 1775, when the colony again had need of men who knew how to organize and lead an army.[97]

Veteran officers performed one more vital service for Connecticut, ten years after forcing the confrontation with imperial authority. In 1775 they were the indispensable element in making armed rebellion a success. Leading commanders like Putnam and Durkee, along with many less well known veterans, steadied the raw American troops in the early battles against the British. They were the ones from whom the rest learned how to be soldiers. Imperturbable and inspirational leadership from French and Indian War veterans, including George Washington himself, helped the American Revolution to survive its crucial first year and grow from a rebellion into a successful war for independence.

97. As soon as it was clear that Parliament was vacillating over enforcing the Act, Lyman wrote to Trumbull from London supporting the colonial cause: "the mother country must consent that her American children must remain free." He knew that "if the Americans insist on freedom . . . perhaps they must see some red coats to try the experiment" (CHS-JT/27 Sep 1768). By then, Trumbull too supported the cause of American rights (CHS-JT/18 Jul 1769).

Chapter Six

From Colony to State

TOWARD INDEPENDENCE

Connecticut underwent a profound transition in the fifteen years after the fall of Montreal in 1760, as pride in being part of the British empire turned into a rebellion to preserve its traditional privileges of self-government. The way in which Britain fought the final French and Indian war had the unintended effect of hastening this transition. The vast expansion of the regular army in North America ended Connecticut's isolation from the empire, and reinforced the distaste the colony had always felt for imperial authority. For the first time, large numbers of Connecticut men came into close contact with British regulars, who showed more disdain for their colonial counterparts than they had at Carthagena in 1740 or Louisbourg in 1745. Disputes between regular and colonial officers about rank and the proper role of the colonial levies helped to poison imperial relations.[1]

Negative impressions were not confined to camps on the New York frontier. The imperial government's decision to recruit and quarter regulars in the colonies brought more Connecticut men and women into daily contact with the agents of imperial authority than ever before. Recruiting

1. Historians have yet to explore how fighting the final French war set the stage for the Revolution. On imperial politics, see Greene, "Seven Years' War." On how the defense of political rights became a drive for independence, see Morgan, *Challenge.* On antagonisms between regulars and colonists, see Leach, "Brothers"; Leach, *Roots,* pp. 107–33; Anderson, *People's Army,* pp. 111–41; and Rogers, *Empire,* pp. 59–74.

parties became familiar sights as they went from town to town looking for volunteers, a difficult job because few colonists were attracted to the regular service. In November 1756 the earl of Loudoun complained that his recruiters had "not got one man yet" in New England, and in March 1757 he reported that the region was "drained of that sort of men" who might enlist. Recruiters were so desperate that they used methods which left the impression that imperial authorities were capricious and cruel, and thus helped to shape colonial attitudes about larger political issues.[2]

The lengths to which recruiters would go was seen in December 1757, when a Stonington peddler stopped to sell a turkey to the owner of a New London tavern where a recruiting party was resting. The owner did not have exact money, and before he could send for change, a soldier offered to pay for the bird. The peddler took the money and was instantly told he was "a King's soldier, for he had got the King's money." The sheriff eventually rescued the unwilling recruit, but only after a scuffle between the regulars and some local sailors. Governor Fitch complained that the recruiters were "guilty of very unjustifiable conduct," and Loudoun concurred when he received a full account of the incident. But nothing was done to change the image of imperial tyranny left in the minds of the New Londoners.[3]

Lingering resentment about recruiting methods made it difficult to find volunteers for the rest of the war. On 30 March 1759 Fitch complained to General Amherst that recruiters had again engaged in "that scandalous practice of shaking hands and leaving money." Even an increase in the bounty in May 1762 did not help the situation. Only two Connecticut officers accepted Amherst's suggestion that they recruit for the regulars while enlisting men for their companies, and one later regretted it. Fitch reported that "as soon as he let people know he had such orders, men appeared shy of him, so that he could not get a man" for his own company. Connecticut men might want bounty money, but most of them were not going to serve in the regulars to get it.[4]

2. On recruiting, see Pargellis, *Loudoun*, pp. 104–31; Rogers, *Empire*, pp. 37–50; and CO-5:II/124 and 262 (quotations).

3. On the episode, see Pargellis, *Loudoun*, p. 128; and Rogers, *Empire*, p. 46 (quotations).

4. On the "scandalous practices," see WO-34:XXVIII/42. On colonial officers recruiting for the regulars, see WO-34:XXVIII/85 (quotation), 87, 93, 181, 187. Fitch hoped in vain that "after the provincial levies [were] completed," regular recruiting would have "better success" (WO-34:XXVIII/77).

Recruiting parties were a nuisance compared with the burden of quartering regular regiments over the winter. The troops were a strain on the five Fairfield county towns that housed the 1,300 men, women, and children of Fraser's Highlanders in 1757–58, and the 1,100 men and women of the Forty-eighth Regiment in 1758–59. For example, Stamford added 250 soldiers, 17 women, and 9 children to its 2,800 people in 1757, and Norwalk's 3,100 people made room for 200 soldiers, and 14 women, in 1758. The towns did not have enough taverns to house all the soldiers and had to quarter many with local families, by compulsion when necessary; senior officers leased entire houses. The towns would have preferred to have had the regulars billeted around the colony, but they realized that the troops had to be kept together to maintain discipline, to reduce the risk of desertion, and to speed their mobilization in the spring. The Assembly reminded the towns "it would not be good policy to make a breach" with imperial generals over quartering, and shared some of the burden by adding 2 pence sterling to the imperial government's 4-pence victualing allowance and by agreeing to reimburse their costs in supplying the regulars with bedding, firewood, candles, cider, and utensils. The five towns received 4,400 pounds of lawful money for quartering the two regiments in 1757–59, sums which Parliament ultimately repaid to Connecticut.[5]

The presence of so many regulars made the local residents sensitive about the misuse of military force. The towns complained that allowing the Highlanders to carry their muskets when off duty caused "notorious breaches of the peace, to the terror and disquiet of His Majesty's good subjects." Some Highlanders even used the weathervane on the Anglican church at Stratford for target practice. The problems were so serious that Fitch asked imperial officials to take steps "to protect the inhabitants of

5. On quartering regulars, see CA-War:VII/278, 281 (quotation), 288–89; CA-War:VIII/141–42, 208–11; and CPR:XI/339, 341–42. The 1756 census is in CPR:X/618. When a house in Fairfield that had been leased by some officers burned down in December 1758, the Assembly avoided civil suits in a Connecticut court by allowing the owners to raise 100 pounds in a lottery (CA-War:VIII/143; CPR:IX/217–18; *Gazette,* 30 Dec 1758, 3 Mar 1759). On the victualing subsidy, see CPR:XI/176, 304–07; food could not be supplied "for less than 6 pence without manifest loss." The Assembly offered a 4 pence per diem subsidy for recruiting parties five times in the years 1763–71 (CPR:XII/136, 543–54, 608; and CPR:XIII/126, 422). On reimbursement, see CPR:XI/190, 339, 341–42.

the country from insults of those sent into it for its defense." In 1758–59 assaults by soldiers on civilians raised the issue of who had jurisdiction over the troops. There was no disagreement that guilty soldiers should be punished, but problems arose when the victims sued their assailants for damages. Regular officers took a dim view of civil suits, since the soldiers had no money to pay fines or court costs. To prevent their men from languishing in jail, the officers wanted to punish them with martial law, "which is equally sound and repressive of every crime and grievance, tho' not subject to such long confinements as the civil law."[6]

Although the Mutiny Act specified that soldiers were subject to the "ordinary process of law," the regulars did manage to circumvent Connecticut civil law. The most serious incident began on 15 January 1759, when three soldiers convicted of beating a Fairfield man were taken from the sheriff's custody by fifteen or twenty soldiers armed with clubs and swords. Fitch was incensed: the mob had violated "the known laws of the land, the rights of His Majesty's subjects and [was] in open contempt of the legal authority of the civil magistrate." Amherst promised to punish the rioters, and asked Fitch to persuade local authorities to allow martial law to supersede civil action. Fitch agreed in the interest of maintaining "a good harmony" between the army and the colony. His pragmatism was tested again on 25 February 1759, when a hundred soldiers took two comrades out of New Haven jail, action which the *Gazette* condemned as "tending to obstruct that harmony and good will that ought to subsist" between the colonists and the regulars. Although Fitch complained that if a jail could be "opened at pleasure by lawless multitudes the law of the community must be at an end," he hoped martial law would prevent any further disorder. That proved to be the case, as this was the last incident before the regulars left the colony for the 1759 campaign. Because the regulars thereafter spent their winters in the French forts they had captured, friction with Connecticut residents did not again explode into violence. Beatings and riots had not been common, but they did cause many in the colony to question the morality and value of the imperial relationship.[7]

6. On the Highlanders, see CPR:XI/178 (quotation); Wilcoxson, *Stratford*, pp. 310–11; and WO-34:XXVIII/8 (quotation), 14–15. Only one case of a Highlander assaulting a civilian came to Fitch's attention; it was apparently resolved by martial law (WO-34:XXVIII/18, 136). On the desire for martial law, see WO-34:XXVIII/139 (quotation). On an incident at Stratford in 1759, see CA-War:X/265; and CPR:XI/293, 296.

7. On the Mutiny Act, see Williams, *Constitution*, p. 35 (quotation). On

While Connecticut gained new perspectives on the imperial government during wartime, imperial officials also began to look at the colony in new and unfavorable ways. The most divisive issue for Connecticut residents was how to defend the highly popular efforts of the Delaware and Susquehannah land companies to create new settlements in northeast Pennsylvania. Faced with the massive task of ensuring that Canada stayed conquered, Amherst worried that overzealous land speculation might provoke an Indian war. Because Fitch feared that continuing settlement might "hazard . . . the public peace, in the blame whereof this government may possibly become involved," he convinced the Assembly in May 1762 to issue a proclamation prohibiting more settlements, a stance that made him very unpopular in eastern Connecticut but did not stop the companies. The imperial government put the governor in the first of many tight corners in mid-April 1763, when it ordered him to prevent all new settlements. The companies were unwilling to defy this edict, and they reluctantly suspended their activities until they could plead their case in London. A decision was still pending when the companies were overtaken by the outbreak of the long-feared war. On 15 October hostile Indians destroyed the settlements, an outcome which, one proprietor bitterly noted, saved "the government the trouble" of evicting them. The companies reestablished the settlements in the late 1760s, but by then attention had shifted to broader issues at the heart of the imperial relationship.[8]

Fear of an Indian war was one of the reasons why the imperial government decided to keep ten thousand British regular troops in North America after the end of the war. While they were also intended to keep order

---

the riot, see WO-34:XXVIII/23–33 (quotations 23–24, 33), 139–41. Fitch reserved the right of the injured to sue in Connecticut courts. On the jail break, see CPR:XI/326; *Gazette,* 3 Mar 1759; and WO-34:XXVIII/36–37, 140–41 (quotation). Two soldiers broke out of Norwich jail on 30 January 1759 without outside help (*Summary,* 4 Feb 1759). Two regulars (presumably recruits) who had been committed to Norwich jail on criminal prosecutions broke out on 30 January 1763 (*Summary,* 11 Feb 1763). The Assembly billeted 136 regular recruits in New Haven, Branford, and Wallingford in 1767–68 (CA-War:X/257–60; CPR:XII/541–43, 562–63).

8. On the land companies, see CHC:XVIII/98, 124–26, 128–29; *Summary,* 18 Jun 1762 (quotation); and Zeichner, *Years,* p. 32. Fitch had opposed western expansion since at least November 1754 (CHC:XVIII/72). On imperial censure, see CHC:XVIII/224–25, 229–30, 250–51; and *Summary,* 29 Apr and 24 Jun 1763. Eliphalet Dyer's comment is in Boyd, *Susquehannah Company,* pp. 25–26 (quotation).

in Canada, many of them were gradually moved to seacoast towns in the old colonies where they "had the added attraction of putting teeth in the imperial system." Imperial officials did not doubt that the system had to be tightened: trade regulations had been grossly violated during the war. At a time when Britain was paying enormous sums to subsidize colonial troops, colonial ships were trading with the French West Indies, enough of them from Connecticut so that London included it in accusations of helping the enemy.[9]

Connecticut merchants freely admitted that they thought trading with the French islands was a vital part of their economy. In August 1751 Governor Wolcott had claimed it allowed the colony to pay for British imports and "to have some money or credit to withstand the French in time of war." In June 1757 the earl of Loudoun, out of step with his colleagues, actually offered some military reasons to continue the trade. He suggested that "the smuggling trade to the West Indies and Holland" stimulated colonial commerce to the extent that it was able to provide him with both the ships and the sailors he needed to transport his intended expedition against Quebec. In and after 1758, Parliamentary subsidies removed the economic reasons for the trade and the massive investment of British money and manpower ensured that imperial commanders always had enough transports and seamen. Still, a letter in the *Gazette* of 6 June 1760 argued that trading should be legalized because it meant the "voluntary surrender" of the French West Indies trade for the duration of the war. Merchants in other colonies had made fortunes supplying provisions and horses to the French islands, and Connecticut merchants wanted to share in the opportunity.[10]

The imperial government took a very dim view of colonial trade with the enemy, and was not mollified by Connecticut's good wartime record. Aware that some imperial officials wanted to revoke the charter, Fitch reported in April 1761 that he had no evidence that Connecticut ships were trading with the French. But he had no proof only because he did

9. On putting teeth in the system, see Shy, *Lexington,* p. 67 (quotation); and Bullion, "'Ten Thousand Men.'"

10. On Wolcott, see CHC:XVI/97–99 (quotation). Loudoun's opinions are in YU-MS:Loudoun/8 (quotation). Connecticut's trade was primarily coastal (*Summary,* 15 Aug 1760). On the West Indies, see Weaver, *Trumbull,* pp. 32–34. There were only a few Connecticut ships at Monti Cristi on Hispaniola, where goods were re-exported to the French islands: four of twenty-seven in February 1759, one of thirty-five in May 1761 (Beer, *Policy,* p. 98).

not want it. Merchants continued their illegal activities, even smuggling with the complicity of the New London customs collector. When Amherst asked for an embargo in May 1762 to prevent the hoarding of provisions for export to the French West Indies, the Assembly quickly enacted it, and asked Fitch to investigate Connecticut's complicity in illegal trading. Not surprisingly, the governor found no violations: he was "informed by such as are most likely to know (except the persons concerned) . . . that no attempts are made by any inhabitants in the colony to supply provisions to the enemy." Fitch was still protesting Connecticut's innocence after the war ended, but by then the imperial government was not listening.[11]

Anger about wartime trade with the French contributed to Parliament's decision to tighten trade regulations and to raise a revenue to keep the regulars in North America. Few colonists were willing to deny Parliament's right to regulate and tax colonial trade in the Sugar Act of 1764, because to do so would have been too close to asserting outright independence. But the Sugar Act by itself could not produce the needed revenue, so on 22 March 1765 Parliament passed the Stamp Act. It thought a stamp tax on paper was a good way to raise money to extend imperial control, but its decision aroused enormous resentment in the colonies. The colonists reacted like Englishmen who feared a standing army outside their control. At the Glorious Revolution in 1688, Parliament had asserted its right to consent annually to fund the army and navy. At a time when a vocal minority of Englishmen still thought that Parliament should have more control over how the king used the standing army, the colonial assemblies sought to have the same right to oversee funding for the regulars in their jurisdictions that Parliament had in England. The Stamp Act crystallized opposition to closer imperial supervision, and pushed the colonists further down the intellectual and emotional road to independence.[12]

---

11. On threatening to revoke the charter, see Great Britain, *Privy Council,* IV/446. On Fitch's response, see CHC:XVIII/112 (quotation). On smuggling in October 1760, see New-York Historical Society, *Collections,* IX/26–28; and Stout, *Royal Navy,* pp. 16–17. On the charges, see WO-34:XXVIII/79 (quotation), 86 (quotation), 182–83; CPR:XII/63–65; and CHC:XVIII/250.

12. On the Sugar Act, see Morgan, *Prologue,* pp. 4–8. On using force to support imperial authority, see Morgan, *Prologue,* p. 184; and [Knox], "Imperial Reform," 122–25. Merchants claimed that taxing trade or imposing a stamp tax would worsen economic conditions in a colony exhausted by the war (CHC:XVIII/296). Customs officials in Connecticut netted 1,025 pounds sterling in the year

Governor Fitch knew the imperial government was scrutinizing Connecticut closely, and his wartime experience convinced him it intended to increase its control. He took the oath to support the Sugar Act because he feared that "some might endeavor to take advantage of any neglects or omissions on my or the colony's part." In the same way, he thought failure to take the Stamp Act oath "would be fatal" to the charter. "If the Governor and Council . . . should refuse obedience, the King . . . would deprive the people of the privilege of electing such officers; and then the whole charter would be at once struck up." Fitch and four like-minded assistants, like some senior leaders in the late 1680s, went along with imperial plans in order to preserve maximum local control. They had been impressed by imperial military power, but their cautious approach was out of step with the anger many voters felt toward the empire. When Fitch took the oath he precipitated a political crisis. He tried to persuade voters that he had acted only to preserve the charter and had never intended to carry out his oath. He failed to do so, and in May 1766 voters sacked him and the four assistants who had administered the oath to him.[13]

Fitch ruined his political career to shield the charter, a sacrifice that proved to be unnecessary when Parliament repealed the Stamp Act on 18 March 1766. The governor was betrayed and humiliated by the imperial government's inability to adhere to a consistent colonial policy. Repeal only encouraged the advocates of unyielding opposition to imperial edicts and absolved the perpetrators of mob violence from the consequences of their actions. Fitch must have smoldered when he read a letter from the imperial government, written on 24 October 1765 but received only on 10 May 1766, in which he was told to call on imperial military support to make sure that those who used "public violence . . . [got] nothing but severity and chastisement." The words meant nothing: they were merely

---

after the Sugar Act took effect on 29 September 1764 (CHC:XVIII/361). It was estimated the Stamp Act would bring in from 2,500 to 5,000 pounds sterling per annum in Connecticut (Ingersoll, *Letters,* p. 49). On the constitutional issues, see CHC:XVII/304–05, 370–73; Fitch, *Reasons Why*; and Schworer, *Standing Armies.* The best account is Morgan and Morgan, *Stamp Act.*

13. On the Sugar Act oath, see CHC:XVIII/299, 303–04 (quotation). On the Stamp Act oath, see [Fitch], *Some Reasons,* pp. 8 (quotations), 9; and Ingersoll, *Letters,* pp. 46, 49. On the mood in Connecticut, see CHC:XVIII/355–56, 366–67. The four assistants were all experienced political leaders: Ebenezer Silliman of Fairfield, John Chester of Wethersfield, Benjamin Hall of Wallingford, and Jabez Hamlin of Middletown.

a reminder of the fatal inconsistency of imperial policy. Using armed force was not necessarily a better idea; coercion is very risky and difficult to apply in an explosive political situation. Moreover, it is hard to imagine how a limited number of British troops could have forced the colonies to comply with the Stamp Act. But it is clear that threatening to use force and then backing down in the face of violent colonial opposition was the worst possible policy. [14]

The overthrow of Fitch and the four assistants did not herald a new political age. Politics in Connecticut remained an intra-group contest among men of similar outlook and social position. They had real temperamental and ideological differences about how to keep the colony free from imperial control—political life was not just a sterile contest for office—but it was a question of means, not ends. The Stamp Act crisis did not create a revolution in the patterns of political participation or in the social standing of the principal leaders. All five ousted leaders continued to hold, or were reappointed to, judicial and militia positions, and they remained prominent local political leaders. They were replaced by men of similar backgrounds, who also had long careers in public service. Even turnover among deputies, which some contemporaries implied was very high in 1765–66, had been regularly exceeded during the final French and Indian war. [15]

The Stamp Act crisis saw the introduction of purposeful violence into the political process. The inclination to use force was in part a product of an inflated military self-esteem stemming from the war which had just ended in unprecedented victory. Many militiamen fancied themselves as soldiers because they could play on the parade ground without the slightest danger of actually being called to fight. In 1762, while the real soldiers were joining the expeditionary regiments, militiamen in both North Haven and Stratford held a "mock Indian fight" at their annual musters in

14. On the letter, see CHC:XVIII/362–63 (quotations). The imperial government might have split colonial opinion by forcing colonial merchants to use stamped paper to stay in business (CHC:XVIII/364–65). In May 1766 Fitch reminded imperial officials of Connecticut's autonomy within the empire by rejecting the New York governor's demand for command of the Connecticut militia (CHC:XVIII/393–96). Seventy years earlier, King William III had confirmed Connecticut's charter right to control its militia in peacetime. Since the charter had not been revoked, that right still stood.

15. On patterns of politics, see Selesky, "Patterns," pp. 175–77; and Ingersoll, *Letters*, p. 45.

May. These exercises had an air of unreality—no militiamen had been asked to fight Indians for forty years—but that did not stop both musters from ending in tragedy. When a man was accidentally killed at North Haven and another was shot in the leg at Stratford, it only emphasized the average militiaman's lack of military skill and experience.[16]

A belligerent attitude carried over into the opposition to the Stamp Act. At Wallingford in January 1766, the local Sons of Liberty (as opponents of the act called themselves) pledged to resist the act "to the last extremity, even to take the field." New York Sons, expecting—incorrectly—that "troops would be sent from England to enforce their submission," received a conditional pledge of military support from a gathering of Sons of Liberty at New London in December 1765. The imperial government never forced any colonist to act on these pledges because it feared provoking a civil war. The Sons learned that they could intimidate their less enthusiastic neighbors and raise the price of enforcement higher than what the imperial government was willing to pay. The Stamp Act resistance was a bluff that worked. By not calling that bluff, the imperial government let the colonists believe they could defend their political rights by force of arms.[17]

Successful posturing during the Stamp Act crisis increased interest in military affairs in the decade after 1765. Militia companies split whenever they reached the statutory minimum of sixty-five men, and the Assembly had to create three new regiments by October 1772, with another six during 1774, to supervise the new companies. One of the principal reasons for interest in the militia was a desire to purge officers who were not enthusiastic about using military force to defend charter rights. Turnover among company officers from 1765 to 1774 rose by nearly 50 percent over the level of the preceding decade, and appointments to field rank tripled (table 6.1). Turnover peaked in October 1774, when the Assembly confirmed the election of 169 men as company officers, and appointed 37 men as field officers. Replacement was largely unforced. Men like William Samuel Johnson of Stratford, an Anglican and an assistant, were genuinely unsure and anxious about the breakdown of relations with Britain, and they chose to resign their militia commands rather than be asked to do things they would not do. Their replacement by men who had fewer doubts

16. On the musters, see *Gazette,* 8 May 1762 (quotation).

17. On Wallingford, see *Gazette,* 3 Feb 1766 (quotation). On New London, see Morgan, *Prologue,* pp. 117–18; and CHC:XVIII/385 (quotation). On the Sons of Liberty in general, see Maier, *Resistance.*

Table 6.1
Number of Militia Officers Commissioned, 1745–84

	1745–54	1755–64	1765–74	1775–84
Field	31	34	104	236
Company	1,338	1,588	2,324	3,305
Total	1,369	1,622	2,428	3,541

allowed the militia to function as "a police force and an instrument of political surveillance." It became the officially sanctioned intimidator of the timid and the uncertain, and silenced the few men who might have supported increased imperial control. The turnover did not improve the militia's military capacity, however, since only 53 former expeditionary officers were elected or appointed to militia command by April 1775. The militia was almost wholly officered by men who had little knowledge of war. [18]

Just as the militia began to assume its new role, it faced a major challenge. In what amounted to an unrehearsed test of its ability to mobilize quickly, the militia turned out on 2 September 1774 when word circulated that British regulars were searching the countryside around Boston for stocks of colonial arms and ammunition. The reports were false, but they afforded militiamen in Massachusetts and Connecticut an invaluable opportunity to experience an actual military emergency. The musters at home a few days later were the culmination of nearly a decade of preparation, and marked the start of the *rage militaire* that would grip Connecticut for the next eighteen months. [19]

18. On the regiments added to the original thirteen, see CPR:XII/607–08; and CPR:XIII/238. For the first time in a century, the Assembly created elite militia companies, at Hartford in October 1771 and at New Haven in May 1775 (CPR:XIII/544–55; and CPR:XIV/404). Johnson advised caution in using force. In April 1769 he reported that because "many" imperial officials would be "very glad to have this kind of excuse for employing the military," the colonies should not "give them any plausible pretences for intermeddling in our affairs" (MHC:5,IX/333; also McCaughey, *Johnson,* p. 168). Illness made it easier for him to resign. On the militia's political role, see Shy, "Hearts and Minds," pp. 174–78 (quotation 176). Among the fifty-three were twenty militia officers who were elected or appointed to higher rank after service in the final French and Indian war.

19. On the September alarm, see Alden, *Gage,* pp. 212–14; Warden, *Boston,*

The strength of the commitment to locally controlled military force as the guarantor of political rights is seen in the resolves of forty-one delegates from towns in New London and Windham counties who met at Norwich on 8 September 1774. The events of the past few days had rekindled fears that a standing army controlled by the imperial government would subvert colonial liberties. These fears were compounded by the fact that Lieutenant General Thomas Gage had been both imperial commander-in-chief and governor of Massachusetts since April, offices the delegates thought were "too great to be given to any [one] person in a free country." For "Americans" to be in "the power of a lawless army, not under the control of the [locally elected] civil magistrate, we humbly conceive is a situation terrible beyond description." The delegates, only a dozen of whom were established members of the colony's leadership, were "extremely apprehensive" that "we shall be under the disagreeable necessity of defending our sacred and invaluable rights, sword in hand." They petitioned the October Assembly to raise five thousand men to repel any British invasion of Connecticut and to sanction the flourishing of the martial spirit by commissioning officers for newly organized militia companies. These were the sentiments of activists in eastern Connecticut, and, while other leaders might have been more reluctant to take up arms, everyone agreed it was prudent to upgrade the colony's military capacity.[20]

An optimistic view of their military abilities made the colonists willing to challenge British authority after 1765, and the measures the Assembly adopted in October 1774 helped make them think they could win a war against the British. The leaders ordered each militia company to repair all firearms and to train for twelve half-days before 1 May, enacted fines and bounties to make sure militiamen appeared at musters, and ordered militia colonels to hold a day of regimental exercises by 10 May. Finally, they accepted the suggestion of the Norwich meeting and agreed to commission officers elected by any company of sixty men "not now included in any militia rolls."[21] By April 1775, Connecticut possessed the confidence it needed to join its neighbors in a war against the most formidable armed forces in the world.

pp. 298–99; and Tarbox, *Putnam*, pp. 78–80. Royster popularized the term *rage militaire* in *Revolutionary People*, p. 25.

20. On the resolves, see CHC:XX/215–17 (quotations). Seventeen of twenty-one eastern towns sent delegates to the meeting.

21. On the new regulations, see CPR:XIV/327–28.

THE LAST COLONIAL WAR

The war to win American independence began as the last war of the colonial period, one in which the people of Connecticut fought to protect the political rights they already possessed. According to Roger Sherman, a Connecticut delegate to the Continental Congress, they were "more zealous in the cause of liberty than the people of other states" because they had "more to lose than any of them." Continuity was also the hallmark of how the leaders organized their resources for war. They successfully applied the experience of the final French and Indian war to the new situation, but they never imagined that fighting to preserve traditional political rights would impose unprecedented strain on their political system, society, and economy. The decision to go to war was not revolutionary: waging the war itself was. Richard V. Buel has brilliantly examined that complex process in *Dear Liberty: Connecticut's Mobilization for the Revolutionary War*; the focus here is on how Connecticut adapted its most recent military experience to its last colonial war.[22]

Connecticut responded to the outbreak of hostilities on 19 April 1775 with a spontaneous burst of military enthusiasm; only the frontier emergency of 1704 and the Fort William Henry alarm of August 1757 had been similar in size and speed. In some towns, local militia officers set out immediately for Boston with some of their most enthusiastic neighbors; from Wethersfield, it was said, "the men march fast and are in high spirits." More frequently, officers took the time to combine men from several companies into temporary units. In the Fifth Regiment in Windham county, for example, officers of the thirteen companies organized 20 percent of their men into three composite companies. Enthusiasm sometimes outstripped the ability of local leaders to guide it into appropriate channels. Militia officers in Farmington thought it was dangerous to march to war without the approval and support of the Assembly: there was "such a spirit of zeal in the soldiers . . . that it was with difficulty that they were prevented" from setting out immediately. In New Haven, the enthusiasts were not thwarted, although Benedict Arnold had to threaten to break open the powderhouse before town leaders supplied his

22. On why Connecticut went to war, see Commager and Morris, *Spirit*, p. 275 (quotation). Jonathan Trumbull, who had succeeded William Pitkin in September 1769, was the only governor to lead a colony into statehood and through the Revolution. Buel's account is the finest study of how a colonial society met the challenge of a revolutionary war.

volunteers with ammunition. A total of about 4,000 men turned out, 15 percent of 26,000 militiamen, a response that proved the militia was still an asset in an emergency. Connecticut began the war at a peak of determination it would not reach again during the next eight years.[23]

Despite the impressive turnout, the true military value of the militia was low, principally because militiamen were not organized or equipped for long service; as had always been the case, they could not stay away from their farms and shops for very long. Over half the 4,000 men served for less than a week, barely enough time for men from the towns closest to Boston to march there and back. Many militiamen did not even leave Connecticut. For example, of the 93 men from Mansfield who were paid for serving in the alarm, 43 marched the fifteen miles to Pomfret and then marched home; only 50 men, presumably those who could stay away longest, were equipped and provisioned to continue to Boston. About 1,000 militiamen served for two weeks or more, but virtually all returned home before replacements began arriving at the camps around Boston in early June. This was only the first of many times that the inability to keep forces in the field without interruption would jeopardize the success of the Revolution.[24]

The creation of an effective military force was also hampered by the militiamen's expectations that their officers would govern them as though a military company were a New England town meeting. At least two companies subscribed to a set of "regulations and orders" which display in exaggerated form the cooperative style of discipline typical of the militia. After vowing that their conduct would be exemplary—they promised to avoid "drunkenness, gaming, profaneness, and every vice of that nature" because they were not "mercenaries whose views extend no farther than pay and plunder"—the soldiers agreed "to submit on all occasions to such decisions as shall be made and given by the majority of the officers we have chosen; the captain . . . [to have] a turning or casting vote in

23. Muster rolls of the Lexington alarm companies are in Johnston, *Record,* pp. 3–28. On Wethersfield, see CHS-IP/25 Apr 1775 (quotation). On the Fifth Regiment, see Storrs, "Farmers," p. 84. On Farmington, see French, *First Year,* pp. 83–84 (quotation). On New Haven, see Osterweis, *Three Centuries,* pp. 130–31. Connecticut reported to London in October 1774 that it had 26,260 militiamen (CPR:XIV/499).

24. On the Mansfield militiamen, see Johnston, *Record,* p. 16; and Storrs, "Farmers," p. 84. On militiamen returning home, see CHC:XX/220–21; and MHC:5,IX/493.

all debates." Any man who transgressed would "be turned out of the company as wholly unworthy of serving in so great and glorious a cause, and be delivered over to suffer the contempt of his countrymen." These sentiments were appropriate for gentlemen playing at being soldiers, but they would never serve as the basis for organizing a revolutionary army.[25]

Everyone realized that the militiamen were only a temporary answer to Connecticut's need for an army. As soon as Governor Jonathan Trumbull received word of the fighting at Lexington and Concord, he called the Assembly into special session to decide how to create a more permanent force. When it met at Hartford on 26 April, it agreed to raise 6,000 soldiers for seven months. This was nearly a quarter of the militia, the largest army the Assembly had ever authorized, although it was actually a smaller fraction of the population (3 percent of 200,000 people) than the 5,000 men authorized annually between 1758 and 1760 (3.7 percent of 135,000 people). The men were organized into six regiments of ten companies each, and each regiment was centered in one of the six counties. The three eastern regiments served at Boston, while the three western regiments were sent to help protect Manhattan and the Champlain valley. When the special session in July authorized 1,400 more soldiers for Boston, demands on the colony's manpower exceeded those reached in any year between 1755 and 1762.[26]

In creating the new army, the Assembly followed the methods of raising troops and organizing logistics that had worked so well during the final French and Indian war. Despite the enthusiastic response to the Lexington

25. The regulations were drawn up by Silas Deane, and used by Benedict Arnold's New Haven company and John Chester's Wethersfield company (Webb, *Correspondence*, I/55–57). A man was expelled from Chester's company, but on his "promising good behavior and asking pardon we have accepted him again. He said he had rather die than return" (CHS-IP/25 Apr 1775).

26. On raising troops in April, see CPR:XIV/417; and Storrs, "Farmers," pp. 85–87. The census of 1774 is in CPR:XIV/483–91. The leaders thought six thousand men were a quarter of the militia (CPR:XIV/417). On the regiments, see CPR:XV/92–93; and Lesser, *Sinews*, pp. 2–12. The three eastern were the Second in Hartford county, the Third in Windham county, and the Sixth in New London county; the three western were the First in New Haven county, the Fourth in Litchfield county, and the Fifth in Fairfield county. There was initially some doubt if the Seventh (east) and Eighth (west) would be paid by Congress (Smith, *Letters*, I/618). General Washington thought Connecticut soldiers were "as good troops as any we have" (Washington, *Papers*, II/148). He also praised Connecticut's commissary system (Washington, *Papers*, I/88).

alarm, the Assembly understood that men would need some financial incentive to show them clearly that it was in their interest to defend their political liberties. It therefore offered a package of bounties, wages, and subsistence money that was competitive with what an agricultural laborer could earn in civilian society. Every volunteer who equipped himself with clothing, a blanket, and a knapsack received a bounty of 2 pounds, 12 shillings lawful money. Those who brought a musket, bayonet, and cartridge box got 10 shillings more. And everyone received a month's wages in advance (2 pounds for a private) and 15 shillings in subsistence money. A fully equipped private thus received 5 pounds, 2 shillings now and 2 pounds, 15 shillings a month for six months. By comparison, an agricultural laborer might earn as much as 5 pounds a month when he could get work. While wages were the same as during the last years of the final French war, the bounties were lower. As in 1745 and 1755, financial incentives at the start of the war were intended to tap popular enthusiasm at the lowest possible cost.[27]

Connecticut succeeded in raising the number of soldiers it wanted, despite a noticeable cooling of patriotic ardor. From Wethersfield on 12 May, Captain John Chester told his brother-in-law, the first lieutenant of a company from Norwich, that "I hear your company is near or quite full. Ours is not. We have about thirty-six more men to enlist [to reach the authorized strength of one hundred men]. Our people seem hardly so forward as when they went out before." Chester reached his goal two weeks later and marched to Boston at the head of a full company which was also notably well equipped. The colony as a whole was nearly as successful, raising 93 percent (6,880) of the 7,400 men authorized in April and July. Windham county had the best record and New Haven county the worst; the First Regiment had only 75 percent of its full complement.[28]

Leadership was the most important element in creating the new army, but as always the most prominent local leaders did not go to war. A third of the officers (107 men) held commissioned rank in the militia, almost all of them only since 1772 (table 6.2); as in 1745 and 1755, militia officers were most prominent during the first year of the war. The militia

27. On the incentives, see CPR:XIV/417–19.

28. On Chester, see CHC:XX/221 (quotation). The numbers are from strength reports for July–November 1775, using the highest figure for each regiment (Lesser, *Sinews,* pp. 2–12). Chester's company wore blue coats faced with red (Webb, *Correspondence,* I/89).

Table 6.2
Experience of Officers, First through Eighth Regiments, 1775

	French and Indian War	Militia	New	Total
Field officers	17 (63%)	10 (37%)	0	27*
Captains	21 (40%)	24 (45%)	8 (15%)	53
1st Lieutenants	23 (29%)	39 (49%)	18 (22%)	80
2d Lieutenants	19 (24%)	26 (32%)	35 (44%)	80
Ensigns	31 (39%)	8 (10%)	41 (51%)	80
Totals	111 (35%)†	107 (33%)	102 (32%)	320

*Field and general officers also commanded companies.
†Nine veterans were or had been militia officers.

officer's principal asset was his ability to attract volunteers from his home region; he gathered the men without whom there would have been no army. Political leaders had always let others do the fighting, and the Revolution was no exception. Only 14 officers were members of the Assembly that decided to fight the British army, and only one, First Brigadier General Joseph Spencer of East Haddam, was an important political figure. While it is true that many of the 132 deputies and 10 assistants present in April 1775 were not physically able to undertake military service, their enthusiasm to protect their rights by force of arms was not matched by a similar desire to bear arms themselves.[29]

Veterans of the French war gave the regiments a leaven of experienced leaders. The first regiments of the Revolution virtually picked up where the last regiments of the French war had left off. Former officers generally received commissions at or above their previous rank, in effect being promoted to replace the men who had died, emigrated, or resigned in the past dozen years. Ensigns were drawn from among men who had formerly been noncommissioned officers and privates. The new war gave veterans the chance to be leaders again, and their psychological value was enormous. They trained recruits who had never experienced camp life or military discipline, and held the army together while the men learned to be soldiers. As had been the case ever since the Pequot War of 1637, the mere fact that the colonists knew how to use weapons did not make them a formidable force.[30]

29. Spencer was also a veteran of three campaigns in the final French and Indian war (1758–60).
30. On veteran soldiers, see MHC:5,IX/500. The Massachusetts Congress

Veteran officers rendered their most important service almost as soon as the regiments arrived in the camps around Boston. They were indispensable in inspiring and guiding their soldiers in the pivotal battle at Breed's Hill on 17 June 1775. Veterans like Israel Putnam and Thomas Knowlton (and William Prescott of Massachusetts and John Stark of New Hampshire) projected the confidence of men who had been in battle before. We have fought Frenchmen and Indians in the open, they seemed to say, and we will show you how to fight the British from behind breastworks, stone walls, and rail fences. By their example, veteran officers showed men who had no firsthand knowledge of war how to survive in combat. The redoubt atop Breed's Hill was built under the direction of Prescott, who walked the parapet contemptuous of British fire while his regiment worked furiously at his feet. Putnam, who had won an intercolonial reputation as a ranger against the French and who was now Connecticut's second brigadier general, worked tirelessly, if haphazardly, to forward men and ammunition to the Charlestown peninsula. Stark, also a ranger captain in the last war, led his raw troops across the isthmus with an imperturbable calm which kept them from panicking. Stark's attitude best illustrates the impact a veteran could have. "My company being in front," recalled Captain Henry Dearborn long afterward, "I marched by the side of Colonel Stark; who moving with a very deliberate pace, I suggested the propriety of quickening the march of the regiment, that it might sooner be relieved of the galling cross-fire of the enemy. With a look peculiar to himself, he fixed his eyes upon me, and observed with great composure, 'Dearborn, one fresh man in action is worth ten fatigued ones,' and continued to advance in the same cool and collected manner."[31]

Stark's New Hampshire men, along with two hundred men from the Third Connecticut Regiment under Captain Thomas Knowlton (later reinforced by, among others, John Chester's company), prevented British troops from turning the American left flank. Had the British broken through, the Americans would have been routed from Breed's Hill. The losses in men, equipment, and morale might have so demoralized the rebels that the Revolution might have been strangled in its cradle. Instead,

---

thought the soldiers, "for want of experience in military life, have but little knowledge of divers things most essential to the preservation of health and even of life" (Washington, *Papers,* I/55). Washington expected that "whatever deficiencies there may be" would "soon be made up by the activity and zeal of the officers, and the docility and obedience of the men" (Washington, *Papers,* I/60).

31. On Stark, see French, *First Year,* p. 226 (quotation).

Sir William Howe, in tactical command of the battle, was forced to order a series of hideously expensive frontal assaults on the hastily prepared American positions. Although the British eventually pushed the Americans off Breed's Hill and back across the isthmus, heavy casualties crippled their army. Even more important, the Americans learned that they could stand against the best troops in the world, and, under certain circumstances, inflict losses they could not afford to bear. The best assessment of the importance of Breed's Hill came from Thomas Gage, the British commander-in-chief, who witnessed at a distance the debacle his subordinate had wrought. "These people show a spirit and conduct against us, they never showed against the French, and every body has judged of them by their former appearance and behavior, when joined with the King's forces in the last war; which has led many into great mistakes. They are now spirited up with a rage and enthusiasm, as great as ever people were possessed of, and you must proceed in earnest or give the business up."[32]

But "rage and enthusiasm" were not a solid foundation on which to build an army trying to win a revolutionary war. Discipline had to be established and maintained, a structure of command erected in the new army, and inadequate officers replaced. Despite the gallant conduct of many officers at Breed's Hill, a few months of service revealed serious shortcomings in leadership, on the excellence of which all else depended. Although he had no prior military experience, thirty-two-year-old Colonel Jedidiah Huntington of the Eighth Regiment shrewdly analyzed the failings of some of his peers. "There are many here who pass for agreeable, clever men in common life that make but an indifferent figure in the army. They have no idea of the discipline and government which are absolutely necessary among military men." Huntington should have been more circumspect: while he turned out to be an able officer, he was appointed in the first place largely because he was the son of Assistant Jabez Huntington and the son-in-law of Governor Trumbull.[33]

Many officers, veterans as well as militia officers and newcomers, had neither the desire nor the ability to impose rigid discipline on their neighbors. Colonial soldiers had never been ruled with an iron hand, even when they had operated with British regulars during the final French and

32. On Breed's Hill, see French, *First Year,* pp. 211–73 (quotation 258); Storrs, "Farmers," p. 92; Webb, *Correspondence,* I/87–89; Johnston, *Record,* p. 58; and Gage, *Correspondence,* I/405–07.

33. Huntington's opinions are in CHC:XX/236 (quotation); and MHC:5,IX/501–02.

Indian war. The colonial regiments had maintained a tradition of loose discipline and lack of subservience to officers because they had generally undertaken nothing more demanding than garrison service and construction work. Although the demands on the troops rose radically with the start of the rebellion, officers and men brought up in the old tradition were slow to realize that they had to change their attitudes to create a more efficient and professional army. Indeed, disciplinary regulations were less stringent than they had been twenty years before. Regimental courts martial used fines as their principal form of punishment, even for serious offenses. One soldier paid 5 shillings for "disobeying orders," another 10 shillings for "intemperate drinking," and a third 10 shillings for "being out of camp contrary to orders." Corporal punishment was used to deter some crimes like theft, but the number of lashes was limited by law to a maximum of thirty-nine, substantially lower than during the final French war. Only desertion in combat and betraying the password were capital offenses. The absence of a solid framework of discipline made good leadership even more important than it had been between 1755 and 1762.[34]

The prospects of creating a better army began to improve on 14 June when Congress adopted the New England troops as a Continental army, bound them together with uniform articles of war, and put them under the command of George Washington, himself a veteran Virginia colonel who looked every bit the commander-in-chief in his blue-and-buff uniform; a Connecticut delegate to Congress reported that he was "well adapted to please a New England army and much better suited to the temper and genius of our people than any other gent[leman] not brought up in that part of the country." The Connecticut troops, who were held in "high esteem" by Congress, accepted this incorporation; their only anxiety was quelled when they were reassured that the new arrangements did not require them to serve longer than their original term of enlistment. New Englanders did have to consider some new ways of organizing an army, in deference to their new "continental" status. General Washington wanted to exclude blacks from the army, and to raise the pay of ensigns because low pay was "one great source of that familiarity between the officers and men which is so incompatible with subordination and discipline." A conference of Congressional delegates and senior New England leaders catered to the general's sensibilities about blacks, but persuaded

34. On courts martial, see CHC:VII/64–65 (quotations). On capital crimes, see Wright, *Continental Army*, p. 39.

him to accept other New England traditions: "raising the pay of the officers would be inconvenient and improper," just as "lowering the pay of the troops would be attended with dangerous consequences." Any reduction in pay was "absolutely impracticable" since "a bare proposal of this nature would cause such discontents, if not mutinies as would perhaps prove the ruin of the army."[35]

Connecticut had a long record of cooperating as a junior partner in a New England army, so the transition to a Continental army was not traumatic, especially as Congress was careful to recognize its efforts with a fair share of the general officers. Second Brigadier General Israel Putnam was named a Continental major general ("his fame as a warrior had been so far extended thro' the continent that it would be in vain to urge any of our general officers in competition with him"), but the appointment nonetheless caused considerable controversy because it violated Connecticut seniority. Major General David Wooster and First Brigadier General Spencer were incensed that Putnam had been promoted over them. Wooster emphasized his command experience ("thirty years' services" in King George's War and the final French and Indian war), and Spencer, who threatened to resign, actually did leave his post, something for which he was roundly condemned. Personal relationships and prestige still counted for more than military subordination in the leadership of the army.[36]

35. On adopting the army, see Wright, *Continental Army,* pp. 21–29; and Washington, *Papers,* II/24–25. The opinion of Washington, by Eliphalet Dyer, a delegate to Congress, is in Smith, *Letters,* I/494–95 (quotation), 499. On the opinion of Congress, see Smith, *Letters,* I/642 (quotation), 647. Huntington reported that "some officers are suspicious they shall be holden in service if they accept" Continental commissions, and thought the soldiers would "in general decline signing the Continental Articles of War, lest they should be retained thereby longer than the term of their first engagement" (MHC:5,IX/504). Connecticut troops in the Northern Army were also reassured about their term of service (Ryan, *Salute,* p. 15). On blacks, see Washington, *Papers,* I/90, II/199. On pay, see Washington, *Papers,* II/26 and 191 (quotations); and Smith, *Letters,* II/243 (quotation). Washington exaggerated the changes when he told General Spencer that "the establishment is entirely new, all provincial customs therefore which are different in different provinces must be laid out of the question" (Washington, *Papers,* II/55).

36. On Putnam, see Smith, *Letters,* I/521 (quotation), 539, 638–39. On Wooster, see Smith, *Letters,* I/522, 540, 626–27 (quotation); Washington, *Papers,* II/241–42; and Johnston, *Record,* p. 37. On Spencer, see Webb, *Correspondence,* I/79–81; and Smith, *Letters,* I/521, 626–27, 634, 638–40, 643, 673–

The officers who led their neighbors to war were not easily interchanged or replaced because, as had been the case since the first days of settlement, men wanted to serve under officers they knew. Like Governor Fitch during the final French war, Governor Trumbull had the Assembly's permission to fill vacancies as the need arose, but he understood that Washington should exercise this most important power. When he did meddle, he caused much controversy. He named twenty-year-old Ebenezer Huntington, brother of Colonel Jedidiah, as the first lieutenant in the Wethersfield company of their brother-in-law John Chester, who accepted him because his subordinate officers were "not much of military men." But the deficiencies of others did not prevent Ebenezer from becoming the object of "a determined and almost universal opposition to any new officers coming into vacancies." He won acceptance only by "giving close attention to his duties." Despite Washington's bitter objections—to yield to the soldiers would "in effect surrender the command of the army to those whose duty it is . . . to obey"—the pace of operations was still slow enough so that New England soldiers could insist on their traditional voice in selecting officers. Washington would eventually win his case to appoint officers on merit, but New Englanders did not quickly change the way they had always chosen their officers.[37]

Helping to create a Continental army took more effort than Connecticut had expended in any one year during the final French and Indian war. But the field army was not the full extent of the burden because the situation was more dangerous in 1775 than it had been twenty years earlier. The Assembly realized that British warships posed an immediate danger to Connecticut towns, a menace it had not faced since French

---

74. Congress thought he "acted a part inconsistent with the character either of a soldier, a patriot, or even of a common gentleman to desert his post in an hour of danger" (Smith, *Letters,* I/639). Governor Trumbull wished "the order we adopted had been pursued" because Wooster and Spencer were "gentlemen held in high estimation by our assembly and by the officers and troops under their command" (Washington, *Papers,* I/113). Both Wooster and Spencer eventually accepted commissions as Continental brigadier generals.

37. On soliciting the Assembly for a commission, see CHC:XX/225. On Huntington, see Washington, *Papers,* II/320–21; CHC:XX/226–27, 229–30 (quotation), 231, 236–37, 240–41 (quotation), 245, 248 (quotation), 253; MHC:5,IX/499–501; Huntington, *Letters,* pp. 18–19, 22, 24–25; and Webb, *Correspondence,* I/104–06. Deserving noncommissioned officers were generally appointed to commissioned rank (MHC:5,IX/506–07). On Washington's objections, see Washington, *Papers,* II/55 (quotation).

privateers threatened the coast in 1690. The leaders got very nervous as warships cruised up and down the coast, and wanted their Continental troops to stay home to defend shoreline towns against seaborne raiders. Washington, who faced a still-potent British army in Boston, did not want any forces diverted, and reiterated the resolution of Congress "that each province should depend on its own internal strength against these incursions." The militia was "deemed competent for that service." The leaders eventually faced up to the danger, and were "obliged actually to raise more men for their security." The Continental troops raised in July went to Boston.[38]

The newly created Continental army faced its first crisis as December approached and enlistments neared expiration. The initial problem was to get the Connecticut troops to stay until 1 January, a few weeks after the expiration of their enlistments. While officers were generally willing to continue, the men were not. In the Sixth Regiment, 220 noncommissioned officers and soldiers (of a total of 635, or 35 percent) agreed to stay, but only "on condition they can have a reasonable time granted them to go home and prepare their winter clothing." The sentiments were similar in the Third Regiment, where soldiers complained that the cost of winter clothes was the same whether they agreed to stay until January or reenlisted for another year. Although they were "repeatedly solicited . . . to tarry longer," the soldiers had a "universal determination" to go home at the end of their enlistment in mid-December.[39]

Some Connecticut soldiers were so unhappy that they left the siege lines around Boston "without leave" on 1 December. Washington, who had been reassured by their officers that the soldiers would stay until 1 January, condemned their conduct as "reprehensible" and "scandalous," especially because he expected the British to take advantage of the reduction in American strength. He called on the governors of the surrounding colonies to send their militias to fill the gap, and sent an express to Governor Trumbull with the names of the returnees so that "they may be dealt

38. On the delay, see Washington, *Papers,* I/267, 276, 406, 416. On Washington's opinions, see Washington, *Papers,* I/407 (quotation), 437 (quotation); II/34. On the new troops, see Washington, *Papers,* I/468–69 (quotation).

39. On Washington, see Washington, *Papers,* II/25, 190–91. On the two regiments, see Washington, *Papers,* II/221–24; and Lesser, *Sinews,* p. 8. On determination to go home, see Huntington, *Letters,* p. 25 (quotation); CHC:XX/24; CHC:VII/128–31; Washington, *Papers,* II/408, 446, 456–57, 464; and French, *First Year,* pp. 503–26.

with in a manner suited to the ignominy of their behavior." When Silas Deane, a delegate to Congress, heard what the soldiers had done, he was angry but not surprised: "The behavior of our soldiers has made me sick, but little better could be expected from men trained up with notions of their right of saying how, and when, and under whom they will serve." By 12 December, Washington gave "what remains of the Connecticut gentry who have not enlisted . . . liberty to go to their firesides." According to Brigadier General Nathanael Greene of Rhode Island, the Connecticut soldiers had had enough of "the fatigues of the campaign, [and] the suffering for want of wood and clothing . . . [and] went off in spite of all that could be done to prevent it," enduring the jeers of the other New England regiments as they did so. (Connecticut troops in the Northern Army also set out for home around this time.) Trumbull condemned their conduct, but tried to explain to Washington why it had happened. "The pulse of a New England man beats high for liberty. His engagement on the service he thinks purely voluntary. Therefore in his estimation, when the time of enlistment is out, he thinks himself not holden, without further engagement; this was the case in the last war."[40]

The next problem was to create a new army to maintain the siege of Boston after 1 January. Two senior Connecticut leaders told Washington, who had been worrying about the problem for months, that the Assembly could raise eight thousand men for a year if it offered them the same bounties as in 1775. But that was not to be, since Congress offered less than what the Assembly had granted eight months earlier; southern delegates refused to offer enlistment bounties and what they thought were exorbitant wages to a largely New England army. Some senior officers were optimistic about the number of troops they could raise. On 5 October, Colonel Huntington believed that most soldiers "after they have been home a while will be glad to join the army again." But recruiting went badly in the camps of the old regiments. By 23 November, Huntington reported that "we shall not with all our rhetoric be able to retain many." Con-

40. On troops going home on 1 December, see Webb, *Correspondence*, I/123–24n (quotation); and Washington, *Papers*, II/471, 475, and 484 (quotations). On the call for the militia, see Washington, *Papers*, II/492, 533, 585. Deane's comment is in Smith, *Letters*, II/489 (quotation). On the departure in mid-December, see Washington, *Papers*, II/533 (quotation); and Greene, *Papers*, I/173 (quotation). On the northern troops, see Smith, *Letters*, II/397. Trumbull's explanation is in Washington, *Papers*, II/511 (quotation).

necticut men had always signed on for a summer's campaign at a time, and they had no intention of changing that practice now.[41]

Because the weakened Continental army faced the danger of a British attack, the officers worked hard to create the new regiments. The "unfavorable reception" people in Connecticut gave the troops who returned home in December prompted "many" of them to reenlist by the end of the month, and it was said that "recruiting in Connecticut goes on exceeding well." But after the fiasco of 1 December, Washington had no intention of relying on enthusiasm to recruit soldiers. As early as 4 December he recommended the introduction of a quota system based on the model of the early years of the final French and Indian war, and the next day he effectively asked the New England governments to draft their constituents. He was "convinced of the impracticability of recruiting . . . by voluntary enlistments," and claimed that "the present soldiery are in expectation of drawing from the landed interest and farmers a bounty equal to the allowance at the commencement of this army, and that therefore they play off" their service for additional money. By mid-January officers were still reporting that "men are much wanted." According to Colonel Huntington, "recruits come in slowly; the regiments on average are not more than four hundred strong. We have, however, more men than arms."[42]

Washington was absolutely correct: Connecticut, and all New England, had always raised expeditionary troops by bounty, starting the system during the early wars against the French and bringing it to a peak of success between 1755 and 1762. The most difficult military lesson American leaders and soldiers had to learn was that the situation after 1775 demanded radical solutions different from all past experience. The American cause might not survive another occasion when one army dissolved before a new one was created. Leaders like Washington realized, partly

41. On raising eight thousand men, see Washington, *Papers*, II/197; Deputy Governor Matthew Griswold and Nathaniel Wales, Jr., a member of Governor Trumbull's Council of Safety, conferred with Washington. On wages, see CHC:XX/252; and Greene, *Papers*, I/170, 174. On Huntington, see CHC:XX/243–44 and 252–53 (quotations).

42. On the reception in Connecticut, see Greene, *Papers*, I/173 (quotation). On recruiting at home, see Greene, *Papers*, I/160, 179; and Washington, *Papers*, II/555. On Washington's ideas about quotas and drafting, see Washington, *Papers*, II/485, 492–93 (quotations), 607. On the lack of men, see CHC:XX/260 (quotation); and MHC:5,IX/509 (quotation).

from their own experience on the southern frontier where multiple-year enlistments were more common, that they had to raise troops for longer terms. But he also had to cater to traditional ways of organizing and leading troops. He knew, for example, that soldiers from each colony did not want "officers of other governments mixed in their corps." As Eliphalet Dyer, a Connecticut delegate to Congress, told his colleagues, "You can't raise an army if you put officers over the men whom they don't know. It requires time to bring people off from ancient usage." Washington always tried to induce Congress and the states to raise a professional army capable of matching the British regulars, but tradition, politics, and the personal inclinations of American soldiers were all against him. He never got the long-service, well-trained army he wanted, and it was part of his genius that he kept the American cause alive with a mix of troops on all terms of enlistment.[43]

The dissolution of the 1775 army marked the cooling of Connecticut's *rage militaire* after eighteen months during which it had fueled an enthusiastic defense of political rights by force of arms. This was a natural reaction to the fact that the policy had achieved its goals. The power of the imperial government hit bottom in March 1776, when the British army in Boston was evacuated to Halifax, thus effectively ending the imperial presence in the colonies. Colonial leaders were in charge from New Hampshire to Georgia. Their military problems were now defensive, to defeat any British attempt to reestablish imperial control. All they had to do was maintain the authority they already possessed. Although they would eventually be involved in military operations of unprecedented scope and cost, it was difficult to generate enthusiasm for defensive measures prior to an actual attack. Connecticut faced the challenge with some trepidation, since its resources would be stretched to the maximum if Britain tried to take Manhattan, a place of obvious strategic importance. While the most extreme enthusiasm had dissipated by early 1776, the leaders remained confident that they could solve their military problems. The road ahead was more arduous than they could ever have imagined, but in the end they were right. Colonial military traditions endured enormous, nearly fatal strain during the Revolution, but ultimately they did not fail the cause of American independence.

43. On traditions, see Washington, *Papers*, II/607 (quotation); and Smith, *Letters*, II/155–56 (quotation).

Conclusion

Wars against local Indians, Frenchmen in Canada, and finally the imperial government were the most complicated, difficult, and expensive problems Connecticut faced during the colonial period. In each case, the leaders showed great skill in bending the colony's resources to war, and in striking a balance among competing demands and the available money and manpower. Until well after the turn of the eighteenth century, their military activity was limited to situations where they could not avoid a fight. They compelled their neighbors to serve only when the threat was clear and close at hand, as in the wars against the local Indians in 1636 and 1675–76, and after French raids on the adjacent frontiers in 1690 and 1704. Because the colony was not exposed to constant danger from the French, for twenty years after 1689 the leaders had no incentive to help the imperial government defend the New York frontier. This view changed when London threatened to revoke their charter right to control their internal affairs. To deflect imperial anger at their independent behavior, in 1709 they agreed to raise troops for the first of many expeditions against Canada. The way they made war also began to change. After five years of helping to defend the Connecticut valley against French raiders, they refused to strain their authority further by impressing men to serve so far from home. Instead, they began to use financial incentives to raise soldiers by voluntary enlistment.

By mid-century, the growth of population and the increase in economic activity allowed the leaders to rely even more heavily on money to attract volunteers. Enthusiasm for military service meant they could keep bounties low at the start of each conflict in 1740, 1745, and 1755. As the final

French and Indian war dragged on, British subsidies enabled them to underwrite the higher bounties required after 1757 to induce men to volunteer. By the last years of the war, they had created a sophisticated military system that did not unduly strain the fabric of their society. After the collapse of the French empire, the old bargain of military cooperation against Canada in return for loose imperial supervision no longer applied, and their relations with London progressively deteriorated. The success of the colonial military system inflated their confidence in Connecticut's military abilities to a level where recourse to force seemed not merely possible but desirable. When war broke out in 1775, the leaders applied the methods they had developed originally for annual expeditions against Canada, and, largely because enthusiasm was high, they met the challenge of the opening campaign. But a system perfected when the colony was not exposed to constant danger and could make liberal use of imperial subsidies was ill suited to the relentless and unprecedented burden of resisting the most powerful army and navy of the day. Had the leaders realized that a war of independence would make revolutionary demands on the resources of their society, they might have thought twice about an appeal to arms.

Bibliography

MANUSCRIPTS

THE CONNECTICUT STATE LIBRARY, HARTFORD
Lucius B. Barbour Collection of Vital Statistics
Connecticut Archives
    Civil Officers (two series)
    Crimes and Misdemeanors
    Ecclesiastical
    Finance and Currency (two series)
    Finances, Treasurer's Accounts
    Foreign Correspondence (two series)
    Indians (two series)
    Lotteries
    Militia (three series)
    Miscellaneous (two series)
    Towns and Lands
    Trade and Maritime
    Travel
    War, Colonial:
        Vol. 1. 1675–1737, mostly 1675–76
        Vol. 2. 1688–96
        Vol. 3. 1695–1736
        Vol. 4. 1728–50
        Vol. 5. 1753–55
        Vol. 6. 1756–57
        Vol. 7. 1757–58
        Vol. 8. 1758–60
        Vol. 9. 1760–63

Vol. 10. 1751–96
War, Colonial, Series 2:
Vol. 1. 1690–1801, mostly 1747
Miscellaneous French and Indian War Papers
Sherman W. Adams Collection
Capt. George Crary, Orderly Book, 1759
Capt. Benadam Gallop, Accounts and Muster Roll, 1757
Capt. Aaron Hitchcock, Receipts, 1760
Corp. Abner Meacham, Diary and Orderly Book, 1757
Wesley U. Pearne Collection
Col. John Pitkin, Receipts, 1755
Capt. John Spaulding, Orderly Book, 1761
Treasurer Joseph Talcott, Account Book, 1755–1770
Capt. Edmund Welles, Diary, 1756–57
Capt. Charles Whiting, Arms Roll, 1758
Col. Nathan Whiting, Orderly Book, 1758
Lt. Giles Wolcott, Letter, 1759
Probate District Records (various districts)
Record Groups:
No. 1. Early General Records, 1629–1820
No. 2. General Assembly Records, 1636–1975:
Journals of the Upper and Lower Houses, 1708–40
No. 7. Treasurer's Account Books, 1748–74
Jonathan Trumbull, Sr., Papers
Robert C. Winthrop Collection, 1664–1707

THE CONNECTICUT HISTORICAL SOCIETY, HARTFORD
French and Indian War Papers (on microfilm)
General Assembly Papers
Hoadly Collection
Miscellaneous French and Indian War Papers:
Clerk John Barnard, Jr., Diary, 1756
Capt. Benadam Gallop, Orderly Books, 1757–59
Lt. Col. Nathan Payson, Orderly Book, 1758
Sgt. Daniel Sizer, Diary, 1759–60
Capt. Tarball Whitney, Account Books, 1759
Israel Putnam Papers
Jonathan Trumbull, Sr., Papers
Roger Wolcott, Sr., Papers
Wyllys Papers

THE MASSACHUSETTS HISTORICAL SOCIETY, BOSTON
Letter Book of John Winslow
Parkman Papers
Israel Williams Papers

PUBLIC RECORD OFFICE, LONDON

Colonial Office, Class 5, Library of Congress Transcripts, French and Indian War Papers (University Publications of America microfilm).

War Office, Class 34, Amherst Papers (Public Record Office microfilm).

YALE UNIVERSITY, NEW HAVEN

Beinecke Rare Book and Manuscript Library:
  Ezra Stiles Papers
Manuscripts and Archives, Sterling Memorial Library:
  Loudoun-Cumberland Collection
  Waterbury Family Papers:
    Capt. David Waterbury, Jr., Orderly Book, 1758–59
  Nathan Whiting Papers

NEWSPAPERS

Connecticut Courant [Hartford], beginning 29 Oct. 1764.
Connecticut Gazette [New Haven], 12 April 1755 to 19 Feb. 1768.
Connecticut Gazette [New London], beginning 18 Nov. 1763.
Connecticut Journal [New Haven], beginning 23 Oct. 1767.
New London Summary, 8 August 1758 to c. Nov. 1763.

PUBLISHED DOCUMENTS, LETTERS, AND SERMONS

Adams, William. *A Discourse . . . On the . . . Reduction of Montreal.* New London, 1761.

Allyn, John, and William Pitkin. *Their Majesties Colony of Connecticut in New-England Vindicated, from the Abuses of a Pamphlet . . . Intituled Seasonable Considerations for the Good People of Connecticut.* Boston, 1694. Reprinted in *The Collections of the Connecticut Historical Society* 1 (1860): 83–130.

Amherst, Jeffery. *The Journal of Sir Jeffery Amherst,* edited by J. C. Webster. Toronto, 1931.

Bates, Albert C. *The Two Putnams: Israel and Rufus in the Havana Expedition 1762 and in the Mississippi River Exploration 1772–1773.* Hartford, 1931.

Bates, Albert C., ed. *Simsbury Births, Marriages, and Deaths.* Hartford, 1898.
———. *Some Early Records . . . of Windsor, 1639–1703.* Hartford, 1930.

Beckwith, George. *That People a Safe, and Happy People, Who Have God For, and Among Them.* New London, 1756.

Bidwell, Adonijah. "[Journal, 1745]." *The New England Historical and Genealogical Register* 27 (1873): 153–60, 192–93.

Bird, Samuel. *The Importance of the Divine Presence with Our Host.* New Haven, 1759.

Booth, Joseph. "[Journal, 1760]." In Charles E. Booth, *One Branch of the Booth Family,* 142–44. New York, 1910.

Boyd, Julian P., and Robert Taylor, eds. *The Susquehannah Company Papers*. Vols. 1–11. Wilkes-Barre, Pa., and Ithaca, N.Y., 1930–71.

Buckingham, Thomas. *The Private Journals Kept by Rev. John {sic} Buckingham of the Expeditions Against Canada in . . . 1710 and 1711.* New York, 1825. Reprinted as *Roll and Journal of Connecticut Service in Queen Anne's War, 1710–1711.* Hartford, 1916.

Bulkeley, Gershom. *The People's Right to Election or Alteration of Government in Connecticut Argued.* Philadelphia, 1689. Reprinted in *The Collections of the Connecticut Historical Society* 1 (1860): 57–81.

————. "Will and Doom, or the Miseries of Connecticut." *The Collections of the Connecticut Historical Society* 3 (1895): 69–270.

Byles, Mather, Jr. *A Sermon, Delivered . . . As a Public Thanksgiving.* New London, 1760.

Champion, Henry. "Journal [1758]." In Francis B. Trowbridge, *The Champion Genealogy,* 417–39. New Haven, 1891.

Cogswell, James. *God the Pious Soldier's Strength.* Boston, 1757.

Colden, Cadwallader. *The History of the Five Indian Nations.* New York, 1727.

Connecticut. *An Account of the Number of Inhabitants* [includes 1756 census]. Hartford, 1774. Reprinted in *The Public Records of the Colony,* vol. 14 (1887): 483–92.

————. "Correspondence of Connecticut with the British Government, [1755–1758]." *The Collections of the Connecticut Historical Society* 1 (1860): 257–332.

————. *The Public Records of the Colony.* Vols. 1–15. Hartford, 1850–90.

    Vol. 1. *1636–1665* (1850).

    Vol. 2. *1665–1678* (1852).

    Vol. 3. *May 1678–June 1689* (1859).

    Vol. 4. *Aug. 1680–May 1706* (1868).

    Vol. 5. *Oct. 1706–Oct. 1716* (1870).

    Vol. 6. *May 1717–Oct. 1725* (1872).

    Vol. 7. *May 1726–May 1735* (1873).

    Vol. 8. *Oct. 1735–Oct. 1743* (1874).

    Vol. 9. *May 1744–Nov. 1750* (1876).

    Vol. 10. *May 1751–Feb. 1757* (1877).

    Vol. 11. *May 1757–March 1762* (1880).

    Vol. 12. *May 1762–Oct. 1767* (1881).

    Vol. 13. *May 1768–May 1772* (1885).

    Vol. 14. *Oct. 1772–April 1775* (1887).

    Vol. 15. *May 1775–June 1776* (1890).

Connecticut Historical Society. *The Collections.* Vols. 1–29. Hartford, 1860–1967.

    Vols. 4–5. *The Talcott Papers: Correspondence and Documents during Joseph Talcott's Governorship, 1724–1741. Vol. 1. 1724–36* (1892). *Vol. 2. 1737–41* (1896).

Vol. 6. *Hartford Town Votes, 1635–1716* (1897).

Vol. 7. *Orderly Books and Journals Kept by Connecticut Men in the American Revolution, 1775–1778* (1899).

Vol. 8. *Rolls and Lists of Connecticut Men in the Revolution, 1775–1783* (1901).

Vols. 9–10. *Rolls of Connecticut Men in the French and Indian War. Vol. 1. 1755–1757* (1903). *Vol. 2. 1758–1764* (1905).

Vols. 11, 13, and 15. *The Law Papers: Correspondence and Documents during Jonathan Law's Governorship, 1741–1750. Vol. 1. October 1741–July 1745* (1907). *Vol. 2. August 1745–December 1746* (1911). *Vol. 3. January 1747–October 1750* (1914).

Vol. 16. *The Wolcott Papers: Correspondence and Documents during Roger Wolcott's Governorship, 1750–1754* (1916).

Vols. 17–18. *The Fitch Papers: Correspondence and Documents during Thomas Fitch's Governorship, 1754–1766. Vol. 1. May 1754–December 1758* (1918). *Vol. 2. January 1759–May 1766* (1920).

Vol. 19. *The Pitkin Papers: Correspondence and Documents during William Pitkin's Governorship, 1766–1769* (1921).

Vol. 20. *Huntington Papers: Correspondence of the Brothers Joshua and Jedidiah Huntington during the American Revolution* (1923).

Vol. 21. *The Wyllys Papers: Correspondence and Documents Chiefly of Descendants of Gov. George Wyllys, 1590–1796* (1924).

Vol. 24. *Hoadley Memorial: Early Letters and Documents Relating to Connecticut, 1643–1709* (1932).

DeForest, Louis E., ed. *Louisbourg Journals.* New York, 1932.

Demos, John P., ed. *Remarkable Providences, 1600–1760.* New York, 1972.

dePeyster, J. Watts, ed. *Commissary Wilson's Orderly Book (1759).* Albany, 1857.

Dibble, Ebenezer. "Diary, [1759]," edited by T. S. Woolsey. In *Papers and Addresses of the Society of Colonial Wars in the State of Connecticut* 1 (1903): 313–29.

Dickinson, Moses. *A Sermon Preached Before the General Assembly.* New London, 1755.

Douglas, William. "Letters Written during the Revolutionary War by William Douglas . . . July 19, 1775 to December 5, 1776." *The New-York Historical Society Bulletin* 12–14 (1929–30).

Dwight, Nathaniel. "Journal, [1755]." *The New York Genealogical and Biographical Record* 33 (1902): 3–10, 65–70, 164–66.

Dwight, Timothy. *Travels in New England and New York,* edited by Barbara M. Solomon. Vols. 1–4. Cambridge, Mass., 1969.

Eliot, Jared. *God's Marvellous Kindness, Illustrated . . . by Taking . . . Louisbourg.* New London, 1745.

Estabrook, Hobart. *The Praying Warrior, or the Necessity . . . of Praying Unto, and Trusting in God.* New Haven, 1758.

Fish, Joseph. *Christ Jesus the Physician.* New London, 1760.

Fitch, Jabez, Jr. "Diary, [1756–58]," edited by Frederick W. Parker. *The May-flower Descendant* 1–13 (1899–1911).

Fitch, Thomas, [and a General Assembly committee]. *Reasons Why the British Colonies in America Should Not Be Charged With Internal Taxes, By Authority of Parliament*. New Haven, 1764.

———. *Some Reasons That Influenced the Governor to Take, and the Councillors to Administer, the Oath Required By . . . the Stamp Act*. Hartford, [1766].

Ford, Worthington C., ed. *General Orders of 1757*. New York, 1899.

Gage, Thomas. *The Correspondence of General Thomas Gage,* edited by Clarence E. Carter. Vols. 1–2. New Haven, 1931.

Gardener, Lion. "His Relation of the Pequot Warres." *The Collections of the Massachusetts Historical Society,* 3d ser. vol. 3 (1833): 136–60. Reprinted in Orr, *History.*

Graham, Gerald S., ed. *The Walker Expedition to Quebec, 1711*. London, 1953.

Graham, John. "Journal [1756]." *The Magazine of American History* 8 (1882): 206–13.

Great Britain. *Acts of the Privy Council of England, Colonial Series,* edited by William L. Grant and James Munro. Vols. 1–6. Hereford, England, 1908–12.

———. *The Calendar of State Papers, Colonial Series {1574–1737},* edited by W. Noel Sainsbury et al. Vols. 1–43. London, 1880–1963.

———. *Proceedings and Debates of the British Parliaments Respecting North America, 1542–1754,* edited by Leo F. Stock. Vols. 1–5. Washington, D. C., 1924–41.

———. *Proceedings and Debates of the British Parliaments Respecting North America, 1754–1783,* edited by R. C. Simmons and P. D. G. Thomas. *Vol 1. 1754–1764*. Millwood, New York, 1982.

Greene, Nathanael. *The Papers of General Nathanael Greene, Vol. 1. December 1766-December 1776,* edited by Richard Showman et al. Chapel Hill, N.C., 1976.

Gridley, Luke. *Diary of 1757,* edited by F. M. [sic] Hartford, 1906.

Hawks, John. *Orderly Book and Journal of Major John Hawks, 1759–1760,* edited by George B. Spalding. New York, 1911.

Hayden, Augustin. "[Journal, 1758–59]." In *Records of the . . . Hayden Family,* 120–23. Windsor Locks, Conn., 1888.

Henderson, James. "Journal, 1758–59," edited by Harold C. Durrell and Alexander B. Ewing. In *The First Half Century of the Society of Colonial Wars in the Commonwealth of Massachusetts, 1893–1943,* 195–209. Boston, 1944.

Hubbard, William. *A Narrative of the Troubles with the Indians*. Boston, 1677.

Huntington, Ebenezer. *Letters Written by Ebenezer Huntington during the American Revolution,* edited by G. W. F. Blanchfield. New York, n. d.

Hutchinson, Thomas. *The History of Massachusetts Bay,* edited by Lawrence S. Mayo. Vols. 1–3. Cambridge, Mass., 1936.

Ingersoll, Jared. *Letters Relating to the Stamp-Act*. New Haven, 1766.

Ingersoll, Jonathan. *A Sermon Preached Before the General Assembly.* New London, 1761.

Johnson, Sir William. *The Papers of Sir William Johnson,* edited by James Sullivan et al. Vols. 1–14. Albany, 1921–65.

Johnston, Henry P., ed. *Connecticut Military Record, 1775–1848: The Record of Connecticut Men in the Revolution.* Hartford, 1889.

Kimball, Gertrude S., ed. *The Correspondence of the Colonial Governors of Rhode Island.* Vols. 1–2. Boston, 1902.

[Knox, William]. "A Project for Imperial Reform: Hints Respecting the Settlement for Our American Provinces, 1763," edited by Thomas C. Barrow. *The William and Mary Quarterly* 24 (1967): 108–26.

Livingston, Robert. "The Camp at the Wood Creek Reviewed, with an Account . . . of the Expedition Against Canada," edited by Bruce T. McCully. In Bruce T. McCully, "Catastrophe in the Wilderness: New Light on the Canada Expedition of 1709," *The William and Mary Quarterly* 11 (1954): 440–56.

Lockwood, James. *Man Mortal: God Everlasting.* New Haven, 1756.

Lyon, Lemuel. "Military Journal of 1758." In *The Military Journals of Two Private Soldiers, 1758–1775,* edited by Abraham Tomlinson, 11–45. Poughkeepsie, N.Y., 1855.

Mante, Thomas. *The History of the Late War in North-America.* London, 1772.

Manwaring, Charles W., ed. *A Digest of the Early Connecticut Probate Records: Hartford District, 1635–1750.* Hartford, 1904–6.

Mason, John. *A Brief History of the Pequot War,* edited by Thomas Prince. Boston, 1736. Reprinted in *The Collections of the Massachusetts Historical Society,* 2d ser., vol. 8 (1819): 120–53; and in Orr, *History.*

Massachusetts. *The Records of the Governor and Company. Vol. 1. 1628–1641,* edited by Nathaniel B. Shurtleff. Boston, 1853.

Massachusetts Historical Society. *The Collections* (Boston).
   2d ser., vol. 8 (1819).
   3d ser., vol. 1 (1825); vol. 3 (1833); vol. 6 (1837).
   4th ser., vol. 6, *The Winthrop Papers,* part 1 (1863).
   5th ser., vol. 8, *The Winthrop Papers,* part 4 (1882); vol. 9, *The Trumbull Papers,* part 1 (1885).
   6th ser., vol. 3, *The Winthrop Papers,* part 5 (1889); vol. 5, *The Winthrop Papers,* part 6 (1892); vol. 7, *The Belcher Papers,* part 2 (1894); vol. 10, *The Pepperrell Papers* (1899).

Minor, Thomas. *The Diary of Thomas Minor, 1653–1684,* edited by Sidney H. Miner and George D. Stanton. New London, 1899.

Morgan, Edmund S., ed. *Prologue to Revolution: Sources and Documents on the Stamp Act Crisis, 1764–1766.* Chapel Hill, N.C., 1959.

New Hampshire. *Town Charters.* Vols. 25 and 26 of *The State Papers,* edited by Albert S. Batchellor. Concord, 1895–96.

New Haven Colony. *The Records* (Hartford).

Vol. 1. *1638–1649* (1857).

Vol. 2. *May 1653-Union* (1858).

New Haven Town. *The Records* (New Haven).

Vol. 1. *1649–1662* (1917).

Vol. 2. *1662–1684* (1919).

Vol. 3. *1684–1769* (1962).

New-York Historical Society. *The Collections* (New York).

Vol. 9. (1876).

Vol. 24. *Muster Rolls of Provincial Troops* (1892).

Niles, Samuel. *A Brief and Plain Essay on . . . the Reduction of Louisbourg.* New London, 1747.

O'Callaghan, Edmund B., ed. *The Documentary History of the State of New York.* Vols. 1–4. Albany, 1850–51.

———. *Documents Relative to the Colonial History of the State of New York.* Vols. 1–15. Albany, 1853–87.

Orr, Charles, ed., *The History of the Pequot War.* Cleveland, Ohio, 1897.

Pargellis, Stanley M., ed. *Military Affairs in North America, 1748–1765.* New York, 1936.

Pepperrell, William. "The Journal of Sir William Pepperrell Kept during the Expedition against Louisbourg, 1745," edited by Charles H. Lincoln. *The Proceedings of the American Antiquarian Society* 20 (1909–10): 132–83.

Peters, Nathan. *The Correspondence of Nathan Peters, April 25, 1775–February 5, 1777,* edited by William H. Guthman. Hartford, 1980.

Peters, Samuel. *General History of Connecticut.* London, 1781. Reprint. New York, 1877.

Pitt, William. *The Correspondence of William Pitt When Secretary of State,* edited by Gertrude S. Kimball. Vols. 1–2. New York, 1906.

Pynchon, John. *The Pynchon Papers. Vol. 1. The Letters, 1654–1700,* edited by Carl Bridenbaugh. Boston, 1982.

Ryan, Dennis P., ed. *A Salute to Courage: . . . Writings of Officers of the Continental Army and Navy.* New York, 1979.

Russell, William. *The Duty of an Army of Professing Christians.* New London, 1760.

Saltonstall, Gurdon. *A Sermon Preached Before the General Assembly.* Boston, 1697.

Shirley, William. *The Correspondence of William Shirley, 1731–1760,* edited by Charles H. Lincoln. Vols. 1–2. New York, 1912.

Slotkin, Richard, and James K. Folsom, eds. *So Dreadful a Judgment: Puritan Responses to King Philip's War, 1676–1677.* Middletown, Conn., 1978.

Smith, Joseph. "Journal [1758]," edited by Welcome A. Smith. *Papers and Addresses of the Society of Colonial Wars in the State of Connecticut* 1 (1903): 305–10.

Smith, Paul H., ed. *The Letters of Delegates to Congress.* Vols. 1–3. Washington, D.C., 1976–78.

Stiles, Ezra. *Extracts from the Itineraries,* edited by Franklin B. Dexter. New Haven, 1916.

Stiles, Isaac. *The Character and Duty of Soldiers.* New Haven, 1755.

Storrs, Experience. "Connecticut Farmers at Bunker Hill: The Diary of Colonel Experience Storrs," edited by Wladimir Hagelin and Ralph A. Brown. *The New England Quarterly* 28 (1955): 72–93.

Syrett, David, ed. *The Siege and Capture of Havana, 1762.* Greenwich, England, 1970.

Taylor, Nathaniel. *Praise Due to God For . . . His Wise and Holy Providence.* New Haven, [1762].

Throop, Benjamin. *Religion and Loyalty, the Duty and Glory of a People.* New London, 1758.

Underhill, John. *News From America.* London, 1636. Reprinted in *The Collections of the Massachusetts Historical Society,* 3d ser., vol. 6 (1837): 3–28; and in Orr, *History*.

United Colonies of New England. *The Acts of the Commissioners.* Vols. 9 and 10 of *The Records of the Colony of New Plymouth,* edited by David Pulsifer. Hartford, 1859.

Vincent, Philip. *A True Relation of the Late Battle.* London, 1638. Reprinted in *The Collections of the Massachusetts Historical Society,* 3d ser., vol. 6 (1837): 29–43; and in Orr, *History*.

Washington, George. *The Papers of George Washington, Revolutionary War Series,* edited by W. W. Abbot et al. Vols. 1–2. Charlottesville, Va., 1985–86.

———. *The Writings of George Washington,* edited by John C. Fitzpatrick. Vols. 3–6. Washington, D.C., 1931–32.

Webb, Samuel B. *The Correspondence and Journals of Samuel Blachley Webb,* edited by Worthington C. Ford. New York, 1893.

Webster, Robert. "Journal [1759]." *The Bulletin of the Fort Ticonderoga Museum* 2 (1931): 120–53.

Whiting, Nathan. "Letters [1747–63]," edited by Lemuel A. Welles. *The Papers of the New Haven Colony Historical Society* 6 (1900): 133–50.

Williams, E. N., ed. *The Eighteenth-Century Constitution.* Cambridge, England, 1965.

Williams, Solomon. *The Duty of Christian Soldiers.* New London, 1755.

———. *The Relation of God's People to Him: . . . A Thanksgiving Sermon on . . . the Reduction of Quebec.* New London, 1760.

Williams, William. *Journal Kept by William Williams of the Proceedings of the Lower House of the Connecticut General Assembly, May 1757 Session,* edited by Sylvie J. Turner. Hartford, 1975.

Winthrop, John. *The History of New England from 1630 to 1649,* edited by James M. Savage. 2d ed. Vols. 1–2. Boston, 1853.

———. *The Winthrop Papers. Vol. 3. 1631–1637,* edited by Allyn B. Forbes. Boston, 1943.

Wolcott, Roger. "Journal of Roger Wolcott [Sr.] at the Siege of Louisbourg, 1745." *The Collections of the Connecticut Historical Society* 1 (1860): 131–62.

SECONDARY WORKS

Alden, John R. *General Gage in America.* Baton Rouge, La., 1948.

Anderson, Fred W. "A People's Army: Provincial Military Service in Massachusetts During the Seven Years' War." *The William and Mary Quarterly* 40 (1983):499–527.

———. *A People's Army: Massachusetts Soldiers and Society in the Seven Years' War.* Chapel Hill, N.C., 1984.

———. "Why Did Colonial New Englanders Make Bad Soldiers?: Contractual Principles and Military Conduct During the Seven Years' War." *The William and Mary Quarterly* 38 (1981): 395–417.

Andrews, Charles M. *The Colonial Background of the American Revolution.* New Haven, 1931.

———. *The Colonial Period of American History.* Vols. 1–4. New Haven, 1934–38.

———. *Connecticut and the British Government.* New Haven, 1933.

Andrews, Charles M., and Albert C. Bates. *The Charter of Connecticut, 1662.* New Haven, 1933.

Axtell, James. *The School Upon the Hill: Education and Society in Colonial New England.* New Haven, 1974.

Ayling, Stanley. *The Elder Pitt.* New York, 1976.

Baldwin, John D., and William Clift. *A Record of the Descendants of Capt. George Denison.* Worcester, Mass., 1881.

Barnes, Viola. *The Dominion Of New England.* New Haven, 1923.

Bartlett, Joseph G. *The Newberry Genealogy: The Ancestors and Descendants of Thomas Newberry.* Boston, 1914.

Beer, George L. *British Colonial Policy, 1754–1765.* New York, 1907.

———. *The Origins of the British Colonial System, 1578–1660.* New York, 1908.

Berkeley, Francis L., Jr. "The War of Jenkins' Ear." In *The Old Dominion,* edited by Darrett B. Rutman, 41–61. Charlottesville, Va., 1964.

Bickford, Christopher P. "The Lost Connecticut Census of 1762 Found." *The Connecticut Historical Society Bulletin* 44 (1979): 33–43.

Black, Robert C., III. *The Younger John Winthrop.* New York, 1966.

Bodge, George M. *Soldiers in King Philip's War.* Boston, 1906.

Boyd, Julian P. *The Susquehannah Company: Connecticut's Experiment in Expansion.* New Haven, 1935.

Boynton, Lindsay *The Elizabethan Militia, 1558–1638.* London, 1967.

Brown, M. L. *Firearms in Colonial America: The Impact on History and Technology, 1492–1792.* Washington, D.C., 1980.

Buel, Richard V., Jr. *Dear Liberty: Connecticut's Mobilization for the Revolutionary War.* Middletown, Conn., 1980.

Buffinton, Arthur H. "The Canada Expedition of 1746: Its Relation to British Politics." *The American Historical Review* 45 (1940): 552–80.

———. "The Puritan View of War." *Transactions of the Colonial Society of Massachusetts, 1930–1933,* 67–86. Boston, 1935.

Bullion, John L. "'The Ten Thousand Men in America': More Light on the Decision on the American Army." *The William and Mary Quarterly* 43 (1986): 646–47.

Bushman, Richard L. *From Puritan to Yankee: Character and the Social Order in Connecticut, 1690–1765.* Cambridge, Mass., 1967.

Childs, John. *The Army of Charles II.* London, 1976.

———. *The British Army of William III, 1689–1702.* Manchester, England, 1987.

Christie, Ian R. *The Crisis of Empire: Great Britain and the American Colonies, 1754–1783.* New York, 1966.

Clark, David S., ed. "Journals and Orderly Books Kept by Connecticut Soldiers During the French and Indian War, 1755–1762." *The New England Historical and Genealogical Register* 94 (1940): 225–30; and 95 (1941): 18–20.

Clark, Delphina L. H. *Phineas Lyman: Connecticut's General.* Springfield, Mass., 1964.

Cohen, Ronald D. "The New England Colonies and the Dutch Recapture of New York, 1673–1674." *The New-York Historial Society Quarterly* 56 (1972): 54–78.

Collier, Christopher. *Roger Sherman's Connecticut: Yankee Politics and the American Revolution.* Middletown, Conn., 1971.

Collier, Christopher, with Bonnie Collier. *The Literature of Connecticut History.* Middletown, Conn., 1983.

Conkey, Laura E., Ethel Boissevain, and Ives Goddard. "Indians of Southern New England and Long Island: Late Period." In Trigger, *Handbook,* 177–89.

Corbett, Julian. *England in the Seven Years' War.* London, 1907.

Craven, Wesley F. *The Colonies in Transition, 1675–1715.* New York, 1968.

Cress, Lawrence D. *Citizens in Arms: The Army and the Militia in American Society to the War of 1812.* Chapel Hill, N.C., 1982.

Cronon, William. *Changes in the Land: Indians, Colonists, and the Ecology of New England.* New York, 1983.

Cruickshank, C. G. *Elizabeth's Army.* 2d ed. Oxford, 1966.

Daniels, Bruce C. *Connecticut's First Family: William Pitkin and His Connections.* Chester, Conn., 1976.

———. *The Connecticut Town: Growth and Development, 1635–1790.* Middletown, Conn., 1979.

———. "Economic Development in Colonial and Revolutionary Connecticut: An Overview." *The William and Mary Quarterly* 37 (1980): 429–50.

Destler, Chester M. *Connecticut: The Provisions State.* Chester, Conn., 1973.

Dexter, Franklin B. *Biographical Sketches of the Graduates of Yale College.* Vols. 1–2. New York, 1885–1907.

Dunn, Richard S. *Puritans and Yankees: The Winthrop Dynasty of New England, 1638–1717.* Princeton, N.J., 1962.

Eccles, W. J. "The Battle for Quebec: A Reappraisal." In Eccles, *Essays on New France,* 125–33. Toronto, 1987.

———. *The Canadian Frontier, 1534–1760.* New York, 1969.

———. *France in America.* New York, 1972.

———. *Frontenac: The Courtier Governor.* Toronto, 1959.

———. "Frontenac's Military Policies, 1689—98: A Reassessment." *The Canadian Historical Review* 37 (1956): 201–24.

Fairchild, Byron. "Sir William Pepperrell: New England's Pre-Revolutionary Hero." *The New England Historical and Genealogical Register* 130 (1976): 83–106.

Ferling, John E. "The New England Soldier: A Study in Changing Perceptions." *The American Quarterly* 33 (1981): 26–45.

———. *A Wilderness of Miseries: War and Warriors in Early America.* Westport, Conn., 1980.

Firth, Charles H. *Cromwell's Army: A History of the English Soldier during the Civil Wars, the Commonwealth, and the Protectorate.* 3d ed. London, 1921.

Fregault, Guy. *Canada: The War of the Conquest.* Toronto, 1969.

French, Allen. "The Arms and Military Training of Our Colonizing Ancestors." *The Proceedings of the Massachusetts Historical Society* 67 (1945): 3–21.

———. *The First Year of the American Revolution.* Boston, 1934.

Frey, Sylvia R. *The British Soldier in America: A Social History of Military Life in the Revolutionary Period.* Austin, Tex., 1981.

Galvin, John R. *The Minute Men—The First Fight: Myths and Realities of the American Revolution.* 2d ed. McLean, Va., 1989.

Gates, Stewart L. "Disorder and Social Organization: The Militia in Connecticut Public Life, 1660–1860." Ph.D. diss., University of Connecticut, 1975.

Gipson, Lawrence H. *Jared Ingersoll: A Study of American Loyalism.* New Haven, 1920.

———. *The British Empire before the American Revolution.* Vols. 1–15. New York, 1936–1970.

The British Isles and the American Colonies. Vol. 3. *The Northern Plantations, 1748–1754* (1967).

Zones of International Friction. Vol. 5. *The Great Lakes Frontier, Canada, the West Indies, India, 1748–1754* (1942).

The Great War for the Empire. Vol. 6. *The Years of Defeat, 1754–1757* (1946); Vol. 7. *The Victorious Years, 1758–1760* (1949); Vol. 8. *The Culmination, 1760–1763* (1953).

The Triumphant Empire. Vol. 9. *New Responsibilities within the Enlarged Empire, 1763–1766* (1956); Vol. 10. *Thunder-Clouds Gather in the West, 1763–1766* (1961); Vol. 11. *The Rumbling of the Coming Storm, 1766–1770* (1965); Vol. 12. *Britain Sails into the Storm, 1770–1776* (1965).

A Bibliographical Guide. Vol. 14 (1968).

A Guide to Manuscripts. Vol. 15 (1970).

———. *The Coming of the Revolution, 1763–1775.* New York, 1954.

———. *Connecticut Taxation, 1750–1775.* New Haven, 1933.

Goodwin, Nathaniel. *Genealogical Notes, or Contributions to the Family History of Some of the First Settlers.* Hartford, 1856.

Graham, Dominick S. "British Intervention in Defence of the American Colonies, 1748–1756." Ph.D. diss., University of London, 1965.

Graham, Gerald S. *Empire of the North Atlantic.* 2d ed. Toronto, 1958.

Grant, Charles S. *Democracy in the Connecticut Frontier Town of Kent.* New York, 1961.

Greene, Jack P. "'A Posture of Hostility': A Reconsideration of Some Aspects of the Origins of the American Revolution." *The Proceedings of the American Antiquarian Society* 87 (1977): 27–68.

———. "The Seven Years' War and the American Revolution: The Causal Relationship Reconsidered." *The Journal of Imperial and Commonwealth History* 8 (1980): 85–105.

———. "An Uneasy Connection: An Analysis of the Preconditions of the American Revolution." In Kurtz and Hutson, *Essays,* 32–80.

Groce, George, Jr. "Eliphalet Dyer: Connecticut Revolutionist." In *The Era of the American Revolution,* edited by Richard B. Morris, 290–304. New York, 1939.

Gwyn, Julian. "British Government Spending and the North American Colonies." *The Journal of Imperial and Commonwealth History* 8 (1980): 74–84.

Haffenden, Philip. *New England in the English Nation, 1689–1713.* New York, 1974.

Hall, Charles S. *The Life and Letters of Samuel Holden Parsons, Major General in the Continental Army.* Binghamton, N.Y., 1905.

Hall, Edwin. *The Ancient Records of Norwalk.* Norwalk, 1847.

Hamilton, Edward P. "Colonial Warfare in North America." *The Proceedings of the Massachusetts Historical Society* 80 (1968): 1–15.

———. *The French and Indian Wars: The Story of Battles and Forts in the Wilderness.* Garden City, N.Y., 1962.

Hanna, Archibald, Jr. "New England Military Institutions, 1693–1750." Ph.D. diss., Yale University, 1951.

Harkness, Albert, Jr. "Americanism and Jenkins' Ear." *The Mississippi Valley Historical Review* 37 (1950): 61–90.

Hatch, Nathan O. *The Sacred Cause of Liberty: Republican Thought and the Millenium in Revolutionary New England.* New Haven, 1977.

Henretta, James A. *"Salutary Neglect": Colonial Administration under the Duke of Newcastle.* Princeton, N.J., 1972.

Higginbotham, Don. "The Early American Way of War: Reconnaissance and

Appraisal." *The William and Mary Quarterly* 44 (1987): 230–73. Reprinted in Higginbotham, *War and Society,* 260–312.

———. "The Military Institutions of Colonial America: The Rhetoric and the Reality." In Higginbotham, *War and Society,* 19–41.

———. "Military Leadership in the American Revolution." In *Leadership in the American Revolution* (Library of Congress Symposia on the American Revolution), 91–111. Washington, D.C., 1974. Reprinted in Higginbotham, *War and Society,* 84–105.

———. *War and Society in Revolutionary America: The Wider Dimensions of the Conflict.* Columbia, S.C., 1988.

———. *The War of American Independence: Military Attitudes, Policies, and Practice, 1763–1789.* New York, 1971.

Higginbotham, Don, ed. *Reconsiderations on the Revolutionary War.* Westport, Conn., 1978.

Higham, Robin, ed. *A Guide to the Sources of United States Military History.* Hamden, Conn., 1975.

Higham, Robin, and Donald J. Mrozek, eds. *A Guide to the Sources of United States Military History. Supplements 1 and 2.* Hamden, Conn., 1981 and 1986.

Higonnet, Patrice L. "The Origins of the Seven Years' War." *The Journal of Modern History* 40 (1968): 57–90.

Hinman, Royal R. *The Early Puritan Settlers of Connecticut.* Hartford, 1852.

Hirsch, Adam J. "The Collision of Military Cultures in Seventeenth-Century New England." *The Journal of American History* 74 (1988): 1187–1212.

Holmes, Charlotte L. *A Genealogy of . . . John Steevens.* Elmira, N.Y., 1906.

Hooker, Roland M. *The Spanish Ship Case: A Troublesome Episode for Connecticut, 1752–1758.* New Haven, 1934.

Humphreys, David *The Life and Heroic Exploits of Israel Putnam.* Hartford, 1833.

Huntington, Elijah B. *The History of Stamford.* Stamford, Conn., 1868.

Huntington, Elijah B., ed. *A Genealogical Memoir of the Lo-Lathrop Family.* Ridgefield, Conn., 1884.

Jacobus, Donald L. *The Families of Ancient New Haven.* New Haven, 1923–32.

———. *The History and Genealogy of the Families of Old Fairfield.* Fairfield, Conn., 1930.

———. *Lists of Officials . . . of Connecticut . . . {and} of New Haven {1636–1677}.* New Haven, 1935.

Jacobus, Donald L., and Edgar F. Waterman. *Hale, House, and Related Families.* Hartford, 1952.

James, Sidney V. *Colonial Rhode Island.* New York, 1975.

Jennings, Francis. *The Invasion of America: Indians, Colonialism and the Cant of Conquest.* Chapel Hill, N.C., 1975.

Johnson, Richard R. *Adjustment to Empire: The New England Colonies, 1675–1715.* New Brunswick, N.J., 1981.

————. "The Search for a Usable Indian: An Aspect of the Defense of Colonial New England." *The Journal of American History* 64 (1977): 623–51.

Johnston, Henry P. *Yale and Her Honor-Roll in the American Revolution, 1775–1783.* New York, 1888.

Jones, E. Alfred. "The American Regiment in the Carthagena Expedition." *The Virginia Magazine of History and Biography* 30 (1922): 1–20.

Judd, Sylvester. *The History of Hadley.* Springfield, Mass., 1905.

Kammen, Michael. *Colonial New York.* New York, 1975.

Kellogg, Louise P. "The American Colonial Charters." *The Annual Report of the American Historical Association, 1903,* 185–341. Washington, D.C., 1904.

Kohn, Richard H. "War as Revolution and Social Process." *Reviews in American History* 5 (1977): 56–61.

Kupperman, Karen O. *Settling with the Indians: The Meeting of English and Indian Cultures in America, 1580–1640.* Totowa, N.J., 1980.

Kurtz, Stephen G., and James H. Hutson, eds. *Essays on the American Revolution.* Chapel Hill, N.C., 1973.

Labaree, Benjamin W. *Colonial Massachusetts.* Millwood, N.Y., 1979.

Lax, John, and William Pencak. "The Knowles Riot and the Crisis of the 1740s in Massachusetts." *Perspectives in American History* 10 (1976): 161–214.

Leach, Douglas E. *Arms For Empire: A Military History of the British Colonies in North America, 1607–1763* New York, 1973.

————. "Brothers in Arms? Anglo-American Friction at Louisbourg, 1745–1746." *The Proceedings of the Massachusetts Historical Society* 89 (1977): 36–54.

————. *Flintlock and Tomahawk: New England in King Philip's War.* New York, 1959.

————. *The Northern Colonial Frontier, 1607–1763.* New York, 1966.

————. *Roots of Conflict: British Armed Forces and Colonial Americans, 1677–1763.* Chapel Hill, N.C., 1986.

Leder, Lawrence H. *Robert Livingston, 1654–1728, and the Politics of Colonial New York.* Chapel Hill, N.C., 1961.

Lesser, Charles H., ed. *Sinews of Independence: Monthly Strength Reports of the Continental Army.* Chicago, 1976.

Lovejoy, David S. *The Glorious Revolution in America.* New York, 1972.

McCaughey, Elizabeth P. *From Loyalist to Founding Father: The Political Odyssey of William Samuel Johnson.* New York, 1980.

McCully, Bruce T. "Catastrophe in the Wilderness: New Light on the Canada Expedition of 1709." *The William and Mary Quarterly* 11 (1954): 440–56.

Mackesy, Piers. *The War For America, 1775–1783.* Cambridge, Mass., 1965.

Mahon, John K. "Anglo-American Methods of Indian Warfare, 1676–1794." *The Mississippi Valley Historical Review* 45 (1958): 254–75.

Maier, Pauline. *From Resistance to Revolution: Colonial Radicals and the Development of American Opposition to Britain, 1765–1776.* New York, 1972.

Main, Jackson T. *Connecticut Society in the Era of the American Revolution.* Hartford, 1977.

————. "The Distribution of Property in Colonial Connecticut." In *The Human Dimensions of Nation Making,* edited by James K. Martin, 54–104. Madison, Wis., 1976.

————. "The Economic and Social Structure of Early Lyme." In *A Lyme Miscellany,* edited by George J. Willauer, Jr., 29–47. Middletown, Conn., 1977.

————. *Society and Economy in Colonial Connecticut.* Princeton, N.J., 1985.

Malone, Patrick M. "Changing Military Technology Among the Indians of Southern New England." *The American Quarterly* 25 (1973): 48–63.

————. "Indian and English Military Systems in New England in the Seventeenth Century." Ph.D. diss., Brown University, 1971.

Marcus, Richard H. "The Connecticut Valley: A Problem in Intercolonial Defense." *Military Affairs* 33 (1969): 230–42.

————. "The Militia of Colonial Connecticut, 1639–1775: An Institutional Study." Ph.D. diss., University of Colorado, 1965.

Martin, James K., and Mark E. Lender. *A Respectable Army: The Military Origins of the Republic, 1763–1789.* Arlington Heights, Ill., 1982.

Melvoin, Richard I. *New England Outpost: War and Society in Colonial Deerfield.* New York, 1989.

Morgan, Edmund S. *The Challenge of the American Revolution.* New York, 1976.

————. *The Puritan Dilemma: The Story of John Winthrop.* Boston, 1958.

Morgan, Edmund S., and Helen M. Morgan. *The Stamp Act Crisis: Prologue to Revolution.* Chapel Hill, N.C., 1953.

Morrow, Rising Lake. *Connecticut Influences in Western Massachusetts and Vermont.* New Haven, 1936.

Murrin, John M. "The French and Indian War, the American Revolution and the Counter-factual Hypothesis." *Reviews in American History* 1 (1973–74): 307–18.

Nash, Gary B. *The Urban Crucible: Social Change, Political Consciousness, and the Origins of the American Revolution.* Cambridge, Mass., 1979.

Nelson, Paul D. "Citizen Soldiers or Regulars: The Views of American General Officers on the Military Establishment, 1775–1781." *Military Affairs* 43 (1979): 126–32.

Niven, John. *Connecticut Hero: Israel Putnam.* Hartford, 1977.

Nutting, Parker B. "Charter and Crown: Relations of Connecticut with the British Government, 1662–1776." Ph.D. diss., University of North Carolina, 1972.

Olson, Alison G. *Anglo-American Politics, 1660–1775: The Relationship Between Parties in England and Colonial America.* New York, 1973.

Osgood, Herbert L. *The American Colonies in the Eighteenth Century.* Vols. 1–4. New York, 1924.

————. *The American Colonies in the Seventeenth Century.* Vols. 1–4. New York, 1904–07.

Osterweis, Rollin G. *Three Centuries of New Haven, 1638–1938*. New Haven, 1953.

Palsits, Victor H. "A Scheme for the Conquest of Canada in 1746." *The Proceedings of the American Antiquarian Society* 16 (1905): 69–92.

Pares, Richard. *War and Trade in the West Indies, 1739–1763*. London, 1936.

Pargellis, Stanley, M. *Lord Loudoun in America*. New Haven, 1933.

Parker, K. Lawrence. "Anglo-American Wilderness Campaigning, 1754–64." Ph.D. diss., Columbia University, 1970.

Parkman, Francis. *Count Frontenac and New France under Louis XIV*. Boston, 1877.

———. *A Half-Century of Conflict*. Boston, 1892.

———. *Montcalm and Wolfe*. Boston, 1884.

Peckham, Howard H. *The Colonial Wars, 1689–1762*. Chicago, 1964.

Pencak, William. *War, Politics, and Revolution in Provincial Massachusetts*. Boston, 1981.

———. "Warfare and Political Change in Mid-Eighteenth-Century Massachusetts." *The Journal of Imperial and Commonwealth History* 8 (1980): 51–73.

Peterson, Harold L. "The Military Equipment of the Plymouth and Bay Colonies, 1620–1690." *The New England Quarterly* 20 (1947): 197–208.

———. *Arms and Armor in Colonial America, 1526–1783*. Harrisburg, Pa., 1956.

Poteet, James M. "The Lordly Prelate: Gurdon Saltonstall Against His Times." *The New England Quarterly* 53 (1980): 483–507.

———. "More Yankee Than Puritan: James Fitch of Connecticut." *The New England Historical and Genealogical Register* 133 (1979): 102–17.

———. "Unrest in the 'Land of Steady Habits': The Hartford Riot of 1722." *The Proceedings of the American Philosophical Society* 119 (1975): 223–32.

———. "'What Interest Has Governed Mr. Allyn': John Allyn and the Dominion of New England." *The Connecticut Historical Society Bulletin* 39 (1974): 1–9.

Radabaugh, Jack S. "The Military System of Colonial Massachusetts, 1690–1740." Ph.D. diss., University of Southern California, 1965.

———. "The Militia of Colonial Massachusetts." *Military Affairs* 28 (1954): 1–18.

Rainbolt, John C. "The Creation of a Governor and Captain General for the Northern Colonies: The Process of Colonial Policy Formation at the End of the Seventeenth Century." *The New-York Historical Society Quarterly* 57 (1973): 100–20.

———. "A 'great and usefull design': Bellomont's Proposals for New York, 1698–1701." *The New-York Historical Society Quarterly* 53 (1969): 333–51.

Rawlyk, George A. *Nova Scotia's Massachusetts: A Study of Massachusetts–Nova Scotia Relations, 1630–1784*. Montreal, 1973.

———. *Yankees at Louisbourg*. Orono, Maine, 1967.

Reid, Ronald F. "New England Rhetoric and the French War, 1754–1760: A

Case Study in the Rhetoric of War." *Communications Monographs* 43 (1976): 260–86.

Rodger, N. A. M. *The Wooden World: An Anatomy of the Georgian Navy.* Annapolis, Md., 1986.

Rogers, Alan. *Empire and Liberty: American Resistance to British Authority, 1755–1763.* Berkeley, Calif., 1974.

Rogers, H. C. B. *The British Army of the Eighteenth Century.* London, 1977.

Rosenberry, Lois K. M. *Migrations from Connecticut Prior to 1800.* New Haven, 1934.

Roth, David M. *Connecticut's War Governor: Jonathan Trumbull.* Chester, Conn., 1974.

Rowse, A. L. *The Expansion of Elizabethan England.* New York, 1955.

Royster, Charles. *A Revolutionary People At War: The Continental Army and American Character, 1775–1783.* Chapel Hill, N.C., 1979.

Russell, Peter E. "Redcoats in the Wilderness: British Officers and Irregular Warfare in Europe and America, 1740 to 1760." *The William and Mary Quarterly* 35 (1978): 628–52.

Sainsbury, John A. "Miantonomo's Death and New England Politics, 1630–1645." *Rhode Island History* 30 (1971): 110–23.

Saladino, Gaspare J. "The Economic Revolution in Late Eighteenth Century Connecticut." Ph.D. diss., University of Wisconsin, 1964

Salisbury, Neal. *The Indians of New England: A Critical Bibliography.* Bloomington, Ind., 1982.

———. *Manitou and Providence: Indians, Europeans, and the Making of New England, 1500–1643.* New York, 1982.

Salwen, Bert. "Indians of Southern New England and Long Island: Early Period." In Trigger, *Handbook,* 160–78.

Savage, James. *A Genealogical Dictionary of the First Settlers of New England.* Boston, 1860–62.

Savelle, Max. *The Origins of American Diplomacy: The International History of Angloamerica, 1492–1763.* New York, 1967.

Schutz, John A. *William Shirley: King's Governor of Massachusetts.* Chapel Hill, N.C., 1961.

Schworer, Lois G. *'No Standing Armies!': The Antiarmy Ideology in Seventeenth-Century England.* Baltimore, 1974.

Scouller, R. E. *The Armies of Queen Anne.* Oxford, 1967.

Selesky, Harold E. "Military Leadership in an American Colonial Society: Connecticut, 1635–1785." Ph.D. diss., Yale University, 1984.

———. "Patterns of Officeholding in the Connecticut General Assembly, 1725–1774." In *A Lyme Miscellany,* edited by George J. Willauer, Jr., 166–98. Middletown, Conn., 1977.

———. "Recruiting in Connecticut During the French and Indian War." In *The Military and Society in Colonial America,* edited by John M. Murrin (forthcoming).

Sharp, Morrison. "Leadership and Democracy in the Early New England System of Defense." *The American Historical Review* 50 (1945): 244–60.

Sheldon, George. *The History of Deerfield*. Deerfield, Mass., 1895–96.

Shepard, James. *Connecticut Soldiers of the Pequot War*. Meriden, Conn., 1913.

Shipton, Clifford K. *Sibley's Harvard Graduates: Biographical Sketches of Those Who Attended Harvard College {1690–1770}*. Vols. 4–17. Cambridge, Mass., and Boston, 1933–75.

Shortt, S. E. D. "Conflict and Identity in Massachusetts: The Louisbourg Expedition of 1745." *Histoire sociale/Social History* 5 (1972): 165–85.

Shy, John. "The American Revolution: The Military Conflict Considered as a Revolutionary War." In Kurtz and Hutson, *Essays*, 121–56. Reprinted in Shy, *A People Numerous*, 193–224.

———. "Armed Forces in Colonial North America: New Spain, New France, and Anglo-America." In *Against All Enemies: Interpretations of American Military History from Colonial Times to the Present*, edited by Kenneth J. Hagen and William B. Roberts, 3–20. Westport, Conn., 1986.

———. "Hearts and Minds in the American Revolution: The Case of 'Long Bill' Scott and Peterborough, New Hampshire." In Shy, *A People Numerous*, 163–79.

———. "A New Look at Colonial Militia." *The William and Mary Quarterly* 20 (1963): 175–85. Reprinted in Shy, *A People Numerous*, 21–33.

———. *A People Numerous and Armed: Reflections on the Military Struggle for American Independence*. New York, 1976.

———. *Toward Lexington: The Role of the British Army in the Coming of the American Revolution*. Princeton, N.J., 1965.

Sibley, John L. *Biographical Sketches of the Graduates of Harvard University {1642–1689}*. Vols. 1–3. Cambridge, Mass., 1873–85.

Stark, Bruce P. *Connecticut Signer: William Williams*. Chester, Conn., 1975.

———. "The Upper House in Early Connecticut History." In *A Lyme Miscellany*, edited by George J. Willauer, Jr., 137–65. Middletown, Conn., 1977.

Steele, Ian K. *Guerillas and Grenadiers*. Toronto, 1969.

———. "The Empire and Provincial Elites: An Interpretation of Some Recent Writings on the English Atlantic, 1675–1740." *The Journal of Imperial and Commonwealth History* 8 (1980): 2–32.

Stiles, Henry R. *The History of Ancient Wethersfield*. New York, 1904.

———. *The History of Ancient Windsor*. New York, 1859.

Stout, Harry S. *The New England Soul: Preaching and Religious Culture in Colonial New England*. New York, 1986.

Stout, Neil. *The Royal Navy in America, 1760–1775*. Annapolis, Md., 1973.

Syrett, David. "American Provincials and the Havana Campaign of 1762." *New York History* 49 (1968): 375–90.

Tarbox, Increase N. *The Life of Israel Putnam*. New York, 1876.

Taylor, Robert J. *Colonial Connecticut*. Millwood, N.Y., 1979.

Trelease, Allen. *Indian Affairs in Colonial New York: The Seventeenth Century.* Ithaca, N.Y., 1960.

Trigger, Bruce G., ed. *The Handbook of North American Indians. Vol. 15. Northeast.* Washington, D. C., 1978.

Trumbull, Benjamin. *A Compendium of the Indian Wars of New England,* edited by Frederick B. Hartranft. Hartford, 1926.

————. *A Complete History of Connecticut.* New Haven, 1818.

Vaughan, Alden T. *The New England Frontier: Puritans and Indians, 1620–1675.* Boston, 1965. Rev. ed., 1979.

Wallace, Anthony F. C. "Origins of Iroquois Neutrality: The Grand Settlement of 1701." *Pennsylvania History* 24 (1957): 223–35.

Waller, G. M. *Samuel Vetch: Colonial Enterpriser.* Chapel Hill, N.C., 1960.

————. "Samuel Vetch and the Glorious Enterprise." *The New-York Historical Society Quarterly* 34 (1950): 100–23.

Ward, Christopher. *The War of the Revolution.* New York, 1952.

Ward, Harry M. *Unite or Die: Intercolony Relations, 1690–1763.* Port Washington, N.Y., 1971.

————. *The United Colonies of New England, 1643–1690.* New York, 1961.

Warden, G. B. *Boston, 1689–1776.* Boston, 1970.

Washburn, Wilcomb E. "Seventeenth-Century Indian Wars." In Trigger, *Handbook,* 89–100.

Watkins, Walter K. "The Capture of Havana in 1762." *Year-Book of the Society of Colonial Wars in the Commonwealth of Massachusetts, No. 5,* 125–68. Boston, 1899.

[————]. "The Expeditions against Port Royal in 1710 and Quebec in 1711." *Year-Book of the Society of Colonial Wars in the Commonwealth of Massachusetts, No. 3,* 81–143. Boston, 1897.

————. "Massachusetts in the Expedition under Admiral Vernon in 1740–1 to the West Indies." *Year-Book of the Society of Colonial Wars in the Commonwealth of Massachusetts, No. 5,* 65–124. Boston, 1899.

Weaver, Glenn. *Jonathan Trumbull: Connecticut's Merchant Magistrate.* Hartford, 1956.

Webb, Stephen S. "Army and Empire: English Garrison Government in Britain and America, 1569 to 1763." *The William and Mary Quarterly* 34 (1977): 1–31.

————. *The Governors-General: The English Army and the Definition of the Empire, 1569–1681.* Chapel Hill, N.C., 1979.

————. *1676: The End of American Independence.* New York, 1984.

Wheeler, Richard A. *The History of . . . Stonington.* New London, 1900.

White, David S. *Connecticut's Black Soldiers, 1775–1783.* Chester, Conn., 1973.

Wilcoxson, William H. *The History of Stratford.* Stratford, Conn., 1939.

Willingham, William F. *Connecticut Revolutionary: Eliphalet Dyer.* Hartford, 1976.
Wright, Robert K., Jr. *The Continental Army.* Washington, D.C., 1983.
Zeichner, Oscar. *Connecticut's Years of Controversy, 1750–1776.* Chapel Hill, N.C., 1949.

Index